DANISH DESIGN OR BRITISH DISEASE?

Peter Nannestad

DANISH DESIGN
OR BRITISH DISEASE?

Danish Economic Crisis Policy 1974-1979
in Comparative Perspective

ACTA JUTLANDICA LXVII:2
Social Science Series 20

AARHUS UNIVERSITY PRESS

AARHUS UNIVERSITY PRESS
Building 170, Aarhus University
DK-8000 Aarhus C, Denmark

Published with financial support from
the Danish Social Science Research Council

Contents

Preface

This book is not about economics. It is about economic policy. While to some such a distinction may appear overly subtle, it nevertheless deserves to be stressed at the outset. It carries implications not only for what shall be dealt with in the following but also for how the subject of the present study shall be approached. The guiding theoretical perspective will not be taken from economic theories of stagflation (cf. for instance Bruno and Sachs, 1985) or other relevant economic theories, but from the theory of rational political behavior (commonly known as "New Political Economy" or "Rational Choice" theory). Consequently, the method of investigation will be rather different from the model-based, axiomatic-deductive reasoning typical of modern economics. We will stay rather close to mainstream empirical methods of inquiry well-known from other parts of empirical social science. The primacy of the empirical will be strictly adhered to. What thereby is lost in elegance will hopefully be gained in realism.

The distinction thus drawn between an economic and a political science approach is not intended to fortify more or less arbitrary boundaries between the two disciplines. Increasingly it has come to be acknowledged that our understanding of the complexities of macro-economic policy making can nothing but benefit from closer cooperation between economics and political science, where each discipline brings its own paradigms, concepts and methods to the study of the subject.

There is, however, in the work of many economists a tendency to equate the "political" and the "institutional" aspect of economic policy making. Institutions have always been important to political science, but political science can offer much more to the analysis of economic policy. In the border region between economics and politics the broader conception of the "political" as embodied in the well-known Eastonian definition of politics as everything relevant to the authoritative allocation of values for a society (Easton, 1953, pp. 125-148) appears to me to be far more attractive than a narrow institutionalist conception. It directs the focus of interest not solely towards institutions, but towards the preferences of people with respect to different possible outcomes of such an allocation and to the patterns of consensus and conflict related to any authoritative allocation of values in society.

Adopting a political science perspective rather than a purely economic approach does not, of course, absolve one from the duty of respecting stylized facts and relevant insights established by the economics profession. Therefore I consider myself very lucky to have had the opportunity to discuss aspects of my work with colleagues from the Institute of Economics at the University of Aarhus. While he should certainly not be held responsible for any of my points of view or my interpretations, nor for errors, omissions or mistakes of any kind, Martin Paldam put in great efforts to set me straight about many economic details. He also read the manuscript in its various stages and made a great number of valuable suggestions for its improvement. Moreover, he spared me for hours on hours of tiresome data retrieval by kindly making his collection of political-economic data-series available to me whenever I asked for it. I also want to thank Claus Vastrup, chairman of the Danish Council of Economic Advisers,

----

for kindly reading and commenting on chapter 4 and Svend Hylleberg for useful technical advice. Also in their case the usual disclaimer applies.

Likewise I am indebted to colleagues and staff from the Institute of Political Science for their willingness to read and discuss pieces, parts and versions of the manuscript, although they did not always like the gist of what was put before them. Erik Damgaard, Jørgen Elklit, Øystein Gaasholt, Jørgen J. Poulsen and Søren Winter all contributed helpful criticisms as well as much welcomed encouragement during various phases of the project. Jørgen J. Poulsen also made many and great efforts to improve the language, while Anette Riber demonstrated on various occasions that she knows words in English I did never hear before. Besides she readily and reliably assisted in transferring files between various data formats and storage media. She also did the final proof-reading.

Further I gratefully acknowledge the financial assistance to the project I have received from several sources. The Institute of Political Science, out of its scarce appropriations, provided the necessary means for acquiring the statistical software on which part of the analysis is based. It also made it possible to obtain important OECD data series in machine readable form. The publication of the present book was supported by a grant from the Social Science Research Council.

Chapter 1
Introduction

"Le Danemark est si peu de chose": Despite the passing of more than a century this condescending utterance attributed to the French diplomat Cadore[1] at the eve of the French-German war 1870-71 has not lost any of its validity. In political, economic, or military terms Denmark still does not amount to much. When the Danish economy sneezes, no one else catches a cold - hardly anyone even notices. What interest, then, can possibly attach to the intricacies and peculiarities of Danish economic policy making?

The aim of this chapter is to argue that examining the Danish case may nevertheless be of more than just parochial interest. Furthermore, the design of the study and the theoretical approach taken shall be presented and discussed.

1. Paradise(s) lost

In the span of the last 15 - 20 years we have been witnessing the erosion of what in the jargon of trendy social scientists would probably be called a "grand project": *The idea and the practice of the political control of the macro-economy.*

This development has had its most dramatic and most highly publicized manifestation in the final and rather sudden abdication of the economic system of state socialism and its political superstructures in a number of Eastern European countries in the late 80s. Exit (possibly) the idea and (certainly) the highly discredited practice of a centrally, politically planned and controlled economy.

In the industrial countries of the West developments may have been more gradual and less spectacular, but here, too, the theory and practice of state intervention in the economy has been in profound crisis ever since the post-war period of unparalleled prosperity gave way to an unexpectedly long-lasting and deep recession. Right up to the economic turning point it had been a widely held belief among decision makers, economic advisers and the general public alike that the instruments needed to forestall economic crises had finally been identified by economic theory and put at the disposal of those in charge. Keynesianism held a truly hegemonial position in the interpretation of economic problems and in economic policy making in Western industrial countries in the beginning of the 70s.

While Keynesianism undoubtedly meant somewhat different things to different people in different places at different times, it is probably not too crude a simplification to claim that the following tenets had come to constitute the basic

---

[1] Sjøqvist (1965, p. 108).

----

conceptual foundation for state intervention in the macro-economy in all Western industrial countries:[2]

- The goals of economic policy making are defined with reference to the key indicators in the "magic square" as
    - constant, high economic growth
    - full employment
    - stable prices
    - balanced external accounts.

- Since a market economy is inherently unstable, the achievement of these goals cannot be left to the market. Hence the need for governmental stabilization policies in order to correct market failures.

- Stabilization policies are aimed at influencing aggregate demand.

- The main policy instruments are fiscal and monetary policy, supported by other instruments, depending on the target(s).

When the oil price hike of 1973/74, on top of a number of other supply shocks in the beginning of the 70s, finally sent the economies of Western industrial countries spinning, Keynesian stabilization policy along the lines sketched above was put to its critical test[3] - and, as it would seem, largely failed it: Figure 1.1 clearly brings out the average deterioration in the four key economic indicators experienced in the OECD-countries as a whole since 1974, bearing witness to the failure of economic stabilization policy.

As can be seen, economic growth came to a near-stop in 1974 and even became negative in 1975. After that the average growth in the OECD-countries turned positive again, but as a whole it remained at a lower level than prior to the first oil price hike 1973/74. There was also a sharp rise in unemployment in 1975. Joblessness by and large stayed at its new, higher level throughout the remaining part of the seventies. Inflation made a dramatic upward jump already in 1974, and although it was curbed somewhat during the subsequent years, it was not forced back to its pre-1974 level in the remaining part of the decennium. Finally, beginning in 1974 and with 1975 and 1978 as sole exceptions, the balance of current accounts of the OECD-countries (average) became negative.

----

[2] Cf. Glastetter (1987, pp. 151-163).

[3] Thus with respect to Keynesian economic policy the period after 1974 may indeed be called a crisis in the original Greek meaning of this term.

Figure 1.1.: Average GDP-growth,[a] unemployment,[b] consumer price inflation, and
surplus on current transactions with rest of the world (in percent of GDP)
in OECD-countries 1966-80

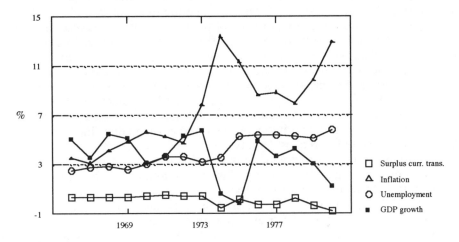

[a] At market prices
[b] Standardized rates from 15 countries[4]

Data: OECD Economic Outlook (1983)

Having thus failed (albeit to different degrees in different countries, cf. below) to
fight off the international recession and its consequences following in the wake of
the first and the second oil price shock, the once near-universally accepted
Keynesian doctrines and instruments for a "global steering" and "fine tuning"
of the macro-economy were finally recognized not to be a panacea for securing
enduring economic growth and prosperity. Competing theories - some of which
even challenge the very feasibility of sustained economic effects of any economic
policy[5] - have appeared, and recipes very different from the traditional Keynesian demand management schemes have been devised and tried out in various
countries. With the ascent to power of Margaret Thatcher in the UK in 1979, of
Ronald Reagan in the US in 1980, and of Helmut Kohl in Germany in 1982 a
conscious break with Keynesian stabilization policies was attempted in three
major Western industrial nations.

Also in Western industrial countries, then, the question of the feasibility of
political control of the macro-economy has made its way back onto the agenda
from which it seemed to have disappeared with the break-through of Keynesian-

---

[4] USA, Japan, Germany, France, United Kingdom, Italy, Canada, Australia, Austria, Belgium,
Finland, Netherlands, Spain, and Sweden.
[5] What is refered to is the well-known "Lucas-critique", cf. Andersen (1987, p. 143).

ism. Both the "if" and the "how" of state intervention in the economy have become subjects of a renewed debate.

Obviously, the question of the feasibility of political control of the macro-economy is of profound importance for practical politics and policy making. But it is no less important from the point of view of political theory. If the recession in the wake of the first oil price hike meant that the political authorities lost control of the economy, then the scope of politics was reduced. This conclusion is important to our understanding of the extent and scope of political participation.

In the broadest of terms, it is the problem of political control of the economy - or the problem of the relationship between state and market, or between the political and the economic system of society - the present study is about. But obviously, in order to make it operational and manageable, the scope of the problem has to be reduced considerably.

As a first step in this process of simplification the type of political control of the economy represented by centrally planned economies will be excluded from consideration. Instead the study will focus on the feasibility of a Keynesian-type state interventionism broadly characteristic of economic policy in most, if not all, of the Western industrial countries at the beginning of the 70s. The obvious question to be addressed, then, is why after 1974 the Keynesian approach apparently did not work out as well as expected.

Table 1.1.: OECD-means and measures of variability on four economic indicators, 1966-73 and 1974-79.

	GDP-growth		Unemployment*		Inflation		Curr. transact.	
	66/73	74/79	67/73	74/79	66/73	74/79	66/73	74/79
Mean	4.80	2.70	3.07	4.93	4.85	9.98	0.30	-0.28
Stdv.	1.01	1.99	0.41	0.71	1.47	2.04	0.11	-0.35
Var.coeff.	0.21	0.74	0.13	0.14	0.30	0.20	0.36	-1.25
Spearmans ρ	0.61		0.83		0.70		0.67	

*Standardized rates, 15 OECD-countries, see note to figure 1.1.
Data: OECD Economic Outlook (1983).

In this context it is important to take note of the fact that Keynesian stabilization policy did not fail everywhere. But, as can be seen from table 1.1., the economic crisis in the 70s deepened the differences in economic performance between different countries. With respect to three of the four key economic indicators the variation between countries did increase (relative to the mean).[6] Nor was the

---

[6] Scharpf (1987, p. 24) finds increased variability with respect to inflation also. His figures are based on only 16 countries and cover the periods 1963-73 and 1973-83, which may explain the difference. It should, however, also caution us as to the generally low stability of such computations which makes the selection of countries and the choice of time periods non-trivial.

ranking of countries with respect to the four indicators unaffected by the crisis, as is indicated by the less than perfect rank correlation of the countries' rankings before and after 1974.

What these inter-country differences regarding the outcomes of stabilization policies immediately suggest, then, is that the success (or failure) of a Keynesian stabilization policy may have been critically dependent on circumstances that varied from country to country. This leads to the second and more precise formulation of what the present study is about: it is about the circumstances that contributed to the differences in the performance of Keynesian stabilization policies in the post-1974 recession.

The questions implied by this formulation of the problem are by no means new or original. They have been taken up in a literature too voluminous to be reviewed here. However, the answers suggested in the following are not quite the usual ones: where the existing body of literature shows a marked tendency to emphasize the role of institutional arrangements, especially with respect to the labor market and to labor market - government relationships, the present study will stress the importance of the incentive structures of politicians and trade union leaders for the enacting and the outcomes of Keynesian stabilization policies.

2. Fallen from grace: The small, rich welfare state of Denmark in distress

From the point of view of the researcher the events of the 1970s may be looked at as a series of replicated "natural" experiments. The supply shocks, especially the oil price shock of 1973/1974, act as input. The national circumstances and conditions of economic policy making - be they political, economic, historical, etc. in nature - act as experimental variables, and the countries' economic performance in the recession serve as the experimental outcomes.

Now, although it is normally not said in methodology classes or written in textbooks, experiments that fail may easily outperform successful experiments when it comes to producing new insight.[7] Successful experiments can tell us only what we in a sense do already know in advance. By confirming that knowledge they make us tread with greater confidence on grounds we already walk, which is nice. But only experimental failures will ultimately force us to seek out entirely new paths to travel. Experiments that do not work out as expected are a necessary step in generating new scientific knowledge.

---

[7] The reason for the bad reputation of experimental failures - how often does one get published? - must be found in the sociology of the scientific community and in the psychology of its members.

This is why we may hope to learn more about the side-conditions that were crucial to the outcomes of a Keynesian stabilization policy by looking at a country where such a policy failed than by searching out as the focus of interest a country where things went as would have been expected from standard economic texts. The question "why did Keynesian stabilization policy fail in country X?" is interesting, since according to theory it should have worked, while the question "why did Keynesian stabilization policy work in country Y?" is not, since the answer is in the theory already.[8] Enters the case of Denmark.

As a pivotal case for studying the conditions affecting the outcome of a Keynesian type of stabilization policy, Denmark is endowed with three distinct advantages. The first advantage (from the point of view of the researcher) is that judged by its results post-1974 stabilization policy in Denmark must be deemed unsuccessful.[9]

Figure 1.2.: Economic performance 1966-79, Denmark and OECD-average

(a) Growth in real GDP (per cent, at market prices)

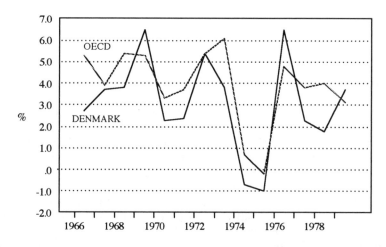

(continued)

---

[8] Except for the case where the latter formulation is actually a short-hand expression for "why did Keynesian stabilization policy work in country Y *when it failed in country X?*".

[9] A less attractive feature of an analysis focused on a policy failure is that at times it may easily come to look like a rating and grading of the performance of decision makers on the cheap basis of hindsight, and the role of Sixtus Beckmesser was never a likeable one. It must therefore be stressed that it is not the intention of the present study to take to school politicians and others for what they actually did or failed to do, nor to lay blame on any particular person.

(b) Unemployment (per cent, 1967-79)*

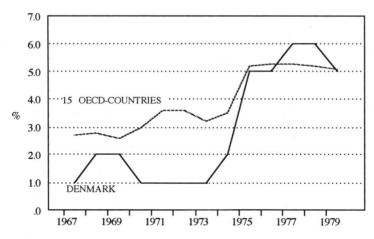

*See note to figure 1.1.

(c) Consumer price inflation (per cent)

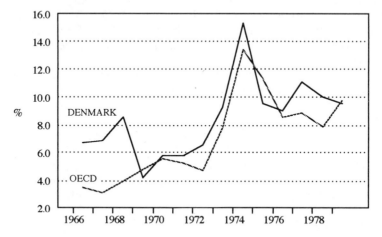

(continued)

d) Surplus on current transactions with rest of world (per cent of GDP)

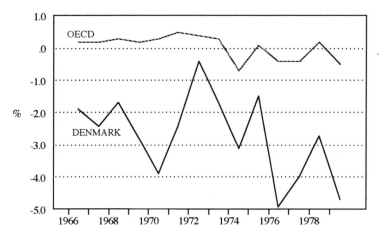

Data: Same as figure 1.1.

The lack of success of Danish stabilization policies is brought out by figure 1.2 which compares Danish economic performance prior to 1974 and after that year with the average OECD-performance by means of the four indicators of the "magical square".[10] The most striking feature is the poor performance of the Danish economy with respect to unemployment. While Danish unemployment figures are not directly comparable to the standardized OECD-rates as far as absolute values are concerned, the trends in both series lend themselves to comparison.

As can be seen, the impact of the recession on employment was much more adverse in Denmark than on average in the 15 OECD-countries. The reappearance of large-scale unemployment is probably the most dramatic evidence of the failure of Danish crisis policy.

With respect to the balance on current transactions with the rest of the world between 1966 and 1979 the performance of the Danish economy was well below the OECD-average for the whole period. But the data suggest that under the impact of the recession this performance gap has tended to widen. Also with respect to GDP-growth and inflation there has been a tendency for the Danish economy to generally perform below OECD-average, and again the distance to the average increased with the onset of the recession.

---

[10] Actually the impression of the relative Danish performance conveyed by the figures is even a bit too positive, since the OECD-performance measures do also include Denmark. With Denmark removed from the OECD-data the differences would have been marginally greater. On the other hand, the weight of Denmark is too modest in the OECD-context as to influence the overall picture unduly.

Thus it is in the area of full employment - the defense of which is the very hall-mark of Keynesianism - that the Danish crisis policy 1974-79 failed most ostensibly when compared to the OECD average.

The second advantage of Denmark as a pivotal case for investigating Keynesian policy making is the fact that economic thinking in Denmark used to be Keynesian in the extreme. "The Danish economic profession is, till this day, dominated by Keynesianism. The same applies to everybody else engaged in economic policy making" (Paldam, 1990, p. 26).[11] This is clearly demonstrated by the two most important models of the Danish macro-economy (ADAM and SMEC).[12] These models originated in the early seventies. Both were - and remain - demand-driven in the sense that any economic impulse is assumed to work through changes in demand, while the supply-side is assumed just passively to accommodate such demand changes (Andersen, 1988). Thus one can rest assured that the shortcomings of the Danish crisis policy were not caused by contamination from elements of other theories, such as monetarism or supply-side economics.

The third and final advantage of focusing on the case of Denmark is that it tends to elude the various explanations to inter-country differences in economic performance suggested in the literature (Scharpf, 1987, p. 26). In many analyses, especially within the neo-corporatist framework, Denmark has shown a persistent tendency to end up in the residuals. Such deviant cases are often considered particularly fruitful in hypothesis building (Pedersen, 1977).

3. Design of the study

3.1. Comparative design: Choice of countries

Looking at the case of Denmark in isolation would, however, be like looking at the outcome of an uncontrolled experiment. While it might give rise to a wealth of competing hypotheses, it would be very difficult to choose among them. The outcome would be theoretically overdetermined. There would be too many potential explanatory factors left. As long as we cannot command laboratory conditions we cannot reasonably hope to reduce the number of potential explanatory factors to just one as in an ideal experiment, but a comparative design (Przeworski and Teune, 1971) may still take us a few steps in the right direction.

---

[11] For an account of the early Keynes-reception in Denmark see Topp (1987).

[12] ADAM is the model used by the ministry of economic affairs. SMEC is used by the Council of Economic Advisers.

As is well known,[13] the choice of countries (and of the time period) to be covered in studies of the determinants of economic performance may critically influence the results. Therefore these choices require a sound rationale.

In many relevant studies the countries included are simply the 24 OECD-countries or some subset, often consisting of the 16-18 most highly developed OECD-countries.[14] The reasoning governing this choice is rarely made explicit, but this type of design can be criticized for being either overambitious or not ambitious enough.

If the researcher chooses to study all or most of the OECD-countries, his design will be theoretically overambitious. Considering the differences between the OECD-countries with respect to numerous potentially important political, economical and historical variables, any attempt to arrive at an explanation covering all or most of them is tantamount to striving for a theory with a considerable degree of generality. This may be a reasonable ambition as long as the investigation is restricted to economic variables, since a body of fairly general macro-economic theory exists. While such general theory should certainly be the ultimate goal of political science as well, for now it is hardly a realistic one, given the limited and fragmented knowledge and understanding available so far. Therefore the level of ambition with respect to the number of countries included has to be adjusted downwards.

The selection of countries may also simply reflect the working of the bit-principle (where bit stands for "because it's there", the "it" often designating data series). To the extent this is the case there is really no conscious design at all and consequently no attempt on the part of the researcher to delineate the scope of validity of the results. Such "designs" are underambitious because they can be improved.

The selection of countries to be included in the present study alongside Denmark has been guided by two prime considerations. Firstly, the countries should exhibit a wide range of economic outcomes during the recession. Obviously, if we have no variance in the dependent variable, we cannot explain anything. Therefore we need to compare countries with good, medium and poor crisis performance - if we can find them.

Secondly, the countries included should be as similar to each other (and to Denmark) as possible with respect to variables we want to control in the sense of reducing the probability that inter-country differences in these particular variables are the cause of observed differences in the outcome of stabilization policies. There is especially one such potential source of inter-country variation in the outcome of crisis policies that should be controlled for (to the extent possible). This source is the possibly different priority orderings of macro-economic goals set up by the political authorities in different countries.

It is quite commonly assumed that Socialdemocratic or socialist governments

---

13 Cf. the discussion following the publication of Hibbs (1977).
14 A noteworthy exception is Scharpf (1987) who uses the same countries as the present study, with the exception of Denmark.

will have the fight against unemployment as their top priority, while bourgeois governments will be more concerned about inflation. Various empirical studies (e.g. Hibbs (1977a); Alt (1985)) have tended to confirm that view, although it is probably most correct to say that the "do politics matter"-issue has not yet been conclusively decided. Given the problem of the present study, however, variations in policy outcomes due to different political priorities should be controlled for. This is done (to the extent possible) by concentrating on "essentially Social-democratic"[15] countries. The governments of these countries can be assumed to adopt similar priority orderings of the goals in the magical square.

The countries chosen in the light of the two central requirements set out above are - besides Denmark - Austria, Germany, Sweden, and the UK. Their economic performance after the first oil price hike is surprisingly different as demonstrated by figure 1.3. This difference is most obvious with respect to unemployment and inflation.

Figure 1.3.: Development in four economic indicators in Austria (A), Germany (D), Denmark (D), Sweden (S) and the UK, 1973-79

(a) Growth in real GDP (per cent, at market prices)

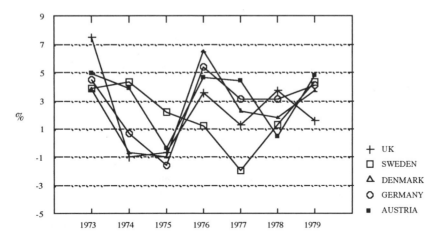

(continued)

---

15 The meaning of this awkward concept will become clear in a little while.

(b) Unemployment (per cent)

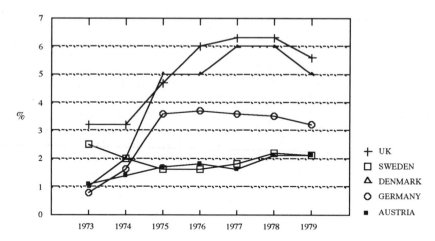

(c) Consumer price inflation (per cent)

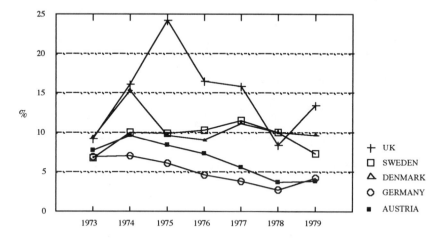

(continued)

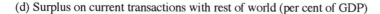

(d) Surplus on current transactions with rest of world (per cent of GDP)

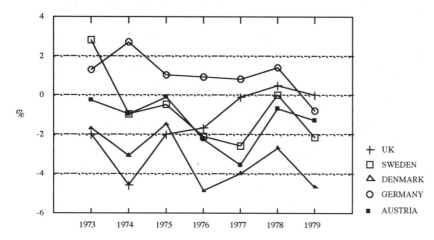

Data: As figure 1.1.

Two countries stand out as largely successful in keeping down unemployment, viz. Austria and Sweden, while the other three countries failed (to various degrees). Austria's performance is also quite good when it comes to fighting inflation, as is Germany's, while Denmark, Sweden and, most clearly, the UK failed to manage this problem well. With respect to the surplus on the current account Germany ranks top and Denmark bottom. The other countries take up the intermediate positions with varying degrees of success. Ranking the growth performance of the five countries is rather difficult. Here the most interesting feature appears to be the differences in the time paths of the individual countries. Three countries - Germany, Denmark and the UK - tend to follow similar trends, while Sweden, and to some extent Austria, exhibit trends of their own.

Thus the five countries included in this study do indeed give us considerable variation when it comes to economic performance in the recession. If their economic performance, as exhibited in the figures above, is summarily assessed using the indicators in the "magical square", one case may be counted as a near-total success (Austria)[16] and two cases as near-total failures (Denmark and the UK). Germany and Sweden occupy the middle ground, but with widely differing performance patterns. The German economy performed well with respect to price stability and the external balance, but less well when it comes to unemployment. Sweden, on the other hand, did very well with respect to unemployment, but not very well with respect to inflation and to economic

---

16 The reservation is due to Austria's relatively minor, but persistent, balance of payment problems.

----

growth.

Our five countries are in several respects politically similar. They are among the most stable post-war democracies, and they all have parliamentary systems of government. Moreover, three of the five countries (Austria, Germany and Great Britain) had Socialdemocratic governments (or, in the case of Germany, a coalition government dominated by Socialdemocrats) throughout the whole period under consideration. In Denmark a Socialdemocratic government regained power in 1975[17] after a short 13-months intermezzo with a liberal cabinet. The liberal government, however, pursued economic policies that did not differ all that much from the policies a Socialdemocratic government would have pursued.[18] In Sweden the Socialdemocrats lost power in 1976, but also in this case the macro-economic goals set up by the new liberal-conservative government did in the most relevant respects not differ significantly from the goals of the Socialdemocratic government.[19] For the period under consideration it seems justified to speak of the five countries as "essentially Socialdemocratic" countries as far as their economic policies are concerned.

However there is one important political difference between the five countries to be considered in the present context. Their party systems differ. Thus the foundations of coalition building and majority formation in the five parliaments will be different. In the period considered, the (Socialdemocratic) government commanded a majority in parliament only in Austria, and in the UK between 1974 and 1976. In Sweden and Germany, the government commanded a majority as well, but this majority was based on a coalition of parties. In Denmark, finally; weak minority governments were the order of the day, excepting the ill-fated coalition government formed by the Socialdemocrats and the

----

[17] Thus the statement of the new Socialdemocratic leader, Svend Auken, at his party's 1988-congress: "Socialdemocrats in government and Agrarians and Conservatives in opposition. That was the situation when things went well for Denmark" (according to Jyllands-Posten, September 18, 1988) can hardly be called a precise historical description.

[18] As can be seen from the diaries of Anker Jørgensen, the Socialdemocratic party leader 1972-87 and prime minister 1972-73 and 1975-82, while in opposition the Socialdemocrats had considerable problems in formulating a stance on especially employment policy that really differed from what the government stood for. Thus on September 30, 1974, he noted: "At 10 am group meeting on formulation of employment policy. We are not very creative, the only difference to the government is subsidized interest to housing; besides that, only some tightening up of things, the government has proposed itself." On October 9, 1974, he wrote: "Meeting on unemployment ... We try to formulate a program for the debate tomorrow, but it is difficult. The government is all too appeasing!!" On December 2, 1974, finally, he remarked: "We say that the government must start more public works, but the fact is that it starts about everything possible." (Jørgensen, 1989, p. 353, 362, 402)

[19] Cf. Olsson (1986); Scharpf (1987). In good agreement with this opinion Alt (1985) found that neither the shift to a bourgeois government in Sweden in 1976 nor the shifts in Denmark to a bourgeois government in 1973 and back again to a Socialdemocratic government in 1975 did produce any significant impact on unemployment.

Agrarians 1978-79.[20] Thus in terms of their parliamentary position the governments in the five countries faced widely differing conditions for policy making and policy implementation.

In his econometric study of the impact of shifts in government on unemployment in 14 countries in the period 1960-83 Alt (1985, p. 1036) reaches the conclusion that differences with regard to possession of a parliamentary majority do matter. It appears that single party majority governments were most likely to be able to significantly influence unemployment, followed by majority coalition governments and minority governments (in that order).

Problems with the validity of the model[21] and the proper definition of a parliamentary majority[22] aside, the pattern of the relationship between shifts to a majority government and political impact on unemployment changes considerably when the focus is narrowed to our five countries. This relationship stands up only in the case of Great Britain: all government shifts included in the Alt-study are to majority governments[23] and in all cases they produce significant political impacts on unemployment. But in the case of Austria Alt's model does not show a significant political impact of government shifts on unemployment at all, neither in the period following a shift to a single party majority government of the ÖVP in 1966 nor in the period following the shift to a SPÖ minority government in 1971. In the case of Denmark the model returns only one instance of a significant impact which, however, happens to occur after the shift to a Social-democratic minority government in 1971. In contrast, the shift to a majority coalition government period 1968-71 apparently had no significant impact on unemployment. In the case of Germany, where there were majority coalition governments all the way through, significant political impacts on unemployment are found after two out of four government shifts only. Finally, in the case of Sweden there are no significant impacts at all in the wake of the two government

---

20 In a technical sense it was a minority government, too, but in practice it was impossible to defeat in parliament and could hence act as if it was a majority government.

21 Alt's model fits Danish and Swedish data considerably poorer than data from other countries. Moreover, two Danish elections had to be left out due to estimation difficulties, cf. Alt (1985, p. 1023, note 15).

22 In the Danish case, for instance, the distinction between a majority and a minority government may easily become somewhat blurred. In some cases, e.g. 1964-66 and 1966-68, the government, although formally a single party minority government, could rely on support from a party outside the government and was hence quite close to the situation of a majority coalition government. In 1978-79, on the other hand, the coalition government formed by the Social-democrats and the Agrarians did not command a majority in parliament, but it could only be defeated in the - extremely unlikely - situation where all other parties united against it. Thus its parliamentary situation was rather like that of a majority government.

23 Strictly speaking the shift from a conservative to a Labour government in 1974 was not a shift to a majority government. The Labour government did obtain a (paper-thin) majority in a new election in the autumn of 1974, however.

shifts included in Alt's study, although in both cases the government taking over is registered as a majority coalition government.[24] Thus with the five countries under consideration here there is very little in the results from Alt's study to support the claim that in general the possession of a parliamentary majority did matter much to the political impact on unemployment. It can hardly be claimed to have been the decisive factor.

Nevertheless, the importance of the different parliamentary situations facing the governments in the five countries in this period for the formation and implementation of crisis policy cannot be entirely dismissed, but the experiences can hardly be generalized.[25] Undoubtedly, however, policy formation was normally considerably more tedious and time consuming for the shifting Danish minority governments than it would have been for a government based on a reliable parliamentary majority (Damgaard, 1989). The necessity of securing a parliamentary majority from situation to situation may conceivably have influenced both the content and the speed of the policy reactions to the economic crisis.[26] The question is, of course, if this might suffice as the sole explanation of the poor overall performance of the Danish crisis policy after the first oil price hike.

My answer is: most probably not. This answer is based on a counterfactual argument[27] which - although not attractive as such - may be the best way to seek an answer to the central hypothetical question: would Denmark have fared better during the first phase of the economic crisis, if there had been a Social-democratic majority government?

In order to answer this question in the affirmative, two conditions would to have to be fulfilled. In the first place one would have to assume that there was indeed a Socialdemocratic strategy that could have succeeded in fighting off the economic crisis. In the second place one would have to assume that a Danish Socialdemocratic government would have found and implemented it.

The Austrian case may be cited as evidence for the existence of such a

---

24 The government formed after the 1982-election in Sweden is registered as a majority coalition government by Socialdemocrats and Communists which in a formal sense it was not since the Communists did not hold cabinet posts.

25 Thus at one time the German chancellor Helmut Schmidt warned his parliamentary group against deluding itself into believing that the world could be substantially improved or made much more beautiful if only the Socialdemocrats had no coalition partner (Webber, 1983, p. 41, note 5). On the other hand the policy choice of the British Labour government in 1976 was considerably constrained by the fact that it had to rely on its continued toleration by the Liberals (Flanagan et al., 1983, pp. 430-431).

26 With an eye to the situation in, e.g., Germany and the UK it might also be claimed that a main side-effect of having big parties able to form majority governments is the existence of in-party factionalism and that the absence of a parliamentary need for the government to bargain and compromise in order to get a majority is compensated for by its need to compromise and bargain with various factions within the party in order to obtain internal acceptance.

27 On counterfactual arguments in general, see Lewin (1984).

successful Socialdemocratic economic-political strategy. As can be seen from figure 1.3, Austria was by and large successful (on all accounts) in making a Keynesian stabilization policy work. Hence the first condition can be met. The second condition poses tougher problems. Several central elements in the Socialdemocratic Austrian crisis policy would have been plainly unpalatable to a Danish Socialdemocratic government. One example is the position of the SPÖ on income inequality and solidaristic wage policies, cf. chapter 2. In their general approach to economic policy making Danish Socialdemocrats were much more in line with the British Labour Party. The crisis policy of that party did not fare any better than that of the Danish Socialdemocrats, even though Labour commanded a majority in Parliament for part of the period. Had the Danish Socialdemocrats commanded a parliamentary majority, things might well have looked different but not necessarily much better. It was probably not the lack of a parliamentary majority that prevented the Danish Socialdemocrats from implementing a potentially effective and coherent crisis policy.[28]

With respect to basic social-economic characteristics Austria, Denmark, Germany, Sweden, and the UK can all be counted among the "big" welfare states (Ringen, 1987). This implies a strong involvement of the state in the economy. The average total outlays of government as a percentage of GDP 1974-79 ranges from 44.4% (UK) to 54.4% (Sweden). This is clearly above the period average for all OECD-countries (37.1%, cf. OECD (1988)).

Finally, the organization in the labor market is in some respects also quite similar in the five countries. In each of them we find one single trade union movement with close ties to the Socialdemocratic party. The degree of working class organization is rather high, ranging in 1979 from 35.9% (Germany) to 79.1% (Sweden).[29] The wage earner / population ratio lies between .38 (Austria and Germany) and .48 (Denmark and Sweden). Thus all five countries can be characterized as "wage earner states".

3.2. Period of investigation

The discussions so far have implicitly refered to a particular span of time. It remains to make the time frame of the present study explicit and to explain the rationale underlying the choice.

The period under investigation is 1974-79 - roughly the period between the first and the second oil price hike. While the starting year hardly needs any justification, terminating the analysis in 1979 does. 1979 was chosen as the terminating year of this study for two main reasons.

---

[28] It is in good agreement with this point of view that Paldam and Zeuthen (1988) did not find minority government status (nor for that sake the ideological position of the government) to have a significant impact on the growth of the public sector in Denmark 1948-85.

[29] According to Scharpf (1987, p. 234).

In the first place, the conditions for national economic policy-making changed radically around 1979-80 (Scharpf 1987, pp. 298-306). From about that time the internationalization of capital markets effectively blocked any national attempt to stimulate the economy through a low-interest policy, i.e. by keeping national interest rates below the dollar rate.[30] The effect of this was a double one: a Keynesian expansionary policy could no longer be based on a coordinated use of fiscal and monetary instruments - the fiscal instrument had to do the job alone. Deficit spending had to be larger in order to achieve the same effect as a combined use of fiscal and monetary instruments on aggregate demand.[31] At the same time it became more expensive to finance a deficit, due to the appearance of positive real interest rates in the dollar market. Thus after 1979 political authorities found themselves in a new, serious predicament. The trade unions, too, had to face a new reality after 1979. The rising real dollar interest and the increasing mobility of capital opened up an attractive alternative to productive (and employment creating) investments. The resulting dilemma to the trade unions has been most succinctly formulated by Scharpf (1988, pp. 23-24): "Any strategy aiming at increasing private sector growth must today be paid for by redistribution in favor of capital ... There remains the crucial strategic insight that for the time being full employment cannot be brought back either at no cost by a Keynesian policy of growth or at the expense of others by redistribution in the disfavor of capital."[32]

In the second place, the period 1974-79 is a relatively short period. This should be considered appropriate when analyzing economic crisis policies and their outcomes. In general, such policies can be expected to be designed in such a way as to have their most visible effects in the short and possibly medium range. There are two reasons for this.[33] Firstly, what Keynesian stabilization policies are about is, after all, to counteract short- and medium-term fluctuations in economic activity. They do not aim at the redress of structural imbalances.[34] Secondly, crisis policies are enacted by politicians, and rational, re-election seeking politicians tend to have a rather short time horizon. (More will have to be said about this later).

Concentrating on such a short period of time has one important methodological drawback, however. It usually leaves us with too few observations from which to estimate reasonably stable quantitative relationships. Even with quarterly data, there are just 24 observations to analyze. In order to overcome this difficulty, the period of observation will often have to be extended backwards

---

[30] The ill-fated French attempt 1981-82 to stimulate the economy by fiscal and monetary expansion did make that point abundantly clear to everyone.

[31] In fact, one of the policy instruments pointed to by Keynes himself (cf. Spahn 1976, p .213) had thus be rendered inoperative.

[32] My translation.

[33] Some economists might even argue that they can only have short run effects.

[34] Cf. Glastetter (1987, p. 163).

and/or forwards. The validity of this practice depends on whether the estimated relationships were stable or did change under the impact of the crisis (structural changes). In order to pick up possible changes in the relationships that might have occurred during the period 1974-79, "crisis dummies" will routinely have to be included in the estimation, if this is partly based on data from outside this period.[35]

4. Approaches

The observable inter-country differences in economic performance during the economic recession have attracted the interest of researchers from both economics and political science. The subject has been studied from various theoretical perspectives, emphasizing different aspects and utilizing different concepts. In the following we shortly discuss three broad approaches that may be identified in the literature. They are classified according to the variable they treat as crucial. One is the economic-structural approach exemplified by the discussion of the impact of economic openness on crisis performance. The second one is the "do politics matter"-approach. Finally there is the institutional approach exemplified mainly (but not exclusively) by the discussion of the role played by neo-corporatist decision making structures for crisis performance.[36] Following this discussion a short account of the approach underlying the present study is given.

---

[35] Cf. Johnston (1963, pp. 221-228).

[36] The Marxist approach is deliberately left out. The reason is that for Marxist scholars the main research question must necessarily be a somewhat different one. As is aptly noticed by Offe (1984a, p. 36) "(f)or Marx, the point was to examine the 'laws of motion' of capital in order to prove that capitalism as a social formation was - contrary to the usual belief in harmony of vulgar economics - in fact a 'dynamic', historical and transitory social formation. Today, by contrast, the tantalizing and baffling riddle (in a political as well as in a theoretical sense) is why capitalist systems have so far been able to survive - in spite of existing contradictions and conflicts - even though an intact bourgeois ideology that could deny these contradictions and construct the image of a harmonious order no longer exists." Since, according to Marxist theory, crises are endemic to capitalism, there is no need to explain the crisis following the first oil price hike. According to Mandel (1978, p. 34) it is just the 20. overproduction crisis since the formation of a world market. What must be interesting, from a Marxist point of view, is rather how to explain the periods of "non crisis" in capitalist countries. For a presentation and critical discussion of Marxist work pertaining to the post-1974 recession the reader is referred to Mazier (1982).

4.1. The role of structural economic factors. Is economic openness a good or a bad thing?

Probably few would doubt that there was a strong international element in the economic recession following the first oil price hike in most Western industrial countries.[37] Hence one approach to the study of inter-country differences in the response to the crisis has been to search for structural economic factors in the individual countries that may account for differences in the impact of the international economic development on the national economies. By structural economic factors I mean factors that cannot - at least not in the short run - be changed by political means, but must be considered "givens" by policy makers.

One such factor that suggests itself is a country's degree of economic openness. The "contact hypothesis", as it will be called,[38] suggests that the more open a country's economic system, the more susceptible to the international economic crisis it will be.[39]

This point of view does not stand unchallenged, however. Katzenstein (1985) has attempted to show that the small European countries with their very open economies have tended to perform better in the economic crisis than have the big industrial countries with their less open economies. This difference he ascribes to the fact that since small, open economies are accustomed to being strongly exposed to international economic fluctuations, they have developed the necessary institutional and attitudinal prerequisites to deal with these fluctuations and to adapt to rapidly changing conditions.

Thus both the "contact hypothesis" and the Katzenstein hypothesis assume a relationship between degree of economic openness and crisis performance, but they disagree as to its direction. According to the "contact hypothesis" one should expect a negative relationship between economic openness and indicators of economic performance during the crisis, while according to the Katzenstein hypothesis it should be positive.

A crude empirical test[40] of the two competing hypotheses for the period under investigation here, based on data from 17 OECD-countries for the period 1960-79, can easily be performed using the ratio between average GDP growth

---

[37] Among those few one must count Dencik and Madsen (1978, pp. 79-80) who claim that Denmark went into a recession even before the international economic set-back could affect production and employment in the export sector. According to their interpretation, then, the Danish recession was essentially home-made. We shall return to that question in chapter 3.

[38] Cf. Paldam (1979a, especially pp. 338 - 345).

[39] This point of view is very popular in the Danish political debate as well: If the economy is not performing satisfactorily, governments use to be quick to point to adverse foreign developments as the real culprits, while the opposition stresses the responsibility of government. When things are improving, the odds are that the roles will be reversed.

[40] As usual the numerical results are sensitive to the choice of countries and time period(s). The signs of the coefficients, however, turn out to be quite robust.

1974-79 and 1960-73 (GR) as indicator of crisis performance[41] and the average import quota 1974-79 (in percent of GDP) as indicator of economic openness (IMPQ).[42] Since the recession was triggered by the oil price hike it seems appropriate to take into account the special kind of economic openness which stems from dependency on oil imports. This variable can be measured as the mean fraction of a country's total energy consumption covered by oil imports (OIMPQ).[43]

Using stepwise OLS the following model is found to provide the best description of the relationships in the data:

$$GR_i = a + b_1 IMPQ_i + b_2(IMPQ_i * OIMPQ_i)$$

Coefficient values and statistics are given in table 1.2. At first sight the result seems to support the Katzenstein hypothesis rather than the "contact hypothesis". The relationship between economic openness and crisis performance as measured here tends to be positive. On the basis of the data the best overall guess is that a (hypothetical) country with a totally closed economy and no oil imports would have an average GDP growth rate 1974-79 that was about 40 per cent of its average GDP growth rate 1960-73. For each additional percent of economic openness the average GDP growth rate 1974-79 as percentage of the average growth rate 1960-73 *ceteris paribus* tends to increase by about one percentahe point.

Table 1.2.: Coefficient values, standard errors and statistics for economic openness model

Variable	Coeff. value	S.E.
Constant	0.424	0.138
IMPQ	0.011	0.005
IMPQ*OIMPQ	-0.020	0.007
R^2(adj.)	0.304	
D.W.	2.004	

While economic openness taken by itself thus appears to be a good thing as far as economic performance 1974-79 is concerned, dependence on imported oil is clearly less so. Although there is no independent impact of oil import dependen-

---

[41] Cf. Lange and Garrett (1985, pp. 802 - 803).

[42] Data: OECD (1988).

[43] See the tables pp. 149 - 150 in OECD (1980). Figures from these tables are used, although they do not cover 1979.

cy on economic performance,[44] there is a negative interaction between economic openness and oil import dependency, meaning that the negative impact of oil import dependency varies with the level of economic openness. The more open the economy the more negative the impact of oil import dependency on crisis performance tends to be.

Alternatively the occurrence of an interaction between economic openness and oil import dependency can be interpreted as indicating that the impact of economic openness on economic crisis performance varies with the level of oil import dependency. If on average more than about one half of a country's total energy consumption 1974-78 is covered by imported oil, then the country's mean GDP growth 1974-79 (as percentage of the average growth 1960-73) tends to be lower the higher its degree of economic openness (since the numerical value of b_2(IMPQ*OIMPQ) becomes greater than the value of b_1IMPQ).

This pattern still holds when the focus is narrowed down to the five countries of the present study. Of the two countries with relatively low dependence on imported oil (Austria and the UK), Austria, being the economically most open country, also has the best average growth performance 1974-79 (relative to 1960-73). Of the three other countries, all with relatively higher dependence on imported oil, Denmark, being the economically most open country, has the poorest average growth performance 1974-79, while Sweden, which is economically a little less open than Denmark, does somewhat better in this respect, and Germany, being the least open country of the three, comes out with the best performance.

There can be little doubt that differences in structural economic conditions - in the present context economic openness and dependency on imported oil - did contribute to inter-country differences with respect to crisis performance in the period 1974-79. On the other hand, these differences offer only part of an explanation. As can be seen in table 1.2, for all 17 OECD-countries together economic openness and oil import dependency in combination "explain" about 30 percent of the variation in growth performance. Differences with respect to economic openness and oil import dependency had some impact on the economic performance of the five countries in this study during the recession 1974-79, but these structural factors are not the sole explanation. Blaming the oil sheiks or the inflation averse Germans for the economic difficulties in Denmark may have been politically convenient but does not exactly qualify as an accurate description of reality. It is quite generally agreed that there is ample room left for the inclusion of non-economic institutional as well as political and policy factors in explanations of inter-country variations in economic crisis performance.[45] It will be shown in the next section that political scientists have not backed off from this challenge.

---

[44] Including this variable in the model actually decreases the adjusted R^2 with a factor of about 0.05. Thus there is no "explanatory" power (in the statistical sense) left in this variable, once the economic openness variable and the interaction term have been included.

[45] Cf. Therborn (1987, p. 260).

4.2. Does (party-)politics matter?

Where tentative explanations based on economic structural factors focus on conditions that cannot be manipulated by economic policy makers, one branch of political science work has concentrated on a factor which is very much inside the policy makers' reach: the order of priority of the goals to be achieved by economic policy.

In empirical studies this problem has mostly been approached in an indirect way. In a number of quantitative cross-national studies - for example Hibbs (1977a), Cowart (1978), Tufte (1978), and Alt (1985)[46] - the focus has been on the party-political orientation of governments and the impact of this orientation on inter-country variations in economic performance. Thus one of the central explanatory variables suggested and tried out by political science in order to account for variations in economic performance has traditionally been the party-political orientation of governments.

By virtue of the design of the present study, the potential impact of differences in the party-political orientation of governments has from the outset been minimized. For that reason the "do politics matter"-approach in its conventional form shall be treated very briefly.

The connection between the party-political orientation of governments and their order of priority of economic goals is invariably furnished by the somewhat simplistic assumption that socialist or Socialdemocratic governments assign top priority to fighting unemployment (at the expense of inflation), while in contrast bourgeois governments have the fight against inflation as their top priority (at the expense of unemployment). The rationale behind this assumption is, as given by Hibbs (1977a, p. 1468), that these orders of priorities of socialist and bourgeois governments respectively are " ... broadly in accordance with the objective economic interests and subjective preferences of their class-defined core political constituencies."[47]

Empirical results have been somewhat mixed. In his analysis, consisting of both a comparative cross-national study of 12 Western industrial nations in the 60s and a time series analysis of the development in the US and the UK, Hibbs (1977a) found the party-political orientation of governments to matter for economic performance in the way expected. His results could not be reproduced using Norway as a test case (Madsen, 1981) nor in a study based on 23 OECD-countries (Schmidt, 1983a).

Alt has reported a large-scale replication of the time series part of the Hibbs-study, covering 13 countries and allowing for two types of party-political impact on unemployment (transitory and sustained). The evidence in favor of the existence of partisan effects is not overwhelming (Alt, 1985, p. 1035).

---

[46] This focus is also represented, although not to the exclusion of others, in i.a. Wilenski (1976; 1981), Cameron (1978; 1984), Schmitter (1981), Schmidt (1982; 1983a) and Paloheimo (1984).

[47] A considerably more sophisticated analysis is given in Hibbs (1979a).

In general empirical findings concerning partisan effects on economic performance seem to be extremely sensitive to the selection of countries and time frame.[48] The variability in performance with respect to unemployment in the period 1974-79 in the five "essentially Socialdemocratic" countries considered in the present study bears strong witness to this lack of stability in the relationship between the party composition of the government and economic performance.

There can be various reasons for this instability. One rather obvious weak spot in the "do politics matter"-framework is the basic assumption that socialist governments will go for full employment and bourgeois governments for price stability because this agrees with the objective economic interests and subjective preferences of their class-defined core political constituencies. There are (at least) two problems with this assumption.

In the first place a considerable weakening of time-honored ties between social groups and parties has been taking place in many Western countries during the last 20 years.[49] Speaking of "class-defined core political constituencies" has therefore become increasingly problematic in connection with the party systems of these countries. Correspondingly it has become increasingly difficult for governments to cater to the political tastes of just one clearly defined social group.

In the second place it is not necessarily true that there actually is a preference for full employment over price stability among left wing voters and for price stability over full employment among voters of the right. Data from the Danish electoral survey in 1979 support such doubts. The respondents were asked if they agreed most to a policy of fighting unemployment at the possible cost of higher inflation, or to a policy of fighting inflation at the possible cost of unemployment.[50] The opinion balance[51] on that question turns out to be in favor of fighting unemployment, regardless of the ideological left-right position of the respondents (Nannestad, 1989a, p. 173).[52] But to conclude from this that politics do not matter is to throw out the baby with the bath water. Actually the present study will corroborate the thesis that politics does matter a lot. What the unstable empirical relationship indicates is that the postulated underlying relationship

---

[48] See the critique of Hibbs' 1977-study (Schmidt, 1979; Payne, 1979) and Hibbs' rejoinder (1979b).

[49] The Danish case is analyzed in Pedersen (1988).

[50] The wording was: "A says: It is most important to fight unemployment, even if this should lead to higher inflation. B says: It is most important to fight inflation, even if this should lead to higher unemployment" (V270).

[51] The opinion balance is simply the percentage agreeing with A (cf. preceding note) minus the percentage agreeing with B.

[52] The majority favoring a policy of fighting unemployment at the expense of price stability decreases monotonically as one moves from the left to the right, however. It is 62.9 in the left-most quartile of the respondents as against 9.1 in the right-most.

between the party-political composition of government and its order of priorities among macro-economic goals is misspecified. In chapter 4 an alternative that fits the empirical evidence much better will be suggested.

4.3. Institutional approaches

Quite naturally the difficulties encountered when trying to explain inter-country variation in economic performance solely from differences in the party-political composition of governments have tended to shift the focus of inquiry to inter-country differences with respect to the institutional set-up within which economic policy is formulated and implemented, and to the constraints hereby placed on governmental choice. Many political scientists - and quite a few economists as well[53] - have pointed to the importance of the institutional framework for macro-economic policy making and wage setting and to its impact on policy outcomes as the central explanatory factor.

To one influential group of political scientists (e.g. Wilensky (1976; 1981), Cameron (1978; 1984), Schmitter (1981), Schmidt (1982; 1983a; 1984), Palo-heimo (1984), Katzenstein (1984; 1985), Czada (1987), Lehner (1987)) the key variable in this approach has been "(neo-) corporatism". Economists have tended to adopt a somewhat more restricted view of what appears to be basically the same phenomenon. They concentrate on the degree of centralization of wage bargaining in the labor market (e.g. Bruno and Sachs (1985), Calmfors and Driffill (1988), Freeman (1988)). Generally the hypothesis consists of the proposition that the higher the degree of corporatism (or centralization of the labor market bargaining system in the work of economists) in a country, the more adequate is the national economic-political response to the crisis. This is especially true when high degrees of corporatism are combined with left-of-center governments. Empirical findings have given some support to the hypothesis. Still, there are some problems with this corporatist institutional approach, at least in its political science version.

In the first place, as pointed out by Scharpf (1987, pp. 27-29) among others, the explanatory power of quantitative models built around the corporatism-variable was never high and has, moreover, tended to diminish with time. Obviously corporatism is not *the* answer. One reason for the relatively low explanatory power of neo-corporatism based models could be that the central corporatism-variable itself is a slippery concept, difficult to operationalize (Therborn, 1986, pp. 98-101) and hence "noisy". But this is hardly the main problem. As can be seen from table 1.3 the rank orderings of countries with respect to their degree of corporatism in studies by Schmidt (1983a), Lehmbruch (1984), Bruno and Sachs (1985) and Lehner (1987) are reasonably close.

---

[53] This is one of the few examples of a theoretical spill-over from political science to economics.

Table 1.3: Correlations (Spearman's ρ) between rank orderings of 13 European
OECD-countries* on corporatism scales in five studies

	Schmitter	Bruno/Sachs	Lehmbruch	Lehner	Schmidt
Schmitter	-	0.73	0.82	0.82	0.92
Bruno/Sachs	-	-	0.90	0.88	0.84
Lehmbruch	-	-	-	0.98	0.93
Lehner	-	-	-	-	0.93

*European OECD-countries (except Greece, Island, Ireland, Luxembourg, Portugal,
 Spain and Turkey)

With respect to the five countries in the present study, their rank ordering on a
corporatism scale is not problematic: Austria and Sweden are universally
considered the most corporatist systems, followed by Germany and Denmark
which rank medium, while the UK ranks as the least corporatist country. But
when this ordering is compared to the ordering of economic performance of the
five countries 1974-79 - roughly the time period for which the corporatism
explanation performs best - difficulties do appear. While the top position of
Austria and Sweden and the bottom position of the UK with respect to economic performance seem to agree well with their rank orderings with respect to
corporatism, the Danish economy did too poorly or the German too well to fit
the model. Moreover, differences in the degree of corporatism can hardly explain
why Austria did so much better than Sweden during this period (except for
unemployment, where both countries did about equally well). Trying to predict
the relative economic performance of our five countries from their ranking on a
corporatism-scale would not be very successful.

In the second place, corporatism-based explanations are theoretically somewhat unsatisfying because most often[54] they are vague as to the exact relationship between the neo-corporatist decision-making structure and the policy
contents of the decisions arrived at.[55] What would have to be provided - but
normally is not - in order to make the corporatism-argument stick is an explanation of *why and under what conditions* economic-political decisions arrived at
through a corporatist decision making system should be qualitatively better,
more adequate, or in other respects superior to decisions arrived at within
different institutional frameworks.[56] As often is the case in macro-level analysis,

----

[54] But not exclusively, cf. Katzenstein (1985). According to Katzenstein, the superiority of
corporatist to non-corporatist systems in coping with the economic crisis can be ascribed to the
greater ability of small, corporatist nations to adjust quickly to new circumstances.
[55] CF. Regini (1984).
[56] In the work of economists it is usually assumed that centralized wage bargaining structures
in the labor marked make it more easy to enforce wage restraint or various kinds of income
policy. The same line of thought appears in some instances to be implicitly contained in the

the theory lacks the specification of the "transmission belt" between institutional structure and economic performance. Without this link between the mode and the content of decision making, the corporatist approach easily ends up resembling pure institutional determinism.

Researchers working from quite different theoretical points of view - and sometimes in direct opposition to the (neo-) corporatist approach - have tended to end up with essentially institutionalist explanations of inter-country differences in economic performance. The participation of strongly and centrally organized interests in the formulation and execution of economic policies is, according to the corporatists, the key to a successful fight against the economic crisis. Olson (1982) takes essentially the opposite view. He agrees that only "encompassing" organizations will be able to forego instant advantages in the interest of future gains to its members and thus be able to enter into a "social contract". Nevertheless he sees the predominance of organized interests and "distributional coalitions" among them as responsible for the "institutional sclerosis" that ails advanced western societies. According to Olson it is this "institutional sclerosis" that has prevented the necessary social and economic adjustments after the onset of the crisis and is responsible for the loss of welfare experienced in the countries considered. Although founded on the logic of collective action (Olson, 1965) with its individualist rational-choice perspective Olson's crisis theory can be read as essentially institutionalist. His central variable is the institutional structure of interest representation in society.

Although the work of Scharpf (1987; 1988a) is one of the most careful and complete works available it should be mentioned in the present context because it also contains a strong and pervading element of institutionalism.[57] The main focus in his work is on "economic-political strategy" and on the coordination of such strategies between the primary economic agents, mainly the government, trade unions and central banks. According to Scharpf's analysis success in fighting off the consequences of the economic crisis - not the least mass unemployment - was critically dependent on a "Keynesian coordination" between fiscal and monetary expansion by the authorities and (restrictive) wage policies of the trade unions, especially in the period up to the second oil crisis in 1979-80. Differences between countries with respect to their ability to bring about the necessary strategic coordination ("Strategie-Fähigkeit") are primarily explained by differences with regard to institutional arrangements and structures such as the degree of central bank autonomy, trade union centralization, the centralization of wage negotiations, etc. Thus, like the corporatists, Scharpf is basically institutionalist with respect to the "ultimate cause". But at the same time he does

---

work of political scientists as well. For a critique see Therborn (1987, pp. 264-268).

[57] As witnessed by, i.a., the following quotation (Scharpf, 1987, p. 205): "Wenn also sozialdemokratisch geführte Länder und Regierungen, die doch ebenfalls auf den Primat der Vollbeschäftigung festgelegt waren, Arbeitslosigkeit dennoch nicht vermeiden konnten, dann sind die Gründe dafür offenbar weniger in den ökonomischen als in den unterschiedlichen institutionellen Bedingungen der einzelnen Länder zu suchen. *Auf sie konzentriert sich deshalb die nachfolgende vergleichende Analyse.* " (emphasis added)

provide a link between institutional structure and policy outcomes that is usually not made explicit in the corporatist-approach.

Finally the attempt of Therborn (1986; 1987) to explain "why some peoples are more unemployed than others" (that is the ambitious title of his 1986-book) appears to end in institutionalism, albeit an institutionalism of a rather unique kind. In his view the deciding factor is the existence of a long-standing institutionalized commitment to full employment prior to the onset of the crisis.[58]

Different as various institutional approaches to the explanation of inter-country variations in economic performance may be they appear to have one trait in common. Most concern themselves very little - if at all - with the *incentive structures* of economic policy makers and with the potential influence of these incentive structures on adopted policies and economic performance.

4.4. Rational Choice theory

Institutionalists seem to hold the tacit assumption about advanced Western economies in general and countries led by Socialdemocratic governments in particular that - given existing institutional strictures and constraints - politicians will as a rule strive to optimize economic performance and try to achieve full employment. This assumption undoubtedly agrees with how politicians are seen in much of the macro-economic and welfare theory, how politicians see themselves, and how they want to be seen. But it does not necessarily agree with reality.

The approach underlying the present study is based on Rational Choice theory. Basically what I hope to achieve by adopting this framework is to steer clear of the institutional determinism lurking just beneath the surface of much (neo-) corporatist as well as comparative economic work in the field and to succeed in bringing back politics (in the broad definition of Easton (1953)) as a central explanatory variable.[59] I want to do this without having to succumb to the empirically less fruitful assumptions about the policy goals of governments of different party compositions that is embedded in the conventional "does politics matter"-approach.[60]

---

[58] The empirical part of Therborn (1986), which is intended to support his basic viewpoint, is open to criticism on both logical and methodological grounds, however. A special problem is how to distinguish between an effective institutional commitment to full employment (like the Swedish Saltsjöbaden-agreement) and a not effective institutional commitment (like § 75 (1) in the Danish constitution) without recourse to circular reasoning.

[59] A number of prominent Rational Choice economists would certainly object to this point of view. Frey (1990) and Pommerehne (1990), for instance, have urged a stronger interest in institutions within the Rational Choice framework.

[60] For some reason the Rational Choice approach has never been popular in Danish political science. In that respect the situation appears different in Sweden, as can be seen from works by prominent Swedish political scientists, for example Lewin (1984) or Elvander (1988).

I prefer to consider Rational Choice theory as a paradigm or an approach rather than as a theory proper. It provides the researcher with one basic assumption and one research principle: the assumption that political behavior is rational, utility maximizing behavior (as is economic behavior), and the principle of methodological individualism meaning that in the last resort the units of analysis and explanations have to be individuals and that macro-analysis and results must have a micro-foundation.

While these assumptions and principles by and large are standard in economics, they still cause debate within political science.[61] That is why it is important to stress the function of Rational Choice theory as a research paradigm for the present study. By adopting it one does not necessarily subscribe to the view that its assumptions are true or even *the* truth. What counts is that the application of this framework leads to fruitful questions and that the answers will enhance our understanding of the subject under study. (In the last resort every reader will have to decide this question for himself).

The core of the Rational Choice approach has been nicely formulated by Katzenstein (1984, p. 31): "The analysis of political economy aims to explain political strategies and, so far as possible, economic and political outcomes by showing how these strategies and outcomes result from the self-defined interests of actors." Thus within a Rational Choice framework the main emphasis is on actors (or agents), their goals and interests, and the strategies employed by them in order to maximize their utility defined with reference to their goals and interests. While there is a multitude of potential and actual actors in various phases and stages of economic policy making, the present study will concentrate mainly on two types of (collective) strategy-producing actors: political authorities, primarily governments, and trade unions. They are the crucial actors in economic policy making in the countries studied here. Because they are collective actors we need to provide some micro-level foundation for the interests and strategic goals ascribed to them.

In contrast, the policy-relevant activities of business and business organizations etc. will be considered only occasionally. It has been convincingly argued by Scharpf (1987, pp. 210-211) that business decisions concerning investments, production, employment and prices are very important to economic policy making and cannot be neglected by policy makers, but are nevertheless most adequately considered mainly reactive and adaptive with respect to existing situations and conditions. The same applies to voters. Ultimately they play a central role (cf. chapter 4) but this role can safely be assumed to be reactive (Nannestad, 1989a).

One distinguishing feature of Rational Choice theory compared to welfare economics appears in the treatment of the behavior of authorities. Welfare economics tend to assume a benevolent dictator bend on maximizing some utility or welfare function. In Rational Choice theory authorities maximize their own utility derived from the set of personal interests characterizing the individuals that

---

[61] For a classical account of the opposing points of view see Barry (1970).

make up the particular authority.62 Thus in attempting to understand and explain the policies adopted or not adopted by governments or trade unions we shall have to take our point of departure in the interests of the individual politicians or trade union leaders.

The actor perspective embodied in Rational Choice theory does not imply that structures and institutions are unimportant. To the contrary, institutions do matter to rational utility maximizing individuals for better or worse. *For better,* because institutions can help reduce the cost of rational decision making by structuring and simplifying complex situations. This lessens information (over)load and information requirement by reducing uncertainty about the reactions to be expected from other actors. It also renders the effects of various alternative strategies calculable.63 *For worse,* because basically institutions do perform these functions through processes of selection and filtering which imply that certain aspects of a situation will be kept out of focus and that certain strategic alternatives may not receive any attention at all (Scharpf, 1987, p. 27).

From the perspective of Rational Choice theory institutions and institutional settings can be resources as well as constraints in policy making and may be both at the same time. But as constraints they are rarely, if ever, so tight as to determine the outcome of strategic choices entirely.64 That is why institutional explanations of differences with respect to economic performance, as they abound in the literature, must normally be incomplete. This is also the main reason why the focus of the present study will be on the actors mentioned above, their incentives and strategies, rather than on institutions.

Thus, in a sense, the present study can be said to be heavily biased towards stressing the role of non-institutional political factors. The justification for this is that one-sidedness is unavoidable on theoretical as well as practical grounds. For theoretical as well as practical reasons no single study can conceivably encompass all variables relevant to an understanding of the formulation, implementation, and outcome of crisis policies in the five countries selected. All studies have to be partial. As long as this basic fact is kept in mind - by the reader as well as the researcher - no harm should result from it.

---

62 Cf. Sandmo (1990).

63 The right institutional setting may even override the destructive logic of a prisoners' dilemma and secure cooperative behavior, cf. Axelrod (1984).

64 Thus institutional explanations may be more successful in explaining why a certain strategy was not adopted than in explaining the actual choice. It is, for instance, easily explained why, as part of their crisis policy, German governments did never attempt to impose a statutory incomes policy by law. The reason is that such a law would infringe on the constitutional contractual freedom in the labor market ("Tarifautonomie") and would most probably be overthrown by the Constitutional Court (Bundesverfassungsgericht). But the monetary policy adopted by the German Bundesbank after 1974 is not in any sense explained by pointing to the highly independent position of this authority vis a vis the German government.

5. Outline

The main thesis underlying the following is that *politics is central to economic performance*. It will be demonstrated that the economic performance of the five countries in the period of stagflation 1974-79 was highly dependent on policy choices by governments and trade unions, as well as on the successful coordination of these policies, cf. Scharpf (1987).

But neither governments nor trade union leaderships are free to choose whatever policy they want. Both are in need of popular support in order to stay in power. Acting rationally, neither can afford to neglect this basic facet of democratic politics.

As far as the strategic choice of governments is concerned it will be argued that *the political cost of unemployment* (in terms of loss of electoral support) was crucial in determining the degree to which governments chose to adopt an accommodating economic strategy in order to keep down unemployment, even - if need be - at the expense of higher inflation ratios or other economic imbalances.

With respect to the strategic choice between a wage- and an employment-goal facing the trade unions it will be argued that *the degree of wage structure stability* played a central role. It will be demonstrated that for rationally behaving union leaderships a high degree of wage structure stability is conducive to the adoption of an employment- rather than wage-oriented strategy. Conversely, with an instable wage structure it becomes rational for unions to choose an aggressive wage strategy, even if this may lead to adverse consequences with respect to employment levels.

As in any fair trial, before the merits of the case can be judged the relevant facts have to be established and presented. This is the main function of chapters 2 and 3. Chapter 2 contains a short Keynesian discussion of the effects of a supply-shock like the oil price hike of 1973/74 on the economy, an outline of the basic configuration of problems facing all five countries, and an examination of the policy responses in Austria, Germany, Sweden and the UK. Against this background chapter 3 deals with the onset of the crisis in Denmark in 1974 and the development of Danish economic policy 1974-79. Since an excellent and up to date account of Danish economic policy is available elsewhere (Hansen et al., 1988), chapter 3 is kept rather brief.

In chapter 4 and 5 the facts are interpreted and the conclusions are drawn. Chapter 4 is devoted to government strategy. Chapter 5 analyzes the strategic choices of trade unions. Readers who are interested in the plot more than in the details of documentation may hence skip chapters 2 and 3 and proceed directly to chapter 4 without too much loss of continuity.

Chapter 6 summarizes the central findings. They are briefly related to the basic issue of the political control of the economy. The chapter also contains some reflections of a more speculative nature concerning the possibility that an incipient erosion of the "big compromise" underlying the Danish welfare state may be at the bottom of the problems encountered in the attempts to arrive at an adequate policy response to the economic crisis in the 70s.

Chapter 2
Four Ways to Meet a Challenge

The oil price hike of 1973-74 was not an isolated phenomenon. It came on top of a series of similar price hikes on various goods and raw materials in the early 70s. This posed a twofold challenge to the Western industrial countries. They had to confront the simultaneous threat of escalating inflation *and* mass unemployment. Besides, economic growth diminished and balance of payment problems developed almost everywhere. The two latter problems, however, did not emerge in isolation, but always as companions to either inflation or unemployment (or both).[1]

In section 1 of the present chapter I shall take a closer look at this challenge and the way the oil price hike brought it about. The main emphasis will be on the effects of the oil price hike on employment and price levels. I shall also consider the economic policy responses suggested within a Keynesian framework and some of their problems. This treatment will follow conventional paths and the point of view presented will not diverge - except for its (low) level of formalism - from what can be found in a number of economic studies.[2]

In subsequent sections (2 - 5) the strategic economic-political responses chosen in each of the four countries selected as comparison cases in the present study are examined in turn. These accounts of national policies reflect the fact that the strategic reactions varied widely between countries despite their common foundation in Keynesianism. The individual accounts may seem innocently descriptive, but - paraphrasing Easton (Easton, 1953, pp. 52-55) - all descriptions are particular orderings of reality in terms of a theoretical interest.

1. The challenge

An oil price hike like the one of 1973-74 will affect macro-economic activity through both the supply- and the demand-side of a small, open economy heavily dependent on imported oil. The overall macroeconomic effects will depend on the interaction between these demand- and supply-side effects.

With respect to domestic demand an oil price hike implies a transfer of real income to oil-exporting countries. This transfer acts like an excise tax levied by OPEC (McCracken et al., 1977, p. 67) in reducing total disposable income and hence domestic demand. This in turn leads to a reduction in domestic production and the level of economic activity. Demand will further be reduced by the drop in foreign demand resulting from the reduction in the level of economic activity in oil-importing foreign countries. In the short run this effect cannot be expected to be offset by an increased demand from oil-exporting countries (Hefting and

---

1 Scharpf (1987).

2 For example Dornbusch (1980); Hefting and Nielsen (1983); Nielsen (1984); Scharpf (1987).

Nielsen, 1983, pp. 207-209). Finally the reduced level of economic activity exerts pressure on profits, too. This may in turn lead to a reduction in investments thus reducing domestic demand still further.

Turning to the supply-side effects increasing energy costs will lead to increasing unit costs, provided that the price of capital and labor is kept constant. In order to supply the same quantity of a good as before firms will hence have to raise prices. If wages are inflexible, e.g. by virtue of indexation, rising prices on domestic and imported goods will lead to even stronger price increases. A third potential source of price increases will be higher prices on imported raw materials other than oil.

On the other hand the reduced level of economic activity in the wake of an oil price hike may tend to curb price raises somewhat. The reduction in foreign or domestic demand may lead business to accept a reduction in profit per produced unit. This, however, may in turn translate into a demand-effect due to falling investments.

The sum of the three types of demand-effects must be assumed to be negative. Thus an oil price hike will result in a lowering of demand and, consequently, in (Keynesian) unemployment. In the longer run substitution effects may be expected to counteract rising unemployment to some degree, for instance as substitution occurs between energy and labor (dependent, of course, on the development in wages), or less energy-intensive goods are substituted for highly energy-intensive ones.

The effect of an oil price hike on the rate of inflation initially depends on the degree to which the increased unit costs due to higher energy prices are passed on in the prices of goods rather than being paid for by a reduction in profits. The further development depends on the flexibility of wages: the more inflexible they are, the more likely an accelerating inflationary price-wage spiral will develop.

The most likely short run impact of an oil price hike on a small, open economy will be a simultaneous increase in the rate of unemployment and of inflation. If the situation is left unattended these imbalances might even end up reinforcing each other.

The stagflationary macroeconomic development set in motion by the oil price hike of 1973-74 put economic-political decision makers in a serious dilemma. If inflation was considered the main evil, then any attempt to break inflationary expectations by means of Keynesian demand management (i.e. by contractive fiscal and monetary policies) would necessarily have to worsen the unemployment situation by depressing demand still further.

If, on the other hand, first priority was given to unemployment, and expansionary fiscal and monetary policies were enacted in order to compensate for the reduction in demand brought about as a consequence of the oil price hike, then there was a real danger of inflation running rampant. The restoration of demand could easily remove what incentive there might have been for trade unions to accept some wage flexibility as well as any incentive for business to hold back on price increases. Under the umbrella of governmental full employment policies both parties could thus keep trying to distribute between them the real income already lost to the oil exporting countries (Franz, 1988). With Socialdemocratic governments in power this risk was especially pertinent since both trade unions and business might well be willing to try to exploit the fact that Socialdemocratic governments have traditionally had a strong ideological commitment to full employment. They could be relied on not to remove the umbrella of full employment policies as readily as bourgeois governments might be suspected to do.[3]

Thus the problem put before policy makers by the oil price hike of 1973-74 could not be solved by Keynesian demand management policies alone. If demand management was the only policy option, either increasing inflation or growing unemployment had to be accepted, at least in the short run. Either way, the result would have to be some kind of stop-go or go-stop policy. The choice between stop-go and go-stop would depend on the expected development in international economic activity.

The authorities could choose to concentrate on inflation first. They could try to bring it down quickly by restrictive policies. With inflation at bay they could then turn to the unemployment problem and try to stimulate employment by expansionary measures. If, as was widely expected at the beginning, the recession was going to be short-lived, this procedure might even be considered advantageous as the expected revival of international economic activities brought about by the eventual recycling of the surpluses from oil-exporting countries would aid domestic economic policies in restoring full employment. If the anti-inflationary policies had succeeded, the country's international competitiveness would have been kept intact or might even have improved relative to other countries. It could then take advantage of an international upswing. But if inflation did not break quickly, or if the international economic recovery did not materialize in due time, this type of stop-go strategy risked creating structural unemployment that would not easily yield to expansionary policy measures later on.

If, in line with the expected preferences of Socialdemocratic governments, unemployment was dealt with first, then inflation would have to be left alone for a time while employment was stimulated through expansionary policies. In this scenario a rapid international economic recovery would also be vital. Otherwise high or accelerating inflation would make any full employment policy unsustainable through the erosion of the competitive standing of domestic firms both abroad and at home. If the international economic recovery came quickly enough it might relieve the need for expansionary fiscal and monetary policies. This would reestablish the degree of freedom necessary to combat inflation without doing much harm to employment. On the other hand such a go-stop strategy might end with both the unemployment and the inflation problem unsolved. This would happen if the inflationary development ended up undermining the full employment policies enacted.

---

3 Cf. Andersen (1987, pp. 145-146). For this reason one of the most widely accepted axioms of Danish politics saying that Socialdemocratic governments are in a better position than others when it comes to securing the cooperation of trade unions in economic policy making should probably be relegated to the realms of political folklore.

The best chance of avoiding the risks inherent in a stop-go or go-stop strategy would be for labor and business to adopt a cooperative strategy with respect to wage and price policy. If government could rely on business to pass through in the prices the increased energy costs only and on labor to refrain from seeking compensation for the loss of income directly and indirectly attributable to the oil price hike, then it could afford to regard the increasing rate of inflation as a passing phenomenon that would die out by itself. Government could then concentrate on stabilizing the employment situation through expansionary measures (Scharpf, 1987, pp. 208-209). What this "Keynesian policy coordination" - the term is borrowed from Scharpf (1987) - of governmental and (primarily) trade union strategy[4] entails, then, is a combination of expansionary fiscal and monetary policies to stimulate employment and the acceptance of a (temporary) loss of income by both labor and business in order to avoid an accelerating inflationary development due to the attempt to have the other part pay the bill to the oil exporting countries all alone.

Obviously this type of coordination cannot be expected to emerge spontaneously. Scharpf (1987) has examined the institutional preconditions of establishing a "Keynesian coordination" of strategies in Austria, Germany, Sweden, and the UK in considerable detail. In the present study, the emphasis will be on the political preconditions of such a coordination - an aspect which is largely ignored in the work of Scharpf.[5] I will return to a comparative analysis of this topic in chapters 4 and 5 below.

In theory one might escape both horns of the stagflation-dilemma. Even supposing that governments as well as trade unions were eager to find the escape (they might or might not have been), they could easily misjudge the situation created by the oil price hike. At least three factors tended to cloud the picture and to impair the foresight of decision makers.

In the first place, the energy supply problem initially drew much of the attention away from the economic implications of the oil crisis 1973-74. Not only did the OPEC-countries quadruple the price of oil. Following the outbreak of the Yom Kippur war in October 1973 the Arab oil-producing countries announced a cut (10 per cent initially, 25 per cent later on) in oil production. Moreover an embargo on oil shipments to the Netherlands and the US was initiated because of the position of these countries in the Arab-Israeli conflict.[6]

---

[4] With regard to price setting by firms, competition in the market can be relied on to do most of the job.

[5] The possibility of enforcing the "Keynesian coordination" by means of a statutory incomes policy and a system of rigid price controls existed, at least in theory, in all countries except Germany. Still, experience has shown this kind of policy to be ineffective, except perhaps in the very short run. That is why the feasibility - or lack of feasibility - of a voluntary coordination of strategies is of much greater interest.

[6] Denmark just managed to avoid being hit as well by the embargo as a consequence of a quite explicit statement by the then prime minister, Anker Jørgensen, expressing some measure of understanding of the Israeli position vis à vis the Arab countries. The official Denmark learned

Although both production cuts and embargo turned out to be ineffective in the end, they succeeded in creating fears of massive energy shortages in the populations and among the decision makers in oil-importing countries. In most countries plans were hastily devised and put to work in order to reduce energy consumption and to make ready for emergency allocations of oil. Only then were the policy makers ready to confront the economic consequences of the crisis.

In the second place the inflationary effect of the oil price hike led the unemployment impact by several months. Given the inclination of politicians to attend to problems in the order of their arrival there was a strong temptation to deal with inflation as it made itself felt (ahead of unemployment) and hence to initiate contractive fiscal and monetary policies in order to contain it. Thus a homemade element was added to the ensuing drop in the level of economic activity brought about by the oil price hike.

In the third place simple inertia may also have contributed in pushing the initial policy reaction in the direction of anti-inflationary measures. In order to cool off a boom accompanied by an over-rapid expansion of demand and strong inflationary tendencies most - but not all - countries had already, at the eve of the oil price chock in 1973, planned or adopted restrictive economic measures (McCracken et al., 1977, pp. 65-66). Thus unwillingly many countries moved into the crisis with a foot on the economic brake. Readjusting policies to the new circumstances (hitting the speeder instead of the brake) took time.

2. The Austrian response

There is some debate in the literature whether there really is such a thing as a specifically Austrian version of Keynesianism which might merit the use of the term "Austro-Keynesianism"[7] to designate the foundation of Austrian economic policy in the 70s. Some writers insist on the basically a-theoretical character of Austrian economic policy making. They claim that the only principle continuously obeyed by Austrian policy makers has been not to obey any principle (e.g. Rothschild, 1989, pp. 121-122). According to this view Austrian economic policy making is just "muddling through" turned into fine art.

It is indeed hard - at least to the outside observer[8] - to detect a theoretical foun-

---

this lecture quickly and well.

[7] This term is often attributed to Hans Seidel who is said to have coined it in 1979, cf. Rothschild (1989, p. 123, note 7).

[8] And not to them only. "The main problem in explaining the principles of the Austrian success-story is the lack of a full understanding by Austrian economists themselves. The country's economic policy does not stem from a logical consistent theory, it built up over time as a hotch-potch (sic!) of many ideas thought up by daring politicians and meek economists alike ..." (Tichy, 1984, pp. 363-364).

dation of Austrian economic policy making akin to that of the "Scandinavian model". Nevertheless there appears to have been an overarching principle adhered to in all of the period considered here. If it were to be formulated as a slogan, "Verstetigung durch Verständigung" (stabilizing through compromising) would probably best catch the gist of it. An overriding concern of Austrian economic policy making was to stabilize expectations and to make future developments calculable to the economic agents by keeping the economy on a steady development path.[9]

Table 2.1.: Coefficients of variation (Standard deviation / mean) on four indicators

	Austria	Germany	Denmark	Sweden	UK
Growth (GDP)					
1966-80	0.48	0.71	0.86	0.76	1.10
1974-79	0.77	1.02	1.34	1.25	1.42
Inflation (cons. prices)					
1966-80	0.41	0.40	0.33	0.42	0.58
1974-79	0.39	0.34	0.22	0.14	0.33
Unemployment					
1967-80	0.21	0.60	0.69	0.18	0.32
1974-79	0.16	0.25	0.30	0.14	0.23
B-o-P (pct. of GDP)					
1966-80	1.63	1.37	0.45	2.53	4.27
1974-79	0.84	1.26	0.37	0.75	1.4
Rank sum					
1966-80	9	10	11	12	18
1974-79	11	14	12	7	16

The way to achieve this was by policy measures agreed upon through continuous and extensive compromising involving primarily the authorities, labor, and capital in a tripartite cooperative setup. As can be seen from table 2.1., Austrian economic policy was actually quite successful with respect to its self-chosen stabilization goal. Thus the country's economic performance during the crisis was not only generally good[10] but it was also quite reliably so.[11]

---

[9] Cf. Tichy (1988, pp. 338-341).
[10] Some observers, e.g. Bös, Genser and Holzmann (1979, pp. 485-489) have claimed that a considerable part of the good-looking Austrian economic performance during the crisis really was a statistical artefact, owing a lot to a suitable (re)definition of central macroeconomic

----

Figure 2.1.: Unemployment in Austria 1974-79, quarterly data

(a) Series

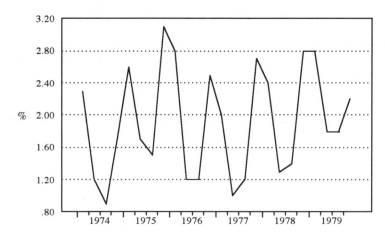

(b) ACF of residuals from Box-Jenkins model

LAG	CORR	SE
1	.122	.224
2	-.112	.227
3	.036	.230
4	-.207	.230
5	-.285	.239
6	-.049	.256
7	-.130	.256
8	-.072	.259
9	.018	.260
10	-.041	.260
11	.090	.261
12	.018	.262
13	.039	.262
14	.226	.263
15	.272	.272

Data: OECD, Economic Surveys: Austria (var. years)

indicators like unemployment. Even if this were to be conceded - it is actually rejected by Tichy (1984) - by and large the same thing would be true for other countries, so the relative performance of the Austrian economy would still stand out as good.

11 It is interesting to notice that the rank order of our five countries with respect to stability (both for the period 1966-80 and the recession period 1974-79) conforms much better to their conventional rank ordering on a corporatism scale than does their rank order with respect to economic performance. This would seem to suggest that (neo)-corporatism is good at stabilizing economic development at whatever level of performance, but not so good at influencing performance levels.

The Austrian performance in stabilizing is especially impressive with respect to the development in unemployment during the recession. This, of course, reflects the high priority assigned to that macroeconomic goal in Austrian economic policy making. Figure 2.1. (a) shows the quarterly development in unemployment figures in Austria 1974-79. On analysis, the fluctuations turn out to be all seasonality and serial dependency. The systematic part can be satisfactorily represented by a $(1,0,0) \times (0,1,0)_4$ model. As can be seen in figure 2.1. (b) the residuals from that model are not different than white noise. The Durbin Periodogram White Noise Test statistic for the residuals is 0.0796. This is far below any critical point. Thus there is no discernible trend in the series.

Pursuing this type of stability-oriented policy successfully requires all principal actors to exercise a measure of self-restraint in order to maintain the necessary level of basic social consensus. Obviously economic expectations cannot easily be stabilized if the political parties were continuously striving to "move ideological fences"[12] by proposals which - if enacted - would profoundly change the very framework of economic activity in society. Nor is stabilization the most likely result if labor and capital are continuously trying to make inroads into each others' shares of factor income, or if there is ongoing pressure on the wage structure with a view to change it in favor of one group of wage earners or another.

Little wonder, then, that Austrian policy making in the period considered here was characterized not only by an unusually high degree of basic social and economic consensus, but also by a likewise unusually strong emphasis on consensus building.[13] With good reason Scharpf (1987, p. 242; my translation) speaks of the "... inexorable Austrian determination to reach a mutual understanding between the social partners (labor and capital) and their political camps."

It is also most probably this concern about consensus that lies at the base of the remarkably low saliency of questions concerning distribution and redistribution in the Austrian labor market which has been noticed by many scholars.[14] The low saliency applies to the question of the wage rate as well as of the wage structure, both of which have exhibited considerable stability. Winckler (1985, p. 301) even speaks of an implicit wage- and price-contract between employees and employers (business) containing a mutual renouncement of attempts at redistributing income in Austria through wage- and price-setting.[15] At the same time

---

[12] This term was coined by the Danish Socialdemocrats in the beginning of the 70s.

[13] There is, of course, a seamy side to this strong consensus orientation as well. It is the weakening of democratic control with the authorities and those in power. A number of political scandals which have surfaced during the later years illustrate that danger.

[14] Cf. for example Sawyer (1976, pp. 22-23); Suppanz and Wagner (1981); Teschner and Vesper (1983, p. 34); Flanagan et al. (1983, p. 53); Tichy (1984, p. 374); Winckler (1985, p. 296), Guger (1989).

[15] The reason why there has nevertheless been a drop in profit shares in Austria 1974-79 (Faxén, 1982, p. 372) seems to be that "Lohnnebenkosten" which amount to about 70 per cent of the wage sum have increased during that period. Even so, in a comparison of 11 countries,

the Austrian labor market stands out as one of the most peaceful labor markets in terms of industrial conflict level (cf. chapter 4; Paldam and Pedersen, 1987).

The Austrian consensus orientation has strong historical roots. There is, for one, the bad experience of what divisiveness can do, stemming from the civil warlike situation leading up to the Dollfuˇ-coup in 1934 and the victory of Austro-fascism over the Socialdemocrats. This, ultimately, opened for the "Anschluß" of the weakened Austrian republic to Nazi Germany in 1938. There is, of more recent vintage, the experience of being an occupied country with limited sovereignty. From 1945 to 1955 all Austrian laws had to be put before the allied commanders for approval. In order to avoid a veto from especially the Soviets, many regulations were based on agreements negotiated by the interested parties instead of on formal laws. In that way a tradition of regulation through agreements was created. This tradition survived the end of occupation.

In order to achieve its prime goal, a high and stable level of employment, Austrian (Keynesian) stabilization policy primarily targets four economic policy fields and activities. The first is wage policy. Wages are the main cost factor to business as well as the most important determinant of income for wage earners. A stable development of wages is hence deemed imperative for the general stabilization of the economy. The second target is price policy. This is viewed as a precondition for a stable development in wages. The third target is investment policy and monetary policy (to keep interest rates low and stable). This is important because interest rates influence investment decisions in business. The fourth and final target is exchange rate policy viewed as the decisive factor in foreign trade development (Tichy, 1988, p. 339). In relation to these four types of policy demand management by fiscal policy primarily plays the role of a fire brigade (Teschner and Vesper, 1983, p. 43). It is used in a discretionary manner to fight instabilities not taken care of by one or several of the four main policies.

2.1. Crisis onset in Austria: Five "good luck" factors and one mistake

Examining figure 1.3. in chapter 1 it is easily seen that the development of the Austrian economy after 1973 took a different path than in the other countries in this study (with the exception of Sweden). While most countries plunged into the recession during 1974, the Austrian economy was still booming. GDP growth diminished only moderately from 4.9 per cent in 1973 to 3.9 per cent in 1974. Unemployment stayed at a low level. Consumer price inflation, on the other hand, was on the upturn running at 9.5 per cent in 1974 compared to 7.6 per cent the year before, and the current account turned negative (-1 per cent of GDP) where in the preceding half decade it used to show a slight surplus (on average 0.3 per cent of GDP).[16]

gross profit rates in Austrian manufacturing were second to those in Finland only (Faxén, 1982, p. 385).
16 OECD, Historical Statistics (1988).

It was not until 1975 that the international economic crisis struck at Austria, too. That year economic growth turned slightly negative (-0.5 per cent GDP growth) and there was an upward tendency in unemployment (extremely weak by international standards). Inflation went down a bit, however, while the current account remained in the red. Still, in international comparison, the Austrian economy got just scratched but not seriously hurt in 1975.

The reason why Austria managed to steer clear of the international recession in 1974 was not primarily a superior, more adequate economic policy making. Rather she owed her good fate to a number of fortunate circumstances combined with a measure of pure luck (Grande and Müller, 1985, pp. 12-15; Scharpf, 1987, pp. 81-84). It was only after the onset of the crisis in 1975 that Austrian crisis policy went into gear and proved itself highly effective.

The first "good luck factor" was the relative economic backwardness of Austria, prior to 1973, compared to most other industrial economies. The period of strong, continuing economic growth which in most countries had begun in the 50s did not come to Austria before the mid-60s. In 1960 an unusually high proportion of the Austrian labor force (22.6 per cent) was still employed in the agrarian sector. GDP per capita was only 75 per cent of the contemporary level in the UK (which among the countries in the present study had the lowest GDP per capita at that time, except for Austria). But beginning in 1968 Austria entered a period of rising prosperity. It was led by an export sector taking advantage of a de facto 12 per cent depreciation of the Austrian Schilling between 1969 and 1973 (when Austria chose not to follow suit in repeated German appreciations of the D-Mark).

Austria had a strong incentive to cling to the economic upswing for as long as possible in order to close the perceived gap to other industrial countries (Chaloupek, 1985, p. 73). Therefore there was very little political incentive to dampen economic activity in the beginning of the 70s, even though at that time wages and prices began to rise sharply in Austria, too. Contrary to many other industrial countries Austria did not move into the worldwide recession with a foot already on the brakes. She thus avoided getting hit by the combined effect of contractive domestic policy measures (enacted while the economy was still overheated) and the likewise contractive demand reduction due to the oil price hike.

The second "good luck factor" was a direct consequence of the first. The belated economic upturn in Austria had consequences for the demand side of the Austrian labor market. It could, in the short run, absorb some part of the unemployment effect of the recession. At the onset of the recession in Austria there was still a reservoir of unfilled vacancies in the (private and public) service sector. During the pre-recession boom wages in the service sector had tended to fall behind wages in industry. The prosperity period had not lasted long enough to allow the service sector to adjust either by letting its wages approach the wage level in industry or by shedding positions that could not be filled. The strong increase after 1974 in the fraction of the Austrian labor force employed in the service sector indicates that the service sector was at least initially instrumental in cushioning some of the employment effects of the international recession.

The third "good luck factor" also relates to the demand side of the labor

----

market. Many observers have pointed to the role played by the Austrian natio-nalized industries in keeping up employment.[17] For political reasons the national holding company (ÖIAG) has to exercise restraint in laying off employees. In 1975, for instance, the nationalized industries (which employ about 17 per cent of the total labor force in industry) shed only 1 per cent of its workers as against the 7 per cent laid off in private sector industry.[18]

There was a (fourth) "good luck factor" on the supply side of the labor mar-ket as well. Several factors combined to bring down labor supply. In the first place the participation rates - especially of women[19] - were elastic enough to make for some adjustment of supply to downward changes in demand. In the second place a reduction in 1975 of the weekly working hours from 42 to 40 hours, agreed upon long before the onset of the recession (Scharpf, 1987, pp. 83-84), worked in the same direction. Thirdly a considerable number of foreign workers had work permits of limited duration. They could be used as shock-ab-sorbers in the Austrian labor market. Between 1974 and 1975 about 33,000 were repatriated. This made for a reduction of the total labor force in Austria by 2 per cent.[20]

The fifth and final "good luck factor" relates to the structure and the geo-graphical orientation of Austria's foreign trade. In the first place the Austrian economy is very open. At the same time the Austrian dependency on oil import was relatively low even before the first oil price hike. As has been shown in chapter 1 this combination of a high degree of economic openness and a relative-ly low degree of oil import dependency was a good one from the point of view of economic crisis management.

In the second place a sizeable part (about 15 per cent)[21] of Austrian foreign trade has by tradition been with Eastern European countries and the Soviet Union. Although this market is certainly not crisis-proof[22] its fluctuations do not necessarily follow those in the world markets. While the OECD-market contract-

----

[17] There is, however, some disagreement. According to Tichy (1984, p. 365) the development in GDP per employed does not suggest that labor hoarding was important. According to Teschner and Vesper (1983, p. 37) other factors (reduction in hours worked and in the number of foreign workers) were more important in keeping unemployment down than labor hoarding in the nationalized industries.

[18] OECD, Economic Surveys: Austria (1976), p. 33.

[19] For 1975 the elasticity (with respect to the employment situation) of women's labor supply has been estimated to 0.89, as against 0.22 for men, cf. Coen and Hickman (1989, p. 171).

[20] Flanagan et al. (1983, p. 41, note 1). On the other hand there was a development in the opposite direction as well: about 15,000 Austrian workers went home in 1975, primarily from Germany and Switzerland, cf. OECD, Economic Surveys: Austria (1976), p. 18.

[21] OECD, Economic Surveys: Austria (1976), table 2.

[22] This claim can still be found in the literature as late as in 1988, however, cf. for example Leaman (1988, pp. 199-200).

ed by 7.8 per cent in 1975 (measured in terms of imports into that area), the Eastern European market grew by 9.7 per cent, measured in terms of imports from OECD-countries. Thus the relatively high share of exports to Eastern Europe in total Austrian exports initially contributed to stabilizing Austrian foreign trade.

Finally the Austrian export was able to draw advantage from the boom in raw materials and semi-manufactured goods following in the wake of the first oil price hike. There was then a widespread fear of the OPEC-example being followed by other producers of raw materials, with similar effects upon supply and prices. Consequently large-style hoarding was taking place. Since about 10 per cent of Austrian exports consist of raw materials and semi-manufactured goods, the increased international demand did the Austrian economy good[23] - while it lasted.

It lasted until early 1975. With the inventories of the main trade partners filled, there was a sudden and severe drop in Austrian exports - not the least of raw materials. Altogether exports decreased by 232 mill. Schillings in 1975.[24] This again had strong repercussions on domestic demand and domestic economic activity. All of a sudden "felix Austria" in 1975 found herself facing the prospect of stagflation. Inflation ran high (8.4 per cent) and the labor market was getting tight.[25]

This development initially caught the Austrian economic-political decision makers by complete surprise. As late as in mid-1974 an expert prognosis foresaw a 4 per cent real growth in GDP in 1975. Even in December 3.5 per cent of real growth was still foreseen (Lehner, 1982, p. 26). It was generally expected that Austria would be able to duck the international recession. On this optimistic basis the round of collective bargaining in the Austrian labor market in the autumn of 1974 had resulted in agreements bringing about large wage rises for 1975 (about 13 per cent on average) to which had to be added the cost of the earlier agreed upon reduction in working hours from 42 to 40 hours a week that was to become effective in 1975 as well. These strong increases in labor cost[26] were not exactly adequate to the export-led recession situation developing in 1975. They could not but further impair the competitive standing of the export sector and hence hurt Austrian exports even more. On the other hand rising wages also helped in temporarily stabilizing domestic demand (Scharpf, 1987, p. 84).

---

[23] From 1973 to 1974 the Austrian export of raw materials grew by 167 mill. Schilling, cf. OECD, Economic Surveys: Austria (1976), table F.

[24] OECD, Economic Surveys: Austria (1976), p. 5.

[25] Although unemployment rose only very moderately, the number of unfilled vacancies was reduced to half its size in 1974 (Statistisches Handbuch für die Republik Österreich, 1980, p. 300).

[26] Unit labor cost in Austrian manufacturing rose by 17.2 per cent in 1975, cf. OECD, Historical Statistics (1988), p. 94. This was more than two times the increase in Austria's main trading partner, Germany.

In this situation there was a general consensus that stabilizing the employment situation was to be the central economic-political goal. Not the least the SPÖ--government which had been in power since 1970 had reason to dread the prospect of serious unemployment developing during 1975. That year was an election year with elections to the parliament (Nationalrat) scheduled for October.

In keeping with the main tenets of Austro-Keynesianism, stimulating demand through expansionary fiscal and monetary policy was not relied upon as the sole remedy in Austrian crisis policy. It was certainly used to the limit in 1975, but besides this corner stone in any Keynesian stabilization policy there were two additional ones in its Austrian version. One was a restrictive wage and price policy jointly agreed upon, implemented and overseen by labor and business. The second was a fixed exchange rate regime. In the following sections these measures will be examined in turn.

2.2. Fiscal policy 1975-79

In anticipation of continuing high economic activity the 1975-budget of the Austrian government[27] had made provision for a small deficit only. The planned overall deficit was -8.5 bill. Schilling and the internal demand effective financial balance[28] of the budget was -7.2 bill. Schilling.

As the economic crisis developed during 1975, these targets were thoroughly revised as the government went into heavy deficit-spending. In the end the internal demand effective financial balance for 1975 stood at -26.1 bill. Schilling (about 4.5 per cent of GDP), or close to four times the size originally voted. It was to stay at approximately that level throughout the rest of the period considered here.

In part the 1975 deficit was due to loss of revenues. Revenues fell by about 6 per cent (9.2 bill. Schilling) compared to the figures in the budget. This can be viewed mainly as an automatic budgetary reaction to the economic slow down.[29]

So can part of the additional expenditures amounting to a 6 per cent increase (9.8 bill. Schilling) compared to the figures in the budget. The Austrian government did not just passively accept lower revenues and higher expenditures as a consequence of the recession. In order to further stimulate domestic demand it

[27] Here and in the following we focus on the federal government, leaving aside the role played by the budgets of state governments and municipalities. The reason is that they have little chance to influence cyclical developments in the economy, cf. Lehner (1982).

[28] Overall deficit minus debt repayment, net payments abroad, and net addition to reserves.

[29] These figures do not contain the effects of the reduction in income taxes becoming effective by January 1975 (which increased disposable incomes by about 2.5 per cent). Although from the point of view of anti-cyclical economic policy the tax reduction came at the right time, it was not part of the government's stabilization policy, having been decided upon prior to the onset of the recession, and perhaps rather with an eye to the upcoming election.

chose to increase public expenditures. Some of this was done by activating the contingency budget, thus making available extra 2.2 bill. Schillings by April 1975 and the rest (4.5 bill. Schilling) by July. This money was used for public investment programs. Furthermore expenditures were increased by having the parliament pass laws allowing the government to exceed certain appropriations. By this means 4.5 bill. Schilling were made available for public construction works by April 1975. Altogether public consumption and transfer payments were both increased by about 16 per cent over their 1974-levels.

The resulting net borrowing requirements were covered by loans, only half of which were raised domestically. The remainder came from abroad (Lehner, 1982, p. 31). Apparently the main reason for the high level of foreign borrowing (which was not continued in subsequent years) was to avoid a "crowding out"-effect on internal credit markets. Besides, interest rates were lower abroad, and a sizeable current accounts deficit had to be foreseen.

Through its deficit spending the government thus attempted to compensate the loss of demand caused by (primarily) the drop in exports in 1975. The attempt did not at once meet with complete success. Despite the various measures, capacity utilization fell below 96 per cent of potential output (Lehner, 1982, p. 27). Some of the stimulating measures simply could not become effective until in 1976. On the other hand "(t)here can be little doubt that the determined anti-cyclical policy adopted during the 1975 recession and its continuation through the early phase of the upswing was the major factor behind Austria's success in maintaining virtual full employment ..." (OECD, Economic Surveys: Austria (1977), p. 39).

The forecast of the economic development in Austria in 1976 was rather cautious. It promised a meagre 1.5 per cent real GDP growth (Lehner, 1982, p. 26). This was certainly better than in 1975, but it was not even enough to make up for the loss that year. Therefore the continuation of large style deficit spending was planned for, albeit at a somewhat reduced scale compared to 1975. The financial balance[30] aimed at was -19.0 bill. Schilling. The government clearly had no intention to cease stimulating domestic demand too early in the upswing, even if this implied running huge budget deficits.

The slight reduction in the deficit planned for 1976 was to be brought about mainly by having revenues grow at a somewhat faster rate than expenditures. Thus by January 1 the VAT was increased from 16 to 18 per cent. By March an indirect tax on gasoline was raised in order to cover an additional 1 bill. Schilling for use in programs of road construction. Taxes on motor vehicles were to be raised by October. Finally a 1 per cent reduction in public employment was announced for 1977.

On the expenditure side the government mainly tried to stimulate private investment still further.[31] An existing investment tax was suspended for the

---

[30] Defined as the internal demand effective financial balance.

[31] With good reason Haas and Svoboda (1978, p. 198) speak of an "... almost breathtaking degree of stimulation of any kind of private investment" in Austria. By 1977 about 40 per cent of domestic credits are estimated to have been subsidized in one way or another, cf. Scharpf

----

whole of 1976 to become effective again (at a 2 per cent rate) for 1977-79. Special depreciation provisions were made for commercial construction work commencing after December 31, 1975 and finished before the end of 1977. In addition, 3.5 bill. Schilling were made available for public investment programs.

The actual, combined effect was not exactly as envisaged, however, as far as the budget deficit is concerned. Instead of the planned reduction the deficit grew slightly compared to 1975. It amounted to 4.7 per cent of GDP in 1976. Contrary to 1975 most of the net borrowing requirement was covered by domestic loans. On the other hand the Austrian economy developed more than satisfactorily in 1976 returning to a higher level of capacity utilization (about 97 per cent) and high GDP growth (5.8 per cent). Employment stayed at its high level. Inflation was moderate.

With forecasts of a real GDP growth between 4 and 5 per cent in 1977 (Lehner, 1982, p. 26) prospects looked bright for the Austrian economy. But the recovery did not come free. The current account deficit had increased significantly (cf. figure 1.3., chap. 1). Mainly for that reason 1977 saw a cautious reorientation of the Austrian fiscal policy.

In order to contain the current account deficit the government strove hard to bring down the planned budget deficit for 1977. At first the government relied on a slow down of the growth in expenditures (planned at 7.9 per cent) relative to the growth of revenues (planned at 10 per cent). Most of the revenue increase was expected to come from tax progression. When at first no result seemed to be forthcoming, the government in the autumn of 1977 decided to tighten the budget still further by increasing revenues and cutting down on expenditures. Thus a 30 per cent VAT-rate was levied on luxury goods - by sheer luck (what else?) primarily on such that were imported, like cars. A transport tax was introduced, and business depreciation rules were tightened in some respects. Together these measures added up to a budget improvement of 14.5 bill. Schilling. Most of this, though, would not become effective before 1978.

Nevertheless the cure had effects in 1977. The internal demand effective financial deficit was reduced by 4.5 bill. Schillings relative to the 1977 budget (and by 3.4 bill. Schilling relative to the result from 1976). This, of course, weakened the demand effect of the federal budget. Public consumption grew only about half as much as in 1976 and the growth rate of transfers to private households was just 75 per cent of last year's. Only subsidies kept growing at an increasing pace (Bös, Genser and Holzmann, 1979, p. 492).

The government did actually succeed in creating a mini-recession or controlled economic downturn in Austria in 1978. The forecast had been for a 1.5 per cent GDP growth only, but in the end not even this modest figure was reached. Real GDP growth was only 0.5 per cent. Consumption and investments fell, mainly reflecting advance purchases in 1977 to avoid some of the effects of the budget tightening measures. On the other hand unemployment only rose by a tiny fraction (from 1.6 per cent in 1977 to 1.8 per cent in 1978). The current account balance improved markedly, although this was not primarily attributable to a fall

(1987, p. 198).

in imports. Rather the improvement originated from significant gains of market shares in Austria's main export markets.[32]

Deficit spending was once more used to control the extent of the economic downturn. While the stated goal of the 1977 policy measures had been to reduce the federal budget deficit, the government adapted its policies swiftly and did instead allow the deficit to grow in 1978. The internal demand effective financial deficit jumped to a new all-times height of -29.1 bill. Schilling (Lehner, 1982, p. 25). This was a 25 per cent increase over the 1977 figure and about 10 per cent more than had originally been planned for. Revenues fell behind targets with 6.3 bill. Schilling. There was an unforeseen increase in expenditures of 3.5 bill. Schilling. Most of this was due to stronger growth in public consumption and transfers to private households. The government also stuck to its traditional policies of creating incentives for investment. In April a new program, extending over several years, was enacted containing subsidized interest and long-term state loans on easy conditions.

Again the cure turned out well. For 1979 a 3 per cent growth was foreseen. In the end this turned out to be too cautious a guess. Real GDP actually grew by 5 per cent in 1979.

With these economic prospects for 1979 it was safe for the government to attend to the size of the budget deficit. This could be done even though 1979 was an election year. The announced goal was to bring down the deficit to 3.5 per cent of GDP by 1979 as a step towards the medium term goal of a budget deficit stabilized at 2 per cent of GDP. To that end revenue increases and budget cuts amounting to 6 bill. Schillings were announced in the autumn of 1978 to become effective in 1979. On the other hand a tax reform which was to ease the tax burden of both wage earners and self-employed also became effective in 1979 so that voters could be kept happy.

As a result, the internal demand effective financial deficit of 1979 was reduced to about the same level as in 1976, without doing any harm to the level of economic activity. The Austrian export sector was strong enough to secure the upswing alone. It took advantage primarily of a slight upturn in German economic activity (Teschner and Vesper, 1983, p. 39). As would have been expected, the Austrian current account balance, however, suffered a new set back.

In figure 2.2. an attempt is made to summarize the impact of fiscal policy on economic activity in Austria 1973-79. In order to facilitate interpretation a short account of the method used is called for.

Measuring the impact of budget changes on demand and economic activity is generally fraught with considerable difficulties. As is well known a budget deficit need not by itself be expansionary, nor a surplus contractive. Even a growth of budget deficits or surpluses is not a reliable indicator of the budget impact, unless it is related to the growth in potential output. Just looking at the absolute or relative size of the deficit or surplus is not enough.

---

32 OECD, Economic Surveys: Austria (1978), p. 5. A different assessment is found in Teschner and Vesper (1983, p. 38).

The budget is neutral with respect to the economic activity in society as long as the public share in present year's potential output is the same as was the share in the preceding year. Thus if the deficit grows, but at a slower pace than potential output, then the impact of the growing deficit will actually be contractive.

Hence one of the central problems becomes how to measure potential output. Here estimations are available for Austria and Germany, but not for the other three countries.[33] Therefore use will be made of a comparatively rough and simple method to assess budget impacts suggested in Teschner and Vesper (1983, pp. 15-16). The purpose of their measure is to indicate the direction (restrictive or expansionary) of the budget saldo impact as well as the size (in percentage of GDP) of this impact.

Their measure of budget impact only covers primary effects. Thus secondary effects (multiplier effects) are not taken into account. While this is certainly a weakness, it renders the computational task feasible.

Teschner and Vesper start from the trend (computed as a five year moving average) of the (nominal) GDP as approximation to potential output. Thus the relevant economic impact of the budget in a given year is defined as the deviation of the year's (actual) revenues and expenditures from their forecast values derived from the preceding year's revenues and expenditures and the trend rate of GDP.

Figure 2.2.: Demand stimulation through public finance in Austria 1973-79, in per cent of GDP

(a) All government

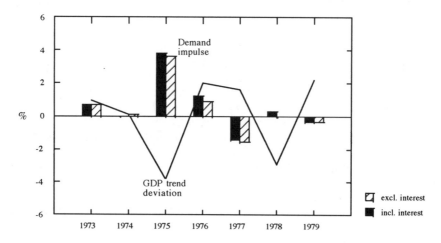

(continued)

(b) Central government

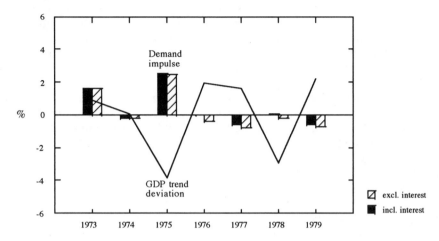

Data: Teschner and Vesper (1983); OECD, National Accounts (1984)

Figure 2.2. shows the economic impulse as defined above originating from the total government budget (a) and the federal government budget (b). The figures clearly bring out the markedly anti-cyclical character of Austrian fiscal policy. The results of the year 1975 stand out with a very strong demand impulse from deficit spending. The impulse was reduced in the following year, but there was obviously no contraction in the interest of short run budget consolidation. It can also be seen that the fiscal impulses become weaker towards the end of the period. This may reflect the fact that the Austrian economy was back on a reasonably stable growth path after the 1975-shock. On the other hand it might also reflect that there was less room for fiscal manoeuvre due to the buildup of a considerable public debt and the resulting interest burden.

In the preceding discussion the possible existence of a political business cycle in Austrian fiscal policy has been alluded to at various points. The timing of this policy as shown in figure 2.2. is in two respects as one would expect in the presence of a Nordhaus-cycle.[34] In the first place there is the strong expansionary impulse of the election year 1975 in order to keep down unemployment. In the second place there is the budget consolidation attempt of 1977, i.e. about at midterm with respect to the election period 1975-79. On the other hand there appears to be "too little" stimulation in 1978-79, but this might simply reflect that little needed to be done to the economy to keep the voters happy.

Neck (1989) has estimated fiscal reaction functions for the Austrian government for the period 1959-86 which also take into account the potential dependence of the fiscal reaction upon the closeness of elections. The basic finding - which agrees well with the results found here - is that the political business cycle

---

[34] Nordhaus (1975).

----

in Austria does not primarily express itself by creating (additional) cyclical movements in the budget deficit. Rather, it may be detected in the response of the
budget deficit to forecast changes in key variables like employment and the
balance of payments deficit. The response of the budget deficit varies with the
closeness of the election. In election years the full employment goal dominates all
others, while the balance of payment goal is given very low priority (Neck, 1989,
p. 102).

In summary, in the period considered here Austrian financial policy was characterized by two main traits. In the first place there was a swift reaction to adverse
economic developments, especially in 1975. After 1975 Austrian financial policy
did not turn to budget consolidation too early during the economic recovery and
thus avoided choking the upswing.

In the second place strong emphasis was given throughout to the stimulation
of private investment. The preferred means was to reduce cost by subsidizing
interest rates. Thus despite its undisputable Keynesian foundation Austrian economic policy was not exclusively demand side oriented but contained a sizeable
element of supply side measures. This happened long before such policies (or
even the term) had become fashionable.

It is, of course, difficult to decide on the effectiveness of this aspect of Austrian
economic policy. Austria stands clearly out with the highest gross fixed capital
formation fraction of GDP (26.4 per cent on average 1974-79), most of which
was in the private sector.[35] This high level of private investment may have been
caused by the supply-side measures of the government.

2.3. Monetary policy in Austria 1975-79

As in textbook-Keynesianism Austrian monetary policy had no independent
function in demand management during the period considered. Rather it simply
accommodated the fiscal policy course defined by the government. Even so, an
easing or tightening of monetary policy at times led the corresponding development in fiscal policy. There was no attempt by the central bank (OeNB) at controlling money supply as a means to control inflation. This reflects the conventional assignment of instruments to goals in Austrian economic policy making.
Controlling inflation is seen as primarily the task of wage and price policy and of
the exchange rate policy.

The prime goals assigned to Austrian monetary policy is to keep stable exchange rates and a stable interest rate level. In the present section we consider
the second goal only. The foreign exchange policy is described in the following
section.[36]

With respect to the goal of stable interest rates OeNB succeeded quite well
(OECD, Economic Surveys: Austria (1976), p. 30). In the period considered here

----

35 OECD, Historical Statistics (1988), p. 65.
36 On possible conflicts between the two goals see Winckler (1989, p. 263).

the largest difference between the highest and the lowest long term nominal interest rate was 1.7 per cent in Austria as against 4.7 per cent in Germany, 4.8 per cent in Denmark, 2.9 per cent in Sweden, and 3.9 per cent in the UK. On the other hand the interest rate was not generally low in Austria. Most of the time it was kept about 1 - 2 per cent above the German level.[37]

The main instruments at the disposal of OeNB are changes in the discount and Lombard rates on one hand and changes in quantitative credit restrictions ("Limes") on the other,[38] as well as open market operations. Besides, OeNB exerts considerable direct influence on the behavior of Austrian commercial banks. Most of these are nationalized.

In January 1975, i.e. even before the recession had really struck at Austria, the first cautious step was taken in the direction of a more expansionary monetary policy. The base time for computing the "Limes" was moved forward from June to December 1974. This was followed by a 0.5 percentage point reduction (from 6.5 to 6 per cent) of the discount rate in April. In June the "Limes" was once more eased as the base time was moved forward to June, and by October "Limes" was suspended altogether pending further notice. The backdrop for these measures was a strong increase in household savings and a shift from real to financial investment or cash by firms as the 1975 recession made itself felt.

Monetary policy stayed expansionary in 1976 in order to help consolidating the economic recovery. In January there was another 1 percentage point reduction of the discount rate. This was followed by a further reduction in June so that by mid-1976 the discount rate stood at 4 per cent. At the same time OeNB moved upwards its ceiling for the rediscount of export credits. To counteract the drop in liquidity due to the loss of foreign currency in the wake of the growing balance of payments deficit a considerable growth in Lombard credits was tolerated.

In 1977 there was some tightening of monetary policy. This was parallel to the tightening of fiscal policy in the same year. By June 1977 the discount rate was raised to 5.5 per cent and "Limes" was put back into effect, but with a 1.1 per cent ceiling on monthly domestic credit expansion. By November "Limes" was lowered considerably for consumer credits, reducing the allowed increase to 0.55 per cent a month. The reason was an excessive growth in consumer credits which between June 1975 and June 1977 had grown by on average 35 per cent a year (or twice the growth rate of commercial credits).[39]

The mini-recession of 1978 brought about primarily by fiscal policy signalled

---

[37] The same is true for real interest, except for 1974 and 1976. But thanks to the Austrian investment programs and the wide-spread subsidization of interests a comparison of Austrian interest rate levels to those of other countries is not very informative.

[38] "Limes" is a 1 per cent a month ceiling on domestic credit expansion that was introduced in 1972. The penalties for exceeding the Limes are an interest charge (equalling the bank rate) on the excess credit granted, and the denial of refinancing (OECD, Economic Surveys: Austria (1976), p. 26, note 18). The most common way of easing Limes is by moving forward in time the base volume of credit used to compute the allowable credit expansion.

[39] OECD, Economic Surveys: Austria (1977), p. 35.

the start of a selective easing of monetary policy in 1978. It was aimed at supporting the government's investment programs introduced in April 1978. Again changes in quantitative credit regulations were the main measures used. By June 1978 these measures were backed by a reduction of the discount rate to 4.5 per cent.[40]

Figure 2.3.: Development in money supply (M1 and quasi-money), discount rate, and credits to the private sector (including local government) in Austria 1973-79, per cent

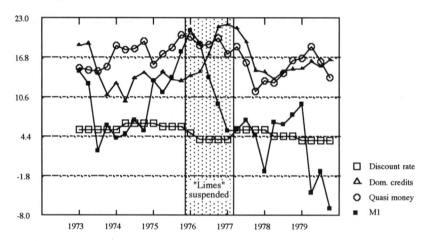

Data: OECD, Economic Surveys: Austria (var. years)

In 1979 the policy of "easy money" continued. By January the "Limes" rate for commercial credits was raised from 1.1 to 1.3 per cent, and the base time was moved forward to December 31, 1978. The discount rate was slightly reduced by knocking off an additional 0.25 per cent. The same was done to the Lombard rate which was lowered from 5 to 4.25 per cent.

By July the base time of the "Limes" was once more moved forward, this time to June 1979. But after that, reflecting the swift recovery from the mini-recession of the Austrian economy, monetary policy tightened slightly. By September discount and Lombard rates above 70 per cent of refinancing quotas were raised 2 percentage points.

---

[40] The frequency of discount rate changes in the period considered here is quite uncharacteristic of Austrian monetary policy. From 1955 to 1974 the discount rate was changed only 9 times, cf. OECD, Economic Surveys: Austria (1977), p. 31. This is probably while some observers have claimed that after 1974 stable interest rates have been abandoned as a goal of Austrian monetary policy. As mentioned above, the long term nominal interest rate did nevertheless fluctuate less in Austria than in the other four countries of this study.

By way of summarizing figure 2.3. illustrates the development in some indicators of monetary conditions in Austria covering the period from 1973 to 1979. If this figure is compared to figure 2.2., the close coordination of monetary and fiscal policy in Austria is easily recognized.

2.4. Exchange rate policy: The hard currency option

The main reason why Austrian fiscal (and monetary) policy could be aimed primarily at the employment goal was that price stability was taken care of by an exchange rate or "hard currency" policy in combination with wage and price policy, cf. below. Among the five countries studied here this way of using exchange rate policy is quite unique.

The basic idea in keeping a fixed exchange rate also after the break-down of the Bretton Wood-system in 1973 was to make it contribute to price stability in Austria even in a situation with a balance of payment deficit. Else a small, open economy like the Austrian economy would run the risk of asymmetric exchange rate fluctuations where the domestic price level would only be pushed up by international inflation but not be pulled down by international price stability. Instead of the threatening vicious circle inflation - devaluation - more inflation the hard currency policy was an attempt at establishing a "good circle" where domestic prices were kept stable through the fixed exchange rate. On the other hand the inflexibility of this rate depended on domestic price stability.

In 1973 the value of the Austrian Schilling was tied to a basket of foreign currencies representing Austria's most important trade partners and weighted in accordance with their weight in Austrian foreign trade. The maximum permissible fluctuation of the Schilling was fixed at ±4.5 per cent, paralleling the arrangements in the European monetary cooperation (Hansen et al, 1988, p. 245).

By July 1976 the basket was abandoned and the Austrian Schilling was pegged at the German mark (DM).[41] After that Schilling was allowed to fluctuate between 7,19 and 7,05 Schilling per DM. This corresponded to the highest and lowest exchange rate since 1975. This meant a tiny depreciation of Schilling against DM (0.6 per cent).[42] By October 1978 intervention points were raised somewhat, corresponding to a Schilling depreciation against DM of about 1 per cent.

The main consequence of pegging the Austrian Schilling at the DM was that the Austrian inflation rate could no longer be higher than the German rate, except in the short run. From figure 1.3. in chapter 1 one can see how the Austrian and the German inflation rates actually tend to converge after 1976. Hence the Austrian hard currency policy which pegged the Schilling at the DM implied

---

[41] For reasons of foreign policy Schilling was tied to the Dutch Gulden as well, but this was of no practical importance.
[42] OECD, Economic Surveys: Austria (1980), p. 49.

----

that Austria "imported" the effects of the German anti-inflation policies which
were rather effective, cf. below.[43] It also meant a continuous, albeit moderate
appreciation of Schilling (following DM) against a number of other currencies,
primarily US$ and UK£. While this put some pressure on Austrian industry, the
effect was limited since about 1/3 of Austrian exports went to and close to 1/2 of
Austrian imports came from Germany and were hence unaffected.

The hard currency policy did contribute to the enforcement of restrictive wage
and price policies, especially in the exposed sectors of the Austrian economy.
Without the devaluation-option world market prices had to be accepted and the
only way to keep up profits was to keep down costs. Wage earners likewise had
to accept a development in wages that was determined by world market prices
and the development in productivity. Otherwise they would endanger their jobs.
Thus the hard currency policy put pressure on labor and capital alike to adopt
restrictive wage policies. It gave business strong incentives to adopt a firm stance
in wage negotiations. Any concessions exceeding what was warranted by world
market prices and productivity gains would in the last resort have to be paid out
of profits. At the same time stable import prices were an excellent carrot and the
threatening loss of jobs in the exposed sector an equally excellent stick for the
union leadership to use in case there were internal opposition to a moderate
wage policy. The leadership of the ÖGB agreed to the necessity of such a
moderate wage policy.

Thus the hard currency policy was quite essential in creating the climate necessary for a restrictive wage policy to win broad acceptance. In the end the hard
currency policy made the restrictive wage policy work (Tichy, 1984, p. 373).

2.5. Incomes policy

Incomes policy is probably the one aspect of Austrian crisis policy that has met
with greatest interest by foreign observers. Sometimes they have even tended to
focus on income policy to a degree where its interaction with and dependency on
other elements of Austrian economic policy has become obscured.[44] In international comparison Austria stands out as one of the few countries where it was
possible during the recession to make the trade unions adopt a rather restrictive
wage policy even in a full employment situation. This contributed to a swift
solution of otherwise intractable economic problems.

By tradition Austrian incomes policy is voluntary. It has no statutory basis
whatsoever. It works through a multitude of institutional arrangements that
integrate labor, business and government in the complex tripartite system called
economic and social partnership (Wirtschafts- und Sozialpartnerschaft). Incomes

-----

43 Scharpf (1987, p. 89) uses the expression "imported monetarism".
44 See for example Hansen et al. (1988, pp. 211-212).

policy is an important but far from the only aspect of this partnership.[45]

As mentioned above a high level of consensus concerning questions of distribution and redistribution exists in Austria. This consensus implies that labor as well as business will abstain from attempts to alter existing distributive relationships decisively.

With redistribution disposed of as a means to improve the economic situation of their members Austrian trade unions have had to opt for economic growth as their prime objective. Their attitude towards wage policy has primarily been informed by this goal. With productivity growth as its main guidepost this policy has, according to the Benya-formula,[46] aimed at a long term 2.5 - 3 per cent real wage growth per year.

This does not mean, however, that in Austria wage claims always need to be moderate. Rather, since the 1960s the aim has been to follow an anti-cyclical wage policy in order to stabilize wage development over cyclical fluctuations in the economy.[47] During the initial stages of an economic upswing (nominal) wage claims may be kept below what would be "warranted" by the development in productivity and inflation. In later stages they may be above that level. Thus in the early 70s wages rose sharply in Austria: from 1970 to 1973 wages in manufacturing went up on average 11.9 per cent (nominal) and 5.8 per cent (real) a year. But this was generally considered a kind of compensation Austrian wage earners were entitled to by virtue of moderate wage increases in the late 60s. This moderation had been instrumental in initiating the economic upswing during these years.[48] The wage increases in the early 70s did not aim at changing the functional distribution of income in disfavor of capital.

The wage increases agreed upon for 1975 - which quickly turned out to have been much too high given the incipient recession - demonstrate that the wage setting mechanism of the economic and social partnership is not infallible when it comes to adapting the development in wages to the Austrian economic situation. During the following years, on the other hand, wage increases were gradually reduced, e.g. from 13.4 per cent in 1975 to 5.5 per cent in 1979 in manufacturing.

This trend reflects that the wage policy of Austrian trade unions paid very close attention to the situation in the labor market after 1975. Although proper

---

[45] For an account of the institutional structure of the economic and social partnership in Austria see for example Nowotny (1989).

[46] Named after a chairman of the ÖGB.

[47] It has to be admitted that traces of such an anti-cyclical wage policy have been difficult to find by econometric analysis. If output growth (in fixed factor prices) is added to the wage equation suggested in Paldam and Pedersen (1987) the coefficient does in fact turn out to be negative, but its numerical value is small compared to the standard error, so it is hardly reliable.

[48] This is still another reason why Austrian economic policy did not turn restrictive in the early 70s (cf. above), as did economic policy in many other countries, despite sharply rising wages and prices.

unemployment did not occur in Austria during the period considered here, the trade unions became very sensitive to tightening labor market conditions. This is brought out by fitting the following union reaction function to quarterly data 1974-79 on nominal wage development in manufacturing:[49]

$$WM_t = a + b_1 WM_{t-2} + b_2 CPI_t + b_3 L/A_{t-2} + b_4 d75$$

where

WM_t = Nominal wage increase in manufacturing
CPI_t = Consumer price inflation
L/A_{t-2} = Ratio of unfilled vacancies to unemployed
$d75$ = Dummy for reduction in working hours 1975

Coefficient values and statistics for this model are given in table 2.2. As can be seen changes in labor market tightness (measured as the ratio of unfilled vacancies to number of unemployed) have a strong effect on nominal wage growth. This occurs at a lag of half a year. An increase in the number of unfilled vacancies relative to the number of unemployed tends to lead to a stronger growth in nominal wages. A reduction, reflecting a tighter labor market situation, tends to reduce the rate of nominal wage growth.

Table 2.2.: Coefficient values and statistics

Variable	Coeff.value	S.E.
Constant	-3.64	1.73
WM_{t-2}	-0.23	0.11
CPI_t	1.29	0.21
L/A_{t-2}	11.74	2.64
$d75$	4.90	1.36
R^2 (adj.)	0.897	
Durbin's h	0.795	
Q(9)	12.731	

Table 2.3. summarizes the main trends in wage development in Austria 1973-79. Despite the gradual reduction in nominal wage growth after 1975 real wages kept growing throughout, albeit at a moderate pace. This happened because inflation was reduced simultaneously with nominal wage growth through the combined effects of the hard currency policy and the restrictive wage policy. Thus Austrian wage earners did not as a whole suffer a setback in economic

---

[49] The data are from OECD, Economic Surveys: Austria (var. years). Estimation method is OLS.

well-being from the restrictive wage policy. Neither did they suffer a clear set-back with respect to the functional distribution of income. By 1979 the (adjusted) wage share was a bit higher than it had been in 1974.

Table 2.3.: Main trends in wage development in Austrian manufacturing, 1973-79
(increases in percentages), and adjusted wage share

	1973	1974	1975	1976	1977	1978	1979
Nominal	12.7	15.9	13.4	9.9	8.4	5.8	5.5
Real	4.8	5.8	4.5	2.4	2.7	2.2	1.7
Inflation	7.6	9.5	8.4	7.3	5.5	3.6	3.7
Unit costs	10.8	9.7	15.1	0.5	5.6	1.2	1.8
W. share	56.7	56.8	59.1	58.4	58.4	58.9	57.3

Data: Scharpf (1987, p. 90); Bayer (1981, p. 45)

2.6. Summary

The success of Austrian crisis policy rested, as has been shown in the preceding sections, on the highly coordinated use of primarily three policy instruments: demand management (by fiscal and monetary policy), hard currency policy, and wage policy. These policies supported and reinforced each other and each of them was at the same time dependent on the effects of the others.

Thus the extensive deficit spending used to stabilize employment was possible primarily because hard currency and wage policy together could be relied on to take care of inflation. The price stabilizing effect of the hard currency policy was a precondition for the restrictive wage policy and in turn depended for its continuing feasibility on a moderate wage growth. Full employment oriented fiscal and monetary policy was also a quid pro quo for a moderate wage policy.

Obviously this system of mutual dependencies is as fragile as it is complex and would hardly have been sustainable for long without the glue of a basic consensus keeping distributional conflicts at bay. This consensus rather than the much eulogized elaborate neo-corporatist institutional structure of economic-political decision making seems to provide one key to the understanding of Austrian success in the period 1974-79.

3. The German response

Among the five countries of this study Germany was the one that had the shortest practical experience with Keynesian economic policies when the country had to face the economic consequences of the first oil price hike and of the subsequent international recession. Up to 1966/67 the dominating doctrines in German economic policy making had come from the "ordo-liberal" or "Freiburg school", the most prominent representative of which had been the popular father of the "German economic miracle", minister of economic affairs (and chancellor 1963-66) Ludwig Erhard, a former professor of economics. In the "Great coalition" cabinet formed by the Christian Democrats (CDU) and Social-democrats (SPD) in 1966 the ministry of economic affairs was taken over by Germany's then leading Keynesian economist, Karl Schiller (another professor of economics). With him, Keynesiansim entered as the central doctrine in the economic policy planning and making of the federal government.[50]

On the other hand Germany was also the only country to have had a proper trial-run of most of the set of Keynesian instruments. This had happened during the short-lived but nevertheless full-blown mini-recession of 1966-67 which had been the prime reason for the ousting of the Christian Democratic-Liberal coalition government and the formation of the "Great coalition", as well as for the shift in the economic regime. The swift economic recovery from this recession was generally credited to Schiller and his Keynesian policies.[51]

There can be little doubt that the experience of the economic crisis of 1966-67 is crucial to an understanding of the economic-political reactions of the main economic agents - federal government, the Bundesbank, and trade unions - in the period leading up to the onset of the recession in Germany in 1974 and during its initial stages.[52] This experience had both a direct and an indirect bearing on the agents' perception of the situation and on their way of approaching it.

The direct influence of the 1966-67 recession was on crisis perception. At first the post-1973 recession was very much seen as a remake of the earlier crisis.

---

[50] But then Germany may also be the only country (it certainly is among the countries in the present study) in which Keynesianism was actually promulgated to law. This was done by "Gesetz zur Förderung der Stabilität und des Wachstums der Wirtschaft" (StWG) of July 8, 1967.

[51] Actually the swift economic recovery owed probably more to the easing of monetary policy by the Bundesbank, the restrictive wage policy adopted by the trade unions, and a strong growth in foreign demand (cf. Basler, 1981, p. 29) than to Keynesian demand management by deficit spending. The investment programs enacted in order to increase demand got a lot of publicity, but their implementation was delayed so much that in the end their effect became pro-cyclical rather than anti-cyclical (Kock, 1975). From the point of view of New Classical Macroeconomic theory it could even be argued that the reason why the German economic policy worked so well in 1966-67 was not that it was Keynesian, but that it was new: thanks to the political and economic regime shift in 1966 the economic policies of the authorities could not be fully anticipated in the private sector and hence the usual reason for the inefficiency of macro-economic policy does not apply in this situation.

[52] The degree to which the 1966-67 recession did determine the frame of reference applied to the events of 1974-75 is also clearly brought out by the numerous references to the experiences from 1966-67 in the influential "Monatsberichte des Ifo-Instituts für Wirtschaftsfragen" (Ifo, 1974; 1975).

This was not altogether unjustified. There is indeed a striking parallelism between the two crises in at least two respects. In the first place there was an overheating of the German economy prior to both of them, giving rise to cost-push inflation in which an aggressive trade union wage policy played an important role.[53] In the second place a politically motivated pro-cyclical fiscal policy did in both situations contribute to the overheating of the economy by a demand-pull. In 1965 a large scale tax reduction (with more than an eye to the upcoming federal election) had been the main culprit. Up to 1973 it was the ambitious reform policies of the new Socialdemocratic-Liberal government aiming at a strong and (too) rapid increase in public services, public consumption and public investments that posed problems (Scherf, 1986, pp. 16-33).[54]

The indirect effect of the 1966-67 experience was through creating an extremely strong belief in the effectiveness of Keynesian demand management, both among decision makers and in the public. This was not just the economic steering optimism still to be found in many countries at that time. It was sheer steering euphoria where everybody trusted blindly that from now on all aspects of the economy could be managed at will by "global steering" and "fine tuning" (Baring, 1982, pp. 647-648). This opinion was, to some extent, based on the "upswing made to measure" (a phrase coined by Schiller) that had followed the recession of 1966-67. This upswing was generally (and unjustly) seen as the effect of Keynesian demand management. It was further due to the skills of Schiller in popularizing key concepts of the new economic doctrine in a way that made them appear like modern magic (Baring, 1982, pp. 137-138). Thus up to and during the initial stages of the post 1973-recession there was undoubtedly a deep-rooted conviction that a recession was just an unfortunately necessary, but passing, situation. It could easily be turned into a new "upswing made to mea-

---

[53] As mentioned above the restrictive wage policies originally adopted by the trade unions after 1967 had been instrumental in the swift recovery of the German economy. But with profits growing rapidly these policies became increasingly unpopular with the rank and file. A series of wildcat strikes in September 1969 resulted in considerable wage increases to the participants (Schumann et al., 1971). At that time the trade unions were bound by collective agreements and hence unable to do anything, which lost them a lot of prestige. In order to reestablish their reputation with the membership the trade union leadership was more or less forced to adopt a considerably more aggressive wage policy in the following bargaining rounds in the German labor market.

[54] Even Baring (1982, p. 660) - himself certainly not inimical to the Socialdemocratic-Liberal government and its aims - speaks of " ... the ambition to use as much money as possible, misunderstood as being identical to the zeal for reforms." (my transl.). In 1971 the minister of finance left the cabinet as a protest against the level of government spending and in 1972 Schiller himself followed suit, also he giving cabinet rows about the proper level and increase of government expenditures as part of his reason to leave. In 1970 already he had characterized his cabinet colleagues' attitude to public expenditures by comparing them to a battalion of soldiers who have got hold of the war chest and hurry to go on the spree with its contents (Baring, 1982, p. 665).

sure" by Keynesian policies.[55]

This (once) strong belief in Keynesianism in Germany is somewhat paradoxical because among the five countries of this study Germany is the one with the greatest institutional obstacles to an effective Keynesian policy making. The main reason for this is historical. Due to the bad experiences with the strong central government of the Third Reich, the German constitution provides for an unusual amount of checks and balances. These limit the powers of the federal government and the federal parliament to a degree where the German system of government is sometimes characterized as fragmented. Moreover there is also a wide-spread popular distrust in too much state intervention in the economy[56]. This is rooted in memories of the over-regimentation of the German economy during the Third Reich as well as in the general dislike of the East German version of a planned economy (v. Beyme, 1979, pp. 176-177).

The aspects of the fragmentation of the German system of government relevant to effective economic policy making have both a vertical and a horizontal dimension. With respect to the horizontal dimension the German constitution bars the government from interfering with the trade unions' freedom of collective bargaining and with wage contracts ("Tarifautonomie").[57] Statutory incomes politics are thus out of the question, even as a threat. The same is true of direct price controls. The constitution does not formally grant autonomy to the the Bundesbank, but its de facto autonomy seems by now to have acquired quasi-constitutional status.[58] Thus it is extremely difficult and potentially very costly in political terms for the federal government to try to force the Bundesbank to adopt an accommodating monetary policy against its will. In addition the government is in no position to force flanking incomes policy measures on the trade unions in order to support demand management by fiscal policy.

The vertical dimension of government fragmentation stems from German federalism. It was explicitly designed as a geographical system of checks and balances where state power is used to counterbalance federal power (Nannestad, 1973). In many areas of state activity this is typically accomplished by a functional division of responsibilities. Law making and revenues are federal responsibilities, while implementation expenditures, not the least public investments, are state responsibilities (v. Beyme, 1979, p. 206). Thus in many areas the states (and municipalities) rather than the federal government decide upon the size of public expenditures and upon their timing. By 1979 only 43.6 per cent of total public expenditure was federal (Scharpf, 1987, p. 265) and about 80 per cent of total

---

[55] How deep-rooted this conviction was can be seen from an editorial in the prestigious weekly *Die Zeit* of May 4, 1973 which said: "The SPD-FDP coalition should ... consciously go for a stabilization crisis, accepting unemployment, mass bankruptcies and social conflicts ... " (quoted from Baring, 1982, pp. 573-574, my transl.). While from today's viewpoint this looks like hybris, it was based on the firm conviction that such a crisis could be turned into a new upswing at will.

[56] While Keynesian-type indirect steering was obviously highly acceptable.

[57] Glastetter (1987, p. 277).

[58] Cf. Emminger (1986, p. 27 and note 3).

public investment was decided at state or municipality level (v. Beyme, 1979, p. 206; Scharpf, 1987, p. 327). This means that an anti-cyclical fiscal policy is hard to implement in Germany unless states and municipalities decide to cooperate with the federal government.

A constitutional reform of 1969 was intended to diminish the size of this coordination problem. There is, however, broad consensus that the reforms introduced were modest in scope and had a marginal impact at best (Kock, 1975; v. Beyme, 1979; Scharpf, 1985; 1987).

Given a measure of uncertainty with respect to the degree of cooperation forthcoming from states and municipalities the federal government will hence have to generate very strong impulses through its budgets in order to influence economic activity. This is reinforced by the fact that the multiplier-effect of revenue-changes is normally smaller than the multiplier-effect of changes in expenditures. But the German constitution actually puts a limit to the size of deficit spending as well. In general the size of the federal budget deficit must not exceed the sum of appropriations for investment purposes.[59]

The institutional obstacles to coordinated (Keynesian) economic policy making in Germany would have been reduced to pure practical inconveniences, however, had economic policy making rested on an Austrian-like consensus among the main actors. But this was not quite the case. Although the German policy making style is described as "rational consensus seeking" (Dyson, 1982), the level of consensus is in a number of respects lower in Germany than in Austria. This is clearly demonstrated by the fate of "Concerted Action" introduced in 1967 (together with Keynesianism) as a forum for the exchange of views and mutual information. It brought together representatives of the government, the Bundesbank, and the main organizations of labor and business. Whatever importance the "Concerted Action" might have had quickly faded away. When the trade unions finally walked out in 1977 - protesting the attitude of business on the issue of labor co-determination in industry - this had no real consequences.[60] The level of consensus had never been so high as to make the "Concerted Action" work.

The lower level of consensus in Germany, compared to Austria, is also visible with respect to issues of distribution and in labor-business relationships. In general the policies of the German trade unions have been growth- rather than distribution-oriented. The German labor market has been one of the most peaceful labor markets in the industrial world (Flanagan et al., 1983, p. 225). Even so, in between long spells of relative tranquility there have been periods of more aggressive union goal setting with respect to distributive issues. This was true of

---

[59] In 1981 the CDU - then in opposition - claimed that this limit had been exceeded every year, except for one, since 1975 and took the matter to the Constitutional Court. Until now the case has not been decided upon.

[60] Ironically the coordination of monetary, fiscal and wage policy in Germany worked best from 1977 onwards, i.e. after the withering away of "Concerted Action".

the early 70s, where such issues got top priority. Moreover, as pointed out by Scharpf (1987, p. 259), the distribution issue continues to dominate trade union rhetoric and self-promotion, regardless of the status quo-oriented policies they mostly pursue. Thus labor-business consensus on distributive issues was pragmatic in Germany (while programmatic in Austria). The issue of the wage structure, on the other hand, appears to have been of as little saliency in Germany as in Austria. Existing data indicate that the wage structure remained essentially unchanged during the period considered (Freeman, 1988, p. 67, table 2). German trade unions had no solidary wage policy goals (Glastetter et al., 1982, pp. 356-372; Esser, 1982, pp. 120-121).

The institutional limits to the powers of the federal government in economic policy making are probably the main reason for the development of a special "twist" of German Keynesianism, viz. the prominent role assumed by monetary policies. In "normal" implementations of Keynesian demand management fiscal policy is considered the most important instrument. Monetary policy is typically used in an accommodating fashion. As will be shown in the following, a situation close to the opposite came to prevail in Germany, especially after 1974.

In summary the German federal government can be said to have moved into the post-1973 recession armed with the tenets of Keynesianism, but also with one hand tied on its back and, moreover, initially manoeuvrering mostly by means of the rear view mirror. Little wonder then that the belief in and support of Keynesian economic policy eroded quite rapidly in Germany. In the process Keynesian ideas were gradually superseded by others, primarily imported from the Neo-Classical Macro-Economy school.[61]

3.1. Crisis onset in Germany: The collusion of two shocks

From figure 1.3. in chapter 1 it can be seen that the German economy was hit earlier and harder by the economic crisis following the first oil price hike than was the Austrian economy, despite the legendary strength of the former. Real growth fell from 4.6 per cent in 1973 to just 0.5 per cent in 1974 and even turned negative in 1975 (-1.6 per cent). Unemployment doubled between 1973 and 1974 (from 0.3 mill. to 0.6 mill.) and once more between 1974 and 1975. Consumer price inflation reached its peak in 1974 (6.9 per cent - a huge figure by German standards) and stayed close to that level in 1975. Only with respect to the current account did things keep going well for Germany. The usual surplus did not disappear.

What had turned the "economic miracle" into an economic crisis? To a considerable degree the adverse economic development in Germany appears to conform to the general explanation to the international post-1973 recession onset suggested in the McCracken-report (McCracken et al., 1977, p. 13). According to this explanation the authorities in numerous countries had by 1973 initiated

---

61 Tichy (1988, pp. 334-338).

measures that by themselves would have resulted in a minor recession in 1974. The effects of these measures were reinforced by the unforeseen deflationary effects of the oil price hike at the end of 1973. The planned economic slow-down then got out of control, not the least because the authorities in some countries continued contractive fiscal and/or monetary policies for too long in order to contain the inflationary pressures from the oil price hike.

Inflation had been rising in Germany during the early 70s. There was an international element in this development, but there were also both domestic "cost push" and domestic "demand pull" factors, cf. above.

In the beginning of 1973 the federal government was under pressure to act. In two steps (in February and May, 1973) fiscal policy was tightened in order to reduce total demand. A 10 per cent surtax was levied on higher incomes and gasoline and oil taxes were raised to curb private consumption. There were also cuts in public consumption. Revenues exceeding the figures in the budget were frozen. Public borrowing was reduced by 5.5 bill. DM, and a number of planned expenditures were either stalled or discarded. In order to reduce liquidity a special federal "stabilization loan" was issued. It was investment, however, that was the main target: an 11 per cent investment tax was introduced, degressive depreciations were postponed until May 1974. In order to cool off the booming building- and construction-industry depreciation rules for buildings were tightened.

On the face of it this was a sizeable fiscal contraction. The deficit in the federal budget was reduced from 13.1 bill. DM in 1972 to 8.8 bill. DM in 1973. But in general the measures taken by the federal government were deemed inadequate. According to Baring (1982, pp. 576-580) "(t)he program was intended to work, but not to hurt anyone. Therefore the harshness was in the appearance rather than in the effects, in the length of the catalogue of measures rather than in the efficiency of the particular measures."[62] The OECD, too, was sceptical.[63]

So was the Bundesbank. Under the regime of fixed exchange rates it had repeatedly found it extremely difficult to influence domestic economic activity and to control money supply and interest rates because any increase in German interest rates had the tendency to bring about a huge influx of foreign speculative capital (Emminger, 1986). But when the block floating of the DM had been decided upon in the first half of 1973, the Bundesbank with its hands freed turned to domestic inflation with a vengeance. It instigated what was quite commonly described as a "monetary shock therapy" (Emminger, 1986, pp. 258-265; Spahn, 1988, p. 71), exactly as it had done in 1965 (Scharpf, 1987, p. 153).[64] The effect on money supply is shown in figure 2.4.

---

62 My translation.

63 "The immediate impact ... is likely to be limited." (OECD, Economic Surveys: Germany (1973), p. 26).

64 Emminger (1986, pp. 137-138), on the other hand, attributes a minor role only to the policies of the Bundesbank in bringing about the recession of 1966-67.

The monetary contraction initiated by the Bundesbank in 1973 was the sharpest ever in the history of the Federal Republic (about 22 bill. DM, cf. Spahn, 1988, table 5). In very short time the free liquidity of the banks was reduced to zero. The unavoidable result was a steep rise in the rate of interest. By July 1973 the bank rate stood at 38 per cent. Short term interest had risen above 14 and long term interest above 10 per cent. Economic activity reacted swiftly and, beginning in September that year, some easing of inflationary pressures was recorded. This was greeted martial-poetically by the Bundesbank as a "silver lining on the horizon of the inflation front."[65]

Against this background the oil price hike of late 1973 could only be seen as a renewed threat to German price stability. The Bundesbank was not willing to let inflation gain momentum again. One had, of course, to accept the direct inflationary effects from the rising energy prices, but the Bundesbank was determined not to allow them to touch off a new wage-price spiral. Therefore the restrictive line in monetary policies was continued well into 1974 and the growth in money supply was kept below its usual level, cf. figure 2.4.

Figure 2.4.: Quarterly growth in money supply (M1) 1969-74, seasonally adjusted

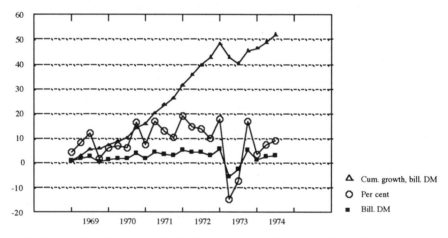

Data: Statistische Beihefte zu den Geschäftsberichten der Deutschen Bundesbank, December 1974.

Developments in the German labor market in early 1974 could hardly make the Bundesbank less determined to stay, for the time being, with its extremely restrictive line. In the regular round of collective bargaining the unions, this time led by the unions of the public employees, ÖTV and DAG negotiated from expectations of a 10 per cent inflation rate in 1974. They managed to obtain wage raises

---

[65] Emminger (1986, pp. 265-270).

around 13-14 per cent.

But in the end this was a true Pyrrhic victory. The settlement certainly reinforced the conviction of the Bundesbank leaders that they should break inflationary expectations once and for all. The wage demands sowed deep suspicion as to the willingness of the trade union leaders to act "responsibly".[66] It was also quite generally interpreted as an expression of the lack of willingness or ability of the Socialdemocratic-Liberal federal government to make the unions adopt a moderate wage policy and in general to pursue effective stabilization policies (Baring, 1982, pp. 694-701). It could nothing but strengthen the perception of the Bundesbank leaders of themselves as the only reliable guardians of price stability and economic order in Germany. They succeeded admirably with respect to the former, but at the price of the deep recession of 1974-75.

Figure 2.5.: Nominal percentage changes in domestic demand components and exports 1973-76

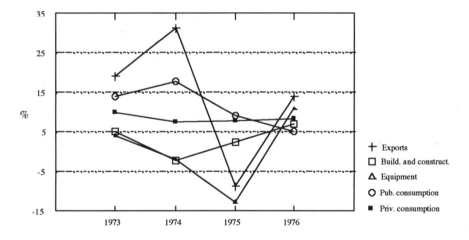

Data: Ifo (1976; 1977; 1978)

While the origin of the German recession was thus primarily domestic in 1974, an external shock contributed to the still deeper recession of 1975. German exports grew by approximately 20 per cent in 1973 and still more in 1974. In 1975 they dropped sharply (approx. -10 per cent nominally) due to the

---

66 Of the wage rises in 1974 Emminger (1986, p. 268) says that they were "a unique demonstration of the divergence of influence and responsibility" (my transl.).

world-wide recession following the oil price hike.[67] Figure 2.5. shows (nominal) percentage changes (relative to the previous year) in a number of important domestic demand components and in exports around the break-through of the crisis in Germany.

Different observers tend to weight the importance of domestic and internal factors differently when explaining the onset of the recession in Germany. Otmar Emminger, ex-president of the Bundesbank, emphasizes the drop in exports in 1975. He points to the fact that despite restrictive monetary policies aggregate domestic demand (in real terms) did not fall in 1975. It increased by 1 per cent (Emminger, 1986, p. 270). There is some support for this interpretation in Alt (1985). He finds that world demand Granger-causes[68] German unemployment. Spahn (1988, pp. 74-77), on the other hand, points primarily to the sharp drop in investments. This occurred in 1974 and continued into 1975. While there are several reasons for this development, Spahn emphasizes the effect of the Bundesbank policies on interest rates and hence on the profitability of investments. Scherf (1986, p. 55) has expressed basically the same point of view.

As can be seen from figure 2.5. private consumption increased (in nominal terms) at an almost constant rate in this period. In real terms the growth was very small. But investment actually decreased in both 1974 and 1975, in nominal as well as in real terms. On top of this, there was the dramatic drop in exports in 1975. This may indicate that the beginning of the crisis in Germany was the combined effect of the (intended) domestic slow-down of economic activity in 1974 - mainly the responsibility of the Bundesbank - and the international recession that hit Germany's exports in 1975.

3.2. Monetary policy

Monetary policy was instrumental in bringing about the recession in Germany 1974-1975. The monetary restrictions (reduction of money supply and increase in interest rates) of 1973 and 1974 had strong, adverse effects on economic activity. On the other hand inflation dropped off, too. Despite the oil price hike, German consumer prices did not rise more strongly in 1974 than they had done in 1973 (about 7 per cent). Inflation was down to 5.9 per cent by the end of 1974. In comparison inflation in the US went up from 6.2 per cent in 1973 to 11 per cent in 1974, and in the OECD-countries as a whole (including Germany) from 7.6 per cent in 1973 to 13.3 per cent in 1974. Thus the German trend of inflation was highly atypical and merits the expression that "Germany had broken away from the inflation convoy" (Emminger, 1986, pp. 267-269).

---

[67] The reason why German exports were hit so hard by the international recession was mainly the big share of investment and consumption goods in total German exports, cf. Glastetter et al., 1982, p. 512).

[68] An introduction to the concept of Granger causality can be found in Freeman (1983).

By the end of 1974 the Bundesbank had reached its prime goal which has always been to stabilize the domestic price level.[69] Therefore monetary restrictions were loosened in small steps. Beginning at the end of 1974 the discount rate was repeatedly lowered, until it stood at just 3.5 per cent at the end of 1975. This was only 0.5 per cent higher than the 1972-figure.

With respect to money supply the Bundesbank introduced a novelty. Beginning in 1974 it made public every year a target for the growth in money supply for the following year.[70] This target was decided upon on the basis of estimated potential output growth, the expected unavoidable inflation rate, and expected changes in the velocity of circulation of money (Tichy, 1988, pp. 175-176; p. 338). It was emphasized time and again, however, that the announced growth target for the money supply was only an intermediate target relative to the central goal of the Bundesbank policy: stable prices (Emminger, 1986, p. 401; p. 403).[71]

Pre-announced targets for money growth was not a totally new idea. Since 1970 such a system had repeatedly been suggested by the German Council of Economic Advisers (Sachverständigenrat). Similar thoughts were at about the same time aired in other countries like the UK and the USA (Whiteley, 1987, p. 185).

The intent of pre-announcing a target for the growth in money supply was, according to Emminger (1986, p. 268) "... to demonstrate strongly to the public the stabilization policy of the Bundesbank by means of a highly visible money supply target."[72] By announcing its target the Bundesbank indicated the amount of growth in demand - primarily from wage increases and from increasing public spending - it was ready to accommodate. The government and/or the trade unions could, of course, choose not to heed this advice. In that case the result would be unemployment.

That the Bundesbank did mean business is indicated by the two reaction functions below. In the first place, the Bundesbank should be expected to reduce the growth in money supply whenever inflation exceeded what was considered unavoidable. This was part of its stabilization oriented money supply policy.

---

[69] According to the law governing the activities of the Bundesbank it has the duty to "protect the currency" (§3). As pointed out by Emminger (1986, p. 25) this has always been interpreted as synonymous with protecting price stability.

[70] The technical definition of money supply was based on the concept of Central bank money stock which is money in circulation plus compulsory reserves at fixed rates (actually the rates of January 1974 were used).

[71] Despite some similarities, the policy of the Bundesbank after 1974 is not just an implementation of the monetarist idea of an exogeneously determined money supply, cf. Spahn (1988, pp. 56-58) for further discussion.

[72] My translation.

Using consumer price inflation as expression of inflation[73] the following reaction function for the quarterly increase in the supply of Central bank money (seasonally adjusted) should hence be expected:

$$CBM_t = a + b_1 CBM_{t-2} + \Sigma b_{2+k} CPI_{t-k}$$

where

CBM_t = Growth in Central bank money
CPI_t = Consumer price inflation

and the summation expression is a sum of lags (running from k=0). Estimating the parameters of this model from quarterly data for the period 1973-1979 (seasonally adjusted),[74] using the Cochrane-Orcutt method (in order to take care of the first order autoregressive structure in the data) and a maximum lag-length of half a year, the values in table 2.4. are found.

Table 2.4.: Coefficient values and statistics

Variable	Coeff.value	S.E.
Constant	21.55	2.73
CBM_{t-2}	-0.55	0.17
ΣCPI_t	-1.73	0.32
ρ	0.42	0.21
R^2 (adj.)	0.758	
Durbin's h	3.796	
Ljung-Box Q(12)	11.037	

As can be seen the development in inflation in the present and the two preceding quarters did indeed influence the development in money supply in the expected direction during the period analyzed. An increase in inflation was followed by a reduction in the growth rate of money supply.

In the second place reductions in the growth of money supply did in turn have an impact on unemployment. It turns out that the main part of the development

---

[73] Actually consumer price inflation is a poor stand-in for unavoidable inflation, because only part of consumer price inflation is unavoidable. This must be expected to primarily influence the fit of the reaction function to data negatively.

[74] Data: Statistische Beihefte zu den Geschäftsberichten der Deutschen Bundesbank (var. years).

in German unemployment can be accounted for by the following reaction funct-ion (using quarterly data from 1973-79, seasonally adjusted)[75]:

$$U_t = a + b_1 U_{t-1} + b_2 BS_{t-4} + b_3 CBM_{t-2}$$

where

U_t	=	Unemployment rate
BS_t	=	Federal budget balance
CBM_t	=	Growth in Central bank money supply

The parameters and statistics of the model are given in table 2.5. For the sake of (statistical) consistency two-stage OLS has been used with CPI as instrument variable with CBM. As can be seen, a slow-down in the growth rate of Central bank money increased unemployment (moderately) half a year after it occurred. In comparison the reaction time to changes in the federal budget balance is longer (1 year). Still, most of the unemployment rate in a particular quarter is accounted for simply by the rate in the previous quarter. This just reflects the fact - brought out in figure 1.3. in chapter 1 - that from 1975 to 1979 German unemployment stayed at a rather stable level (with a weak downwards tenden-cy).

Table 2.5.: Coefficient values and statistics

Variable	Coeff.value	S.E.
Constant	1.11	0.26
U_{t-1}	0.96	0.06
CBM_{t-2}	-0.07	0.02
BS_{t-4}	0.04	0.24
d75	4.90	1.36
R^2 (adj.)	0.936	
Durbin's h	0.716	
Ljung-Box Q(9)	11.015	

Thus from 1975 monetary policy in Germany set explicit limits for a Keynesian demand management through fiscal policy. As long as it stayed within these limits the federal government did not have to worry about whether the Bundes-bank would counteract or cooperate. But if it exceeded them there was sure to be a conflict with the Bundesbank. The outcome of such a confrontation would

---

[75] Data: Statistische Beihefte zu den Geschäftsberichten der Deutschen Bundesbank (var. years).

be uncertain at best, because the position of the Bundesbank had widespread public support as well as the support of the German Council of Economic Advisers.

Table 2.6. shows the pre-announced monetary targets and the actual money supply growth rates 1975-79. As can be seen from the figures the Bundesbank tried to keep a stable money supply growth rate and was reasonably successful in that respect.

Table 2.6.: Monetary targets and actual money supply growth, 1975-79

Year	Target	Actual	Deviation*
1975	8.0	9.8	22.5
1976	8.0	9.2	15.0
1977	8.0	9.0	12.5
1978	8.0	11.4	42.5
1979	6.0-9.0	6.3	0

*in per cent of target value

Data: OECD, Economic Surveys: Germany (1980)

The average deviation 1975-79 was 18.5 per cent.[76] The huge excess growth in 1978 was predominantly technical in character and had no real economic consequences (Emminger, 1986, pp. 411-424). Thus in general the new monetary policy of the Bundesbank worked quite well.

In 1975, however, it looked for quite a while as if the Bundesbank would not be able to achieve the targeted growth in the money supply. The demand for money was clearly below supply during the first half of 1975 (Spahn, 1988, pp. 79-80). The Bundesbank found it unexpectedly difficult to stimulate economic activity through the supply of money alone. Therefore massive (7 bill. DM) open market operations were undertaken. By this move the Bundesbank also "made room" in the credit market for a strong increase in the number of government bonds reflecting the rapid growth in the federal budget deficit.

Against the background of a continuously decreasing rate of inflation (from 6.6 per cent in 1974 to 2.7 per cent in 1978) and a sizeable surplus on the current account the Bundesbank stayed with its cautiously expansive monetary policy until 1978. But in 1979 signs of inflationary pressures re-appeared in the wake of the dollar crisis of 1978. The Bundesbank reacted swiftly with a new

---

[76] In comparison the average deviation between planned and actual money supply growth (M3) in the UK 1980/81-1983/84 was 35.4 per cent. This is part of the background for Whiteley's conclusion from his study of monetary policy in the UK and the USA that it is very difficult for governments in advanced industrial societies to control the money supply (Whiteley, 1987, pp. 191-193 and pp. 201-202). The German experience would seem to indicate otherwise.

monetary contraction. Compulsory reserves were increased. The discount rate went up by 1 per cent every quarter. By mid-1979 the Bundesbank announced that it would aim money supply growth at the lower end of the previously announced interval. By this economic slow-down the way was paved for a new recession following the second oil price hike.

Figure 2. 6.: Central bank money growth and real GDP growth 1973-79 (quarterly data, seasonally adjusted), per cent

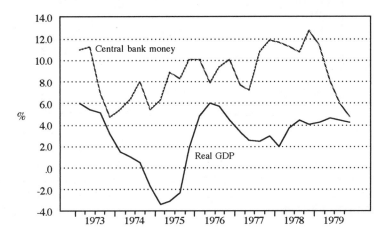

Data: Statistische Beihefte zu den Geschäftsberichten der Deutschen Bundesbank (var. years).

By way of summarizing we may finally try to relate the Bundesbank controlled money supply growth to changes in the level of economic activity in Germany 1973-79. Figure 2.6. suggests that there is such a relationship. Changes in Central bank money growth lead changes in real GDP growth by a rather short period. This pattern is most clearly observed during the earlier years (when variations were strongest).

The relationship shown in figure 2.6. may be quantified by the following simple model with lags of the money supply growth of length k=0 to 3 quarters as exogenous variable:

$$\Delta GDP_t = a + b_2 \Delta GDP_{t-1} + \sum b_{2+k} CBM_{t-k}$$

where

ΔGDP_t = Real GDP growth
CBM_t = Growth in Central bank money supply

We fit this model to quarterly data 1973-79 (seasonally adjusted)[77] and use the Cochrane-Orcutt method. The following coefficient values are found to describe the relationship between Central bank money growth and growth in real GDP:

Table 2.7.: Coefficient values and statistics

Variable	Coeff.value	S.E.
Constant	-2.63	1.81
ΔGDP_{t-1}	0.68	0.16
ΣCBM_t	0.40	0.21
ρ	0.58	0.44
R^2 (adj.)	0.821	
Durbin's h	0.716	
Ljung-Box Q(12)	6.744	

From the results it appears that the Bundesbank by varying the growth in money supply could influence economic activity in Germany rather strongly. As has been shown it did not hesitate to make use of this ability whenever it saw its stabilization goal threatened.

3.3. Fiscal policy

In 1973 the fiscal policy of the federal government aimed at a contraction. The measures taken were insufficient and widely perceived as mainly window-dressing. In the end the main contractive effect came from the tightening of monetary policy. The immediate fiscal reaction to the situation created by the oil price hike of late 1973 was again quite moderate. Fiscal policy did not turn clearly expansionary before mid-1974.

In December 1973 it was still considered sufficient to revoke some of the contractive fiscal measures introduced earlier in the year in order to curb consumption. The 11 per cent investment tax was retroactively abolished. Depreciation rules were restored, and a number of previously postponed structural end regional development programs were reactivated. Only in 1974, with economic activity already in a down-turn and with unemployment rising, the federal government went into larger style deficit-spending. By February a 1 bill. DM

---

[77] Data: Statistische Beihefte zu den Geschäftsberichten der Deutschen Bundesbank (var. years).

"special program" was decided upon. This aimed at supporting regions with special structural problems. By September another "special program" followed. It was intended to support employment locally and regionally at a total cost of 0.95 bill. DM. It was financed out of the revenues that had accrued from the investment tax in 1973.[78] Finally in December a third program, worth 1.73 bill DM, was put to work. The greatest part of the money (1.13 bill. DM) was targeted at subsidizing investment, while 0.5 bill. were direct wage subsidies to employers in specific regions, and 0.1 bill. DM were to be used to further the mobility of unemployed persons. Moreover there was a special investment grant (7.5 per cent of value) for investment goods and buildings ordered or started prior to July 1, 1975. This program was financed out of the revenues from the surtax on higher incomes that had been introduced in 1973.

Besides these programs a long-planned reform of the tax system and the system of child-allowances went into effect from January 1, 1975. The net fiscal impact of an approximately 14 bill. DM loss in revenues and extra expenditures from this reform dwarfed the combined fiscal impact of all three previously enacted "special programs".

All together the measures enacted meant that federal fiscal policy turned expansive by the second half of 1974. But the measures came much too late and were far from strong enough to influence economic activity or employment effectively in 1974. In fact the most comprehensive and ambitious program (of December 1974) did not really make itself felt before 1976 (Scharpf, 1987, p. 179).

In 1975 the expansive impulse from the federal budget deficit grew considerably stronger. This was owing mostly to the revenue effects of the reform of the tax and the child-allowance system and to the automatic stabilizers in the budget. The budget deficit reached an all-time peak of 68.3 bill. DM, or 6.2 per cent of GDP. But the stimulating effect of this deficit on economic activity was partly neutralized by an extraordinarily weak growth in private consumption, despite the sizeable growth in disposable incomes brought about by the reform of the tax and the child-allowance system. Instead the private saving rate went up to more than 16 per cent (Spahn, 1988, table 4).[79] Here the problems associated with a strategy based on the stimulation of private consumption (through tax-reductions etc.) became evident.

The economic development in 1975 posed a dilemma to the federal government. On the one hand the level of and development in economic activity and employment were still more unsatisfactory than had been the case in 1974. On the other hand the budget deficit had reached a size that was deemed unsustain-

---

[78] The revenues from this tax and from the surtax on higher incomes had been frozen in the Bundesbank.

[79] Thus fiscal policy was in the same situation as monetary policy (cf. above): by increasing disposable incomes it could only create the conditions for a growth in private demand, but not make it happen.

able. The main headache was that to a large extent this deficit might be structural and might hence persist even when economic activity and employment recovered (as both were quite generally expected to do in 1976). In such a situation it was feared that a large deficit could exert upward pressure on interest rates and thus impair an incipient economic upswing (Ehrlicher and Rohwer, 1979, pp. 307-308). Moreover, the monetary discipline enforced by the Bundesbank limited the growth of public demand. With a structural deficit the federal government might be handcuffed should another recession occur. Thus the question became urgent if deficit spending of 1976 could and should continue at its 1975-level, or if it was more pressing to begin consolidating the budget.

In that situation an attempt was made to do both at once. Already by August 1975 the hitherto most ambitious program for stimulating investments was enacted at an estimated cost of 5.8 bill DM. But in parallel a catalogue of expenditure cuts and tax hikes was compiled with the intention of reducing the federal budget deficit by 23 bill. DM by 1978. The biggest cuts (7.9 bill. DM in 1976) were made in federal subsidies to unemployment insurance where benefits were to be lowered and contributions raised. At the same time a 2 percentage point rise of the VAT by January 1, 1977 was announced. This would improve the federal budget by an estimated 8.2 bill. DM in 1977. Moreover very little additional expenditure was planned for 1976.

The net effect of the new fiscal course quickly became visible in the 1976 budget. Public expenditures increased by a meagre 4.5 per cent, while revenues went up by 10.8 per cent. The federal budget deficit was reduced to 48 bill. DM (4.3 per cent of GDP). From mid-1976 the impact of the federal budget on economic activity turned restrictive.

Nevertheless there was a marked economic upswing in Germany in 1976 leading a general upswing of economic activity in Europe.[80] Real GDP grew by 5.8 per cent after having been negative in 1975. One main contribution came from private consumption. A drop in the private saving rate (to 14.7 per cent) and a near-doubling of the volume of private consumer credits in 1976 indicate that postponed consumption plans started to become effective. The other main factor contributing to the upswing was the fiscal impact of the programs enacted the earlier years. But despite increased economic activity the employment situation improved only marginally.

It was soon apparent, however, that the economic upswing of 1976 was rather fragile and did not generate its own growth dynamics. By the beginning of 1977 a 5 per cent real GDP growth had been expected for that year, but this assessment quickly turned out to have been far too optimistic. In the end not more than 3 per cent growth was achieved. Private consumption continued growing in 1977, but exports fell off and there was a marked drop in private sector gross investment. But the strongest drop in aggregate demand came from public expenditures (Spahn, 1988, table 4). Obviously budget consolidation had been overdone and threatened to choke the economic upswing.

Consequently federal fiscal policy changed direction and by 1977 once more

---

80 OECD, Economic Surveys: Germany (1976), p. 33.

became expansionary. Already by March 1977 an ambitious "Program for future-oriented investments" (Programm für Zukunftsinvestitionen, ZIP) was adopted. It made available funds for investments in infrastructure, energy, environment protection, and city renewal. In contrast to previous programs this one had a somewhat longer time horizon (4 years). The appropriations totalled 16 bill. DM, 3.5 bill. of which were to be released in 1977.

Moreover the federal government introduced a number of tax relief measures and improvements in allowances and grants. Income taxes were lowered, child allowances increased and tax benefits to housing construction and to investment were made (still) more attractive. For technical reasons the VAT-increase announced to become effective by January 1, 1977 had had to be postponed a year. This contributed to the general easing of fiscal policy in 1977.

Most of the measures introduced in 1977 did not show any effects on economic activity until the second half of 1978, however. In early 1978 prospects for economic activity still looked less than bright.[81] Against this background a new investment program was adopted, this time for furthering investments in energy conserving housing modernization. The program was to run over several years at a total cost of 4.3 bill. DM. Thus the expansionary line of 1977 was carried over into 1978.

The most important impetus for further expansionary fiscal measures in 1978 came from abroad.[82] With her stable surplus on the external balances, low inflation and rather low economic growth rates Germany (together with Japan) had come under mounting international pressure to adopt the role of economic "locomotive" for the international economic development by leading a more expansionary economic policy (Putnam and Bayne, 1987, pp. 73-92).[83] As a result of the economic summit in Bonn in June 1978 the government yielded to the pres-

---

[81] However, this was partly due to the effect of bad weather conditions on building and construction activity. Besides there was a strike in the metal industry.

[82] Putnam and Bayne (1987, p. 79) claim that "(d)uring the spring of 1978 a domestic political process ... led to a situation in which a revision of German economic policy would have been highly likely, even if the international pressure in the end had eased." According to their view the German government just used the external pressure as an alibi for the strengthening of the expansionary line in fiscal policy, which for domestic political reasons might else have been difficult to do. It is by no means inconceivable that this was the strategy of the federal government. In his memoirs a former Danish minister of economic affairs, Nyboe Andersen, relates that during a visit in 1975 chancellor Helmut Schmidt encouraged his Danish hosts to make public their concern about the stagnating German economy, "... because this would strengthen his employment-oriented policy vis à vis the majority in Germany that wants to put all emphasis on fighting inflation." (Nyboe Andersen, 1989, p. 185; my transl.).

[83] This was not exactly a new situation: thanks to low inflation rates and the hard currency Germany had since the mid-50s intermittently been confronted with demands to lead a less stringently stability oriented economic policy and to allow a certain degree of "adaptation inflation" in order to help reducing imbalances in the international monetary system, cf. Emminger (1986).

sure and took on the obligation of creating a fiscal stimulus corresponding to 1 per cent of GDP.

Only a fortnight later the government was ready to present a catalogue of fiscal measures for further stimulating economic activity.[84] The main components were tax relief measures, increases in child allowances, and a new "motherhood grant".[85] Furthermore maternity leave was lengthened from two to six months. The cost of these measures was estimated at 13.5 bill. DM in 1978 and 15 bill. DM in 1979. The net impulse from the federal budget was weakened, however, by the automatic stabilizers which increased revenues.

Under normal circumstances one should have expected a strong economic upswing in Germany in 1979 from these measures. Actually very little happened. Economic growth increased from 3.5 per cent in 1978 to 4 per cent in 1979, and unemployment was reduced from 1 million to 0.9 million. Thus the "locomotive" strategy agreed upon at the Bonn summit largely failed. The main reason was the incipient second oil crisis following the Iranian revolution. It led to a new stage in the world wide recession.

In figure 2.7. the fiscal impulses to German economic activity from the federal government budget and the "all government budget" 1973-79 are summarized. To construct it I use the same method described in connection with the analysis of the corresponding figures for Austria.

As can be seen from figures 2.7. (a) and (b), as far as demand impulses from the budgets is concerned German fiscal policy was no less anti-cyclical than Austrian fiscal policy. This is true despite the institutional obstacles to coherent Keynesian economic policy making in Germany discussed above. As in the Austrian case the strongest impulse came in 1975 (partly due to automatic stabilizers). Measured in per cent of GDP the impulse was of about the same size as in Austria. But the figures also quite clearly demonstrate that budget consolidation was initiated too early during the process of economic recovery and did harm to the upswing.

---

[84] This very swift reaction would seem to indicate that most proposals had been prepared even before the result of the economic summit was known. This would seem to support the claim by Putnam and Bayne (1987) that the summit was just used as an alibi for introducing measures which the government had long wanted to have passed but which were thought to possibly be met with (political) resistance. If this was actually the case then the critique of the measures as a hodgepodge of proposals that just happened to be available in the ministries (Scharpf, 1987, pp. 183-184) seems not quite justified.

[85] According to Putnam and Bayne (1987, p. 82), "(t)he *composition* of the program was clearly determined by domestic politics, and in particular by Lambsdorff's tactical victory over those Social Democrats who wished to increase social spending and investment grants, rather than cut taxes". In fact the major part of the expenditures came from social policy measures (motherhood grant and prolongation of maternity leave), cf. Scharpf (1987, pp. 183-184).

Figure 2.7.: Demand stimulation through public finance in Germany 1973-79, per cent of GDP

(a) All government

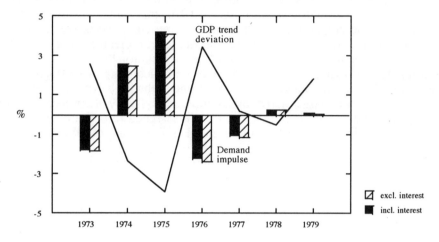

(b) Central government

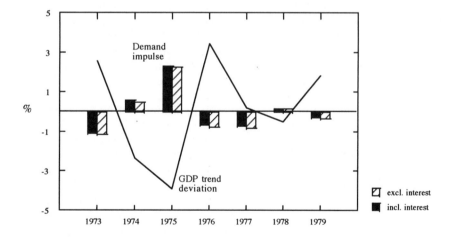

Data: Teschner and Vesper (1983); OECD, National Accounts (1984)

The pattern of timing does not immediately suggest a political business cycle interpretation. Had there been a Nordhaus-type cycle, one should have expected a stronger contraction in 1973 (a federal post-election year), less budget consolidation in 1976 (a federal election year), and possibly less stimulation in 1978 (a federal between-elections year).[86]

The development in central macro-economic figures - inflation, unemployment, etc. - does not indicate the working of a political business cycle either. Although economic growth was very high in 1976, this figure must be seen on the backdrop of the negative growth the year before. Unemployment decreased after 1975, but at a very measured pace, and the federal election year 1976 did not deviate from the trend. The same holds true for inflation.[87]

In summary two features appear particularly characteristic of German fiscal policy during the period considered. The first one is the high concern about the dangers of a structural budget deficit and, consequently, early attempts at budget consolidation. The second is the important role assigned to tax cuts and to increases in some kinds of transfer to households rather than to public expenditures.

3.4. Fiscal policy and monetary policy: Cooperation, conflict, or conspiracy?

In some treatments of German crisis policy after 1973 the Bundesbank is assigned the role of the "evil spirit" of German economic policy making relentlessly pursuing its goal of price stability through restrictive monetary policies. Thus it prevented the government from enacting the expansionary fiscal policy needed to combat unemployment effectively.[88] On the other hand Frey and Schneider (1981) have reported an econometric study of Bundesbank monetary policy vis à vis the policy of the federal government 1957-77. They model the reaction function of the Bundesbank under the assumption that in the case of serious conflict the Bundesbank follows the policy directions of the federal government. They obtain a good fit to empirical data.

Both views rest on the implicit assumption that there can be a clash between the goals and policies of the federal government and the Bundesbank. It is intuitively plausible that in such a case the German institutional set-up - with a near-autonomous Central bank - is unlikely to bring about cooperation. A little formal reasoning (Andersen and Schneider, 1986) supports this conclusion. The interaction of the federal government and the Bundesbank under the monetary regime introduced in 1974 may be modelled as a two-person non-cooperative game with a sequential decision structure (Stackelberg game). Both players are assumed to have an objective function to maximize. The objective function of the Bundesbank is determined by one goal only (price stability). The federal government has two main goals: price stability (as the Bundesbank) and economic

---

86 Essentially the same conclusion is reached by Schmidt (1983b).
87 Cf. Lessmann (1987, pp. 51-57).
88 For an example of this kind of reasoning see Leaman (1988, pp. 216-221).

growth. Because economic growth is related to the employment level the government may be assumed to favor the growth goal over the (low) inflation goal.

Suppose the Bundesbank moves first. Suppose, further, that the Keynesian view relating demand management politics to real output is correct. Then the solution to the game (i.e. the inflation rate and the growth rate realized) will be Pareto-efficient (Andersen and Schneider, 1986, pp. 180-183). This means that neither the federal government nor the Bundesbank can be made better off without making the other worse off. Any outcome that is more preferred by the federal government than the one realized is less preferred by the Bundesbank, and vice versa. Thus there is nothing gained from cooperating. Which solution will be obtained is in the last resort a question of power.

However this result rests on the assumption that there is a different priority ordering of the actors' goals. If this is really the case, one can never know for sure. But when policies are compared for the period 1973-79, it is hard to detect signs of serious clashes where monetary policy and fiscal policy worked in opposite directions. The closest one comes to such a situation is a short period in the second half of 1974 and a period beginning at the end of 1978. For most of the period considered monetary and fiscal policy were either both expansive or both contractive. There was (de facto) coordination, if not cooperation.

This coordination might, of course, just reflect the working of "anticipated reactions" in the policy making of the Bundesbank or the federal government (or both). But it may also reflect that the federal government agreed to the stability course of the Bundesbank[89] but preferred to have it do the "dirty work". By means of the pre-announcement of monetary targets the institutional autonomy, the prestige and the expertise of the Bundesbank could be used to neutralize a potentially highly partisan and politically dangerous issue (Dyson, 1982, p. 37).

3.5. Wage policy: From wage offensive to "reasonable wage formula"

As has been described above the aggressive wage strategy followed by the trade unions in 1974 contributed greatly to the development of the economic crisis in Germany, although mostly in an indirect way. It prompted the sharp monetary contraction policy of the Bundesbank initiating the downturn of the German economy.

In a longer perspective union behavior between 1970 and 1974 was rather atypical. Most of the time, German trade unions have been guided by the "reasonable wage formula" suggested by Meinhold in 1965.[90] According to this formula wage rises should primarily reflect productivity growth and the un-

---

[89] This is also how Scharpf seems to view the issue, cf. Scharpf (1987, pp. 170-171; 177). He also relates that ex-chancellor Helmut Schmidt did himself claim credit for the idea of pre-announced monetary targets, the so-called "monetary overcoat" (Scharpf, 1987, p. 170).
[90] Cf. Altvater et al. (1979, pp. 319-320).

avoidable inflation rate. In figure 2.8. the development in these figures is shown for the period 1965-1979.

As can be seen, there are two peaks in the nominal wage curve, one in 1971 and the other in 1974. The first represents the wage offensive more or less forced upon the trade unions by the September-strikes of 1969 (cf. above). The other represents the nominal wage pressure of 1973 and 1974 which was primarily a function of (exaggerated) inflationary expectations. It is also seen that after 1974 wage development became much more moderate. The figure further suggests that there is a relationship between productivity growth and nominal wage growth with the former leading the development in nominal wage growth. There may also be a similar relationship between inflation and nominal wage growth, but without a lag.

Figure 2.8.: Growth in nominal wages*, productivity* and consumer prices 1965-79, per cent

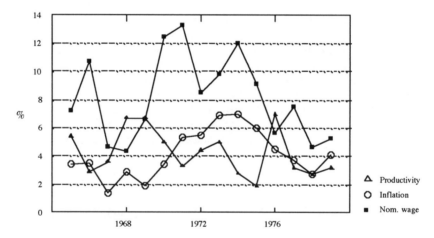

* in manufacturing
Data: Scharpf (1987); OECD, Historical Statistics (1988)

The descriptive power of the "reasonable wage formula" for nominal wage development in German manufacturing 1965-79 may be tested by fitting the following model to the data in figure 2.8.:

$$W_t = a + b_1 W_{t-1} + b_2 \log(PROD)_{t-1} + b_3 CPI_t$$

where

W_t =   Nominal wage growth

$PROD_t$ = Productivity growth[91]
CPI_t = Consumer price inflation

Fitting the model by OLS to data from the period 1965-79 produces the coefficient values and statistics of table 2.8.[92] As can be seen, the "reasonable wage formula" appears to yield a rather satisfactory description[93] of the development in nominal wages in manufacturing 1965-79. Nominal wage increase is influenced in the expected direction by both consumer price inflation and productivity growth changes. The fact that inflation does not lead nominal wage growth could suggest that it is expected inflation rather than actual inflation which influences nominal wage growth.

Table 2.8.: Coefficient values and statistics

Variable	Coeff.value	S.E.
Constant	-6.28	2.46
W_{t-1}	0.41	0.18
$log(PROD)_{t-1}$	5.57	1.19
CPI_t	0.77	0.30
R^2 (adj.)	0.736	
Durbin's h	0.328	
Ljung-Box Q(7)	17.565	

By 1975 already the trade unions were back at a moderate wage strategy very much like the one that had greatly contributed to turning the mini-recession of 1966-67 into a new economic upswing. Between 1975 and 1979 nominal wages (in German manufacturing) grew at a modest 6.4 per cent a year as compared to 8.9 per cent for the period 1965 to 1974.

These moderate nominal wage rises were sufficient, however, to secure a (moderate) growth in real wages as well. This is true because inflation decreased at the same time. But the moderate wage policy meant that the unions had to accept a roll-back of the distributional gains achieved in the early seventies. From

---

[91] The logarithmic transformation was suggested from the results. It implies that changes in the productivity growth rate, rather than the growth rate itself, influence nominal wage growth.

[92] Data: As figure 2.8.

[93] There is, however, some higher order serial correlation left in the residuals, as witnessed by the value of the Ljung-Box Q-statistic. It can be removed by including a dummy variable coded 1 for the years 1971-74 (the years of the wage offensive) and 0 else. This does change all coefficient values proportionally in the same direction while leaving adjusted R2 nearly unaffected.

its peak value of 66.3 per cent in 1974 the adjusted wage rate dropped to 63.5 per cent in 1979, 1.1 per cent below even its 1973 value, cf. table 2.9.[94]

Table 2.9.: Main trends in wage development in German manufacturing, 1973-79
(increases in percentages), and adjusted wage share

	1973	1974	1975	1976	1977	1978	1979
Nominal	9.8	12.0	9.1	5.6	7.5	4.6	5.2
Real	2.6	4.7	2.9	1.0	3.7	1.8	1.1
Inflation	6.9	7.0	6.0	4.5	3.7	2.7	4.1
Unit costs	6.2	9.6	6.6	0.9	5.7	4.5	2.7
W. share	64.6	66.3	66.1	64.9	64.7	64.0	63.5

Data: OECD, Historical Statistics (1988); Kloten et al. (1987, p. 358)

At the same time the German labor market remained peaceful, although there was a slight increase in conflict levels in the last years of the period considered here. Wage differentials stayed by and large unchanged.

What led the German trade unions back to a moderate wage strategy after 1974? Most observers seem to agree that their moderation was not part of an Austrian-style coordinated attempt to solve the economic crisis.[95]

One possible explanation is that the trade unions did react to the development in unemployment. There is indeed a pattern in the data suggesting such a relationship. When unemployment increases then increases in nominal wage increases tend to diminish (at a one-year lag), and vice versa.[96]

If one looks at the simple bivariate relationship between nominal wage rise in manufacturing and the logarithm of unemployment[97] lagged one year (with nominal wage rise lagged one year included), the expected negative relationship can be found for the period 1965-79. An increase in (the logarithm of) unemployment leads to a decrease in nominal wage growth one year later. This relationship stands up also when the period 1974-79 is considered in isolation.

---

[94] Part of the growth in especially 1974 and of the fall in 1978-79 must probably be ascribed to the well-known fact that profits react more quickly to cyclical changes in business activity. Therefore the wage rate will tend to grow in the beginning of a recession and to fall in the beginning of an upswing.

[95] See for example v. Beyme (1979, pp. 120-125); Kloten et al. (1985, pp. 388-401).

[96] On the other hand Hardes (1981, pp. 98-101), going back to 1960, fails to find a relationship for the period 1960-75. Thus the relationship is obviously not very stable.

[97] The fact that the strongest relationship is found with the logarithm to unemployment instead of the unemployment figures themselves is interesting because it indicates that the reaction to a rise in unemployment may be stronger when unemployment is low than when it is high.

Table 2.10. shows what happens when (the logarithm of) unemployment (lagged one period) is included in the nominal wage model formulated above. The main problem in doing so is evidently one of multicollinearity. This makes it difficult to assess the impact of unemployment on nominal wage development precisely.

Table 2.10.: Coefficient values and statistics

Variable	Coeff.value	S.E.
Constant	-2.90	3.54
W_{t-1}	0.21	0.23
$\log(PROD)_{t-1}$	4.34	1.49
CPI_t	0.89	0.30
$\log(u)_{t-1}$	-1.04	0.81
R^2 (adj.)	0.752	
Durbin's h	-0.937	
Ljung-Box Q(7)	21.265	

Another possible explanation of trade union moderation after 1974 could be the new monetary policy adopted that year by the Bundesbank. After all it was designed to put a brake on wage increases. That message was clearly understood (although not much liked) by the unions. But since the introduction of the new monetary policy coincides in time with the return of mass unemployment, it is virtually impossible to separate the effects of this policy on wage development from the effects of unemployment.

In any case, neither actual nor threatened unemployment is a sufficient condition for rationally behaving trade unions to exercise wage restraint. (This will be shown in chapter 5). Consequently the development in the rate of unemployment in Germany and the monetary policy of the Bundesbank after 1974 can only be part of an explanation of union behavior.

A third factor encouraging wage moderation may have been the continuous appreciation of the DM after 1975 - not the least vis à vis US$. This appreciation was a consequence of the relatively low German inflation and a currency system based on floating. The DM-appreciation led to a relative drop in the price of oil (which is traditionally traded in US$) which neutralized part of the 1973-74 oil price hike and in general tended to shield the German economy from international inflationary tendencies. Thus the appreciation of the DM served to stabilize German price levels and through this had an influence on wage development. Furthermore the continuous appreciation of the DM served to put pressure on profits in the economic sectors exposed to competition from abroad. This can hardly but have induced employers to adopt a firmer stand in wage negotiations. At the same time it became easier for trade union leaderships to explain to the rank and file that there was not all that much to give away.

But despite the wage moderation exercised by the trade unions full employment was not restored in Germany during the period considered here. The reasons are many and complex, but the importance of two factors stands out as particularly evident.

In the first place private investments did not return to their pre-1973 level (Spahn, 1988, figure 2). The main reason for this was simply that right up to 1978 profits from investment could not compete with interests earned from financial assets (Teschner and Vesper, 1983, p. 28; Scharpf, 1987, pp. 184-185). Whether this was the fault of a wage policy still not moderate enough or of a monetary policy that was too tight and kept interest rates at too high a level can be endlessly debated.

In the second place, as already mentioned, this time the moderate German wage development did not help to strengthen the competitive standing of the exporting sector and to create more employment in that way. It had done so in 1966-67 under the fixed exchange rate regime, but after 1974 all that could be achieved by wage moderation with respect to foreign trade turned out to be an appreciation of the floating DM.

3.6. Summary

Despite institutional impediments, in the period 1974-79 the main German economic actors managed little by little to establish a reasonably well coordinated and successful set of policy responses. Coordinated policies emerged once the extent and duration of the economic recession had become clear to all of them. While the beginning of the crisis had been marked by a forceful clash between an aggressive wage policy and a contractive monetary policy - a show-down that was won by the latter - from about 1977 monetary policy, fiscal policy and wage policy worked in unison.

What was achieved was a (pragmatic) coordination of policies rather than (consensual) cooperation. This coordination was established largely on terms set by the Bundesbank (at least in the perception of the public). German crisis policies hence became highly stability oriented. This preoccupation with stability did contribute to make employment recovery in Germany extremely slow, although after 1975 unemployment actually was reduced every year.

4. The Swedish response

It is generally accepted that Swedish economic policy in the seventies rested on a well-developed theoretical foundation. This foundation had been created during the previous two decades. It contains two discernible layers: the Rehn-Meidner model of the fifties and the EFO-model added to it in the late sixties and early seventies.

Together these two models led to a unique policy mix in Swedish economic policy.The central pieces of the "Swedish model" was a (negotiated) centralized and solidary wage policy. Responsibility for this policy was assigned solely and jointly to the Confederation of trade unions (LO) and the employers' association (SAF). It was to be flanked by a (public) active labor market policy with the prime task of reducing bottle-neck as well as excess supply problems in the labor market by measures aiding in the structural adaptation of the labor force to changes in demand for labor. It was to be further supported by (restrictive) fiscal and monetary policies designed to manage aggregate demand in such a way as to support the attainment of the solidary goals set for the wage policy.[98]

The foundation of this "Swedish model" was laid in the early fifties through the work of the two trade union economists Gösta Rehn and Rudolf Meidner. Their point of departure may be called Keynesian in the sense that they, too, saw labor bottle-necks in particular occupations and regions, as well as increased unions bargaining power, as the most important factors creating inflationary pressures, even at less than full employment levels.[99] But in such a situation, they argued (well ahead of Phillips), the traditional Keynesian instruments of aggregate demand expansion would be able to reduce unemployment only at the expense of increasing inflation (Hedborg and Meidner, 1984, pp. 74-75). If inflation was to be kept down at the same time, this would have to be achieved by, for instance, a statutory incomes policy which was unpalatable to the main labor market organizations in Sweden (Hedborg and Meidner, 1984, p. 72). Moreover traditional aggregate demand stimulation might produce inefficiencies by preventing or slowing down the necessary reallocation of labor resources from stagnating to expanding firms, industries and economic sectors.

In an unorganized market the reallocation of labor resources in response to changes in the relative demand for or supply of labor in various industries and regions would (theoretically) be accomplished by temporary short-run changes in wage differentials. With increased union bargaining strength this mechanism of labor reallocation might have difficulties in working, however, and even produce inflation instead of adaptation and improved employment. This would happen if organized groups of workers tried to protect their relative wages.

The system suggested by Rehn and Meidner was supposed to outperform this unorganized market with respect to reducing (or keeping down) inflation and unemployment simultaneously, as well as with respect to securing the necessary growth in productivity by allowing for an effective reallocation of labor resources. This system was even supposed to make feasible an ideologically motivated solidary wage policy according to the principles of equal pay for equal work (later on changing in the direction of (more) equal pay for all work), and a gradual diminishing of wage differentials.

The active labor market policy constituted one of the most central elements of

---

98 Cf. Andersson (1987, pp. 168-169).

99 This scenario corresponds roughly to the economic situation in Sweden during the first post-war years.

the Rehn-Meidner model. It was conceived as a set of public programs to subsidize and train unemployed workers who could thereby be moved, at unchanged relative wages, to jobs in expanding firms and sectors of the economy. The main motivation for advocating active labor-market policy was that policies with such specific objectives would be able to reduce unemployment and inflation at the same time (Flanagan et al., 1983, p. 306).[100]

Unemployment would be brought down primarily by ensuring a faster adaptation of labor supply to demand, i.e. primarily by reducing structural and frictional unemployment. This in turn would automatically take away some of the inflationary pressures as both wage pressure emanating from pockets of excess demand for labor and wage pressure originating in inter-union conflicts over relative wage shares would be kept at bay. Demand pressure on wages would be handled through the rapid adjustment of supply to demand and hence the quick elimination of any excess demand for labor. Wage pressure caused by distributive concerns would be forestalled by not relying on changes in relative wages as the main mechanism of reallocating labor resources.

Moreover, the use of active labor market policy measures would allow the economy to reach high levels of employment without having to generate the same increase in corporate profits as would the extent of ordinary (Keynesian) aggregate demand expansion needed to bring about the same employment level. The lower level of corporate profits might serve either to stiffen employer resistance to demands for big wage increases or to keep down union demands and union militancy and hence contribute to reducing (wage) inflation (Flanagan et al., 1983, p. 307).

But active labor market policy was not only intended to sever the link between full employment and inflation. It was likewise intended to help loosening the bond between profitability and (relative) wages (or between marginal productivity and wages), and hence to open up for a solidary wage setting, in two ways.

First, if active labor-market measures replaced changes in relative wages as the primary means of reallocating labor resources between economic sectors, geographical regions etc., then the main economic reason for maintaining unequal pay for equal work across different firms, sectors and regions was removed. In that perspective the original doctrine of solidary wage policy in Sweden - equal pay for equal work - followed logically.[101]

Second, as has always been acknowledged by Swedish trade unionists,[102]

---

[100] Thus the main thrust of the active labor market policy, as envisaged by Rehn and Meidner, can be said to have been to break up the link between inflation and unemployment, or to move the Phillips-curve towards origo and to change its form, cf. Hedborg and Meidner (1984, p. 83).

[101] In comparison the second doctrine - (more) equal pay for unequal work, i.e. a reduction of wage dispersions across different types of jobs - seems much more discretionary or ideological.

[102] In marked contrast with, for example, their Danish counterparts. Actually, to give extra profits to the most productive firms and to shake out the least efficient ones was an intended side-effect of the solidaristic wage policy in the Rehn-Meidner model (Andersson, 1987, p. 168;

solidary wage policy may have adverse employment consequences, typically for those employed in high cost, low productivity firms or sectors. Therefore an important function assigned to active labor market policy has routinely been to look after and bring back into employment those wage earners made redundant when their place of work is crowded out because the relationship between profitability and wages has been severed, or, in short, to neutralize the adverse employment effects of the solidary wage policy which might else endanger its popular support.

Solidary wage policy in its turn was not only meant as a means for achieving the ideological goal of creating greater equality in society. At the same time it was also to contribute to support the non-inflationary full employment policy central to the Rehn-Meidner model. For that reason the solidary wage policy required highly centralized bargaining in order to avoid inflationary inter-union wage competition and the effective containment of wage drift at plant level (Scharpf, 1987, p. 120).

Centralization of bargaining was actually institutionalized in the mid-fifties at the request of the Swedish employers' federation (SAF).[103] The interest of the employers in centralizing collective bargaining at that time came mainly from fear that a structural peculiarity of the mode of the Swedish labor market organization might lead to escalating wage claims. The problem was that only trade unions of blue collar workers, belonging to the central trade union organization (LO), are organized according to industries. White collar unions, on the other hand, most of which belong to the umbrella-organizations TCO and SACO, are primarily organized according to occupation or education. This means that white collar unions negotiate wages for their members across different industries. If these white collar unions set their across-industries wage claims according to the bargaining results obtained by the workers' unions in the most prosperous industries, then workers' unions in less prosperous industries might in turn be induced to set their wage claims according to the results obtained by the white collar unions (Scharpf, 1987, p. 120). To avoid the consequences of such inter-union wage competition the employers wanted wage levels for all industries fixed in central negotiations with LO.

Formally the results negotiated in central bargaining between SAF and LO were not binding on the trade unions under LO.[104] They constituted just "recommendations". But at that time LO (still) wielded sufficient power and moral authority as to ensure that these recommendations were adhered to (Hedborg and Meidner, 1987, p. 64). Furthermore, they were even routinely accepted as guide-lines also by unions not belonging to LO, i.e. primarily white collar unions.

Scharpf, 1987, p. 122).

[103] Meidner (1974, p. 31) sees the collective bargaining process in 1952 as the first centralized round of collective bargaining, but at that time five unions upheld their opposition to centralization.

[104] The formal authority of the SAF over its component organizations was considerably greater, cf. Martin (1985, pp. 407-409).

While the system of centralized bargaining could be counted upon to be effective in keeping down inter-union wage competition, the problem of wage drift at the plant level remained. Significant plant level wage drift would not only run counter to the egalitarian goals of the solidary wage policy. It could also endanger the non-inflationary full employment policy goal embodied in the Rehn-Meidner model. The model's attack at this problem was in principle two-pronged, although the basic idea was the same in both cases: to limit the possibilities of firms to exceed the wage levels agreed upon in the central negotiations by cutting into their profits.

The first approach was to fix wage levels so as to exhaust the ability of firms to pay, leaving (in theory) nothing to distribute in the form of wage drift. But in conjunction with centralized bargaining this approach in isolation would have meant that wage levels would have had to be fixed according to what the most prosperous industries and firms could bear. The result would have been massive shut-downs of less profitable firms and a large scale loss of jobs. For that reason wage levels in the Rehn-Meidner model were assumed to be fixed in accordance with what the more prosperous firms - but not the most prosperous ones - can pay.[105]

The other approach relied on the use of fiscal and monetary policy. According to the Rehn-Meidner model it was the task of the government to prevent excess demand from developing and persisting by leading a generally restrictive fiscal and monetary policy. This was meant as a means to reduce "surprofits" in firms and thus to eliminate one of the supposedly most important sources of plant level wage drift (Hedborg and Meidner, 1987, p. 77).[106]

There was another function assigned to a restrictive fiscal policy in the Rehn-Meidner model as well. It was acknowledged that the way in which the wage level was to be fixed under the solidary wage policy must reduce aggregate profits below what is needed to finance the necessary level of investments. Industry as a whole would be unable to finance the necessary amount of capital formation itself. Thus capital had to be made available from other sources. According to Rehn-Meidner most of it had to be accumulated in the public sector. Thus restrictive fiscal policy was also needed to produce persistent surpluses in the public sector budgets which could then be "recycled" to the private sector as investment capital.

While the Rehn-Meidner model was adopted by the trade unions in the beginning of the fifties already, it took most of a decade until it was also accepted by the employers and the government and made the common foundation of policy making. The period from the late fifties to the mid-seventies is generally con-

---

[105] Hedborg and Meidner (1987) generally refer to the "median firm" (median with respect to profitability) as a guide-line for where to set the wage level.

[106] As a consequence, in disputes over the timing and extent of fiscal and monetary policy measures the positions of trade unions and government in Sweden have often been reversed compared to what can be seen in other countries, the Swedish trade unions accusing the government of showing too much leniency.

sidered the heyday of the Swedish model (Calmfors and Forslund, 1990, p. 64). In that period the Swedish macro-economy was by and large managed successfully (on the model's own premises).[107]

Still there were problems in the practical implementation of the Rehn-Meidner model and its prescriptions. Most of these revolved around wage setting and inflationary tendencies. With respect to wage setting two problems arose.

The first problem was wage drift which showed a marked tendency to increase during the sixties (Flanagan et al, 1983, pp. 312-315). This constantly threatened the solidary wage policy goal.[108] In order to defend this goal complex rules of compensation had to be introduced. They generalized the wage drift by providing for compensation to "disadvantaged" (with respect to wage drift) groups of workers. But these measures tended to lead to stronger wage increases than was planned for and to inflationary pressures.

The second problem was inter-union wage competition. As time went by the white collar unions outside LO were gradually strengthened. In the process they became less and less inclined to accept passively the wage levels agreed upon in central negotiations between SAF and LO (Elvander, 1988, pp. 36-40). Thus a crucial piece of the solidary wage policy - the centralized wage setting for the whole labor market - was in danger of erosion.

Once the unions outside LO would no longer automatically accept the leader role of that organization with respect to their wage claims need arose for an elaboration of the methods of wage setting. The model called for "objective" guide-lines for the negotiators to follow. Such guide-lines were established in the late sixties through the work of the top economists from the three most important labor market organizations (TCO, SAF and LO) which led to the addition of the EFO-model[109] to the original Rehn-Meidner model.

Basically the EFO-model can be seen as an adaptation of the Aukrust-model of inflation transmission in an open economy to the environment of the Rehn-Meidner model. The three authors distinguished between two sectors of the Swedish economy: an exposed sector producing tradable goods in competition with international producers, and a sheltered sector producing non-tradables. They assumed firms in the exposed sector to be price-takers in international markets and prices in the sheltered sector to be set by a simple mark-up pricing. They further assumed parallel development in wages in both sectors and fixed exchange rates.

---

[107] This is not the place to enter into a discussion of the results of the Swedish model prior to 1974. Parts of the Swedish debate are reviewed in Furåker (1976, pp. 152-159) and Hedborg and Meidner (1987, pp. 157-172).

[108] It is worth noticing that wage drift was especially pronounced in the sectors in which wages were relatively high (Flanagan et al., 1983, p. 314). Hibbs and Locking (1991, p. 12) found that wage drift typically favored the high paid. Thus to some extent wage drift may have been a means for higher paid groups to try to escape the consequences of the solidary wage policy and to (partially) restore wage differentials.

[109] Named after the initials of the three authors (Edgren, Faxén and Odhner, 1970).

Under these assumptions the international competitiveness of the exposed sector could only be ensured if nominal wage increases in this sector were determined according to the development in international prices and in productivity. Under the assumption of parallel wage development in the exposed and the sheltered sectors this would put a ceiling on the feasible size of wage increases in the sheltered sector as well. Thus in principle an objective guide-line for the size of "permissible" wage increases in both the exposed and the sheltered sector was established[110] - at least as long as the central assumptions of the model were met (Elvander, 1988, pp. 46-47).

As will have become clear from this short presentation of the "Swedish model", it is a highly complex construction establishing mutual dependencies between (primarily) wage policy, active labor market policy, and fiscal and monetary policy. But due to its complexity it is also a rather fragile construction. It requires a considerable degree of social and political consensus in order to work. Such basic consensus is required to exist both between labor and capital and within each of the two groupings.

The solidary wage policy with its numerous implications is probably the most important concession by the employers in this system. Following the implementation of the model capital in Sweden had to accept the gradual severing of ties between wages and productivity, the pressing down of levels of profits, and the crowding out of less productive firms and whole economic sectors. Labor, in return, had to accept the existing capitalist mode of production. The foundation of the "Swedish model", then, was a "big compromise" between a capitalist mode of production and a socialist mode of distribution.

In the seventies, however, cracks were beginning to develop in the basic consensus underlying the "Swedish model". The wage earner funds issue brought onto the political agenda in the mid-seventies is certainly one of the most dramatic expressions of this erosive process. It openly threatened the central content of the "big compromise".[111]

In a sense the wage earner funds issue emanated directly from the solidary wage policy and its relative success.[112] During the sixties this policy had led to an increasing degree of levelling of wages, but at the same time also to a concen-

-----

[110] Actually it is at times difficult to distinguish between descriptive and normative elements in the EFO-model. In some passages Edgren, Faxén and Odhner (1970) reads like a description of how wages were by and large set in Sweden in the sixties; in others it reads like a suggestion of how they should be set in the future.

[111] For a comprehensive account of the wage earners funds issue see for example Åsard (1985).

[112] This was hardly the only reason why the issue was brought up at this point of time, however. Another important factor was the general radicalization and the swing to the left experienced in Sweden (as well as in many other countries) in the late sixties and early seventies (Lewin, 1984, p. 344). Moreover the trade union movement was in need of a new issue for its members to rally around, since the traditional welfare state issue was gradually losing saliency.

tration of profits and capital formation in the most productive firms. The owners of these enterprises had therefore unintendedly been (indirect) beneficiaries of the trade unions' solidary wage policy. In order to counteract the tendency towards an increasing concentration of wealth and economic power Meidner in his 1975-report to the LO suggested the establishment of wage earner funds. These funds should make it possible for the wage earners to get their part of corporate profits.

The really controversial aspect of the Meidner-proposition was its insistence on collective ownership to the funds and the emphasis assigned to just this aspect. According to Meidner himself the wage earner funds were devised as a technique for gradually transferring the ownership to productive capital from private capitalists to the collectivity of wage earners (Lewin, 1984, p. 344). When the Swedish trade union movement adopted the Meidner-proposal (with minor modifications only) in 1976, one of the two legs of the "big compromise" - the trade unions' acceptance of the capitalist mode of production (in exchange for a socialist mode of distribution) - had manifestly been called into question.

The Swedish employers' federation did not only vehemently reject the idea of collectively owned wage earner funds. It also staged an ideological counter-offensive of its own which was, i.a., aimed directly at one of the trade unions' most sacred cows - the solidary wage policy (Elvander, 1988, p. 353). SAF increasingly stressed liberal market oriented views, not the least with respect to the process of wage determination.

The strained consensus between labor and capital was only part of the problem. Faced with growing internal heterogeneity both sides found it more and more difficult to keep the necessary consensus within their own ranks, too.

Among wage earners the old tensions between blue collar unions under LO and white collar unions outside it persisted and became more salient as the latter continued to grow strongly in membership numbers throughout the seventies. In the process their inclination to follow the lead of LO with respect to wage policy naturally diminished still further. Besides, tensions were also developing between private and public sector employees, the former resenting the evolving claims of the latter for a parallel wage development in the two sectors and for automatic compensation for wage drift in the private sector. Thus despite the frequent and ritualistic invocation and affirmation of the central tenets of solidary wage policy, the conditions for retaining its consensual basis among various groups of wage earners gradually became less favorable.

The worsening general economic situation from the mid-seventies onwards may well have contributed to this erosion of the former consensus about the solidary wage policy. As pointed out by Hedborg and Meidner (1984, p. 188) solidary wage policy may turn from a positive-sum game into a zero-sum game when the economic situation deteriorates. During good times solidary wage policy requires the better-off to give up some of their potential real wage increase in favor of the less well-off, but they may still experience some progress themselves. In a recession the only way to improve the situation of the (relatively) low-paid may well be to take away something from higher income groups. While the solidary wage policy was thus probably advantageous to a majority of

----

LO-workers until about 1976, it may well have stopped being so after that time (Elvander, 1988, p. 265).

A survey from 1974 (Lewin, 1977, p. 131) suggests that at that time already the support of the solidary wage policy among the trade unions' rank-and-file membership was anything but rock-solid. Thus 53 per cent of the rank-and-file respondents indicated that they were not ready to forego wage increases to themselves in favor of low-paid groups in other unions.[113] On the other hand 78 per cent of the rank-and-file respondents agreed that higher paid wage earner groups within LO should back the claims of the lower paid, even if this meant to cut back on their own claims.[114] Finally 60 per cent agreed that LO was wrong in setting its wage claims in a way that might cause crowding out of the least efficient firms. On two out of three questions tapping attitudes towards central aspects of the solidary wage policy in the "Swedish model" a majority among the rank-and-file respondents hence failed to support this policy in 1974.[115]

SAF likewise experienced increasing difficulties in maintaining consensus among its affiliated organizations. In no small measure this was due to a strong growth in the number of small and medium-sized firms which threatened the traditional dominance of the big firms within SAF (Elvander, 1988, pp. 69-70). For obvious reasons the consequences of the solidary wage policy were more easy to live with for big than for small firms - after all it contained built-in tendencies for crowding out small firms and for rapid concentration in production (Andersson, 1987, pp. 168-169). Hence the increasing weight of smaller firms within the SAF constituency was one of the reasons why - beginning in the seventies - the organization was forced to begin showing a more marked ideological profile on issues like solidary wage policy versus productivity based wage setting.

Thus for various reasons the seventies saw a beginning re-intensification of

---

113 As one moves up the trade union hierarchy attitudes become more and more positive towards solidary wage policy. This is a general trait with all questions asked concerning this issue.

114 While at first view the pattern of responses to these two questions may appear strikingly inconsistent, this is not necessarily the case. It should be noticed that the two questions belong to different levels. The second one concerns a norm which is far more abstract and "distant" to most individuals than is the concrete choice situation presented in the first question. It is very commonly found that the closer the questions get to a genuine individual choice, the closer the responses get to economic rationality (and the farther away from altruism).

115 Most surprisingly the survey also showed that the solidary wage policy did not enjoy remarkably strong support among low-paid workers. The main support was rather forthcoming from higher paid groups (Lewin, 1977, p. 204). A possible explanation could be that the solidary wage policy as perceived by the respondents had increasingly turned into a relatively abstract principle or norm, like justice, tolerance, or equality, rather than a set of practical political measures to aid low-paid groups, and in surveys people in higher socio-economic strata are often found to be more prone than people in lower strata to voice their support for such general principles. A similar explanation is given by Lewin himself (1977, p. 231).

distributional conflicts in Sweden, not just between labor and capital, but also within both groupings, not the least labor.[116] The development in the level of industrial conflicts tends to support that interpretation: while still low by international standards (or, more specifically, in comparison with Danish or British levels) there was an increasing tendency in the seventies, compared to for example the sixties, not the least with respect to the number of wild cat strikes.[117]

In summary, then, among the five countries in this study Sweden undoubtedly was the country which was equipped with the most sophisticated model for macro-economic policy making. Furthermore, this model had been designed with a view to the establishing and maintaining of full employment without the creation of inflationary pressures. But the model was vulnerable. It could hardly be expected to function without being grounded in a far-reaching distributional consensus between (as well as among) labor and capital - and this consensus was in the process of eroding when the economic recession in the wake of the first oil price hike hit the country.

4.1. Ducking it? Crisis onset and crisis development in Sweden

From figure 1.3. in chapter 1 it can be seen that the Swedish way into and through the economic recession in the wake of the first oil price hike differs from that of the other four countries[118] - but least so from Austria's - in a number of respects. While the other countries experienced a sharp decline in economic activity and GDP growth in 1974 (except for Austria, where it occured in 1975), GDP growth in Sweden actually rose slightly in 1974. But after 1974 the Swedish economy gradually lost momentum. By 1977 Sweden reached a stage of economic stagnation comparable to the 1974-75 level of the other countries (which by then were experiencing various degrees of recovery). After 1977 a certain (albeit short-lived) recovery in economic activity and GDP growth in Sweden took place, but the weak economic growth, signalling among other things a gradual decline of productivity in Swedish industry, became one of the weak spots of the country's economy.[119]

Complementary to the development in GDP growth there was a slow increase in consumer price inflation until 1977 and a gradual decrease thereafter. Thus

---

116 Cf. also Calmfors and Lundberg (1974, pp. 206-215).

117 The average number of wild cat strikes 1960-69 was 17.6, while for the period 1970-74 the average number was 52.8, cf. Lewin (1977, p. 89). Data on the development in the level of industrial conflicts are discussed and analyzed further in chapter 4 and 5.

118 It differs as well from the typical patterns found with the OECD-countries as a whole, cf. for example Lundberg (1983, pp. 13-15) and figure 1.1. in chapter 1.

119 The rather strong GDP growth in 1979 was simply due to a pre-election boom, cf. Martin (1985, pp. 457-458) and below.

Sweden avoided a dramatic jump in the rate of inflation such as occured in Denmark (1974) and the UK (1974-75). Even so, among the five countries considered Sweden ranked second with respect to the size of the rate of inflation in four out of six years. To make matters worse, the Swedish rate of inflation was out of phase with that of Germany (one of the main competitors of Swedish industry). All together this adds up to a poor Swedish performance with respect to inflation for the period 1974-79.

Things look very much different when we consider unemployment. Swedish unemployment figures actually went down somewhat until 1975 and then stayed almost constant, well below the two per cent mark. There was a slight increase of unemployment in 1978, but in general the development in Swedish unemployment from 1975 onwards is strikingly similar to the development in Austria. It clearly stands out as a success of Swedish crisis policy.

The same similarity to Austria is found with respect to the development in the Swedish surplus on current transactions with the rest of the world. During the period considered here it was mostly negative, but not dramatically so when compared to the situation in Denmark and the UK.

The factors that initially helped Sweden duck the crisis in 1974 were in two respects the same "good luck" factors that helped Austria achieving the same thing. One factor was the general line or direction of the macro-economic policy pursued at the onset of the crisis. The second factor was the composition of Swedish exports.

Contrary to Germany, Sweden did not move into the international recession with a foot on the economic brake. No home-made stabiliziation contraction had been planned for 1973-74. Sweden had been through its own mini-recession in the beginning of the seventies ("the lost years"). In 1970-71 policies aimed at creating a short recession. This, however, had been expected to become short-lived and moderate: for 1971 already a certain degree of economic recovery had been predicted. But things turned out quite differently. During the second half of 1971 the rate of expansion of economic activity fell off rapidly, and unemployment doubled.[120] Therefore - and conceivably also with just an eye to the upcoming national election in 1973 - economic policy turned expansionary in 1972 and stayed so in 1973. The "idiot stop" of 1970-72 was not going to be repeated (Andersen and Åkerholm, 1982, p. 635). Thus the macro-economic policy in Sweden was expansion-bound at the start of the crisis.

The first oil price hike started a boom in raw materials and semi-manufactured goods in 1974. This happened because industrial countries went into a heavy build-up of inventories. They feared the spread of the example of cartel formation and price hikes by the oil-producing countries. This boom was advantageous to parts of Swedish industry, especially the wood and iron ore industries as well as car manufacturing.[121] Export prices rose by 28 per cent, and profits soared. The boom was strong enough to temporarily offset the negative effects of the quadrupled oil price on domestic and international demand, especially since fiscal

---

120 OECD, Economic Surveys: Sweden (1972), pp. 22-31.
121 Elvander (1988, p. 48).

and monetary policy stayed expansionary.

But in 1975, with inventories filled, the boom was coming to an end and Sweden had to face the same stagflationary problem as did other industrial countries. Economic stability was threatened by the simultaneous loss of demand and fuelling of inflation. Conscious macro-economic crisis management was called for. In the following sections various components of Swedish macro-economic policy making 1974–79 will be examined.

4.2. *Wage policy*

In keeping with the tenets of the "Swedish model", wage policy must be considered the corner-stone of Swedish macro-economic policy making. It is the appropriate starting point for our analysis.

The course taken by Swedish wage policy 1974–79 turns out to have been significantly different from that of Austria and Germany. The wage explosions of 1974 (Germany) and 1975 (Austria) were certainly not conducive to the necessary concertation of the various elements of stabilization policy. But once this had become recognized, considerable and sustained wage restraint came to be exercised in both countries during the rest of the period.

In Sweden, on the other hand, the initial wage policy reaction in 1974 was considered to be relatively moderate.[122] But it was then followed by a two-year wage explosion which went far beyond what had been experienced in Germany and Austria. After that, wage policy turned more moderate again. Thus in the Swedish case one can hardly speak of a policy of sustained wage restraint and strategic coordination with other elements of crisis policy.

Under the impression of the economic uncertainty generated by the oil price hike in late 1973 the regular round of collective bargaining 1973-74 was short and peaceful. It ended in the spring of 1974 with the conclusion of a one-year central agreement.

In general this agreement is considered an instance of considerable wage restraint.[123] Wage increases agreed upon in the central negotiations were in fact relatively low by Swedish standards, at least for workers in industry. For this group the wage increases provided for in the central agreement amounted to five per cent only.[124] But to a considerable degree this picture of restraint is shat-

---

[122] At least this seems to be the general view of the central collective agreement in 1974. Some qualifying remarks will be added below.

[123] Cf. for example Martin (1985, pp. 426-427); Scharpf (1987, p. 128); Esping-Andersen (1987, p. 91); Elvander (1988, p. 48).

[124] The figures in the following are from Elvander (1988, p. 55). Martin (1985, p. 427) gives a somewhat deviating figure (8.1 per cent) for increase in hourly wages of industrial workers due to wage drift.

---

tered by the extent of locally negotiated wage drift. For industrial workers wage drift amounted to 6.8 per cent in 1974. Thus the total wage increase was 11.8 per cent for this group, or nearly four percentage points more than in 1973. For white collar employees in industry the total wage increases in 1974 amounted to about the same percentage as for blue collar workers (12.3 per cent). Most of this rise came from the central agreement and only a minor part (1.8 per cent) from wage drift. Wage increases for public employees fell behind those for private sector employees by about 4 percentage points but even they exceeded their 1973-levels.

Adding wage drift does not necessarily give the whole picture. Besides the wage increases agreed upon centrally and locally, pay-roll taxes were also raised by 4.8 per cent in 1974.[125] Seen from a total wage bill perspective the 1974-agreement may have entailed still higher increases in labor cost.

The main argument for nevertheless talking about wage restraint in connection with the 1974-agreement appears to be that it did not prevent a sharp rise in profits that occured in 1974, primarily in those industries that benefited from the boom in raw materials and semi-manufactured goods. Obviously there would have been economic scope for higher wage increases than the trade unions were asking for (and got).

Seen in an international perspective, on the other hand, the 1974-agreement does not necessarily qualify as an outstanding example of wage restraint. In 1974 hourly wage rates in manufacturing rose by 11 per cent in Sweden as against 12 per cent in Germany (one of the main competitors to Swedish industry), while unit labor costs rose 12.4 per cent in Sweden, but 9.6 per cent in Germany.[126] Thus wage increases were at roughly the same level in both countries in 1974 - only that this level of wage increases was considered a flagrant expression of lack of restraint in Germany, to be subsequently brought down by all means!

In the last resort, however, it does not matter much if the 1974-agreement "really" (whatever that means) was moderate or not. The most important thing is that it quickly came to be perceived as (too) moderate by the trade unions. Both the rising profits in parts of the Swedish industry and the high level of wage drift were considered indicative of this. Owing to their preoccupation with distributional matters (compared to the main orientation of trade union policies in Austria and Germany) both developments represented serious set-backs and were hence unacceptable to the Swedish trade unions. Rising profits implied a

---

[125] This rise - as well as a similar one in 1975 and 1976 - had been agreed upon by the government and the wage earner organizations in the so-called Haga-agreements. The increased pay-roll taxes were intended to compensate the government budget for loss of revenues due to changes in the personal incomes tax scales introduced in order to counteract the fiscal drag caused by inflation. In return the wage earner organizations had promised to moderate their wage claims (Calmfors and Forslund, 1990, p. 90).

[126] In national currencies, cf. OECD, Historical Statistics (1988). Since the DM was the dominating currency in the "snake", keeping a fixed exchange rate vis a vis the other currencies in the snake required the Swedish price and wage development to follow the German.

reduction in the wage share in favor of capital, and wage drift threatened the very goal of the solidary wage policy, the levelling of wages.

Thus in the next regular round of collective bargaining the trade unions had strong motivations to try to roll back the distributional gains to capital from the 1974-agreement and to safeguard the goal and principles of the solidary wage policy by limiting the extent of wage drift. A high level of centrally negotiated wage increases obviously would serve both purposes at once.

In the negotiations LO did not only press for big wage increases. It also demanded a two-year agreement. The obvious strategy was to try to use the present, favorable economic situation, which was expected to last throughout 1975, to secure as big wage increases as possible not only for that year, but also for 1976, when the economic situation might be less favorable and employers hence harder to deal with. SAF initially resisted the claim for a two-year agreement[127] but had finally to give in when the public employers concluded a two-year agreement (at a high level of wage increases[128]) with the public employees.

The outcome was a two-year "wage feast". In 1975-76 the wages of Swedish industrial workers increased no less than 31.3 per cent. Close to 13 percentage points of this increase came from wage drift. Obviously even very high centrally agreed levels of wage increases were no longer sufficient to contain wage drift. White collar employees in industry obtained wage increases of 30.2 per cent, while public employees had to content themselves with increases around 25 per cent.[129] Furthermore pay-roll taxes were raised by almost 7 per cent. Taking together that the wage bill in industry was increased by close to 40 per cent in 1975-76.

Two factors amplified the effects of the 1976 explosion in costs. The first of these was that international inflationary pressures were beginning to ease in 1975. The second factor was the rapid appreciation of the DM at this time. This development forced upwards the other currencies in the "snake", among these the Swedish krona. As a result the Swedish economy was simultaneously exposed on three flanks: rising internal costs, appreciation of the currency, and a falling rate of inflation among the main competitors. The consequences were soon to be felt. Current account deficits rose rapidly in 1976 and 1977 and Swedish inflation rates went up as well. Gross operating surpluses in the exposed

---

127 It is sometimes claimed that multi-year wage contracts are conducive to wage moderation, cf. Calmfors and Forslund (1990, pp. 84-85). If this were really the case, it seems hard to understand why LO would press for a two-year agreement in 1975, while the SAF initially rejected such a claim. See also Flanagan et al. (1983, p. 326).

128 Jonung (1989, p. 15) claims that in this situation the public sector became the wage leader, contrary to the stipulations of the EFO-model according to which the exposed sector should be the leading one.

129 But both groups had a break-through with respect to another point of great importance to them: for the first time they obtained a "lönutvecklingsgaranti" (LUG), i.e. an automatic compensation for blue collar wage drift.

----

sector slumped dramatically from a little above 11 per cent of the capital stock in 1974 to just a little above 4 per cent in 1977,[130] and employment in industry began to fall in 1976 (Scharpf, 1987, pp. 129-130).

Thus around 1976-77 the "bridging strategy" by which Sweden had hoped to escape the repercussions of the international recession had broken down. It is hardly unduly harsh to claim that the distribution-oriented wage policy of 1975-76 strained the capacity of the Swedish system of crisis management beyond the breaking point.

Of sheer necessity the following rounds of collective bargaining in Sweden became characterized by attempts to get the baby back into the tub. After pro-tracted and hard negotiations, limited conflicts, and a threatening industry-wide strike among white collar employees in the private sector a one-year agreement was reached for 1977, just a few hours ahead of the outbreak of the strike. It was certainly a more moderate agreement than the one from 1975-76, with wage increases (including drift) reduced to about one half in the private sector, while increases in the public sector were of about the same size as in 1976. To these increases a new 3.2 per cent increase in pay-roll taxes had to be added, however.

When the next round of collective bargaining started, the outlook for the Swedish economy was bleak. GDP-growth was negative, the public budget deficit and the current account deficit were rising, and so were both consumer price inflation and open unemployment (although the latter was still extremely low - 1.8 per cent - by international standards). Thus there was a general agree-ment that wage moderation was called for, even despite the loss in real wages experienced as a consequence of the 1976-77 depreciations of the Swedish krona (see below).[131] But while SAF demanded a three-year agreement, the wage earners organizations were only ready to offer a one-year contractual period.

The outcome was an agreement covering 1978 and 10 months of 1979. It provided for moderate wage increases. Wage drift included, wages for industrial workers rose by 16.2 per cent 1978-79 (of which roughly one half caused by wage drift) and wages for white collar employees in industry by 15.6 per cent. Wage increases in the public sector followed a comparable trend.

As a new feature a price guarantee was added to the central agreements. It gave the wage earners organizations a right to re-open negotitations - complete with the possibility of establishing industrial conflicts - for wage increases in case inflation exceeded a certain threshold. Both sides were in agreement that this might be a way to encourage the government to try to keep inflation down.

Table 2.11. summarizes some of the main trends in wage development in

----

130 OECD, Economic Surveys: Sweden (1984, p. 39).

131 The government's attempt of furthering moderation through "tax bribery" was probably not successful, however, since LO considered the distributional consequences of the reductions in marginal taxes unacceptable (Elvander, 1988, p. 288). But even if it had no influence on the position taken by LO in the central negotiations, it might have increased the readiness of the rank-and-file (or at least the part that benefited from it) to accept nominal wage increases which were lower than what would have been needed in order to offset the effects of the devaluation on real (pre-tax) wages.

Sweden 1973-79 in a way lending itself to comparison with corresponding developments in Austria and Germany. Both the "slip of restraint" in Swedish wage policy in the middle of the period and the adverse consequences of this slip are easily recognized.

Table 2.11.: Main trends in wage development in Swedish manufacturing, 1973-79
(increases in percentages)

	1973	1974	1975	1976	1977	1978	1979
Nominal	8.4	11.1	17.2	13.5	8.2	10.3	7.8
Real	1.7	1.2	7.4	2.2	-3.2	-0.3	0.6
Inflation	6.7	9.9	9.8	10.3	11.4	10.0	7.2
Unit costs	4.6	12.9	19.3	16.7	11.1	8.3	-0.1

Data: Scharpf (1987, p. 90)

It is interesting to notice that the generally more restrictive, growth- rather than distribution-oriented wage policies adopted by Austrian trade unions were nevertheless more successful in defending real wages than was the Swedish wage policy.[132] In Austria the average yearly increase in real wages in manufacturing 1973-79 was 3.44 per cent compared to 1.37 per cent in Sweden.[133] It looks as if the size of the cake is not entirely independent of how it is distributed, after all!

In the sections on both Austria and Germany union behavior with respect to nominal wage setting (in manufacturing) 1974-79 was found to be rather strongly influenced by the general situation in the labor market ("tightness" as defined as the ratio of vacancies to unemployed in the Austrian and unemployment in the German case). For Sweden Calmfors and Forslund (1990, pp. 99-117) have reported results of a series of estimations of real wage equations for the whole of Swedish industry 1969-86. They found that growth in open (registered) unemployment has a tendency to diminish the size of real wage increases. This tendency is rather weak and (statistically) unreliable. They also found that if the relative importance of active labor market programs increases this tends to increase real wage growth

Thus the real wage-reducing effects of increases in unemployment can be counteracted by the wage-raising effects of accommodating labor market policies. Since - as will be shown below - deteriorations with respect to the employment situation in Sweden 1974-79 were regularly met by an accommodating expansion of labor market programs,[134] it can be concluded that during the

---

[132] If Germany were included in the comparison, it would turn out that also the German trade unions were more successful than their Swedish counterparts in defending real wage growth, despite their less distribution-oriented policies. It might be argued, however, that this success was bought at the expense of sizeable unemployment.

[133] The rank order remains the same when 1973 is excluded.

[134] Cf. Calmfors (1990, pp. 55-56).

period considered here the net impact of employment conditions on Swedish wage policy was modest.

4.3. Demand management and exchange rate policy

As has been mentioned above the "Swedish model" assigned to the government a responsibility for supporting wage policy in mainly two ways. Aggregate demand management policies were to be used in order to avoid situations with excess demand in the economy as a whole or in sectors and sub-branches, and active labor market policies were to be used in order to assist in the reallocation of labor resources.

Both types of policies were extensively used in the period considered here, but it may seem that in the process they changed character. Demand management policy (by fiscal and monetary measures) became very much like the (conventional) demand stimulating policy used by most other governments in their fight against unemployment. The active labor market programs were increasingly transformed from reallocation measures into an alternative labor market.

The present section deals with the conventional Keynesian policy instruments of the government, fiscal and monetary policy, and exchange rate policy. The next section deals with more specific Swedish policy instruments, active labor market policies and the policy of public sector employment growth.

In the uncertain and volatile situation created by the oil price hike in late 1973 the Swedish government decided to react with expansionary fiscal and monetary measures in order to counteract an expected drop in aggregate demand, rather than with restrictive measures in order to counteract the foreseeable inflationary consequences of the quadrupled oil prices.[135] By March 1974 a bundle of expansionary fiscal measures was introduced, including a temporary reduction of the VAT from 15 to 12 per cent to be effective from April 1 to October 15, 1974, and a considerable increase in transfer payments to various groups. As a consequence there was a rather strong increase in the deficit of the 1974 central government budget.

Monetary policies were assigned a supporting role with primarily three objectives (which were to remain largely unchanged during the whole of the period under consideration). In the first place it should encourage borrowing abroad in order to finance the current account deficit to be expected and to protect the Swedish foreign currency reserves. In the second place it should stimulate the flow of credit to business in order to keep up investment levels. In the third place it should aim at financing the central government deficit without "crowding out"

---

[135] While the Swedish Central Bank (Riksbanken) is formally independent of the government, the government in power always commands a majority on the board. According to Alesina (1988, p. 41) with respect to independence from the government the Swedish Central Bank belongs in the second least independent category (out of four).

effects and without creating excess liquidity which might reduce incentives to borrow abroad.

By and large Swedish monetary policy was successful in achieving these objectives.[136] The primary instruments used in various combinations were regulations of domestic credit supply through changes in primary reserves and reserve requirements, introduced in early 1974, and an easing of restrictions on capital imports (Andersen and Åkerholm, 1982, p. 617).

Thus in 1974 both fiscal and monetary policies were mobilized to fighting off a recession. But in the short run the recession failed to materialize. Instead there was the world-wide, albeit short-lived boom benefiting primarily the Swedish exporters of raw materials and semi-manufactured goods. Unemployment even decreased, compared to the 1973-figure, and huge profits were created in some sectors of the Swedish economy.

This development did not make the government change its expansionary policies. However, knowing the sensibility of the trade unions to what they considered excess profits in firms special investment funds were introduced by October 1974 in which 15 per cent of the 1974-profits were to be deposited.

As it turned out this measure was far from effective in preventing employers and trade unions from negotiating a central agreement which triggered off the "wage feast" of 1975-76 (cf. above). As an alternative a number of independent economists had suggested an appreciation of the Swedish krona. This would also have reduced profits but, in addition, it would have reduced the impact of the international inflation on domestic price levels in Sweden. But since the "Swedish model" was built on the assumption of fixed exchange rates, the exchange rate option had traditionally been more or less neglected in Swedish economic policy discussions (Scharpf, 1987, p. 129). It was not utilized in this situation either.[137]

When the Swedish economy began its downhill move in 1975, the government once more resorted to demand stimulation through fiscal policy. By October 1975 changes in the central government budget were introduced to the tune of 2 bill. kr. of extra expenditures. Among the measures introduced were favorable borrowing conditions for the purpose of inventory financing, extra depreciation allowances for investment in machinery and equipment, the advancing of certain public investment programs, and large grants to public relief works.[138] But since central government revenues nevertheless grew somewhat faster than expenditures, the budget deficit of 1975 (in percentage of GDP) was actually reduced a bit, compared to 1974. The same pattern was repeated in 1976, so during these two years the impacts of central government fiscal policy were actually pro-cyclical rather than anti-cyclical, despite continuing deficit

---

[136] OECD, Economic Surveys: Sweden (1976).

[137] After the break-down of the Bretton Woods system of fixed exchange rates Sweden had joined the "snake" (as had all the countries included in this study with the exception of the UK).

[138] OECD, Economic Surveys: Sweden (1976, p. 23).

----

spending.

After the general election of 1976 a bourgeois three-party coalition government took over from the losing Social Democrats who were thus out of power for the first time in 44 years.[139] The new government inherited a bleak economic situation, dominated mainly by three problems.

The first one was the cost problem of Swedish industry which had developed primarily during 1975-76. The high Swedish wage increases, the appreciation of the Swedish krona (together with the DM), and the reduction in international inflation rates had combined to bring about this problem.

The second problem were structural difficulties in parts of Swedish industry. Raw material based industries, ship building, and car manufacturing were all seriously hit by the international recession (Scharpf, 1987, pp. 129-130).

Together these two problems spelled the third one: unemployment. Although Swedish unemployment was still low (by all standards) in 1976, there was an incipient loss of jobs in industry to take into account, and the bourgeois government had every political reason to dread mass unemployment. It was not keen at vindicating the claims of the Socialdemocrats to be the only reliable guardians of full employment.

Keeping down open unemployment thus had to be the high priority goal to be achieved by the new government. To that end it relied on three main instruments: devaluation to improve the relative cost position of Swedish industry, large style subsidizing (involving equally large style deficit spending) of firms to preserve jobs, and active labor market policies (to be discussed below) to provide a kind of alternative labor market for those losing their job in the private sector. The structural problem of Swedish industry, on the other hand, was more or less left alone: this was a long-run problem, and the full employment restriction tended to confine the options of the government to short-run strategies.

In three steps between October, 1976 and August, 1977 the Swedish krona was depreciated by 15 per cent, and Sweden left the "snake". The goal of this operation was to restore the international competitiveness of Swedish exports. The outcome was by and large a success: Swedish relative export prices (trade-weighted) went down from an index value of 111 in 1976 to 106 in 1977, 99 in 1978, and 100 in 1979.[140]

This development is remarkable because the devaluation was not flanked by any kind of "social contract" in order to prevent the initial gains to be offset by increases in prices and wages. Instead there was a temporary price freeze which was later replaced by rules of notification before price increases could become effective. Furthermore the general pay-roll tax was abolished in order to reduce labor cost pressures on export and domestic prices (Martin, 1985, p. 454).[141]

---

[139] The wage earners funds issue was one of the factors that contributed to the Social-democratic defeat, cf. Lewin (1984, p. 353).

[140] Index 1970 = 100; OECD, Economic Outlook 38 (1985).

[141] The abolition of the general pay-roll tax did not become effective before the beginning and the middle of 1978, however.

Finally, in order to curtail private consumption and to shift resources into the external sector, the VAT was raised to 17.1 per cent. Together these measures were expected to reduce the inflationary effects of the devaluation, and thus in turn the demand for compensatory wage increases.

The central agreements in the labor market of 1977 and (especially) 1978-79 (cf. above) actually accommodated the government's devaluation policy. Nominal wage increases did not even compensate for the effects of the devaluation.[142] Workers in manufacturing, for example, took a real wage reduction of about 3.5 per cent in 1977 and 1978.[143] There was hence even created scope for a 1.5 percentage point lowering of the discount rate in 1978, although monetary policies by and large remained tight.

Thus, in the words of an observer[144] "... the government had apparently managed to bring off one of the few effective devaluations among the many that have been attempted." Exports did rise in the wake of the devaluation and contributed to a certain recovery of production. From 1978 Swedish output growth turned positive again. An export-led upswing had been initiated.

Still this success alone might have been insufficient to avoid open mass unemployment. To prevent that from happening the bourgeois government continued many of the employment support programs inside and outside the framework of the active labor market policy inherited from its Socialdemocratic predecessor, only on a much enlarged scale. But since it was not willing to finance these activities by raising taxes - always a problem for non-socialist governments[145] - the result was large style deficit spending. Thus from 1977 Swedish fiscal policy turned strongly expansionary again as the central government budget deficit grew at an alarming pace (and well ahead of the trend in GDP-growth). From 2 per cent of GDP in 1976 (when the bourgeois government took over) it rose to 9.6 per cent in 1979.

---

[142] A possible reason for the relative moderation shown by the trade unions in connection with the 1977-agreement might have been political uncertainty about what the course of the new government would be, cf. Sørensen (1990). As far as the 1978-79 agreement is concerned the sense of doom prevailing at the time of its conclusion is possible to be credited.

[143] OECD, Historical Statistics (1988). Martin (1985, p. 455) gives a considerably higher figure for industrial workers ("over 8 per cent").

[144] Martin (1985, p. 455).

[145] Actually the bourgeois Swedish government pursued a curious mix of "socialist expenditure policies and conservative tax policies" (Scharpf, 1987, p. 131, my transl.). Not only did it not raise taxes in order to cover some of the expenditures on employment support, it initiated a series of tax reforms aiming at reducing especially marginal income taxes. The most important step in this process was probably the indexation of the tax scale in order to counteract fiscal drag.

Figure 2.9.: Demand stimulation through public finance in Sweden 1973-79, per cent of GDP

(a) All government

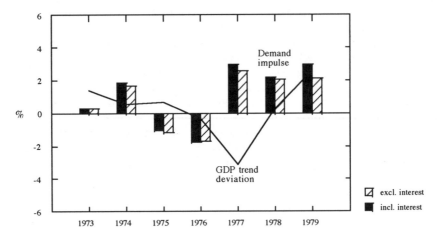

(b) Central government

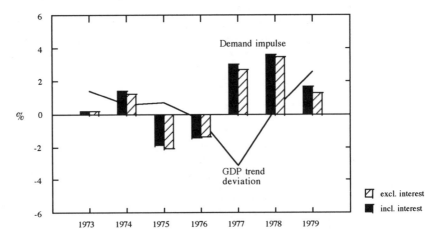

Data: Teschner and Vesper (1983); OECD, National Accounts (1984)

Figure 2.9. summarizes the impact of fiscal policy on aggregate demand in 1973-79.[146] It illustrates the rather dramatic shift in extent of demand stimulation from

---

[146] See section 2 above for computational details.

public sector budgets which occured in the latter half of the period considered here (1977-79), i.e. during the tenure of the first bourgeois government. Between 1973 and 1976 the impulses from the public budgets are seen to have been somewhat weaker. Moreover, half the time they were actually contractive rather than expansionary. Thus fiscal policy in the latter half of the period clearly deviated from the role assigned to it within the framework of the Swedish model.

As has been mentioned the main reason for this development in Swedish fiscal policy is most probably to be found in the political interest of the bourgeois government in preventing open unemployment. More specifically, this interest might also serve to explain the markedly pro-cyclical fiscal policy adopted in 1979.[147]

This raises the question of the possible existence of a Swedish political business cycle (or electoral cycle), i.e. a possible synchronization by the government of the timing of economic policy measures and election dates. Surveying election dates, the timing of certain economic policy measures (monetary policy and government expenditures), and the development in certain macro-economic figures (real GDP growth, unemployment rate, and inflation rate) in 10 industrial countries between 1960 and 1979 Schmidt (1983b, p. 182) found that in the case of Sweden there was some synchronization between the timing of both monetary and fiscal policy measures and election dates. He found only a weak relationship, however, between, on the one hand, variations in GDP growth and the inflation rate and, on the other hand, election dates. There was no link between unemployment and election dates. The attempts of the bourgeois Swedish government to make sure it "looked good" with respect to employment by even increasing deficit spending in 1979 would seem to fit that conclusion.

4.4. In defense of full employment: Labor market policy and public sector employment growth

As in the case of Austrian incomes policy, Swedish active labor market policy has for a long time been met with great interest by foreign observers who have looked to Sweden as a model case for the successful implementation of this type of policy.[148] Rightly so: "Sweden has probably the largest experience of manpower policy (more than three decades), the broadest set-up of activities and the

---

147 According to Martin (1985, pp. 457-458) "... government policy reinforced the effect of the international recovery, fueling a pre-election boom that brought open unemployment down to 1.8 per cent in the last quarter of the year." The same interpretation can be found in Jonung (1989, p. 15; p. 22).

148 The German "Arbeitsförderungsgesetz" of 1969, for example, was in many respects modeled on the Swedish active labor market policy.

best equipped machinery to implement the policy" (Meidner, 1984, p. 255).[149]

Moreover, the record of Swedish active labor market policy as a means to avoid open unemployment is impressive. Together with a strong growth in public sector employment active labor market policy programs were not just instrumental in keeping Swedish unemployment under or close to the 2 per cent mark during the whole of the period 1974-79: Swedish employment actually increased during this first period of the world-wide recession.

Table 2.12.: Percentage of participants in labor market programs, public employment (general government) and unemployment 1974-79

	1974	1975	1976	1977	1978	1979
In labor market progr.	2.9	2.5	3.0	3.3	3.9	4.0
Public empl.*	24.8	..	26.6	27.8	29.0	29.9
Unemploym.	2.0	1.6	1.6	1.8	2.2	2.1

* in per cent of total employment
Data: Webber (1983, p. 33); OECD, Historical Statistics (1988)

Between 1973 and 1979 the total Swedish population aged 15 to 64 remained almost constant (+0.9 per cent). The total labor force, however, grew by 5.5 per cent, and the participation rate in the population aged 15 to 64 went up by 4.6 per cent.[150] This increase was solely due to a higher female participation rate. While the 1974-79 average of the male labor force as a percentage of the male population aged 15 to 64 was almost identical to the 1968-73 average (88.4 against 88.8 per cent), the corresponding female rate increased from an average of 59.9 per cent in 1968-73 to an average of 69.2 per cent in 1974-79.

This increase in the size of the labor force could not be absorbed by the private sector. Between 1973 and 1979 employment in agriculture and in industry as a percentage of civilian employment fell, while there was a modest growth in employment in services (excluding the public sector). The main brunt had to be borne by active labor market programs and growing public sector

---

[149] The institutional set-up of Swedish active labor market policy is described in Schmid et al. (1987, pp. 60-63).
[150] OECD, Historical Statistics (1988).

employment.[151]

The coincidence of strong labor force growth and weakening economic activity led to a considerable expansion of the scope of active labor market programs and public sector employment during the period 1974-79. The development in this "alternative labor market" is clearly brought out by table 2.12. As can be seen, Swedish unemployment might have totalled 6.1 per cent in 1979 - a figure higher than Germany's - had it not been for the impact of active labor market policy - to say nothing about public sector employment.[152]

Table 2.13:. Total expenditures of the Labor Market Authority 1974/75 - 1979/80

	74-75	75-76	76-77	77-78	78-79	79-80
In pct. of GDP	1.9	1.9	2.6	3.2	3.0	2.9
In pct. of total government expend.	5.4	5.4	7.2	8.1	7.7	7.0
Unempl. benefits in pct. of total expend.	14.6	12.6	11.3	11.6	15.3	14.7

Data: SOU (1984), p. 81 (Table 4B:1)

The adverse development in labor demand and supply also led to some reorientation of the contents of active labor market policy. Demand-side oriented programs (sheltered jobs, temporary relief projects, etc.) gained in importance relative to traditional, supply-side oriented activities (training and re-training, increase

---

[151] A continuous reduction in working hours per employee at an average annual rate of 1.3 per cent also helped (Webber, 1983, p. 32). This reduction was brought about by a marked increase in part-time work (mainly by women in the public sector). The trade unions were strongly opposed to a general reduction in working hours which they considered a purely defensive measure with the sole effect of distributing the available work instead of creating new jobs through an offensive policy which was the course they preferred.

[152] There has been some discussion whether the percentage of the workforce taken care of by active labor market programmes should be added to the unemployment rate in order to give the "right" picture of Swedish unemployment in comparison with unemployment in other countries. In my opinion the two figures should be kept apart for the simple reason that obviously the macro-economic effects of changes in unemployment and of changes in the number of people in labor market programmes are very different, cf. above on wage formation. Thus being in labor market programmes of some kind obviously is closer to being in "real" employment than being unemployed.

----

of mobility, etc).[153]

One might also try to assess the importance of active labor market policy in Sweden by looking at the expenditures of the Labor Market Authority (Arbetsmarknadsverket). Table 2.13. shows this cost as a percentage of GDP and of the total government budget for the period 1974/75 - 1979/80.[154] These figures are rather impressive. As (rightly) noted by Meidner (1984, p. 250), "(t)here is no other country which spends 3 per cent of its GNP or 8 per cent of its total national budget for manpower policy."

The last row of table 2.13. highlights another distinguishing feature of Swedish labor market policy in the post 1973-recession. As can be seen, only 10 to 15 per cent of total expenditures financed unemployment benefits. The rest was devoted to active labor market programs.

4.5. Summary

Sweden entered the world-wide post 1973-recession equipped with an elaborate model for macro-economic policy making designed to achieve and safeguard a condition of non-inflationary full employment. Within the framework of this model specific tasks and strategies were assigned to the various macro-economic actors. In principle the problem of strategic coordination was hence removed from Swedish macro-economic policy making.

In practice, due not the least to the beginning erosion of the model's consensual foundations, the coordination problem found its way back into macro-economic policy making in Sweden, too. Especially in the middle of the period the coordination between trade union wage policy and the strategies of other actors was seriously deficient. Thus the Swedish economy owed its undisputable success - the low rate of open unemployment - to a rather uncoordinated use of instruments. Some of these were part of the "Swedish model", like the active labor market policy, and some were instruments foreign to it, like large-style deficit spending and exchange rate policy. Taken together they did not add up to a skilful application of the model. The price that had to be paid for this eclecticism was the development and persistence of other macro-economic imbalances, most notably inflation, and recurring current account deficits.

5. The British response

At the onset of the economic recession in 1973-74 Britain could look back at a long tradition of Keynesian demand management policies. A government com-

----

[153] Meidner (1984, pp. 252-254).
[154] The Swedish fiscal year runs from June 1 to May 31.

mitment to maintain high and stable levels of employment[155] was first stated in a White Paper of 1944 on employment policy (Beveridge, 1944), although such policies were not actually practised in Britain until the late 1940s.

The transition from a regulatory to a Keynesian approach to macro-economic policy making was originally effected by the Labour government around 1948. It was continued by subsequent Tory governments. Initially the emphasis was on "fine tuning" through fiscal policy, primarily by means of variations in tax rates.

The practical implementation of Keynesian demand management in the British setting resulted in a characteristic cyclical "stop-go" pattern (Surrey, 1982). Whenever economic growth slackened and unemployment tended to rise, demand was expanded through fiscal (and accommodating monetary) policies. The ensuing economic recovery then regularly led to an upsurge in wage and price inflation, growth in imports, and a deterioration of the current account. To correct these imbalances, and to defend the sterling, restrictive fiscal policy measures had to be resorted to again, and, in the process, the economic upswing was usually choked.

At least two factors contributed to the "stop-go" pattern in macro-economic policy making. Both were deeply entrenched in the British economy.

The first one was the special vulnerability of the British current account to speculative capital movements. After the war sterling had remained an important reserve currency, and London was still a leading international financial centre.

The second factor was the relatively high (compared to the other four countries in the present study) level of trade union militancy, or, equivalently, the high level of distributional conflict in Britain. Its main effect was that the trade unions (about 600 in number) tended to grasp any chance to negotiate higher wages for their members, using their bargaining power to the very limit. Therefore economic upswings regularily led to wage increases the level of which made the upswing unsustainable in the end.

The reasons for this high level of trade union militancy and industrial conflict are seen somewhat differently by different observers. Some ascribe it to institutional peculiarities of the British labor market:[156] the great number of trade unions and the organization of wage earners according to skills and education rather than according to industry, the high degree of organizational decentralization of the trade union movement as a whole, the autonomous role of the job stewards in wage negotiations at plant level, and the lack of judicial regulations concerning industrial conflicts. Others have pointed to the importance of the incomplete integration of the working class in British society and the persistence of marked class cleavages, despite the integrative stance of the Labour party (Panitch, 1976).

---

[155] The irreducible rate of unemployment envisaged by Beveridge had been as high as 3 per cent, however, and this estimate was even regarded an optimistic one by Keynes himself.

[156] This was the main point of view adopted in the so-called "Donovan report" of 1968 (Cmnd 3623, 1968).

But despite its shortcomings the "stop-go" policy appears to have worked quite well up to the mid-60s, at least with respect to unemployment and inflation. Between 1948 and 1966 the average unemployment rate was 1.7 per cent, and it never exceeded 2.6 per cent, while inflation was low (Levacic and Rebmann, 1989, p. 3).

On the other hand investment rates, growth in productivity, and total output growth were all low in the UK compared to other countries. Obviously high, steady growth was inhibited by the "stop-go" policy[157] and could only be achieved if the upsurge of price and wage inflation in times of economic up-swing, which regularly forced economic policy to turn contractionary, could somehow be forestalled.

That was why Labour and Tory governments alike had been experimenting with statutory price and wage controls since the late 40s and had increasingly resorted to them after 1964 (Flanagan et al., 1983, p. 369). The results, however, had normally been short-lived at best, and incomes policy came increasingly to be resented by the trade unions, even in times of Labour governments (Scharpf, 1987, p. 100). The frequent use of various forms of incomes policies as a means of macro-economic policy making can, nevertheless, be said to have developed as the second distinguishing feature - alongside the "stop-go" pattern - of the British way of practising Keynesianism: prior to 1973 none of the other countries in the present study had used incomes policies at a comparable scale.

5.1. Crisis onset and development in the UK: Heritages, assets and liabilities

Turning once again to figure 1.3. in chapter 1 two traits in the economic development in the UK between 1973 and 1979 are easily recognized. In the first place, and contrary to popular prejudices ("Europe's sick man"), the state of the British economy on the eve of the first oil price hike 1973-74 does not appear to have been significantly worse than the state of the other economies considered. Thanks mainly to the "Barber-boom" real output growth was high in 1973 (actually the highest among the five countries in the present study). Unemployment was only a bit higher than in the traditional country of full employment (Sweden). It was even on the decline. Consumer price inflation stood at about the same level as in Denmark, and not much higher than in the other three countries. The deficit on current transactions with the rest of the world was of about the

----

157 Blackaby (1978, p. 635) suggests a somewhat different interpretation of the connection between "stop-go" policy and slow economic growth: "(T)e problem with the British economy was not so much any 'stop-go' pattern imposed by government policy, but rather the slowness of the rise in the underlying trend in output. Possibly the 'stop-go' pattern appeared more marked in the United Kingdom because in other industrial countries output was still rising significantly when it was below trend, whereas in Britain there tended to be virtually no rise at all in the 'stop' phases."

same size as Denmark's (in per cent of GDP), but in this case the distance to the other three countries was somewhat more marked.

In the second place, as can be seen from figure 1.3., there is a striking similarity of development with respect to the level of economic activity and to unemployment in the UK, Germany, and Denmark between 1974 and 1977.[158] In all three countries real GDP growth fell dramatically in 1974, stayed negative in 1975, only to rise steeply in 1976, and slow down again in 1977. In 1978 the UK experienced its own mini-recovery, but "the winter of discontent" prevented it from participating in the 1979-recovery occurring in the other countries. Also with respect to unemployment a marked degree of parallelism prevailed, albeit at different levels. But with respect to inflation and to the deficit on transactions with the rest of the world the British development does not resemble any of the other four countries.

Besides its momentarily quite healthy economic state Britain enjoyed two further advantages at the time of the onset of the crisis. First, thanks to the position of London as an international centre of finance, a sizeable share of the OPEC-countries' newly acquired wealth could be expected, in due time, to be cycled back via London. The UK would not have difficulties in attracting foreign capital to finance a growing trade deficit. The seamy side of this was, of course, that it might enhance the vulnerability of the British economy to speculative capital movements. Second, within a foreseeable future the UK could look forward to having the revenues from its own North Sea oil production to alleviate the pressures on the current account. Therefore it could afford to consider a current account deficit as a passing problem.[159]

On the other hand, neither the developments in the British labor market nor the actual situation in Great Britain could be considered favorable at the onset of the crisis. Most ominously the relationship between the trade unions and both Labour and Tory governments had been deteriorating since the middle of the 60s, making trustful cooperation increasingly problematic.

The relationships between the Labour government and the trade unions turned sour in 1966[160] when the government sought to enforce a statutory incomes policy. The relationship suffered again in 1968, following the publication of the "Donovan-report", when the government attempted to reform industrial relations with the objective of bringing down the frequency of industrial dispute. The conflict between the Labour government and the trade unions over parts of

---

[158] For statistical reasons the Danish unemployment data are not comparable with the others. Development trends may still be compared, however, although levels may not.

[159] The balance of payments impact of British North Sea oil is discussed in OECD, Economic Surveys: United Kingdom (1975, pp. 39-40). Both Labour and the Conservatives were well aware of these future prospects and eager to exploit them, cf. Wilson (1979, p. 16).

[160] Statutory incomes policy was resorted to in 1966, but it was so widely undermined by plant level union opposition resulting in wide-spread wage drift and wildcat strikes that in 1968 the government had to give up any idea of regulating wages.

the planned industrial relations legislation[161] was generally considered a main reason for Labour's losing the 1970-election to the Conservatives. Although the relationships had subsequently been repaired to some extent during Labour's term in opposition, there was a wide-spread feeling that Labour owed some restitution to the trade union movement.[162]

Upon taking office the new Heath-government wisely shelved any idea it might have harbored concerning incomes policy,[163] thus avoiding a potential conflict with the trade unions over that issue. But it felt compelled by the worsening strike situation and the wage inflation to act on the matter of industrial relations. There were two main trends in its Industrial Relations Act of 1971. The first was an attempt at organizational centralization mainly with a view to weaken the position of the shop stewards and to strengthen the central trade union leadership. The other was a poorly concealed attempt to cut some of the trade unions' teeth by, for example, proscribing "closed shop" arrangements and making provisions for enforcing intra-union democracy and the protection of minorities in unions.

Prior to its becoming law the Industrial Relations Bill had encountered strong resistance from both the Labour opposition in Parliament and from most trade unions. Moreover, after some hesitation the latter continued the fight even after the bill had been passed. The 1971 TUC Congress decided to instruct all affiliated unions not to register under the provisions of the law (and those which had done so to de-register). It was the Transport and General Workers Union (TGWU) and the Amalgamated Union of Engineering Workers (AUEW), however, which most stubbornly opposed the Act in practice.

In the end the opposition of the unions proved successful. The provisions of the Act demonstrably failed to fulfil their intended functions. All that had been achieved by the bill was to sully industrial relations and to nullify most of what chances there might have been of a stable Tory government - trade union co-operation in economic policy making.

As a consequence the Heath-government could, at best, hope for tacit toleration by the trade union movement when in 1972 it was finally forced to resort to incomes policy in order to protect the shift to an expansionary fiscal policy. The

---

161 For a short account of the contents see for example Smith (1980, pp. 120-121).

162 It was hardly a coincidence, but rather an expression of this feeling, that the "Social Contract" signed between Labour and the trade unions in 1973 was very specific as to the obligations of an incoming Labour government, but much less specific as to what the trade unions were going to yield in return.

163 It soon abolished the National Board for Prices and Incomes (NBPI) and advised private sector employers that it was their responsibility to resist "irresponsible" wage claims. Employers were also warned that they would not be bailed out by government intervention if they got into trouble thanks to irresponsible wage settlements. With respect to the public sector the situation was in principle to be the same. But the government itself showed a certain interest in the "n-1 strategy" which implied that each successive wage settlement should be one per cent less than the previous one (Dawkins, 1980, p. 64).

aims were to stimulate economic growth and bring down unemployment which was beginning to approach the "unacceptable" figure of 1 million. Initially the reflationary measures had been expected to have little effect on the rate of inflation. It was quite generally believed that unemployment and demand pressures could not coexist (Westaway, 1980, p. 18), but things went differently - inflation increased markedly.

The government failed (predictably) in an attempt to negotiate a voluntary agreement on wages with the TUC and, on prices, with the Confederation of British Industry (CBI). It then introduced a statutory freeze on wages and prices by November 1972. This measure was to be in force until March 1973, when Stage Two would come into effect which had room for some limited wage increases. As the government was worried about possible union opposition, Stage Three of its pay policy, to commence in November 1973, contained still more flexible limitations on wage increases. Moreover, it contained a provision opening up for threshold agreements whereby employees were to be automatically compensated for price increases in excess of 7 per cent, and this threshold clause came to be widely used.[164]

Although they avoided a formal endorsement, the unions had in practice acquiesced in both Stage One and Stage Two of the government's pay policy.[165] But shortly after the commencing of Stage Three the policy was challenged by the militant National Union of Mineworkers (NUM), pressing claims for wage increases ranging from 22 per cent to 46 per cent for different categories of mineworkers. This corresponded to an estimated average wage increase of 25 per cent. When the Coal Board refused the claims, the union called a strike. This the other trade unions had to support, as they were not bound by any official deal with the government (Scharpf, 1987, p. 103).

The strike of the coal-miners coincided with the oil crisis and produced an acute energy crisis. Declaring a national emergency the government introduced a three-days week to save energy. At the same time elections were called for February 1974 in order to determine who was to rule Britain - the government or the trade unions. The electorate, by a close margin, pointed to the opposition.

When taking office in early 1974 the new Labour government thus inherited two problems from its conservative predecessor. The first problem was the unsettled miners conflict which was ended only when the government gave in to the union's demands. The wage increases conceded to the miners in turn set a standard for other wage settlements and thus helped pave the way for the 1974-75 wage explosion (Scharpf, 1987, p. 104). The second inherited problem

---

[164] Approximately half the work-force was covered by threshold clauses.

[165] The reason was probably that the economy was going well: GDP-growth rose to 7.6 per cent in 1973, and unemployment decreased from 3.6 per cent in 1972 to 2.6 per cent in 1973 (Dawkins, 1980, p. 63, table 3.1). Moreover, growth rates of money wages were largely unaffected: they rose by 12.1 per cent in 1971, 11.2 per cent in 1972, and 12.2 per cent in 1973. Real wage increases were about the same in 1973 (3.0 per cent) as in 1971 (2.7 per cent), while 1972 stands out with a growth rate of close to 4 per cent (3.9 per cent), cf. Dawson (1980, p. 63).

was the threshold clauses agreed upon under Stage Three of the Tory government's pay policy. Although the latter was abolished, the threshold agreements
remained in force, giving further momentum to domestic inflation. Taken together these factors made it extremely difficult to contain the inflationary pressures inherent in the oil price hike of 1973-74.

5.2. Muddling through with blurred objectives: UK fiscal policy 1974-79

Contrary to, for example, the German economy the British economy was not hit
by the post-1973 recession while implementing a full-blown deflationary demand
management policy. Slightly contractionary measures were in force, though: the
prospect of excess demand in 1974 had prompted restrictive demand management measures to be taken by the Tory government towards the end of 1973
(OECD, Economic Surveys: United Kingdom (1975, p. 5)). Fiscal policy furthermore remained mildly restrictive in the first half of 1974, as the first budget of
the Labour government aimed at some reduction in the public sector borrowing
requirement (PSBR). After that there was a marginal boost in July 1974 and a
more substantial one in November.

   Table 2.14. (adapted from Westaway (1980, p. 7)) provides a survey of the
development in policy targets and the fiscal response in terms of the PSBR from
1974 to 1979.

Table 2.14.: Policy targets and governmental fiscal response 1974-79

	Unemploy-ment	Inflation	Growth	Balance of Payments	PSBR
1974	low	high	decline	weakening	rising
1975	moderate	peak	decline	crisis	peak
1976	high	falling	low	crisis	large
1977	high	falling	low	strong	moderate
1978	high	moderate	moderate	surplus	rising
1979	falling	rising	low	weakening	rising

Source: Westaway (1980, p. 7); Scharpf (1987, p. 105).

The somewhat confused fiscal policy signals of 1974 were mainly a reflection of
a confusing situation. At the beginning of the year the rapidly rising inflation
looked like the biggest problem. The retail price index rose by 13 per cent in the
first and by 16 per cent in the second quarter of 1974, relative to the same quarters of 1973. Moreover the balance of payments was deteriorating. Unemploy-

ment, on the other hand, stood at a stable level, well below the 3 per cent mark.

The fiscal measures then taken were intended to dampen inflation in two ways. In the first place the budget would reduce the PSBR from about £ 4000 mill. to £ 2700 mill., thus reducing demand pressure. In the second place food subsidies amounting to £ 500 mill. were introduced to keep down the prices of essential foods. These subsidies were estimated to reduce the general index of retail prices by about 1.5 percentage points, which, in view of the threshold clauses and their effects, could be crucial to the further development in the rate of domestic inflation.

The fiscal measures taken in July, although slightly reflationary since they increased the PSBR by another £ 340 mill., were once more prompted by the increasing rate of inflation rather than by growing unemployment.[166] The intention of the Chancellor was to break the momentum of price increases by acting directly on consumer prices. Therefore food subsidies were raised by a further £ 50 mill. and VAT was reduced from 10 to 8 per cent.

Also the budget presented in November 1974, after the second general election of that year, was expansionary. This time, however, it reflected government concerns about unemployment. It began to rise, albeit slowly. On a yearly basis unemployment was even somewhat lower in 1974 than in 1973 (Scharpf, 1987, p. 105).

Taken together the signals of the fiscal policy in 1974 were set on "go", although the main problem of that year was obviously inflation and the deteriorating balance of payments, and not unemployment. Reflating the economy nevertheless might have worked as part of a deliberate "bridging strategy", had it been flanked by a restrictive wage policy by the unions (which might have served to dampen inflation).[167] But since wage restraint was not forthcoming (cf. below) - owing in part to the wage increases provided for under the threshold clauses - the expansionary stance of fiscal policy in 1974 paved the way for the wage and price explosion of 1975.

The plans for public expenditures presented in January 1975 continued the trend from the previous year's budget. They contained large increases in public expenditure programs in order to stimulate economic growth (which had turned negative in 1974) and employment.

But with the rate of inflation approaching 20 per cent on an annual basis and a

---

166 According to Wilson (1979, p. 28), "(t)he Chancellor stressed 'recession' rather than inflation as the immediate danger." Actually unemployment was 2.4 per cent in the second and 2.6 per cent in the third quarter of 1974, and hence at roughly the same level as the previous year.

167 That wages at that time were rising well ahead of prices was acknowledged by the Chancellor, Denis Healey, in his Budget speech on April 15, 1975. "The general rate of pay increases has been well above the increase in the cost of living and much further still above the level in countries which compete with us ... As a result, by February the retail price index stood 19.9 per cent over a year earlier, and the wage rate index was 28.9 per cent ... pay has been running about 8 per cent or 9 per cent ahead of prices." (Wilson, 1979, p. 112).

----

growing balance of payment deficit in the first months of 1975 the government was forced to adjust the direction of its fiscal policy. The fiscal signals switched from "go" to "stop". The budget introduced in April was clearly an attempt to deflate the economy. It foresaw cuts in public expenditures of £ 1100 mill., mainly in subsidies to nationalized industries, on food, and on housing. There were also cuts in investment plans for the nationalized industries and in defence expenditures. Revenues were to be raised by £ 1251 mill., most of it from increasing income tax rates and from the introduction of a luxury rate for VAT. While these measures could not prevent the PSBR from rising to its maximum in 1975, they contributed to the trend reversal in 1976 when - for the first time since 1970 - the PSBR showed a decline, relative to the previous year.

During 1976 the government stuck to its deflationary course, although unemployment was still rising. But at the beginning of 1976 Britain's inflation rate had been exceeding 20 per cent (on an annual basis) for six quarters straight. The slip into a South American style hyperinflation did no longer appear an entirely impossible event (Caves and Krause, 1980, p. 12). Furthermore a serious pound-crisis developed as the exchange rate of sterling towards US dollars fell from 2.02 US$ in 1975 to 1.70 US$ in 1976 (Scharpf, 1987, p. 109). These developments forced the hand of the government.

The public expenditure plans announced in February 1976 limited expenditure growth to 2.66 per cent annually. This was actually a reduction, since the base for calculating these projections had been cut in the previous budget (Westaway, 1980, p. 22). The budget introduced in April was, by and large, neutral in terms of its impact on the PSBR. Some of its provisions for tax reductions were made contingent upon a continuation of the voluntary incomes policy originally agreed upon by the government and the TUC in 1975 (see below). In this case, "tax bribery" proved efficient. An agreement with the TUC on continuing pay policy was reached in May, releasing the conditional tax reductions which implied a £ 930 mill. loss of revenues.

By July 1976 a package of deflationary measures was introduced, however, although unemployment stayed at high levels without signs of decreasing. But the pound was still in crisis, and a $ 5.3 bill. credit from an international consortium of banks had to be obtained in order to try to defend whatever was left to defend of its international position. "Responsible" fiscal policy, equated with a reduction of the PSBR and the public sector's claims on resources, would, it was hoped, help to re-establish confidence and stabilize the exchange rate. The basic aim of this operation was to re-direct resources to the private sector, especially the export sector.[168] The PSBR was to be reduced to a figure below £ 9000 mill. in 1977-78 by cutting public expenditures by £ 1000 mill. and increasing the

---

[168] The budget speech was couched in terms of export-led growth (Westaway, 1980, p. 22). But there was another line of thought, too: there were fears that an excessive PSBR would lead to a likewise excessive growth in money supply and thereby finally inflation (Westaway, 1980, p. 22). This was a purely monetaristic way of thinking which seems to foreshadow the cautious turn to stronger emphasis on monetary policies and control of the money supply that took place in connection with the agreement about the IMF standby loan at the end of 1976.

contributions of employers to the national insurance by 2 per cent.

As it turned out Britain would not be able to repay the 5.3 bill. $ loan from the international banking consortium by the December 1976 deadline. This necessitated an IMF stand-by loan. As part of the conditions of this loan imposed by the IMF Britain was to cut public expenditures, reduce the PSBR, and thus reduce the growth of the money supply. To this end a £ 500 mill. sale of BP-shares was announced at December 15.

Given the fact that the Labour government pursued a restrictive fiscal policy throughout 1976, despite high unemployment, one might be tempted to speak of this year as a water-shed in its fiscal policy. Furthermore, a basic change in priorities was apparently articulated in the famous speech to the Labour Party Conference by Prime Minister James Callaghan (who had succeeded Harold Wilson in mid-1976): "We used to think that you could just spend your way out of a recession and increase employment by cutting taxes and boosting government spending. I tell you, in all candour, that the option no longer exists, and that insofar as it did exist, it only worked by injecting bigger doses of inflation into the economy followed by higher levels of inflation. The Manifesto was right when it said that the first priority of the Labour Government must be a determined attack on inflation."[169] Obviously the difference to what Milton Friedman might have said about the same topic was not great, if there was any distance left at all, and 1976 saw the introduction of money growth targets in the UK, first in the April budget and, later on, in the letter of intent to the IMF (Dennis, 1980, p. 49).[170]

The question is, of course, the degree to which this speech and the adoption of some monetaristic guide-lines were primarily window-dressing intended to convince a sceptical international financial community (where monetarism reigned) that the Labour government was determined to pursue a stability oriented policy in the future in order to create new confidence in the sterling. After all, the pound crisis was far from over when the speech was given. Looking at the fiscal policy of the Labour government during the last part of its term it can also be seen that attempts at fighting unemployment by means of demand stimulation through fiscal policies were not abandoned. Although the fiscal measures taken were far from powerful enough to return the economy to anything close to a full employment situation, the growth in unemployment was halted in 1978, and a reduction took place in 1979. If there had been a conversion to monetarism in British economic policy making in 1976, it was somewhat incomplete.

Judged by the development of the economic indicators for 1977, the various fiscal operations of 1976, combined with incomes policy (cf. below), were in some respects a success. The rate of inflation continued to decrease (albeit slowly), and the balance of payment was strengthened substantially. But econo-

---

169 Quoted from Therborn (1986, p. 37).

170 Thus, if the speech is taken at face-value, Scharpf (1987, p. 110) is most probably right in speaking of "a reluctant conversion to monetarism" of the top decision makers and their advisers and staffs in the course of 1976.

mic growth stayed low (the growth rate actually decreased relative to 1976, but remained positive), and unemployment increased still further.

The 1977 budget contained a fiscal stimulus to the economy mainly through reductions in personal taxation. As in 1976 tax reductions were linked to a continuation of voluntary incomes policies. Again the method worked. The tax concessions promised in the budget could be introduced in July (Westaway, 1980, p. 23).

Further expansionary measures were introduced in October 1977, mostly by increasing personal allowances. The cost to the economy was estimated at £ 1000 mill. for 1977-78. Public expenditure increases in the magnitude of £ 1000 mill. were also announced. They were confirmed in January 1978.

The "go" policy was continued into 1978. By April 1978 a new set of reflationary measures was announced with the budget, consisting almost entirely of reductions in personal taxes. The stimulus to the economy was estimated at £ 2500 mill. (Westaway, 1980, p. 24). But then the breakdown of the precarious cooperation between government and trade unions precluded further activities before the Labour government was replaced, following a "winter of discontent" and an election in May 1979, by a conservative government with an avowedly monetarist economic policy orientation.

5.3. Incomes policy

Upon their return to power in 1974 the Labour government had at first refrained from taking initiatives which could be interpreted as pointing towards an incomes policy. As part of the "Social Contract" of 1973 with the TUC Labour had committed itself to the implementation of price and rent controls, while the use of statutory pay policies had been explicitly precluded. The trade unions, on their side, had agreed to the principle that wage increases should not exceed what was necessary to keep up with price rises between main settlements. There was also an understanding that there should be a 12 months interval between such main settlements (Dawkins, 1980, p. 66).

While the Labour government dutifully implemented its part of the deal - Barbara Castle was appointed to the newly created post of Secretary of State for Prices and Consumer Protection, and rigourous price controls were introduced - and furthermore kept fiscal policy largely reflationary during 1974, the trade unions failed to deliver on the deal. The wage guide-lines set out by the TUC were widely evaded, and, as had to be admitted by the Chancellor in his budget speech in early 1975 (quoted above), there was a much stronger wage increase in 1974 than warranted under the provisions of the "Social Contract".

The wage explosion of 1974 continued into 1975, and, while wages kept running ahead of prices, a price explosion was triggered. This was followed, naturally, by a run on the pound in mid-1975. It was obvious that the government could no longer afford the free rider attitude of the trade unions in economic policy. The incomes policy complex had to be re-examined.

The trade unions, preferring a different approach, had to realize the relative weakness of the Labour government and the danger of bringing back into office a Conservative Party which was in the process of turning to a clear-cut monetarist stance in economic matters (Flanagan et al., 1983, pp. 430-431). Compared to such prospects cooperation with the government in establishing some kind of voluntary incomes policy was preferable.

A government proposal for an incomes policy designed to reduce inflation, restore international confidence in the currency, and rebuild profitability and competitiveness was announced in July 1975 (Flanagan et al., 1983, p. 429). It was to be in effect into 1976, and the aim was a reduction of wage and price increases to 10 per cent and a reduction in real wages during the first eight months after the implementation of the policy. The incomes policy would not be made statutory, however,[171] and no penal code would be attached to it. It would be enforced under the price code by not allowing employers to pass along any wage increases (i.e. not just excess increases) in prices if these increases exceeded the limits. There was also some supportive legislation in other fields.

In negotiations with the TUC the proposal was revised in several respects. Most importantly the 10 per cent limit originally proposed was changed into a £ 6 a week flat rate limit. Incomes above £ 8500 were not to be allowed any increase at all. The initiative to this solidary twist of the proposal came from the leader of the TGWU which by the early 70s had adopted a strongly solidary wage policy and, together with the AUEW, saw a chance to obtain a narrowing of wage differentials in industry which would favor important groups in their constituency.[172] The government could easily agree to this change since it implied an approximate 10 per cent limit on wage increases for "typical" skilled workers.[173] Lower paid groups, not the least women, might experience wage increases of 20 per cent.[174]

The new incomes policy named "Social Contract mark 2" was inaugurated in a tough statement by prime minister Harold Wilson to the House of Commons on July 11, 1975. He set out the basic principles agreed upon by the TUC and outlined the supportive legislative action that would have to be taken. After a debate on July 21 and 22 the policy was carried by a comfortable majority, and the legislation went into effect in August. In September, following an intense "Give a Year to Britain"-campaign, the TUC Congress voted its assent.

Although the new guide-lines for wage increases were generally observed, the incomes policy came too late to prevent 1975 from becoming a year of wage explosion: nominal wages in industry rose by 30.1 per cent and, since wage

---

[171] The government nevertheless prepared legislation to be introduced in the case the pay limit was endangered (Dawkins, 1980, p. 66).

[172] Flanagan et al. (1983, p. 372). This may partly be explained by the fact that lower paid groups were a majority in the TGWU, cf. Scharpf (1987, p. 107).

[173] Wilson (1979, p. 269).

[174] The government made it a point to emphasize that the £ 6 limit was a maximum, not an entitlement, cf. Wilson (1979, p. 269), but unsurprisingly that turned out to be in vain.

inflation was leading price inflation, real wages went up by 4.8 per cent, the highest increase in real wages since 1972 (Scharpf, 1987, p. 105). But the incomes policy did probably contribute to a slowing down of wage inflation in the following year, when nominal wages rose by "only" 19.8 per cent. This question will be taken up later.

As "mark 1" of the income policy in 1976 came to its close, it was clear that the Labour government needed a continuation of incomes policy under one form or another. In negotiations with the trade unions it could argue by pointing to the trend reversal in wage and, especially, price developments which had occurred under "mark 1". While the rate of price increases had been accelerating through the first three quarters of 1975 - from 20.3 per cent on an annual basis in the first to 26.5 per cent in the third quarter - this trend had been halted in the fourth quarter (25.3 per cent) and reversed in the two first quarters of 1976 when the rise in the retail price index had been 22.4 per cent and 16.0 per cent on an annual basis.[175] Moreover the government could point to the fact that incomes policy notwithstanding there had been a significant increase in real wages.

It was here government strategy picked up. Its 1976-77 budget contained provisions for tax reductions which, however, were made contingent upon a continuation of an incomes policy (cf. above). The idea was, as emphasized by the Chancellor, to protect real wages in exchange for restraint with respect to money wages.

Due to the sterling crisis of 1976 the Treasury wanted the incomes policy "mark 2" tightened considerably. Despite "mark 1" British wage and price increases were still above the levels in most comparable countries. Furthermore, there was concern in the Treasury about the impact of the flat rate limit in "mark 1" on wage differentials.[176] Therefore the Chancellor's opening bid in the negotiations with the TUC was a linear 3 per cent limit on wage increases until 1977.

The result was a compromise. There was to be a 5 per cent guide-line for wage increases (i.e. half the size of the one envisaged prior to "mark 1"), but with a maximum of £ 4 and a minimum of £ 2.5 a week.[177] Thus there was a linear limit - although somewhat higher than in the opening bid - but the small scope provided by the minimum and maximum would in many cases make it work very much like a flat rate limit. In this way TUC support was assured and "mark 2" went into effect by August 1976.

While the government had been able to argue (and to underpin this argument with quite impressive figures) that "mark 1" of the incomes policy had helped to

---

[175] OECD, Economic Surveys: United Kingdom (var. issues).

[176] The Treasury had been sceptical about the adoption of the flat rate limit in 1975 already, cf. Scharpf (1987, p. 107).

[177] Dawkins (1980, p. 66). The same numbers are found in Flanagan et al. (1983, p. 422), while according to Scharpf (1987, p. 108) the maximum was £ 6 and the minimum £ 4.5 a week.

bring about an improvement with respect to price inflation while more than keeping up real earnings, this argument lost some validity while "mark 2" was in effect. After reaching a low in the third quarter of 1976 (when the retail price index rose 13.7 per cent on an annual basis) the rate of inflation accelerated again. It reached a maximum in the second quarter of 1977 (17.4 per cent). Wage increases, on the other hand, were effectively curtailed, so the net effect was a significant drop in real wages under "mark 2". Moreover unemployment kept growing and reached its peak (on an annual basis) in 1977.

To the surprise of none this development kindled trade union opposition to the continuance of incomes policy. But there were other reasons as well why, by 1977, even a Labour government was no longer able to achieve active trade union cooperation in the continuation of incomes policies.

In the first place there was the well-known problem for trade unions and their leadership to legitimize their actions and possibly even the existence of unions to the rank-and-file if, for too long a period, they are perceived to be cooperatively striving for a "public good" (in the sense of the New Political Economy, cf. Mueller (1989)) benefitting all, rather than for a "private good" benefitting only its members (Flanagan et al., 1983, p. 433). At least from time to time trade unions need free collective bargaining as a tool to legitimize their existence. It is probably in this light the TUC resolution of 1977 calling for "a planned return to free collective bargaining" to commence in 1977 (upon termination of "mark 2") should be seen.

In the second place some unions with greater numbers of well-paid members began to object to the solidary line of the incomes policy. For these unions the narrowing of wage differentials had gone too far and they were looking for a chance to redress the situation (Flanagan et al., 1983, p. 433; p. 436).

The government hence failed when it tried to obtain trade union cooperation in still another phase of incomes policy in 1977. "Mark 3" of the incomes policy was unilaterally introduced in August 1977. It contained a 10 per cent limit on increases in "average national earnings" without a flat rate ceiling, and in a number of cases it allowed for higher flexibility than previous limits on the basis of restoring wage differentials or self-financing productivity deals (Dawkins, 1980, p. 66).

Without TUC support[178] the government could only hope for the willingness of the employers to keep within the wage increase limit. While enforcement of the pay guide-lines by price guide-lines was abandoned,[179] employers who broke the limit were threatened with the loss of government contracts, financial aid from manpower training and subsidy programs, and export credits.

---

[178] The TUC continued to support the twelve-months interval between negotiations, however. It further pledged that the collective bargaining would be not only "free" but also "responsible" (Flanagan et al., 1983, p. 434).

[179] Only price increases due to settlements in violation of the twelve-months rule were prohibited. In general price control had been loosened considerably after 1976, mostly in order to encourage new investment.

These measures proved rather inefficient. The government's pay guide-lines were widely evaded. Average earnings in 1978 rose 14.3 per cent above their 1977-level (Flanagan et al., p. 434), about three times the growth rate of the previous year.

While observance of a tight incomes policy under "mark 2" had - somewhat perversely - been accompanied by increasing inflation, the opposite occurred under "mark 3". Although the pay limits were generally not adhered to, inflation fell to a single-digit figure (8.3 per cent on an annual basis) for the first time since 1973. This could be attributed primarily to the lagged effects of the restrictive pay policy in 1977 and an appreciation of the sterling. As a consequence real earnings increased substantially. At the same time unemployment ceased to grow as the government had returned to a cautiously stimulating fiscal policy (cf. above).

Despite the wide-spread evasion of its pay guide-lines the government could hence be quite satisfied with the course of (economic) events in the beginning of 1978, not the least the downwards trend in inflation. In order to hold on to the positive development it decided in July 1978 to unilaterally set a new 5 per cent guide-line[180] for pay increases.

But by this time the TUC was no longer able to unite in even passively tole-rating such an incomes policy. Pressures on the wage structure had become too powerful and triggered a reaction.

On one side there was increasing opposition by skilled workers to a policy maintaining low skill differentials. This was primarily a reaction to the success of semi-skilled workers in reducing skill differentials substantially during the first half of the decade (Flanagan et al., 1983, p. 436). This opposition became mani-fest in a change of leadership in the AUEW and the subsequent alignment of the AUEW, the Electricians, and other unions with many skilled workers in a bloc which opposed primarily the TGWU. The former group demanded a restoration of wage differentials and for that reason rejected incomes policy.

On the other side were primarily unions of public employees and unions with large numbers of public employees, like the TGWU. During the years of incomes policy the various pay guide-lines had by and large been most strictly observed in the public sector, and the relative pay of public-sector employees had, hence, been reduced (Flanagan et al., 1983, p. 436). Discontent with incomes policy was accumulating in these unions and led, i.a., to the defeat on the 1978 TGWU Congress of its leader, Jack Jones (one of the architects of the "mark 1"), on the matter of incomes policy. This group demanded a narrowing of wage differen-tials (between public and private employees) and for that reason rejected incomes policy.

The first clash over the pay guide-lines came in October and November 1978, when the Ford factories offered a 17 per cent wage rise to its striking workers. In accordance with the sanctions announced for exceeding the pay limit the

----

180 It allowed for exceptional cases, though, to be established by independent recommenda-tions, cf. Dawkins (1980, p. 67).

government (which since 1976 had been dependent on the Liberals for a majority in Parliament) took action to exclude Ford from public contracts, but was defeated on that matter in the House. With no sanctions to back it any longer, the government's pay limit had been reduced to a non-binding recommendation in the private sector (Scharpf, 1987, p. 116).

This put extra pressure on the government to remain firm in its dealing with the demands for wage increases from its own public employees. The immediate outcome of that approach was an outburst of strikes in the public sector in "the winter of discontent" between November 1978 and March 1979. In March 1979 the government capitulated.[181] Incomes policy was once again finished - but so was the government. Upon losing a division on the devolution of competence to the regional Parliament of Scotland it called a general election in May 1979 which returned the Conservatives to power.

Despite the erosion of incomes policy in 1978 and its final break-down in 1979, "mark 1" and "mark 2" of the "Social Contract" are widely considered a success. While it is always difficult to evaluate the effects of incomes policies, since one can never know for sure how things would have looked without it, figure 2.10. (a) and (b) indicate that the British incomes policy of 1975-77 did have an effect.

Figure 2.10.: Effects of incomes policy on wage increase and level of industrial conflict

(a) Rise in weekly earnings in manufacturing (Per cent pr. month, annual basis)

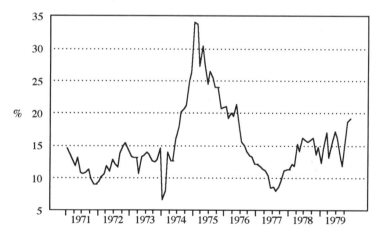

(continued)

---

181 The setting up of the Standing Commission on Pay Comparability (the Clegg Commission) which was to review the public sector wage structure from the principle of equal pay for equal work was mainly a face saving device.

(b) Working days lost due to industrial dispute (monthly data), in 100,000

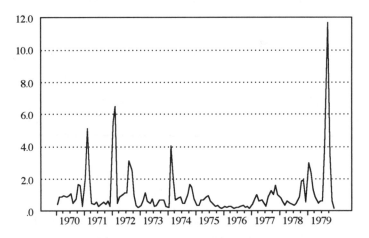

Data: OECD, Historical Statistics (1970-79), files GBRM170 and GBRM270

Figure 2.10. (a) shows the monthly rise in weekly earnings in British manufacturing between 1971 and 1979. The period of co-operative incomes policy is clearly marked by a significant drop in the rate of wage increase. But it is worth noticing that the rate of wage increases had obviously begun to level off even before "mark 1" went into effect in the second half of 1975. The termination of active union co-operation in the implementation of incomes policy in mid-1977 is actually much clearer marked in the data than the beginning of this co-operation.

Figure 2.10. (b) shows another effect of government - trade union co-operation on incomes policy: a drop in the number of working days lost due to industrial conflicts. The level of industrial conflict was remarkably low in the second half of 1975 and during the whole of 1976. During 1977 there are two (relatively) minor upsurges of conflict, the biggest of which came in the second half of 1977, i.e. after the unions had renounced the incomes policy. The final break-down of incomes policy is marked by increasing numbers of working days lost, culminating in the mass strikes during the "winter of discontent".

5.4. Summary

In summary the British case stands out as an example of failing coordination between the economic strategies of the government and the trade unions, despite the existence of the "Social Contract" and the government - TUC cooperation between 1975 and 1977 in the formulation and implementation of incomes policy. It rather appears as an example of mutual, but shifting, exploitation, creating a final economic outcome which was equally undesirable to (and most probably undesired by) both.

There can be little doubt that from the return of Labour to power in 1974 and to the introduction of "mark 1" of the incomes policy in 1975 the trade unions successfully exploited the government. While the government complied with the commitments of the Social Contract on industrial relations and price control, and furthermore led an expansionary fiscal policy, the trade unions did not stick to their (vague) commitments concerning wage restraint. This looks very much like an illustration of the well-known vulnerability of Socialdemocratic governments to extortion from trade unions, exacerbated by the particularly weak position of Labour vis a vis the trade unions after the clashes about incomes policy and industrial relations legislation in the late 1960s.

During the heydays of the incomes policy, on the other hand, the government can be said to have exploited trade union wage restraint. Mainly for reasons not attributable to the government, at least not directly - especially the sterling crises of 1975 and 1976 - the trade unions were not rewarded for their restraint by a demand stimulating policy powerful enough to reduce unemployment. This, in turn, helped to reduce the commitment to incomes policy on the side of the unions.

When the government finally attempted to alleviate the unemployment problem by untightening its fiscal policy (although staying within the limits on the PSBR agreed upon in its deal with the IMF), incomes policy was in the process of disintegration and the trade unions were on their way back to a more aggressive wage strategy. Once more coordination had failed.

Chapter 3
To the Brink of the Abyss: Danish Crisis Policy 1974-79

The preceding chapter has demonstrated a high degree of diversity in the policy responses to the stagflation problem in Austria, Germany, Sweden, and the UK in the aftermath of the first oil price hike 1973-74. Although all were "essentially Socialdemocratic" countries in the sense defined above, and although Keynesianism was the dominating economic doctrine adhered to in all of them, they approached the solution of the "Keynesian coordination problem" in markedly different ways. Nevertheless, common traits have emerged from the single-country analyses as well.

In the first place, all four countries used aggregate demand management, through budgetary policies, in an attempt to stabilize the economy. What differed strongly between them was the extent to which this instrument was employed, spanning from the vigorous deficit spending of the Austrian government in 1975 and of the Swedish (bourgeois!) government 1978-79 to the more cautious approach of the German government. Also the timing varied. Some countries were more successful than others in making the instrument work in a truly anti-cyclical fashion. The reason for these inter-country differences will be explored further in chapter 4.

In the second place, all countries tried to bring about some measure of wage restraint. Here both the extent of restraint aimed at and the means used to achieve it differed strongly between countries, from statutory incomes policy in the UK over the more subtle restraint imposed by the pre-announced monetary growth targets of the Bundesbank in Germany to the reliance on "corporatist" modes of policy making in Austria and Sweden. This point will be further elaborated on in chapter 5.

But possibly the strongest impression conveyed by a survey of the economic policy making in each of the four countries after 1973 is one of continuity and maybe even inertia. To a large extent the economic policies pursued during the crisis tied in with each country's particular experiences with, and traditions of, economic policy making. In each of the countries the particular policy mix, the instruments relied on, and the assignment of these instruments to actors were very much the same both prior to and after the crisis had struck. The size of the economic problems facing the decision makers meant that the scale of operations had to be enlarged, of course, but still Germany's decision makers basically tried to re-enact their successful anti-recession policies of 1966-67. The Labour government in the UK primarily clung to the traditional British combination of fiscal and incomes policy, while Austria and Sweden kept trying to make their respective "models" work. To be fair, there were innovations, as for example the introduction of pre-announced money growth targets in Germany, but they represented a different type of policy implementation rather than a new policy. In all four countries a genuine qualitative shift in the contents of economic policy making did not occur until the second oil price hike.

Where does Denmark fit into this pattern? We must now review Danish crisis policy 1974-79 in order to provide an answer.

This review of the Danish crisis policy will, by and large, follow the chronological order of events. In that respect the period 1974-79 splits roughly into two - actually very different - halves[1] which will be considered separately. The first one, approximately from 1974 to 1976, was a period of rather traditional Keynesian interventionism in the form of a British-style "stop-go" policy. The underlying view was optimistic. The crisis was expected to be short-lived and the economic-political instruments to be effective in fending off its repercussions on the Danish economy. The second period, from 1977 to 1979, was a period of reassessment of goals and reconsideration of means for economic policy making in face of growing imbalances on all important macro-economic indicators and gloomy prospects. The underlying view was now profoundly pessimistic. The crisis was expected to be long-lasting, and the ability of economic policy to do much about its consequences for the Danish economy was considered to be severely limited. There was mainly a Micawberian hope that something might turn up.

1. Economic-political prelude and background

Figure 1.3. in chapter 1 brings out how the economic crisis hit Denmark in 1974. All four macro-economic indicators show a serious deterioration for that year. Real growth became negative, unemployment and inflation soared, and the balance of payment plunged into still deeper deficit. Further, figure 1.3. in chapter 1 illustrates that Denmark followed the international economic trend rather closely, but with a marked tendency to perform worse than the OECD average on all indicators. Obviously the Danish economy was hit harder (or proved less resistant) to the economic crisis than the average OECD-country.

Undoubtedly there were several reasons for this. One of these was that serious imbalances had been allowed to develop in the Danish economy even prior to the first oil price hike and its aftermath. Another contributing factor might well have been that the political system was in a state of turmoil at this time. Denmark was caught on the wrong foot by the onset of the crisis in 1974.

1.1. Good years with troublesome legacies: The period 1958-74 [2]

The period 1958-74 stands out as a period of unprecedented prosperity growth in post-war Denmark. Prior to 1958 economic growth had been low and unem-

---

[1] Cf. Hansen et al. (1988, pp. 44-45).
[2] See also OECD, Economic Surveys: Denmark (1977, pp. 10-18).

ployment had been a permanent problem. A weak balance of payments and the constant lack of foreign exchange reserves had time and again forced governments to put brakes on upswings in economic activity. In that respect the situation had been like the situation of the UK.

But from 1958 onwards Danish growth rates exceeded those of most other European countries, and unemployment virtually disappeared. Opinions differ as to what really made possible this shift from a low growth / high unemployment combination to a high growth / low unemployment situation around 1958. Many Danish economists favor as their main explanation a terms of trade improvement which occurred in 1958 (Hansen et al., 1988, pp. 36-37).[3] Others have pointed to improved international conditions for financing the Danish balance of payments deficit.[4] According to others, again, the shift occurred in 1958 because in that year Danish foreign competitiveness was at a peak (Gelting, 1976).

Whatever the exact reason for the economic trend shift of 1958, it is clear that the ensuing high growth period got most of its momentum from internal sources.[5] In the first place there was a construction boom, primarily in housing, the background of which was a reform of the financing and mortgaging system. In the second place the post-1958 period was a period of extremely strong public sector growth associated with the building up and expanding of the institutions and services of a welfare state.[6] In that perspective the high growth period 1958-74 may be seen as the outcome of conscious political choices (Paldam, 1979, p. 375; p. 377).

During the whole period Danish economic policy followed a "stop-go" pattern. The dominating orientation among professional economists and economic political decision makers had been Keynesian since the end of the second world war. The preferred model of the economy was the one where only fiscal policy matters while money is just a veil (Paldam, 1990, p. 26). Most of the "stop" and "go" was hence accomplished by tightening or loosening fiscal policy. Normally the shifts between "stop" and "go" were triggered by the development in the balance of payments (Hansen et al., 1988, pp. 142-143).

While there hence was a distinctly British touch over the conduct of fiscal policy, the other traditional core instrument of stabilization policies in the UK, (statutory) incomes policy, was not much used in Denmark. There had been an element of incomes policy in the "comprehensive solution" (Helhedsløsningen) of 1963, but when the Socialdemocratic government tried to enact a relatively

---

3 Paldam (1990, p. 35) points to an obvious difficulty with this explanation: there had been more sizeable improvements in terms of trade before, which had not had this effect.

4 This point of view is mentioned in Paldam (1979a), p. 375, but not tested.

5 The relative independence from international economic development exhibited by the Danish economy 1958-74 (cf. Paldam (1979), p. 377) is worth keeping in mind as a supplement (or corrective) to the recurring assertions of some Danish governments and politicians that the economic crisis in Denmark was entirely caused by external forces beyond their control and hence could only be remedied if and when the international economy picked up (cf. below).

6 Cf. Paldam (1990, pp. 25-27).

minor incomes policy measure in the wake of a depreciation of the Danish krone in 1967 (following the depreciation of the sterling), part of the Socialist Peoples' Party, which had secured the parliamentary majority of the Socialdemocratic government, broke away, and the bourgeois parties seized upon this opportunity to topple the "red cabinet" over the incomes policy issue.

Although the expansion of the public sector was accomplished with a continuous budget surplus, fiscal policy 1960-74 was on average strongly expansive (albeit somewhat more so between 1960 and 1967 than between 1968 and 1973) with an average first year growth impulse to the economy around 2 per cent of GDP (Hansen et al., 1988, p. 142). Even though full employment had been achieved early in the period, the growth in public employment most of the time was allowed to exceed the net growth of the labor force. Thus, although there was a strong growth in the labor force, employment in the exposed sector stayed almost constant, while employment in the sheltered sector, especially the public sector, rose rapidly. Furthermore, with increasing public demand labor markets became very tight. This resulted in accelerating wage increases. They came to exceed wage increases among the trading partners by about 20 per cent. As a consequence there were constant inflationary pressures and balance of payments deficits.[7] There is little doubt that the combination of strong public sector growth and (too) expansive fiscal policy 1958-74 contributed heavily to shaping the character of the Danish economy as a full employment / high inflation / constant balance of payments deficit economy.

Despite the grave economic imbalances, the 60s were (and, in retrospect, still are)[8] generally perceived as a "good" period. The balance of payments deficit did not affect people directly and was thus of little interest.[9] Due to the near-universal application of CoL-indexation wage earners were not much affected by inflation either, despite the Danish labor market tradition for having collective agreements negotiated for two years. Much of the distributional conflict was cushioned by persistent high economic growth rates which made the welfare state look like a positive-sum game where everybody won something and nobody lost anything. This is also reflected in the rather low level of industrial conflicts in Denmark during that period which, although higher than in Austria, Germany and Sweden, was far from approaching the UK standard.

When the period of strong economic growth came to its end in 1974, some legacies and liabilities from the past 16 years' development became visible.[10] Denmark came to face the crisis with an economy characterized by a relatively

---

[7] Actually there was only one year (1962) with a balance of payments surplus.

[8] The 60s are quite commonly referred to as "the happy 60s", in contrast to "the crisis 70s" and "the pauper 80s".

[9] Paldam and Schneider (1980).

[10] There had been warnings before that time, most notably in a voluminous report of 1971 from a committee of top civil servants ("Perspektivplanredegørelsen 1970-85"). It would be incorrect to say that they went unheeded, but there was little effective action.

weak exposed sector and a seemingly ever-expanding public sector. In the international economic situation following the first oil price hike the combination of a weak exposed sector and a large balance of payments deficit was ominous. Furthermore, the internal growth dynamics in the public sector reduced the room for budgetary manoeuvre and did not make economic policy formation any easier. Finally, wage earners had grown accustomed to a continuous rise of real wages and could not be assumed to adjust their expectations and aspirations readily.

In metaphorical language, then, the Danish economy at the eve of the recession may be likened to a vessel with its course set into the eye of a storm, equipped with a weak engine and a helm of doubtful reliability. Moreover, as will be seen below, the crew in charge was deeply divided and quarrelsome.

1.2. From tranquillity to turmoil: The political arena

At about the same time as the oil price rises hit the Danish economy (but well ahead of the time when their economic repercussions started to become fully visible) Danish politics were hit by the greatest disruption since the existing party system had taken form around 1920. Overnight the "landslide election" of December 1973 doubled the number of parties in parliament (the Folketing) from 5 to 10, reducing the vote share of the five "old" parties from its established level well above 90 per cent to 64.3 per cent.[11] Never since 1920 had there been a comparable degree of fractionalization in the Folketing.[12]

The "landslide election" of 1973 marked the beginning of a period of political instability in Denmark characterized by continuing high degrees of fractionalization in the Folketing, weak minority governments (with a single exception), and frequent elections. Thus the liberal government taking over after the 1973-election was based on 22 (out of 179) seats in the Folketing only, and it had no reliable support from other parties. Also the Socialdemocratic governments formed after the elections in 1975 and 1977, respectively, were minority governments (based on 53 and 65 seats, respectively) without the backing of an informal working majority. So was the Socialdemocratic - Liberal coalition formed in 1978. It was four seats short of a majority. But since it would have required the joint effort of all other parties in the Folketing (an extremely unlikely situation) to defeat or overthrow it, this government could conduct itself as if it were a majority government. Finally, the Socialdemocratic government formed after the election in 1979 was once more a pure minority government (68 seats) without an informal working majority behind it.

---

11 Cf. Nannestad (1989a, pp. 9-11; pp. 77-81).

12 Rae's index of fractionalization it reached a value of 0.85 in 1973, cf. Damgaard (1977, pp. 92-93).

Thus the problems posed to macro-economic policy making by the economic crisis were aggravated by the difficulties of forming parliamentary majorities in a highly fragmented Folketing to carry through a coherent policy. In 1976 a Social-democratic spokesman aptly summarized the situation in the statement: "When we had greater political stability than we have today, our problems were lesser. Now, as the problems have grown and new ones have emerged, we have the greatest political disruption in memory."[13]

The upshot Progress Party, which had been the big winner of the 1973-election when it obtained 28 seats, and which managed to retain most of its parliamentary strength throughout the period 1974-79, may well have added further to the difficulties of economic policy formation, quite apart from the fractionalization in the Folketing to which it contributed. Although it is hardly possible to verify, the mere existence of the Progress Party as a manifestation of strong anti-tax sentiments in the electorate may conceivably have influenced crisis policy making in an indirect way.

The initial reaction from the other parties, especially the five "old" ones, to the appearance of the Progress Party in the parliamentary arena had been to ostracize it. The party was more or less openly declared a conglomerate of political outcasts. No "responsible" party could or should ever cooperate with it.[14] Thus it was normally shut out from direct influence on the contents of policy making.

But the results of the election of 1973 had also demonstrated that several parties, including the Socialdemocrats, had open flanks towards the Progress Party and were forced to reckon with the danger of losing voters to it. Hence, even if a parliamentary majority could have been found to support such measures, none of these parties could possibly have been interested in enacting policies which in the end might have strengthened the Progress Party still further. In this indirect way the party most probably reduced several other parties' room for manoeuvre in various relevant policy areas, for instance with respect to personal taxes.[15]

Furthermore, the existence of the Progress Party may also have had an indirect influence on agenda setting in economic policy making, although once more such an influence is near-impossible to prove. However, since its adversaries preferably depicted much of the Progress Party's platform as unabashedly

---

[13] Quoted from Damgaard (1989, p. 73).

[14] Nevertheless, under the liberal government in 1974 there were occasional contacts between the government and the Progress Party in an attempt to secure a majority for one of the numerous "crisis packages", cf. Nyboe Andersen (1989, pp. 182-183), according to whom the initiative came from the Progress Party. But thanks to the "wild" and at times bizarre behavior of the Progress Party and its leader the task of ostracizing them was made rather easy. Still, it must be considered a tactical masterpiece by the Socialdemocratic leadership, since it effectively neutralized about 20 per cent of the non-socialist seats in the Folketing.

[15] It is difficult to imagine that there was no relationship at all between the electoral success of the Progress Party with its very strong anti-tax platform in 1973 and the reduction in personal taxes under the liberal government in the following year, cf. below.

anti-social and egoist, no "responsible" party wanted to become identified with Progress Party standpoints. Neither did they want to adopt or support stand-points which could be denounced as "Progress Partist" by others. By declaring the Progress Party "off limits" debates on certain issues and standpoints had in effect been declared "off limits" as well.

But there was still another potential impediment to political consensus forma-tion on economic policy. In 1972 the Socialdemocrats and the Danish trade union federation (LO) had jointly tabled a plan for the introduction of what was labelled "Economic Democracy" (Økonomisk demokrati, ØD) in Denmark, and twice in 1973 the Socialdemocratic government had, without success, introduced bills on ØD in the Folketing. The main features of the Socialdemocratic plan for "Economic Democracy" were not unlike the Swedish plans for the introduction of wage earner funds (cf. chapter 2, sec. 3). The central constituent was a wage earner fund to which employers would contribute. The fund would be under trade union control and its means were to be re-invested in business as risk-bearing capital.

The campaign to drum up support for the ØD-plan was not launched in eco-nomic terms, although this approach would certainly have been possible. But actually very little was made of ØD as a means to help solving problems of capital formation and investment in society. The emphasis was entirely on the plan's political and ideological aspects: ØD was intended to secure wage earner co-ownership and co-determination in business as a whole and in each particular firm. This was to bring about an extension of political democracy and, in the end, as wage earner capital grew in size, a fundamental change in ownership of the means of production and, thus, in the power relations in society.[16] The plan further aimed at a levelling of incomes and wealth.

Other parties as well as employers' and business organizations, then, could (and possibly should) hardly see the ØD-plan as anything other than a large-scale operation to "move ideological fences". The plan met with stiff resistance. There was never a parliamentary majority for ØD in the Folketing - actually the Social-democrats were the only party to support it. While there were certainly nuances, all other parties, both to the left and to the right of the Socialdemocrats, were opposed to ØD in the form envisaged by the Socialdemocrats and LO. To judge from various opinion polls there was no popular backing of ØD either. Quite to the contrary, opposition at the mass level was strong, not the least to the idea of a central wage earner fund, administered by the trade unions - the very heart of the ØD-plan (Buksti et al., 1978, pp. 3 - 10).[17]

---

[16] This is also indicated by the fact that the alternative term to "Economic Democracy" (ØD) became "Wage Earners' Co-Ownership Right" (Lønmodtagernes medejendomsret, LM).

[17] This was politically important because it meant that even if the Socialdemocrats should succeed in somehow marshalling a parliamentary majority behind ØD, the bill stood a fair chance of being defeated if a referendum were called on it, and it would take only 60 members of the Folketing to have a referendum.

However, the Socialdemocrats had invested too much prestige in the ØD-issue to be able just to drop it. They also had their commitments to the trade unions to honor. Thus the ØD-debate kept lingering on, and, time and again, the issue surfaced in negotiations between the Socialdemocrats and other parties over policies to combat the economic crisis. The Socialdemocrats regularly demanded concessions on ØD in return for the enacting of, e.g., incomes policy. Thus ØD contributed significantly to exacerbating the economic-political cleavages separating the political parties and making consensus formation and cooperation on economic policy difficult. In 1979 the Socialdemocratic - liberal coalition government actually broke up over the ØD - incomes policy nexus.

Furthermore, the ØD-issue provided the trade unions with excellent leverage in negotiations on economic policy, if they needed one. At any time they could effectively evade cooperation by demanding ØD as a quid pro quo for wage restraint. The (Socialdemocratic) government could hardly refuse to support such a demand with the certain prospect of a break-down in negotiations. This, then, legitimated the withholding of cooperation and the refusal of wage restraint from the side of the unions.

To sum it all up, the political conditions under which the economic crisis in Denmark had to be tackled were far from fortunate. The fragmentation of the Folketing made majority formation time-consuming and tedious at best. A number of parties, furthermore, lived under the Damocles-sword of still another voter defection to the Progress Party. Finally, the unresolved ØD-issue was an obstacle on the path to inter-party consensus on economic policy.

2. Crisis onset 1974: External or domestic causes?

The repercussions of the oil price hike 1973-74 on the Danish economy did not reveal themselves at once, nor did they emerge simultaneously. Rather, they hit in two or three different waves. This made it difficult to envisage from the start the full extent of the direct and indirect impact the oil price rises would eventually have on the economy. In sequence, the supply-aspect, the inflationary consequences, the employment effects, and the repercussions on the balance of payments came to dominate crisis perceptions. As a consequence the different aspects of the crisis were largely handled in a sequential manner.[18]

---

[18] There appears to be a distinctly "Mosley-like" pattern in the policy reactions 1973-74. According to the model of satisficing government behavior suggested by Mosley (1976) governments are inherently crisis-averters. They will only attend to the economy when some economic variables are seen to go into crisis (i.e. to deviate sufficiently and negatively from usual states, e.g. the trend rate), and their attention will be confined to getting the particular variables out of crisis again.

2.1. A supply-crisis that never quite materialized

At the very beginning of the crisis, in the fall and winter of 1973-74, the supply-aspects dominated crisis perceptions. Oil reserves were small, and in view of a highly unstable supply situation for oil and oil products, of which Denmark had to import quantities covering about 90 per cent of its consumption, various measures were introduced to conserve energy in order to keep industrial production running. Private driving was forbidden on Sundays, speed limits were introduced, there were restrictions on collective traffic as well, room temperatures in public buildings were lowered to 18° C maximum, etc.

In the end the dreaded Arab oil boycott against Denmark never quite materialized, and an unusually mild winter helped in keeping down energy consumption. In early 1974 most of the energy conserving restrictions were revoked.

2.2. The upsurge of inflation and a continuing boom

The next aspect of the crisis calling for attention was inflation. As can be seen from figure 3.1, while inflation rates had been rising slowly throughout the first part of 1973, they began to soar in the last months of the year, and thereafter inflation accelerated for every month.

Figure 3.1.: Increase in Consumer Price Index (CPI) and Monthly Price Index (MPI) 1972-74, in per cent, annual basis

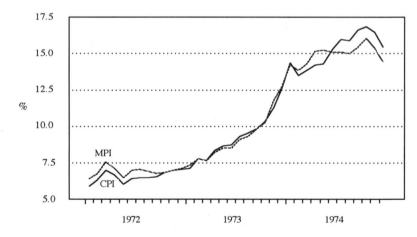

Data: Danmarks Statistik, Statistiske Efterretninger: Konjunkturoversigt (var. years)

In October consumer price inflation reached double-digit figures for the first time (10.33 per cent over October 1972). By November it had reached 11.25 per cent, by December 12.57 per cent, and in January 1974 consumer prices stood 14.33 per cent over January 1973. This meant that by March 1974 three CoL-regulation "portions" would have to be added to wages and salaries. Inflation was feeding on itself.

Due to the political vacuum existing between November 8, 1973, when the general election was called following the parliamentary defeat of the Socialdemocratic government, and December 19, 1973, when the new Liberal government took over, nothing had been done about inflation.[19] It thus became one of the first tasks confronting the new government to decide what to do or not to do about price levels.

On its first day in office the new government made the Central Bank raise the Danish discount rate from 8 to 9 per cent, and restrictions were put on some kinds of foreign loan taking in order to forestall a circumvention of the tightening of monetary conditions. However, the primary intention of these measures was to signal that the situation was considered serious (Nyboe Andersen, 1989, p. 172). But it probably also signalled that the government was aiming at a deflationary strategy.

Right upon taking office the government had been approached by the Council of Economic Advisers[20] who had proffered the view that it would be possible for Denmark to avoid the unilateral use of deflationary measures if the necessary oil supply could be secured (Nyboe Andersen, 1989, p. 172). But according to the government's view the only alternative to deflationary policies was incomes (wage) policy, and on this point it drew a blank when it approached the trade union federation (LO). The then minister of economic affairs, Poul Nyboe Andersen, relates as his impressions from the meeting that there was no hint of any trade union willingness whatsoever to cooperate in solving the inflation problem in a way which would not endanger employment (Nyboe Andersen, 1989, p. 172).[21] Thus the first cautious attempt at bringing about a solution to the "Keynesian coordination problem" failed.

Instead the government proceeded with plans for a (mild) deflation of the economy. In order to gain time - and undoubtedly as a kind of political cadeau to

---

[19] Energy conservation measures, on the other hand, could be introduced by administrative action and were hence less affected by the political impasse.

[20] The "three wise men" in popular language.

[21] Needless to say this could be a "tactical" recollection, possibly in order to exonerate the government from part of the responsibility for the rise in unemployment later on in 1974. But on the other hand the trade unions had probably no incentive to help the bourgeois government. New elections were generally expected within a short span of time, so there was no reason to make the going more easy for this government - the more incompetent it looked, the better, and it would also be a tactical disadvantage to the Socialdemocrats to have the trade unions demonstrate the lack of validity of the old Socialdemocratic claim to being the only party able to bring about trade union cooperation.

the Socialdemocrats - there was a price-freeze during January and February, 1974. As can be seen in figure 3.1, it had a minor effect only on the consumer price inflation. The rate stayed firmly in the double-digit range.

In January 1974 the government put two anti-inflation proposals to the Folketing. The first one was a very traditional one: a 2.9 bill. kr. budget cut. The second one was more innovative: instead of the three CoL-regulation portions to be paid by the employers from March, each tax-payer was to be given a tax-free amount of 1000 kr. in 10 monthly instalments.[22] The idea was to keep down labor cost increases, even if it was not possible to keep down wage increases.[23]

After protracted negotiations a compromise was finally reached in early February bringing together the governing Liberals, the Socialdemocrats, the Center Democrats, and the Christian Peoples' Party. As in the government's proposal the contents were a mixture of deflationary and cost reducing measures. The proposed budget cuts were reduced to 1.55 bill. kr., but as a supplement (and a concession to the Socialdemocrats) a compulsory saving scheme was introduced according to which tax payers in higher income brackets were to save a proportion of their income into blocked bank accounts. The CoL-regulation portions were to be paid out, but most employers were to be compensated for this additional cost by receiving a fixed compensation for each full-time employee in 1974.

In early May the government introduced a new set of mainly deflationary proposals in the Folketing. These proposals were intended to bring down the level of imports and to reduce the balance of payment deficit which was showing signs of alarming growth. In addition the measures aimed at curbing domestic demand in order to shift labor resources from the sheltered to the exposed sector and to make possible a certain easing of the tight monetary policy. During the first months of 1974 the economy was still booming, and there was shortage of labor in some branches.

The government announced that it planned a major income tax reduction, to become effective by the beginning of 1975. This reform would imply a sizeable lowering of marginal tax rates. The reasons for proposing tax reductions in the existing economic circumstances were probably as much political as economic ones. The government led an insecure parliamentary life, and having to meet the

---

22 The original idea had been to substitute a tax reduction to wage earners for the three CoL-regulation portions, but it had turned out that the Danish tax system could not distinguish between wage earners and other tax payers (Nyboe Andersen, 1989, p. 172).

23 With this proposal the government thus may seem to have tried to follow what Scharpf (1987, p. 209) points to as the next best strategy in the developing stagflationary situation: "But even if the Keynesian coordination was not achieved in the first run, there was a second chance, although it was more difficult to grasp: if the central task was to stabilize the price level in face of the oil price hike, but without creating mass unemployment, then firms had to be relieved from certain costs in order to compensate for the higher oil prices. At the same time international competition or other circumstances had to enforce discipline in price setting." (my translation).

electorate without a proposal for income tax reductions could be dangerous for a bourgeois government in view of the Progress Party's continuing strength in opinion polls.

The loss of revenues from the income tax reduction was to be covered, partly by budget cuts, beginning with a 5 bill. kr. cut in 1975, and partly, by raising at once various existing indirect taxes and introducing a new one on consumer durables. Further rises in indirect taxes or the VAT would have to follow. The (already extremely high) indirect taxes on cars were also to be raised for a limited period in order to reduce imports in 1974.[24] Thus the immediate impact of the proposed "package" would be deflationary.

This time the going turned out to be much tougher for the government than it had been in February. While acknowledging that the economic situation with respect to inflation and the balance of payments deficit was grave and called for action, the Socialdemocrats decided to stand off. Their attitude was probably affected by the considerable unrest in the labor market accompanying the parliamentary negotiations and the determined attempts by the left-wing parties to exploit this situation at the expense of the Socialdemocrats.

After much parliamentary drama - more than once it looked as if new elections were the only way out - a compromise was finally reached which could be supported by the non-socialist parties in the Folketing, including the Progress Party. The contents of that compromise (which came to be known as the "black compromise" among opponents) were very much in line with the government's proposals for increasing revenues.[25] Thus, in the short run, the policy was clearly dominated by deflationary measures in the form of raises in various indirect taxes.

The economic-political developments in the first half of 1974 show, then, that despite its parliamentary weakness the government had actually been able to implement a deflationary economic strategy, although this may not in all cases have been done exactly in the way and to the extent it would have preferred most. But did the strategy work in the way expected, i.e. reducing inflation and the balance of payments deficit?

As always this question is hard to answer in the absence of a clear counterfactual. Looking at the behavior of the MPI (the monthly price index which, contrary to the CPI, is net of indirect taxes etc.) in figure 3.1. it can be seen that for a short period after May 1974 the inflation rate actually stayed constant (albeit at high levels). Then there was a short upsurge followed by a markedly declining tendency during the last months of 1974. How much of this development should be credited to the deflationary measures taken in February and May is unclear. As can be seen from figure 3.2., the development in consumer prices closely paralleled the development in the import price index and the index for raw material prices. At least there was probably a considerable international element in

---

24 Since Denmark has no car manufacturing of its own, all cars are imported.

25 The tax reduction issue was finally decided on in September, resulting in a 7 bill. kr. tax cut for 1975.

the domestic price development, which suggests that some dying down of inflation would have occured even in the absence of domestic deflationary policy measures.[26]

Figure 3.2.: Increase in Raw Material Price Index (RPI) and Import Price Index (IPI) 1972-74, in per cent, annual basis

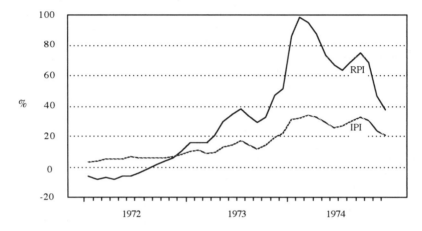

Data: Computed from Danmarks Statistik, Statistiske Efterretninger: Konjunkturoversigt (var. years)

With respect to the balance of payments goal of the government's deflationary measures figure 3.3. shows a marked improvement in the current account in the second, third and fourth quarter of 1974, following an all-time record deficit in the first. The 1974-pattern in the development of the balance of payment deficit is thus quite different from the one in the previous years when the deficit used to diminish towards the middle of the year, only to increase strongly in the last quarter. This would seem to suggest that some intervention had taken place.

Endowed with the wisdom of hindsight it is easy to reproach the deflationary strategy of the government during the first half of 1974 for having paved the way for the recession through "... underestimation of the simultaneous lagged effects of restrictive policies and the external shock of the oil price increase, both acting concurrently in nearly all countries, interacting with - and reinforcing - progressive loss of confidence on the part of both business and consumers." (McCracken et al., 1977, p. 71).

---

26 Cf. Lindbeck (1979).

Figure 3.3.: Quarterly balance of payments deficit, current account, 1971-74, mill. kr.

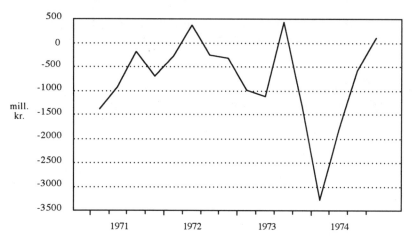

Data: Danmarks Statistik, Statistiske Efterretninger: Konjunkturoversigt (var. years), and
      own computations

On the other hand, it may well be argued that some kind of non-accommodating strategy was unavoidable. The huge balance of payments deficit in the first quarter of 1974 threatened the exchange rate, and a depreciation of the krone would only have fuelled inflation still more.[27] Furthermore, the government had to take into consideration that negotiations for wage settlements 1975-76 were to commence in the fall of 1974, and a run-away inflation up to that time would most certainly be reflected in the wage claims forwarded, triggering off another round of inflationary wage rises. Thus the government could hardly afford "... with a certain equanimity to let the oil price inflation have its course and die down without additional restrictive measures" (Scharpf, 1987, p. 208 (my translation)).

---

[27] To some degree the role played by such very real economic problems in economic policy formation seems to be neglected in the writing of "critical" economists relative to the role they ascribe to more general, ideological motives. Dencik and Madsen (1978, pp. 79-80), for example, ascribe the government's policy to "... the intention to ease the pressure on profits by weakening the relative strength of the working class in the economic class struggle through a minor increase in unemployment" (my translation). A critical examination of the implied "class struggle hypothesis" of unemployment can be found in chapter 4.

2.3. The U-turn into recession

During the first months of 1974 the economy was still booming. Unemployment was virtually non-existing and the number of vacant jobs was still high.

Figure 3.4. : Labor market developments 1970-74

(a) Unemployment (seasonally adjusted), per cent

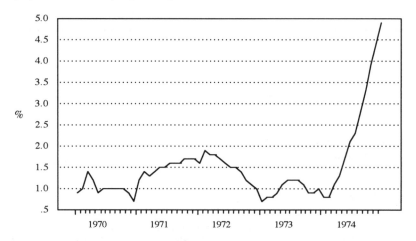

(b) Number of unfilled vacancies (in 1000)

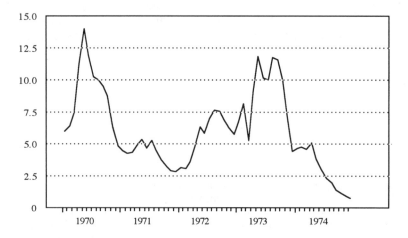

Data: OECD, Historical Statistics (1970-79), file DNKM170

But then, rather suddenly, the picture changed. This is most easily seen from the unemployment figures in figure 3.4. (a). By the middle of 1974 unemployment (seasonally adjusted) passed the 2 per cent mark. It continued to rise steeply throughout the rest of the year. There was a corresponding drop in the number of unfilled vacancies, signalling a slump in economic activity. The recession had finally caught up with Denmark, changing profoundly the agenda for future economic policy making.

Although the government as well as the main opposition party, the Social-democrats, were eager to blame the international recession for much of the Danish economic downturn,[28] the mid-1974 slump was in fact not export-led. Initially the main loss of employment was not in the export sector.

Figure 3.5.: Danish exports 1971-74, quarterly data, value- and volume-index (1971=100)

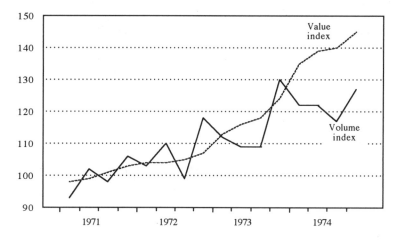

Data: Danmarks Statistik, Statistiske Efterretninger: Konjunkturoversigt (var. years)

As figure 3.5. shows, the value-index for Danish exports kept increasing through-out all of 1974. The development in the volume-index was somewhat more

---

[28] See for instance Folketingstidende 1974-75, 1. saml., sp. 406-575. There was clearly a political interest in both the present and the previous (and future) government party to shift as much as possible of the responsibility for the rising Danish unemployment away from domestic policies and to anonymous and uncontrollable international economic conditions. Left-wing parties tended to buy part of the argument, but re-interpreted it in terms of the inherent crisis proneness of capitalist systems. At the same time they marketed underconsumption explana-tions of the Danish slump. Bourgeois parties, on the other hand, tended to stress problems with Danish cost levels and international competitiveness. The suggested solutions varied according-ly.

erratic, but there was no clear relationship between its ups and downs and the development in, for example, unemployment.[29]

The main factor behind the economic downturn in 1974 was domestic demand. After a relatively stable period in the beginning of the year private consumption began to fall. As can be seen from figures 3.6. (a) - (b) this drop was most clearly marked in the consumption of durables and, especially, cars, which had been some of the main targets for the increase of indirect taxes (and the levying of new ones) under the government's anti-inflation offensive in the spring of 1974.[30] Although wages kept outrunning prices by a safe margin - real hourly earnings in industry increased by 5.4 per cent in 1974[31] - real private consumption decreased by about 3 per cent in 1974, compared to the previous year.[32]

Figure 3.6.: Indicators of private consumption trends 1971-74, monthly data

(a) Index of retail sales and sales of durables, seasonally adjusted (1985=100)

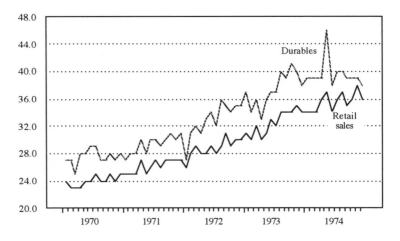

(continued)

---

[29] This agrees well with Alt (1985, p. 1032) who failed to find a clear relationship between Danish unemployment and levels of world demand.

[30] The spikes for May 1974 in the durables and the car registration curves indicate that a considerable amount of hoarding was done during the period of political negotiations prior to the conclusion of the compromise.

[31] OECD, Historical Statistics (1988).

[32] Danmarks Statistik, Statistiske Efterretninger: Konjunkturoversigt (December 1974).

(b) Number of new passenger car registrations, seasonally adjusted (in 1000)

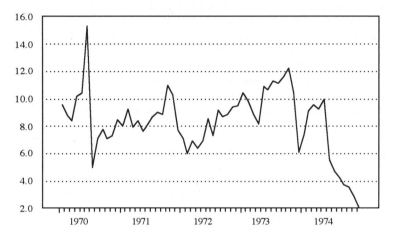

Data: OECD, Historical Statistics (1970-79), file DNKM170

Business expectations concerning future trends in production ("the business climate") deteriorated sharply throughout 1974 and reached an all-time low in the fourth quarter of 1974, cf. figure 3.7.

Figure 3.7.: Index of business expectations of future production 1970-74, quarterly data ("Business climate barometer")

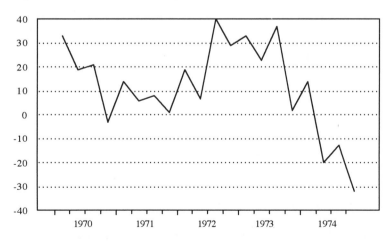

Data: OECD, Historical Statistics (1970-79), file DNKM170

This in turn affected investment decisions. Real gross fixed capital formation in machinery and equipment grew by 3.1 per cent in 1974 (as against 10.7 per cent in 1973) and most of this investment was done in the first half of 1974.[33] Thus in the second half of 1974 demand from private investment was weak, too.

Moreover, there was a huge slump in residential construction in 1974. This is clearly brought out by figures 3.8. (a) and (b).

The sharp decline in the level of residential construction in 1974, compared to 1973, was mainly the combined effect of two factors. In the first place the number of housing constructions started decreasing throughout 1974. This would, by itself, have made for less construction activity in 1974. But in the second place there had been a building boom of unprecedented strength in 1973 which levelled off in 1974 as construction work that had been started in 1973 reached completion.

Some authors - most notably Therborn[34] (1986, pp. 138-139) - have viewed the decline in residential construction in 1974 as the outcome of a deliberate economic-political strategy by the Liberal government.

Figure 3.8.: Residential construction 1970-74, monthly data

(a) Dwelling units under construction (in 10000)

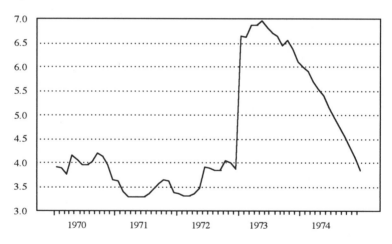

(continued)

---

[33] Danmarks Statistik, Statistiske Efterretninger: Konjunkturoversigt (December 1974), p. 34.

[34] On this point Therborn's source are "helpful observations" by Gunnar Olofsson from the (now defunct) Institute of Sociology at the University of Copenhagen, see Therborn (1986, p. 173, note 162).

(b) Construction permits and residential construction starts (in 1000)

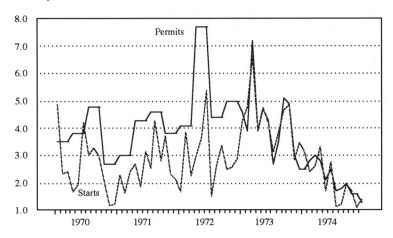

Data: OECD, Historical Statistics (1970-79), file DNKM170

The aim of this strategy is said to have been a transfer of resources to the export sector of the Danish economy.[35] According to this view, then, the government willfully "smashed" the construction sector in order to achieve its goal.

On closer inspection the truth turns out to be somewhat less Machiavellian, however, although "policy failures" certainly did contribute in bringing about the slump in residential construction in 1974. Only, they were not primarily attributable to the incumbent Liberal government. Part of the problem was a legacy from the housing policy of the preceding Socialdemocratic government and its parliamentary support, the Socialist Peoples' Party.

In 1972 the Socialdemocratic government had presented a set of policy proposals concerning the housing and construction sector. Among them was a proposal to abolish the existing VAT-refund[36] on residential construction. After protracted negotiations this proposal became law in 1973. The VAT-refund was to be abolished for residential construction started later than March 9, 1973. The bill was carried by the votes of the Socialdemocrats and the Socialist Peoples' Party.

---

35 Similarly, Ibsen and Jørgensen (1979, p. 306; my translation) claim that "i.a. the Perspective Plan II had pointed to the fact that residential construction did preempt resources at the expense of, for instance, the export sector, and in 1973 the bourgeois government decides to take measures against residential and general construction." This must be called swift action, as the Liberal government did only come into office on December 19, 1973.

36 Strictly speaking there was no proper VAT-refund, but rather a subsidy. The "refund" was given as a fixed amount per square meter (165 kr.) up to a maximum of 100 m2.

The immediate consequence, once the proposal to abolish the VAT-refund became known, had been large-style hoarding of building permits and a boom in construction starts, the traces of which are clearly visible in figure 3.8. (b). As a consequence, the level of residential construction activity sky-rocketed to unseen (and unsustainable) heights in 1973 and in part, as mentioned, the slump in residential construction in 1974 simply reflects the return to more normal levels of activity in this sector. Such a development had long been foreseen by the Council of Economic Advisers.[37] Hence, in the final analysis, part of the reduction in residential construction levels in 1974 must be blamed on the long interval allowed to elapse between the time when the proposal to abolish the VAT-refund on housing construction became known and the time when this policy was enacted. This was what made the ensuing explosion in residential construction levels possible.

The drop in the number of construction projects started in 1974, which contributed further to the slump in construction, may also - at least in part - be a reflection of the 1973-boom. The abolition of the VAT-refund was a strong incentive to hasten the start of residential construction. Conceivably many building projects - which under normal circumstances would not have been started before 1974 - were pushed through in 1973 in order not to lose the VAT-refund.[38]

But also inflation may have contributed to the lowering of the number of building projects started in 1974. It drove up the long-term interest rate, which under the Danish system of financing housing has (some) direct impact on rents and determines the expenditures of home-owners very directly. In 1974 the Danish nominal long-term interest rate stood at 15.8 per cent, higher even than in the UK, and 3.2 percentage points higher than in 1973.[39] Thus costs may have become prohibitive to prospective home-owners, or they may have found it wise to wait and see if the government would succeed in bringing down inflation. In both cases the number of housing constructions started would be affected downwards.

With private demand sluggish, strong increases in public consumption and investment would have been necessary in any case to offset the effect on the overall level of economic activity. But actually real public demand grew only by 1 - 2 per cent in 1974, about the same growth rate as in 1973.[40] This was mainly

---

[37] Dansk økonomi (1973; 1974).

[38] Another unfortunate side effect of the abolition of the VAT-refund and the ensuing construction boom was its expansionary effects on the macro-economy in 1973. Thus one of the "golden opportunities" to solve the recurring conflict between high employment levels and the balance of payments was possibly lost. The marked improvement in terms of trade resulting from the entry into the EEC, together with generally tight economic policies 1972-73, had led to a temporary improvement in the current balance of payments. But, due to strong domestic economic expansion which rapidly restored the balance of payments deficit, this opportunity was missed, cf. OECD, Economic Surveys: Denmark (1978), p. 17.

[39] OECD, Historical Statistics (1988).

[40] Danmarks Statistik, Statistiske Efterretninger: Konjunkturoversigt (December 1974), p. 45.

a consequence of an existing general freeze on public building and construction works and of a round of budget cuts in May 1973.

Thus by the end of 1974 it turned out that Denmark had experienced a real GDP decline. For the whole of 1974 it amounted to 0.9 per cent, roughly the same magnitude as in the UK. Economic policy makers found themselves confronted with new and unfamiliar tasks.

3. 1974-76: The years of Keynesian interventionism

There are few, if any, indications that the economic set-back beginning in the middle of 1974 was at once recognized for what it was: the onset of a full-fledged recession. The then minister of economic affairs preferred to characterize it as an adaptation process in the Danish economy which unfortunately had become aggravated by the consequences of the oil price hike. The Socialdemocrats did not seriously contest that view.[41] This is probably the most important reason why the incipient crisis was not met by an immediate attempt to formulate and implement a multifaceted, coherent economic crisis policy, but rather with policy responses in the style of "piece-meal engineering".

3.1. First reactions to the crisis

The first major policy reaction from the liberal government came in September 1974. All bourgeois parties except the Progress Party[42] joined together in an agreement concerning a 7 bill. kr. cut in personal taxes (6.7 bill. kr. in 1975-prices), to become effective by January 1, 1975. The resulting loss of revenues to the state would have to be covered by a - yet unspecified - 6.7 bill. kr. budget cut. Despite the apparent balance between tax and expenditure cuts the macro-economic net impact of these measures would be expansive, mainly be-

---

[41] Nor did the Socialdemocrats propose solutions that differed radically from the government's (with the exception of "Economic Democracy", the positive employment effects of which remained somewhat nebulous, however). Their policy could well be characterized as "the Liberals plus 10 per cent".

Various left-wing Marxist parties held different opinions on the economic situation, of course, but their long- standing tradition of seeing inherent crises of the capitalist system everywhere and at any time had not earned them a particular reputation as reliable judges of the economic developments and prospects.

[42] The Progress Party kept out because it considered the 6.7 bill. kr. tax cut too small. In connection with the "black compromise", which in the end had been supported by the Progress Party, a 10 bill. kr. cut had been on the table, so the Progress Party felt cheated on.

cause the tax cut would become effective by January 1 while the budget cuts would not become effective before April 1. After much parliamentary drama, with four vain attempts at the government's political life in the course of one day, the tax cut was carried.

But the rising unemployment was only one of Denmark's economic concerns. Prospects for both inflation and the balance of payments in 1975 were not considered rosy either. In this situation the Council of Economic Advisers had recommended a combination of stiff wage restraint and reflationary fiscal policies for 1975.[43]

As the government saw it, the September-agreement had taken care of the momentary need for expansionary fiscal policy (Nyboe Andersen, 1989, p. 212). Its "Comprehensive plan 1975", presented to the Folketing on December 3, was primarily intended to take care of the problem of costs, inflation, and the balance of payments.[44] The main elements in the plan were a proposal to prolong the collective wage agreements in the private and the public labor market, which were to expire in the spring, until the end of 1975. Another proposal was to have the state pay out 100 kr. per month (net of tax) in exchange for the three CoL-regulation portions expected to become due from March. There was also a proposal to freeze domestic agricultural prices as well as dividends, honoraries, etc. until the end of 1975.

When in the government's opinion no sufficient support was forthcoming on the first reading of the 11 bills making up the "Comprehensive plan", prime minister Hartling, his political self-confidence undoubtedly bolstered by his party's permanent good standing in the polls, decided to call elections for January 9, 1975. They were a triumph for the Liberals who managed to nearly double their number of seats in parliament (from 22 to 42 seats). This success occured despite the fact that the government had come to preside over the onset of the worst post-war recession in Denmark and, especially, a sky-rocketing unemployment figure.

But the liberal victory came at the expense of the other bourgeois parties. The Folketing was still highly fragmented and majority formation had not become any easier. About a month after the election the liberal government was forced to resign and, following a long and intriguing political charade,[45] a Socialdemocratic minority government took office in mid-February 1975.

As was soon to become evident, the main tenets of the economic strategy followed by the new Socialdemocratic government were not much different from the previous government's, although there were differences with respect to

---

[43] Dansk økonomi (September 1974).

[44] It has been argued, however, that it was primarily intended as an electoral platform. There are certainly things in the ensuing course of events which may seem to support this view. But then it has to be remembered that undoubtedly - and with good reason - the government expected to win the election and to stay in office. In this situation it would not be able to just drop the "Comprehensive plan" after an election. Therefore the plan had to be something more than an electoral platform.

[45] Vividly described in Kaarsted (1988).

the means preferred by the two administrations. Fiscal expansion combined with restraints on domestic cost development was still seen as a feasible way out of the crisis.

Upon return to office the Socialdemocratic government met an economic situation characterized by somewhat contradictory tendencies. Unemployment had been increasing steadily since the summer of 1974, and up to April 1975 the tendency was for still further increases, cf. figure 3.9.

Figure 3.9.: Unemployment 1973-76, monthly data, per cent

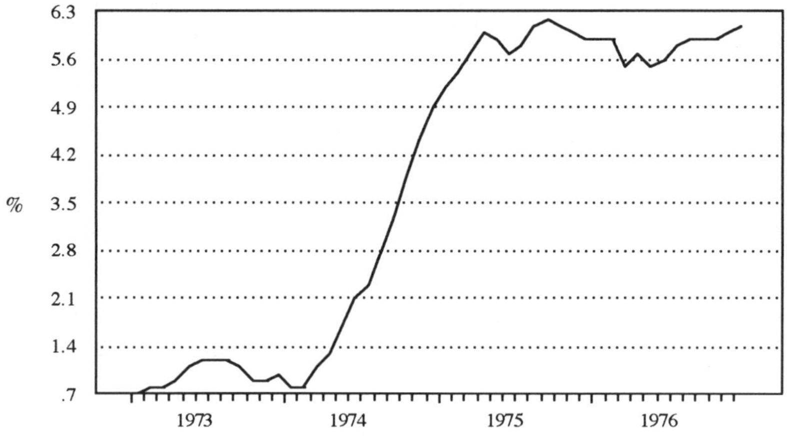

Data: OECD, Historical Statistics, files DNKM170 & DNKM270

The balance of payments deficit, on the other hand, had been improving since the second quarter of 1974, cf. figure 3.10. Unfortunately the main reason for this was a drop in the volume of imports rather than a growth in exports, so it was a reflection of the economic slow-down in Denmark rather than an indication of a stronger standing with respect to international competitiveness. The levelling off of international inflation, as reflected in the development in Danish import prices, also contributed to the balance of payments improvement. Moreover, the continuing slight appreciation of the Danish krone vis a vis the US dollar in conjunction with the other currencies in the "snake" helped in limiting the impact of international price rises still further.

Figure 3.10.: Balance of payments, current account 1973-76, quarterly data, bill. kr.

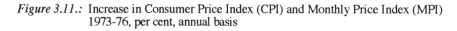

Data: Danmarks Statistik, Statistiske Efterretninger: Konjunkturoversigt (var. years)

With respect to inflation the situation also improved. As can be seen from figure 3.11., domestic inflation rates were sharply de-accelerating towards their 1973-levels.

Figure 3.11.: Increase in Consumer Price Index (CPI) and Monthly Price Index (MPI) 1973-76, per cent, annual basis

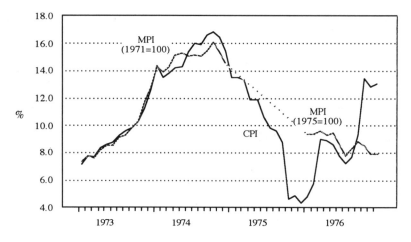

Data: Danmarks Statistik, Statistiske Efterretninger: Konjunkturoversigt (var. years)

Everything considered, there appeared to be some macro-economic scope for stimulating economic activity in the beginning of 1975. In January the discount rate had been lowered from 10 to 9 per cent, not the least in order to encourage housing construction. Further reflationary action had been taken in early February when the (bourgeois) parties behind the September 1974-compromise on tax and budget cuts and the Socialdemocrats had reached an agreement to waive these budget cuts.[46] In late February, finally, the new Socialdemocratic government initiated a sizeable relaxation of existing restrictions on local government investment and a lowering of the share of local government investments which had to be financed out of tax revenues. Further stimulating measures were announced, aiming especially at the housing and construction sector.

3.2. The statutory incomes policy solution of 1975

While thus busying itself with measures to stimulate the economy the Socialdemocratic government came to face its first serious economic-political challenge when the negotiations on a general wage settlement for 1975-76 in the private labor market broke down. Large-style industrial action loomed ahead. This was considered desastrous to the ongoing attempts to stimulate economic activity.

In this situation the Socialdemocratic government, supported by all bourgeois parties, except the Progress Party (and by none of the three left-wing parties), decided to step in by imposing a statutory incomes policy solution. In order to slow down the growth in nominal incomes the existing wage settlements in both the private and the public labor market were prolonged unchanged for two years. As part of the package incomes from entrepreneurship and dividends were likewise to be regulated by law, as were the profit margins of financial institutions (commercial banks etc.).

In order to give the incomes policy a solidary twist, two additional measures were introduced. In the first place provisions were made for special wage increases to low-paid groups. In the second place all future CoL-regulations were to be given as flat rate increases with identical amounts to all wage earners, regardless of income.[47] CoL-regulations in the form of a fixed percentage of

---

[46] As a consequence the projected budget deficit for the financial year 1975-76 came to amount to 9 bill. kr. (as against an estimated budget deficit of 3.5 bill. kr. for the financial year 1974-75).

[47] At the same time the base year from which to compute the price index was shifted forward to 1975.

income, which had been the rule in the public sector, were abolished for all groups but pensioners.[48]

The insertion of a solidary element into the imposed solution undoubtedly reflected ideological motives. To further the levelling of wage differentials was an avowed Socialdemocratic goal. However, it might simultaneously have served a tactical purpose as well. The solidaristic element made the solution less difficult to swallow for the large union of unskilled workers (SiD). But at the same time it was acceptable to the powerful union of skilled metal workers (Dansk Metal), because the imposed solution did not interfere with the right to negotiate wage increases at the local level which existed under the so-called "minimal wage system".[49] Under this system, which covered a large part of this union's members, wage increases based on local productivity improvements etc. could be negotiated even while collective wage settlements were in force. Thus wage differentials could easily be maintained or restored under this system, regardless of the special provisions for low-paid groups in the imposed settlement.

Figure 3.12.: Increase in hourly earnings in manufacturing and in the Consumer Price Index (CPI) 1972-79, per cent, annual basis

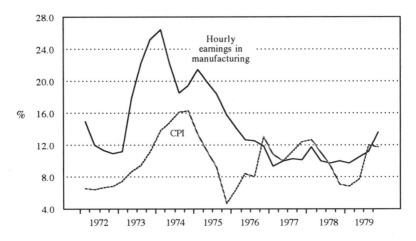

Data: OECD, Historical Statistics, file DNKQ70

---

48 As an incomes policy measure this change was of no more than marginal significance. It probably must be seen as a Socialdemocratic bow to certain populist "anti civil servants"-sentiments whipped up and articulated especially by the Progress Party. As a compensation, public employees were given a regulation mechanism which tied their wage development to wage developments in the private sector, although not on a one-to-one basis.

49 Cf. Ibsen and Jørgensen (1979, p. 368).

The effect of this, the first of a long series of statutory incomes policies, is difficult to assess accurately. As can be seen from figure 3.12., the rate of wage increases slowed down considerably in 1975 and even more so in 1976, compared to 1974. But until the last quarter of 1976 nominal wage increases in manufacturing were still able to outrun inflation, and, to some degree, the falling rate of nominal wage increases observed after the statutory incomes policy had become effective was due to the falling rate of inflation.[50] This in turn partially reflected international price developments.

Thus, despite the Danish government's attempt at bringing about wage restraint through statutory incomes policy, by the end of 1975 nominal hourly earnings in manufacturing had increased by 19.1 per cent[51] over 1974. Although this increase was marginally smaller than the one in 1974 (21.5 per cent), real hourly earnings in manufacturing increased by no less than 8.7 per cent in 1975, as compared to 5.4 per cent during the previous year.[52] With respect to nominal wage increases in the five countries of the present study in 1975 Denmark was second to the UK only. With respect to real wage increases it was second to none.[53]

By the end of 1976, increases in nominal hourly earnings in manufacturing had almost been halved, amounting to 12.7 per cent over 1975 (on an annual basis). While this was still well above the level of wage increases in Austria and Germany (where there was no statutory wage policy), it was also below the level of wage increases in Sweden and the UK. But still the rate of annual increase in real wages was rather high (3.4 per cent) which was surpassed only by the comparable Swedish wages.

With respect to the effect of the solidaristic component of the 1975 incomes policy solution the empirical evidence is mixed, cf. figure 3.13. (a) and (b). It is unambiguous, however, as far as public employees - both civil servants and employees hired on a contractual basis - are concerned: from 1976 onwards these two groups were the real big losers in terms of relative wage shares when their annual wages are compared to the annual wages of all workers. The reason

---

[50] "Eyeball econometrics" would suggest that the reduction in wage increases in 1975 was lagging the decline of the inflation rate by a quarter, cf. figure 3.12. Actually the greatest part of the difference with respect to wage increases in manufacturing in 1974 and 1975 came from indexation which contributed 3.5 percentage points less to the increases in 1975 than in 1974. Wage drift contributed the same amount in both years, while raises due to wage agreements were 1 percentage point lower in 1975 than in 1974, cf. OECD, Economic Surveys: Denmark (1978), p. 27.

[51] Due to a reduction in working hours by December 1974, the effective wage increase for a wage earner in employment during all of 1975 must have been about 4 percentage points lower, however.

[52] OECD, Historical Statistics (1988).

[53] Part of this marked real wage increase may be explained by the fact that the rise in unemployment affected low-paid groups disproportionally, thus raising the average wage level, cf. OECD, Economic Surveys: Denmark (1978), p. 27.

for this loss was the change from a percentage-based to a flat rate CoL-regulation of wages in 1975 which was not adequately compensated for by the new
regulatory mechanism relating wage development in the public sector to wage
development in the private sector. Also salaried employees as a group lost relative wage shares. Thus, if one compares all workers, salaried employees in the
private sector, and public employees, the incomes policy solution of 1975 seems
to have effected a certain compression of the wage structure.

On the other hand, if one compares relative wages within the group of
workers, changes in the wage structure in 1975 and 1976 seem to have been
rather modest, despite solidaristic intentions. Skilled male workers had their
relative wage position reduced a little between 1974 and 1975, but this appears
just like the continuation of a trend which had existed at least since 1970. No
further deterioration in the relative wage position of this group can be observed
in 1976.[54]

Figure 3.13.: Relative annual wages in different groups 1971-79. Index all workers=100

(a) Salaried employees, civil servants, and state employees hired on a contractual basis

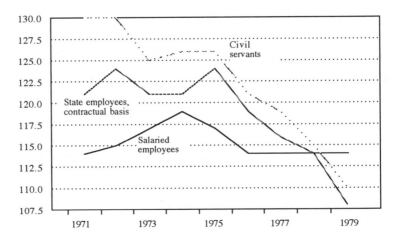

(continued)

<hr />

54 Although this is hardly the sole explanation, it may be worth noticing that the degree to
which the three higher paid groups in this comparison - public employees, salaried employees,
and skilled workers - were "victimized" by the solidary incomes policy is inversely related to
their past record of militancy, the traditionally least militant group (public employees) losing
most in terms of relative wage shares.

(b) Skilled male workers, unskilled male workers, unskilled female workers

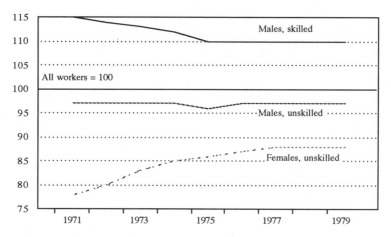

Data: Vejrup Hansen (1982, p. 43)

Unskilled male workers also lost a little with respect to relative wage shares in 1975, compared to 1974, but recouped this loss in 1976. Female unskilled workers, finally, had their relative wage position improved in both 1975 and 1976. But, as with the relative loss of skilled male workers, this appears as the continuation of an ongoing trend rather than a development set in motion by the incomes policy solution of 1975.

It is an intriguing question why the relative wage positions of skilled and un-skilled male workers were apparently so little affected by the solidary incomes policy, while unskilled female workers were able to (allowed to) improve their relative wage position. One (hypothetical) explanation could be that some level-ling of wage differentials between female and male workers was more acceptable than a levelling of wage differentials between skilled and unskilled (male) workers. After all, there are two different principles involved in these two forms of levelling: while the levelling of sex-specific wage differentials represents a principle of "equal pay for equal work", levelling of skill-specific wage differen-tials represents a more far-reaching principle of "(more) equal pay for all work". This may have been met with more resistance and compensating wage claims from the higher paid groups.[55]

---

[55] In this context it is thought-provoking that the level of industrial conflict did increase in 1975 and 1976, compared to 1974 (cf. chapter 5). This increase might well have been brought about by the pressure put on the wage structure by the solidaristic incomes policy and the ensuing attempts to restore previous relative wage positions, cf. OECD, Economic Surveys: Denmark (1979), pp. 14-15; p. 17.

3.3. The big push: The September agreement of 1975

During the early months of 1975 the stimulating actions taken in 1974, not the least the reduction in personal taxes by January 1, did in fact succeed in raising private consumption. But this recovery was short-lived and soon gave way to new stagnation.

Despite a reduction in the discount rate from 10 to 9 per cent in January and a new reduction (to 8 per cent) in April,[56] real long term interest rates were still high, profits were falling, and the "business climate" barometer indicated little optimism, cf. figure 3.14. (a) and (b). Private investments carried their downwards trend from 1974 into 1975. The investment trend in residential and non-residential construction also pointed downwards.

Against this background of continuing stagnation tendencies in the Danish economy, and anticipating an immanent international economic upswing led by the strong nations, not the least Germany, the Danish government summoned the parliament extraordinarily in August 1975 to have it pass a package of measures designed to stimulate the economy mainly by means of a stimulation of aggregate demand.

Figure 3.14.: Indicators of private investment climate 1973-79, quarterly data

(a) Official discount rate and redemption yields on long-term mortgage bonds, per cent

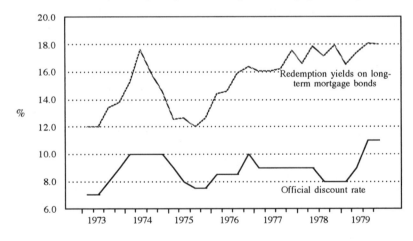

(continued)

---

[56] But when the government few days after the reduction of the discount rate from 9 to 8 per cent decided to issue for 6 bill. kr. state bonds in order to reduce the excess liquidity generated by the big budget deficit, the Copenhagen exchange almost panicked, and the National Bank could only avert a steep increase in long-term interest rates by engaging itself in massive open-market operations.

(b) Index of business expectations concerning future production 1973-79

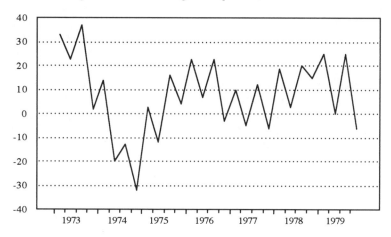

Data: OECD, Historical Statistics, file DNKQ70

Again a period of protracted negotiations between the government and various non-socialist parties was needed to reach an agreement that could be supported by a majority in the Folketing. While the plan presented by the government focused on fiscal measures to support demand and employment, the Liberals met with their own "Comprehensive Plan II" which focused on costs and called for a stabilization of wages, prices and taxes until 1979.[57] In early September a compromise on a comprehensive stabilization program (the so-called September agreement) was obtained between the Socialdemocrats and four bourgeois parties, including the Liberals. Two bourgeois parties (Conservatives and the Progress Party) chose to stay out, as did all socialist parties.

The central element in the agreement was a set of fiscal measures to support demand and employment. The VAT rate was to be temporarily lowered from 15 to 9.25 per cent in the period from September 29, 1975 to February 28, 1976 on all goods and services. Only cars, electricity, gasoline, and public charges were excluded. The compulsory saving introduced in February 1974 (at the bequest of the Socialdemocrats) was to be released, giving back about 1 bill. kr. to about 665,000 persons. Furthermore, a set of selective measures to support manufacturing was introduced, and 500 mill. kr. were set aside for special employment supporting programs, including an increase in public investment.

Primarily as a tribute to the Liberals' views there was also a declaration of intent on incomes policy, pledging the continuation of a policy of reducing the

---

[57] It would probably be too farfetched, however, to interpret this difference between the government's and the Liberals' approach as a difference between a (Keynesian) demand-side orientation and supply-side economics.

----

rate of increase of incomes, prices and costs, and improving the competitiveness of Danish industries. But concrete measures were conspicuously absent.[58] Finally the parties to the compromise agreed on a recommendation of non-monetary financing of the budget deficit in a way which would be consistent with a continuing fall in the long-term bond rate. Here the experiences from April (cf. above) probably played a role.

The measures agreed upon in the September agreement came too late to prevent 1975 from becoming the second year in a row with negative GDP growth in Denmark. But they certainly had a strong impact on economic developments in 1976, although in a way which was most probably neither wholly foreseen nor intended.

Figure 3.15.: Indicators of private consumption developments 1973-79, quarterly data

(a) Index (1986 = 100) of retail and durables sales, seasonally adjusted

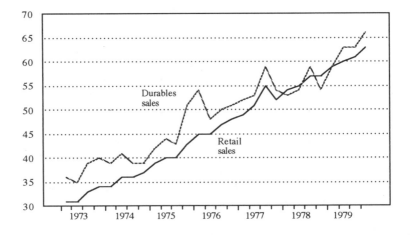

(continued)

----

58 During the debate in the Folketing the leader of the Liberals, former prime minister Poul Hartling, stressed that the parties backing the compromise had taken on an obligation to make the government secure a stable cost development. He admitted that one could not tell beforehand how this should be done, but that the commitment was no less real for this. There was a certain ring of conjuration about this statement.

(b) New passenger car registrations, seasonally adjusted (in 1000)

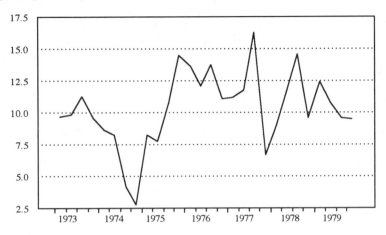

Data: OECD, Historical Statistics, file DNKQ70

As a result of the temporary reduction of the VAT-rate, private consumption increased strongly in early 1976, and there was a certain increase even after the VAT-rate had been restored to its original level.[59] The most marked effect of the reduction in the VAT-rate was on the sale of durables and passenger cars, cf. figure 3.15. (a) and (b).

The reduction of the VAT-rate also led to a temporary increase in residential construction[60] which, however, was soon slowed down again by the steeply increasing long-term interest rate level (cf. figure 3.14. (a)). Business investments grew by about 12 per cent,[61] while public consumption and investment contributed relatively little to the higher level of economic activity, both growing by about 3 per cent in 1976.

Thanks to a certain revival of economic activity in a number of major OECD-countries, especially Japan, Germany and the US, Danish exports also grew in 1976. In the first half of 1976 exports of goods was 13 per cent higher (in Danish kr.) than in the first half of 1975, while in the second half of 1976 exports exceeded the corresponding 1975-figure by 20 per cent.

Altogether, then, the economic policies did in fact succeed in bringing about a much desired spurt of growth in the Danish economy in 1976, which came to

---

[59] Real consumption increased by almost 7.5 per cent in the first half of 1976 relative to the previous half year, cf. OECD, Economic Surveys: Denmark (1977), p. 22.

[60] This development was aided further by making special cash loans as well as mortgage bonds with prolonged maturity available for residential constructions started prior to April 1, 1976.

[61] Special depreciation allowances were provided for, if fixed investments were started in 1976.

amount to 6.5 per cent of GDP. By far the most important contribution to this growth rate came from the growth in private consumption.[62]

Despite the economic growth rate achieved in 1976 - the highest among the five countries in the present study - unemployment was only marginally affected. As can be seen from figure 3.9., the only visible effect was a small drop in the unemployment figure around the middle of 1976, which soon gave way to a rise towards the previous level, however.

If one looks at employment instead of unemployment, the balance appears a little more favorable. Between 1975 and 1976 total employment actually increased by 1.7 per cent (1.5 per cent in the private as against 2.4 in the public sector).[63] But as the total labor force at the same time grew by 1.8 per cent, the growth in employment was not even sufficient to absorb this growth in the labor force.

All together, the expansionary policies adopted in 1975 did achieve little more than to arrest the growth in unemployment in 1976. The improvement hoped for did not materialize.

Furthermore, the economic expansion of 1976 came at the price of an extremely strong growth in imports and a rapidly deteriorating balance of payments. In 1976 imports increased by 29 per cent (in Danish kr.) over their 1975-level. The current account deficit quadrupled (cf. figure 3.10.) and totalled 11.5 bill kr., or close to 5 per cent of GDP. Net foreign debt sky rocketed, increasing from 26.8 bill. kr. in 1975 to 40.6 bill. kr. in 1976.

In the words of the normally cautious OECD-experts, the economic developments in Denmark after the September agreement were "disappointing".[64] They clearly demonstrated that there was a narrow limit to what could be achieved by a demand stimulating policy which was not sufficiently backed by international economic developments nor sufficiently coordinated with the economic strategies of other actors, especially in the labor market.

4. 1976-79: From stop-go to "demand twist"

The general failure of the expansionary policy laid down in the September agreement forced a reconsideration of the Danish economic situation and a reorientation of Danish economic policy, beginning in the second half of 1976. With respect to economics one of the lessons learned was that the recession could not be treated as just a passing problem, but that it was obviously a very resistant one. Furthermore, experience had now shown that for the time being economically strong foreign countries could not be relied on to come to the rescue of weaker countries like Denmark by acting as locomotives driving the whole train

---

62 OECD, Economic Surveys: Denmark (1977), p. 23.

63 The figures are computed from data in Buksti (1984, p. 220).

64 OECD, Economic Surveys: Denmark (1977), p. 49.

forwards towards an economic recovery. With respect to politics one of the lessons of the 1975-election, reinforced by numerous polls taken since then (and, by early 1977, by the results of still another election) was that in terms of popular support the government was obviously not hurt by unemployment. Politically the government could survive even the existent high and persistent unemployment levels.

While regaining full employment undoubtedly remained a central ideological goal of the economic policy of the Socialdemocratic government, it was recognized that the attainment of this goal could only be approached in small, cautious steps rather than in a few big leaps, and that other fundamental imbalances in the Danish economy had to be taken care of simultaneously, not least the balance of payments deficit. Therefore the period beginning in the second half of 1976 saw the development of a new, more multi-faceted approach to crisis policy. New instruments were put to use, and some of those already in use were aimed differently.

With respect to demand management, demand expansion was gradually replaced by "demand twist". Fiscal and budgetary policy increasingly aimed at replacing "import heavy" consumption by labor intensive consumption. In practice this meant curbing private consumption (which is import intensive) in favor of expanding public employment and consumption (which is labor intensive). By this twist it was hoped to achieve an improvement with respect to employment without too strong negative repercussions on the balance of payments.

Statutory incomes policy was continued and even tightened in order to keep Danish wage rises in line with wage developments in the main competitor countries. At the same time attempts continued to use incomes policy to inject a solidary element into the economic crisis policy.

Furthermore, a certain shift occured in the exchange rate regime, too. Between 1972 and 1976 there had been no direct adjustment in the exchange rate of the Danish krone, but as a consequence of the Danish participation in the "snake" there had been an effective 8 per cent revaluation relative to the floating currencies (US$ and sterling). But beginning in 1976 the effective exchange rate of the Danish krone was kept approximately constant by repeated minor exchange rate adjustments.

Monetary policy continued to play a minor role only in connection with stabilization policies. The main task assigned to Danish monetary policy was still to secure the financing of the external deficit.[65]

Finally there was a certain shift from passive to active labor market policy. Although the proportion of total labor market expenditures, which might be labelled active, remained low, not least in comparison with the situation in Sweden, the period after 1976 saw the gradual emergence of a number of programs aimed at the demand- and supply-sides of the labor market.

---

[65] Cf. Thygesen (1979).

4.1. The politics of "demand twist"

The main methods to achieve the desired twist from private to public consumption were repeated increases of indirect taxes, especially the VAT and various conventional indirect taxes (alcohol, beverages and tobacco), in order to curb the growth in private consumption, and a strong increase in public employment and in public outlays. Such tax increases were normally implemented as parts of more comprehensive package deals in the mould of the September agreement of 1975.

Thus in August 1976 a compromise on a restrictive economic policy package was reached between the government (Socialdemocrats) and three small bourgeois parties, primarily as a reaction to the growing balance of payments deficit.[66] As part of this compromise indirect taxes were raised with an estimated revenue effect of 5 bill. kr., and there was also a relatively small one-year employment program in the package (0.6 bill. kr.). By the end of February 1977, following a general election[67] in which - despite the poor economic record - the Socialdemocrats were the big winners (plus 12 seats), there was a raise in other indirect taxes, and a new surcharge on electricity consumption was introduced. This was joined to an agreement on temporary employment supportive initiatives at an estimated cost of 0.8 bill. kr.

But these were just appetizers. The clearest expression of the "twist-policy" was probably the August compromise of 1977, as it combined both rises in indirect taxes and rises in public expenditures on a series of employment promoting measures.

This time the deal was struck between the Socialdemocrats and the three "old" bourgeois parties (Liberals, Conservatives, and Radical Liberals). Negotiations had been extremely difficult, not the least because tactical considerations had played an unusually important role - even by Danish standards - for most participants.[68] The forced 5 per cent devaluation of the Danish krone in the wake of the Swedish devaluation and exit from the "snake" had further complicated the situation. But in the end a compromise was reached.

The annual revenue effect of the indirect tax increases agreed upon in the August compromise was estimated at 7.3 bill. kr. annually. The raises affected

---

[66] As usual, the socialist parties stayed out, as did the Progress Party. But this time the Liberals stayed out, too, while the Conservatives lent support to most of the package. In the subsequent general election of February 1977 this change in policy positions by the two parties was clearly reflected in the voters' perception of their relative positions, cf. Nannestad (1989a, pp. 142-144), the Conservatives reaping a sizeable reward in votes and seats for coming out of their self-chosen isolation.

[67] See Nannestad (1989a, pp. 138-140) for details.

[68] The Liberals had attempted - not without some initial success - to use the situation to forge a four-party cooperation between themselves, the Conservatives, the Center Democrats, and the Christian Peoples' Party; the Socialdemocrats had manoeuvred very much with a view to break up this threatening constellation.

mainly the VAT (the VAT-rate was increased from 15 per cent to 18 per cent) and indirect taxes on cars, gasoline and fuel oil.

On the other hand an agreement was reached on a comprehensive employment program extending (as a novum) over a period of several years (1978-80). By means of investments in energy conservation, measures to stimulate production, growing public employment, and a specific youth employment program it was hoped to increase employment by 40,000 persons on an annual basis. The total cost of this employment package was estimated at 10 bill. kr.

Besides these two "twist-related" sets of measures, a set of cost dampening measures was enacted. They introduced more favorable depreciation rules and the special deductions for investment in equipment, in force since September 1975, were prolonged. Moreover firms were to be compensated for part of their expenditure on sickness benefits.

Altogether the net result of the August 1977 compromise was hoped to be an increase in employment by 20,000 - 30,000 persons a year (according to official guestimates), but there was considerable disagreement on that point.[69] Also the two central imbalances in the Danish economy were expected to improve. The measures were estimated to reduce the budget deficit by about 3 bill. kr. a year and the balance of payments deficit by about 2 bill. kr. a year.

The restrictive line in fiscal policy was continued after the formation of a Socialdemocratic - Liberal coalition government in August 1978. The coalition partners had agreed on a program intended to decrease the budget deficit and to put a ceiling on the increase in incomes and prices. In September the VAT-rate was once more increased (to 20.25 per cent), and an incomes and price freeze was introduced for the period until March 1, 1979, i.e. while negotiations on a central agreement were in progress in the labor market. Prices were not allowed to increase except to compensate the effect of price increases on raw materials and contractual wage gains.

In June 1979 a new round of "demand twist" was entered. This time indirect taxes on all forms of energy were the central object. Taxes on gasoline, fuel oil, gas and electricity consumption were increased, making for price increases on energy of about 20 per cent. These increases were estimated to raise revenues by 4.5 bill. kr. a year.

At the same time the employment stimulating measures, agreed upon in the August 1977 compromise, were to be stepped up for both 1979 and 1980. An additional 0.35 bill. kr. a year were earmarked for this purpose.

The measures of June 1979 were already taken under the impression of the onset of the second oil price hike in the wake of the Iranian revolution and its repercussions on the balance of payments. As in 1973-74 Denmark found itself confronted with deteriorating terms of trade and an international economic recession on top of the existing imbalances. In October the Socialdemocratic -

---

[69] According to the Council of Economic Advisers, and contrary to the more optimistic evaluations by government experts, the net result on employment was actually going to be negative, cf. Dansk økonomi (1977).

Liberal government broke down. The outcome of the general election caused by the break-up of the coalition was still another Socialdemocratic minority government,[70] which found it increasingly difficult to marshal support behind its economic policy. With the prospect of an increasing balance of payments deficit, a foreign debt closing in on the 100 bill. kr. mark (reached in 1980) and a mounting domestic debt,[71] Denmark, in the words of the Socialdemocratic minister of finance, found itself close to the brink of the abyss.

Did the "demand twist" strategy work in the period up to 1979, when new problems complicated the situation still further? As usual this type of question is difficult to answer conclusively. According to Hansen et al. (1988, p. 145) the policy was insufficient at best, given the magnitude of the economic problems facing Denmark.

With respect to unemployment, government experts have estimated the employment effect (net) of the "demand twist" policy to have been 11,000, 15,000 and 22,000 persons in 1976, 1977 and 1978, respectively.[72] This has to be compared to annual unemployment figures of 133,000, 164,000 and 191,000 persons in the three years. Thus it would seem that, at best, the "demand twist" policy was able to prevent unemployment from rising even more. The reduction in unemployment in 1979 was not the effect of the "demand twist" policy. It was caused by a newly introduced labor market program, cf. below.

For the same years (1976, 1977 and 1978) the balance of payments improvement achieved through the "demand twist" has been estimated to have been 1.0 bill., 1.1 bill., and 1.1 bill. kr. This must be compared to balance of payments deficits in 1976, 1977 and 1978 amounting to 12.3 bill., 11.1 bill., and 8.5 bill. kr.

The combined fiscal and incomes policy 1974-76 had not been able to solve the "Keynesian coordination problem", as had become abundantly clear by 1976. But if the "demand twist" strategy was an attempt to circumvent the basic obstacle, at the heart of which were difficulties in achieving a sufficient degree of wage restraint, it did not succeed either. The fundamental idea of the "demand twist", to achieve macro-economic balance without potentially painful real labor cost adjustments (Calmfors, 1990, p. 26), did not work out.

---

[70] Neither the Socialdemocrats nor the Liberals were "punished" in the election of 1979: both gained a little in votes and seats, despite the break-up of the coalition, the trade unions' strong and public denunciation of its formation and policies, and the continuing poor performance of the economy.

[71] The internal debt resulted in an ample supply of high-yield government bonds of short maturity. Thus an excellent alternative to investment in production was created.

[72] OECD, Economic Surveys: Denmark (1979), p. 20.

Figure 3.16.: Indicators of effectiveness of "demand twist" policy 1976-79

(a) Unemployment (monthly data, seasonally adjusted), per cent

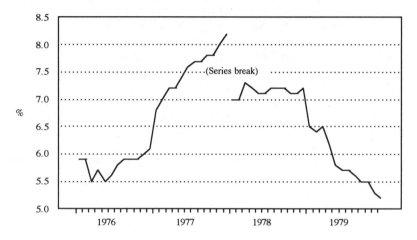

(b) Balance of payments deficit (current account, quarterly data), bill. kr.

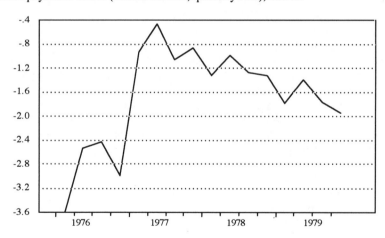

Data: (a) OECD, Historical Statistics, file DNKM270; (b) Danmarks Statistik, Statistiske
     Efterretninger: Konjunkturoversigt (var. years)

Despite a gradual tightening of incomes policy, Danish wage increases did never drop significantly below the 10 per cent mark (cf. below). In order to curb private consumption (in favor of increased public consumption), as required by the "demand twist" strategy, this continuous growth in purchasing power had to be neutralized by means of indirect taxes.[73] There was a long tradition in Danish fiscal policy making for doing just this, but it had negative impacts on the outcomes of the "demand twist" policy in at least two respects.

In the first place, raising indirect taxes did neutralize the effect of wage increases on private demand levels, but not on the domestic cost level. As a contrast, a higher degree of wage restraint would have implied an improvement in Danish competitiveness without a loss in real disposable income to Danish wage earners, since the indirect tax raises needed to keep private demand from growing would have been smaller in a situation with wage restraint. Such growth in competitiveness would have been able to stimulate total output and employment beyond what was achieved through the government's employment programs. The need to curb private consumption by means of deflationary indirect tax increases probably reduced the overall effectiveness of the "demand twist" policy as an instrument to improve the employment situation.[74]

In the second place, the steep increase in various indirect taxes necessitated by insufficient wage restraint may itself have been one of the origins of wage pressures and wage hikes in the Danish labor market (which in turn necessitated new increases in the level of indirect taxation with the consequences described above). While Andersen and Risager (1990, pp. 155-156) found that a 1 per cent rise in direct taxes leads to a similar decrease in real disposable income, this does apparently not hold for increases in indirect taxes.

This assessment of the "demand twist" strategy raises two obvious questions. First, the Socialdemocratic government had the fight against mass unemployment as its acknowledged top priority. Why, then, did it stick to such a relatively inefficient strategy in the fight against unemployment? Secondly, why did the Danish system of wage determination fail to respond to mass unemployment? Why did wage adjustments fail to accommodate to the need of increased employment, as they did in Austria? Both these questions would seem to call for an answer in terms of political variables (see chapters 4 and 5).

----

[73] The total direct tax burden stayed almost constant (as percentage of private gross factor income) from 1975 onwards. After the 1973-election no party had the stomach for increasing direct taxation, although using rising direct rather than in indirect taxes to curb private consumption might in some respects have been advantageous, because there seems not to have been any effect on wage levels from increases in direct taxes (contrary to indirect taxes which do influence wage levels), cf. Andersen and Risager (1990, pp. 155-156). On the other hand, indirect taxes are more easy to vary at short notice than are direct tax rates.

[74] See also OECD, Economic Surveys: Denmark (1979), p. 40. According to Andersen (1989), the employment losses (in the tradables sector) may even have outweighted the gains (in the non-tradables sector).

4.2. Incomes policies

The series of statutory incomes policy solutions, beginning in 1975, was subsequently continued, and there was even a certain tightening of measures in the process. There is little doubt that, given the economic situation and prospects, a majority of leading Socialdemocrats did genuinely believe in the need for an incomes policy. Thus in an article on May 1, 1976 in the Copenhagen daily "Politiken" the Socialdemocratic prime minister Anker Jørgensen defended incomes policy as the only means to escape the dilemma of having to choose between unemployment and inflation. He was remarkably outspoken with respect to what incomes policy implied for his own constituency: "There can be no doubt that a dampening of wage cost development - or, frankly spoken, wage restraint - is a decisive factor."[75] But he also stressed the central Socialdemocratic claim to an incomes policy: in principle it had to be "balanced", i.e. to encompass all kinds of incomes groups in society,[76] and it had to be socially just.

With respect to their attitude on incomes policy the Socialdemocratic government was much closer to the bourgeois parties than to the left-wing opposition. The parties of the left rejected incomes policy out of hand. The main difference separating the government and the non-socialist opposition on the incomes policy issue was primarily one of degree, the bourgeois parties usually wanting incomes policy to be more tight than suggested by the government.

The position of the trade unions was somewhat more complex. In principle and officially they rejected incomes policy. The repeated statutory incomes policy solutions of the period put heavy strains on the relationship between the Socialdemocratic Party and the trade unions. On the other hand there are indications that off the record at least some trade union leaders did accept the need for an incomes policy.[77]

But the trade unions had two concerns with respect to incomes policy. In the first place they had to take into account the activities of a rather small, but well-organized and articulate left-wing (communist) opposition within their own ranks. In connection with the "black compromise" in 1974 this opposition had demonstrated its ability to - given the right circumstances - whip up strong sentiments and mobilize a considerable part of the rank-and-file in strikes and mass

---

[75] Quoted from Bender et al. (1977, p. 116), my translation.

[76] If this is taken to include profits as well, one might, of course, wonder what could be the rationale of an incomes policy which does not allow profits to increase either.

[77] Thus in an entry of March 16, 1977, in his diaries, dealing with a negotiation between an inner circle of Socialdemocratic policy makers and trade union leaders prior to the implementation of the second statutory incomes policy solution, prime minister Anker Jørgensen quotes one trade union leader (Paulus Andersen) for actually saying that an incomes policy solution was necessary (Jørgensen, 1989b, p. 371). Although Anker Jørgensen is not an impartial witness to that meeting where he clashed heavily with the leader of the LO, Thomas Nielsen, there is no obvious reason why the remark by Paulus Andersen should not be reliably referred.

demonstrations. An open endorsment of incomes policy would have played directly into the hands of this opposition.

In the second place statutory incomes policy, especially if it is kept up over a longer period of time, in the last resort threatens the very raison d'etre of distribution-oriented trade unions by removing them from the process of determining wages and conditions of work. Therefore it is likely to draw resistance out of a simple interest in self-preservation. One of the factors in the final break-down of incomes policy in the UK had been increasing unrest among the shop stewards. Incomes policy made them look superfluous and they wanted finally to get "back into business" (Scharpf, 1987, p. 114). There are indications that this line of reasoning - which is actually very much in line with Olson's theoretical reasoning (Olson, 1965; 1982) - was also present in the Danish trade union movements' attitude towards incomes policy. Thus in his diary entry on February 23, 1977 Anker Jørgensen writes about the leader of the LO, Thomas Nielsen, with whom he had repeatedly clashed about incomes policy: "By the way, I understand Thomas' attitude. On behalf of the trade unions - and his own - he has to preserve their raison d'etre, which is a self-evident thing to us, but is not so for many of the rank-and-file."[78]

In this perspective the repeated attempts by the trade union movement to trade acquiescence in incomes policy for "Economic Democracy" (or a profit-sharing scheme) can be seen as an expression of the need for "organizational self-preservation".[79] In a situation where the unions could not offer their members the usual "goods" in the form of wage increases wrung from the employers, a break-through in the "Economic Democracy"-issue would in itself have been a result to present to the rank-and-file as an evidence of the trade unions' continuing role and raison d'etre.[80] Moreover, it would have given the unions new, important, and highly visible roles to play in the administration of the wage earner funds. These roles could then have functioned as replacements for the usual role played by the trade unions in connection with wage determination, should the latter be made obsolete by the continuation of incomes policy over a long period.[81] But as it was, all the unions were able to achieve on the

---

[78] Jørgensen (1989b, p. 360), my translation.

[79] Cf. Elvander (1988, pp. 256-281).

[80] Given the cool to outright hostile attitude towards "Economic Democracy" in broad sectors of the population it is questionable, however, how impressed the rank-and-file would have been by such a "victory".

[81] With incomes policy the trade unions were actually given a very strong argument for "Economic Democracy". If wage earners were to exercise wage restraint in order to improve competitiveness and employment, then it was reasonable to ask for some kind of guarantee that increasing profits were in fact invested in production (rather than in, for example, state bonds, the yields of which in many instances compared favorably with the profits to be expected from investment in production). "Economic Democracy" would have given this kind of guarantee. But the "Economic Democracy"-issue had originally been presented as part of an ideological offensive designed to bring about a basic change in (private) ownership to the means of production, and this ideological "original sin" made it non-negotiable even under radically

"Economic Democracy"-issue was a voluminous report from an expert commission investigating the issue 1977-78.

In the practical implementation of incomes policies evenhandedness with respect to different types of income was usually attempted by putting some restrictions on the development in non-wage incomes, and by tightening price controls. In the following the main emphasis will be on the wage aspect of incomes policies, which was the leading aspect throughout.

The first tightening of incomes policy came with the August compromise in 1976. As part of this compromise a set of incomes policy guide-lines for the upcoming contract period 1977-79 was formulated. Total wage increases were to be limited to 6 per cent per year, of which 2/3 was expected to come from the CoL-indexation. Thus what was left to the employers and trade unions to negotiate in connection with the new central wage agreements, to become effective in the spring of 1977, was a meagre 2 per cent wage increase. If the CoL-indexation resulted in more than two "portions" a year, additional "portions" were to be financed by the government and frozen in individual accounts with the Supplementary Pension Fund. This arrangement would expire by the end of August, 1979, however.

The measures directed at wage development were supplemented by a tightening of the existing price regulation. Furthermore, the Monopoly Board was given wider scope to intervene in price setting.

The incomes policy part of the August compromise of 1976 was promptly denounced by the trade unions and resulted in a wave of (illegal) wild-cat strikes in October and November 1976. Most of the conflicts can be described as an attempt at "wage hoarding" prior to a possibly even tighter incomes policy package in connection with the expiration of the central agreements in the spring of 1977, and an attempt at obtaining compensation for the rise in indirect taxes resulting from the August compromise.

As the labor market situation sharpened, so did the claims to a political reaction put forward by the non-socialist political parties. The Liberals and the Conservatives had initially suggested a total price and wage freeze. Later on they added a proposal to penalize the participation in wild-cat strikes so that participants in such actions could be fined in ordinary courts. This was totally unacceptable to the Socialdemocrats,[82] and for a while it looked as if the only way out of the political impasse was an election and the break-down of the August compromise.[83] In the end a compromise on a price, wage and rent freeze was

changed circumstances.

[82] The government at one point had been pressured into formulating a suggestion for penalty payments (to be administered by the ordinary courts) to both parts if wage increases outside the limits of the central agreement were given. But trade union resistance had been too strong, so the government swung around and ended up rejecting any idea of having ordinary justice involved in the matter of illegal strikes.

[83] Most probably an election would not have changed the composition of the Folketing decisively, and the break-down of the August compromise only three months after it was concluded would have done great harm to the credibility of the Socialdemocrats as a participant

----

reached in early December (when the wave of illegal conflicts had largely subsided). To some degree it plastered over the deep disagreements and suspicions
between the participants in the August compromise which had been uncovered
by the events.

The central element in the compromise consisted of a fairly comprehensive
price freeze. It was to be effective from December 1976 to the end of February
1977. In general only price rises on raw materials or semi-products from abroad
were allowed to be passed on in the prices.

The price freeze was also intended as a means of containing wage drift by
making employers resist wage claims more stubbornly. Besides the incentives to
employer resistance thus provided by the price freeze, the compromise also tried
to create an incentive to refrain from wild-cat strikes. All wage increases obtained
through illegal actions or wild-cat strikes were to be declared nil and void. Obligations concerning wage increases would not have to be honored by the employers
if they were the outcome of an illegal conflict. In that sense the compromise
contained a wage freeze as well.

Only a few months later the government again intervened in the labor market.
The negotiations on a central wage agreement broke down in early 1977.
Through informal contacts the prime minister at first succeeded in reviving the
negotiation process, only to see it break down again for good when a draft for a
compromise drawn up by the State Mediator was accepted by the trade unions,
but rejected by the Employers' Association.[84] The draft was promptly promulgated into law, as it was considered to be in conformity with the incomes policy
guide-lines adopted as part of the August compromise.[85]

The main point in the new incomes policy package was a minimum hourly
wage guarantee of 29 kr.. This clearly represented the continuation of a solidary
line in connection with the governments' statutory incomes policy. Other wage
increases provided for were minor only (2 times 0.7 kr. in both 1977 and 1978).
Both the CoL-indexation of wages and the "flexible wage system" were continued, although the number of CoL-regulation "portions" to be paid out to
wage earners was limited to two a year (at most). Additional "portions" were to
be covered by the state and frozen, cf. above.

In August 1978 the Socialdemocrats and the Liberals agreed on forming a

----

in political agreements of this kind. This in turn would have made it almost impossible for the
government - if it were returned - to find a majority in the future.

[84] One of the central points of disagreement was the impact of a minimum wage and increased
minimum wage levels on wages in higher paid groups. According to the employers a 1 per cent
increase in minimum wages would lead to a 0.8 - 0.9 per cent wage increase in higher paid
groups, while the trade unions estimated the effect to be 0.25 to 0.30 per cent. Interestingly,
prime minister Anker Jørgensen, himself a seasoned trade union leader, believed the employers'
figures to be realistic, at least with high employment levels (while he was less certain in an
unemployment situation), cf. Jørgensen (1989b, p. 374).

[85] It was so in a technical sense, i.e. if there would be almost no wage drift in 1977 and 1978.

coalition government.[86] Part of their common platform was a wage and price freeze running until March 1, 1979, i.e. up to the expiration date of the existing central agreements in the labor market which had been made into law in 1977.

The parties were also in agreement on a declaration of intent concerning incomes policy. The aim would be a tight incomes policy in the coming years, but it was to be mitigated by a real wage guarantee. The new government also planned tripartite negotiations between trade unions, employers and government.

The trade unions strongly resented the formation of this coalition government, the way it had been formed,[87] and the platform agreed upon. They had little incentive to make life any easier for it. Therefore "Economic Democracy" was for the first time formulated as a demand directed at the employers, when negotiations for a new central agreement in the labor market were to begin in late 1978.[88]

The Employers' Federation, on its side, simply refused to negotiate about "Economic Democracy" or, for that sake, about any other claim as long as the claim for "Economic Democracy" was not withdrawn (which in the end it was). But the employers' claims were equally unpalatable to the trade unions. They demanded, i.a., a three-years agreement, abolition of any CoL-regulation, and the suspension of the "flexible wage system".

In the end the government had to step in, putting through the Folketing yet another statutory incomes policy solution. Basically the existing central agreements were prolonged for two years, with minimum wages increased for the sake of solidarity. The problem of what to do with the two CoL-regulation "portions" which, according to the August compromise of 1976, had been paid into frozen individual accounts with the Supplementary Pension Fund was solved by

---

[86] The political background for this strange marriage will not be explored in the present context. It certainly was surprising - after all the Liberals had stayed out of the August compromise in 1976 and had, as a consequence, not supported the incomes policy legislation in March 1977 either. Instead the Liberals had tried, not without success, to forge together a four-party coalition under their leadership which could challenge the Socialdemocratic government.

[87] The trade unions felt that there had been no sufficient consultation between the Socialdemocratic party and the trade union movement prior to the formation of the government, and they singled out prime minister Anker Jørgensen the main target of their wrath. The enstrangement between party and trade union movement had gone so far that according to the trade union newspaper the leader of the Trade Union Federation (LO), Thomas Nielsen, did actually demand a public apology from Anker Jørgensen for having formed this coalition government, cf. AKTUELT, December 11, 1978.

[88] This claim was really "poisoned": provided there was going to be still another statutory incomes policy package, the government would be forced to take position on the "Economic Democracy"-issue, if it was one of the unresolved issues "left over" from the negotiations between trade unions and employers - which it could be confidently expected to be. And on the "Economic Democracy"-issue there was no chance of a compromise between the Socialdemocrats and the Liberals.

having the employers carry the expense as from September 1979. But the "portions" were to be converted into an increase in standard (paid) annual leave in 1980 (two days) and 1981 (one week). In that way the two "portions" were prevented from having an impact on private demand which would have run counter to the target of the "demand twist" policy (cf. above).

The statutory incomes policy measures in the period 1976-79, judged against their declared intentions, did not succeed, neither with respect to wage restraint nor with respect to the nivellation of wage differentials (the solidaristic target).

Despite the six per cent ceiling on wage rises agreed upon in the August compromise of 1976, wage increases in the private sector[89] were close to 10 per cent in both 1977 and 1978, and stayed at the same level in 1979, cf. also figure 3.12. above. The rise in salaries in the public and the private sector was somewhat lower, but only the salary rises of higher paid civil servants were close to the limits set by the August compromise and the subsequent statutory incomes policy solutions.[90]

Another yardstick by which to measure the (lack of) success of Danish incomes policy could be the development of Denmark's international competitiveness, as indicated by the development in relative cost. While the development in cost (and competitiveness) does not depend on wage development alone, the weight of wages in total cost is great enough to merit the use of this yardstick to assess the result of incomes policy. Moreover, the improvement of Denmark's international competitiveness was the primary reason normally given for leading an incomes policy in the first place.

But even according to this criterion Danish incomes policy was unsuccessful.[91] Except for the years 1975 and 1976 Danish wage increases were slightly higher than was the average trade-weighted wage increase abroad, despite the statutory incomes policy solutions in Denmark. Moreover, relative productivity in Denmark was decreasing somewhat after 1975,[92] so in order to offset this development, wage rises should have been even smaller. With the effective exchange rate of the Danish krone approximately constant from 1976 onwards, relative unit labor costs[93] increased somewhat between 1975 and 1979. Most likely,[94] then, Denmark's international competitiveness did not improve in the period of statutory incomes policy. It might even have worsened slightly.

The pessimistic conclusion as to the effectiveness of Danish incomes policies is

---

[89] Hourly earnings in manufacturing.

[90] Cf. Danmarks Statistik, Konjunkturoversigt (1979), p. 34.

[91] The following is based on Finansredegørelsen (1988, pp. 31-39)

[92] This could be taken as an argument in favor of the "efficiency wage" hypothesis.

[93] Defined as the product of the index for relative wages, relative productivity, and the effective exchange rate.

[94] The slight qualification is due to the fact that there must be some degree of uncertainty in measuring productivity, and there is some statistical uncertainty as well.

also supported by OECD-figures.[95] They show that although the rise in real wages per employee slowed down considerably in 1975 and even turned negative from 1976 onwards (due to the repeated rises in indirect taxes), the gap between the rise in real wages per employee and in real national income per employed person created in 1974 was far from closed. Likewise, the slow-down in the growth of real labor costs effected by incomes policy was far from sufficient to close the gap between real labor costs and productivity in the total economy which had opened in 1974-75.

Also with respect to their solidary intention the success of the statutory incomes policies appears highly debatable. As can be seen from figure 3.13., levelling of wage differentials between skilled male workers, unskilled male workers, unskilled female workers, and salaried employees stopped by 1976 (for females 1977). Only wage differentials between public employees (civil servants and public employees hired on contract) and all workers continued to diminish.

There may be several reasons for the (unintended) weakening of the solidary element in the Danish incomes policy. Vejrup Hansen (1982, p. 106) points to the gradual reduction of CoL-regulation of wages, especially by limiting the maximum number of "portions" to two a year in 1976. Since all CoL-regulation had been on a flat rate base since 1975, with the same rate applied to all kinds of wages and salaries, there had been a levelling effect from CoL-regulation, the strength of which depended on the number of "portions" triggered.

Another explanation is suggested by the OECD.[96] They tend to interpret the stop in further wage levelling as a reaction against the egalitarian profiles of the 1975 and 1977 (imposed) wage settlements leading to attempts to restore the previous wage structure through wage drift.[97] Their data show that for skilled labor wage drift did in fact become relatively more important in 1978 than in the past. This explanation appears intuitively plausible also because it makes sense to expect resistance to the solidary elements in the Danish incomes policy to have gained momentum around 1977. At that time the previous years' strong growth in real wages had by and large subsided, meaning that the wage setting "game" was changing from a positive-sum game to a zero-sum game (at best), or even a negative-sum game. This in turn meant that solidarity was becoming more expensive to the higher paid. For higher paid wage earners wage levelling was no longer a question of accepting somewhat lower real wage increases for themselves in the interest of somewhat higher wage increases given to the lower paid. It was now a question of having to accept a greater fall in real wages in the interest of a smaller or no fall in the wages of the lower paid.

---

95 OECD, Economic Surveys: Denmark (1979), pp. 39-42 (especially diagram 9).

96 OECD, Economic Surveys: Denmark (1979), pp. 14-15.

97 This also implies, of course, that the solidaristic element in the Danish incomes policy was actually contributing to continuing wage inflation and in this way counteracting the overall purpose of incomes policy, cf. also Lindbeck (1980, pp. 99-101).

4.3. (Active) labor market policy

Up to 1976 Danish labor market policy had been almost totally "passive". Its main aim had been to compensate the unemployed for their loss of income.[98] Expenditures on unemployment benefits were the all-dominating type of labor market expenditure. This approach possibly reflected the wide-spread expectation that the economic crisis was going to be short, so that the main task called for with respect to labor market policy was one of providing financial "sheltering" to those affected by unemployment. Moreover, there was no tradition in Danish labor market policy for state measures to influence demand and supply in the labor market in a more direct fashion.[99]

When it came to be recognized that the economic recession was not likely to be a mere short-term phenomenon, a certain reorientation of labor market policy in a more active direction was initiated. During the late 70s a number of specific labor market programs were introduced with the intent of influencing labor supply and demand.

In the employment program which was part of the August compromise 1977 special provisions were made to fight youth unemployment. A law of September the same year put the municipalities and counties in charge of initiatives to further youth employment. A wide range of measures were initiated, including the start of specific youth employment projects, wage subsidies to private firms taking in young people for work or training, the establishing of extraordinary positions for young people in municipalities and counties, and the expansion of education and training opportunities.

By October 1978 a job offer program for the long-term unemployed was established. Under this program people unemployed for a certain period of time became entitled to a job offer of at least nine months' duration. In order to bring forward as many job offers from the private sector as possible, the wage was heavily subsidized (close to three quarters of the minimum wage rate was paid as subsidy). But if there was no suitable job offer from the private sector, one had to be provided by the public sector, mainly the municipalities. In the end the public sector came to account for about 75 per cent of the job offers.

The avowed intention behind this program was to keep intact the working routine and work experience of the unemployed and to ease their way back into employment - if possible by using a job offer in the private sector as a stepping stone into permanent employment with that particular firm. But most important-ly, the idea was to keep people from dropping out of the unemployment in-

----

98 Unemployment benefits were quite generous both with respect to coverage and duration. Nevertheless, there is no stable empirical indication of an effect from unemployment benefits on the level of unemployment, cf. Pedersen and Westergård-Nielsen (1984, espec. p. 285).

99 This agrees well with the conventional overall pattern of state intervention in the Danish economy: there is a tradition for very little direct state intervention. For example, there is a strong anti-subsidy tradition in the industrial sector of the economy, and relatively little industrial policy, cf. Paldam (1990).

surance system. According to rules the right to unemployment benefits was lost after a person had been without a continuous work period of at least 26 weeks' duration during the last three years. The job offer program, as it was implemented in 1978, implied that, once inside the unemployment insurance system, people could in principle stay there for ever, even if they did never again find and hold a permanent job - or if, for that sake, they did not care to.

But by far the most important program was the voluntary early retirement scheme negotiated in 1978 and made effective in January 1979. Under this scheme it became possible for members of the unemployment insurance funds aged 60 to 66 to withdraw from the labor market before reaching the ordinary retirement age. If they did so under the provisions of the scheme, they would not suffer a major loss of income as they would receive a pension corresponding to unemployment benefits during the first two-and-a-half years. After that, the pension would be gradually reduced to 60 per cent of unemployment benefits, until at the age of 67 the person was entitled to the general Old Age Pension. Moreover, persons retired under the provisions of the scheme would be entitled to do a limited amount of paid work.

The program was to be administered by the unemployment insurance funds. They were also to foot the bill. The program was to be financed by increasing employers' and employees' contributions to the unemployment insurance funds.

The early retirement program quickly became a big success - a highlight in the complex of Danish crisis policy which as a whole is not exactly noteworthy for its successes. In the first year of the program alone, nearly 50,000 people did avail themselves of this new opportunity for early retirement. The drop in unemployment recorded for 1979 was mainly due to the effects of early retirement (Buksti, 1982, p. 226).

Besides the specific labor market programs various employment programs were implemented as part of the overall "demand twist" strategy, cf. above. But even if expenditures on these programs are added to expenditures on the more specifically labor market directed programs, expenditures on passive labor market measures (unemployment benefits) still exceeded expenditures on active labor market measures by a large margin. In 1978 no less than 78 per cent of all expenditures was on passive measures, while this figure had fallen to 71 per cent in 1979, mostly due to the success of the early retirement scheme.[100] In Sweden, in comparison, the relationship between passive and active measures was almost exactly the opposite.

5. Summary

Surveying the general features of the Danish economic crisis policy 1974-79, "too little too late" would probably appear the most fitting shorthand characteristic of the major part of it. After the cataclysmic years of 1974 and 1975, the

---

[100] Cf. NU (1984).

economic policies enacted sufficed to stabilize the imbalances in the Danish economy at, by and large, their existing levels. For the rest, there was only the Micawberian hope that something might turn up. But, as was to become evident with the second oil price crisis, this was a risky and in the long run unsustainable position.

Nevertheless, politically the Socialdemocratic government could live with the economic situation as it was. Cynics might even say that the party thrived on unemployment: following the "landslide election" of 1973 the Socialdemocrats increased their share of the vote in every election during the rest of the 70s, regardless of the state of the economy in general and of employment in particular.

One of the central impediments to a more successful approach to economic crisis policy making was the failure to obtain sufficient trade union cooperation with the Socialdemocratic government's crisis strategy. While some of the disagreement between these two actors was certainly displayed for tactical reasons, with the purpose of preserving unity in union ranks, there undoubtedly also was a very real core of dispute about the right choice of strategy. In the process the traditionally very close ties between the Socialdemocratic party and the trade union movement were at times strained to a degree which brings to mind the controversies between the British Labour Party and the trade unions in the late 60s and late 70s.

Unable to obtain the consent, not to mention support, of the trade unions and unwilling to practice a "shut up" style of policy making (Damgaard et al., 1989, p. 5) with respect to them,[101] the government hence had to choose a cautious, middle-of-the-road approach which hopefully would accomplish some of what was needed in the situation, without being too offensive to known trade union points of view. Thus the policies implemented were mostly compromises between positions which were hard to reconcile. The outcomes were in a number of cases contradictory or somewhat inconsistent. For example, the degree of compensation through wage indexation was reduced, but the principle of wage indexation was not abolished; tight limits for wage increases were adopted, but the "flexible wage system" with its provision for free wage negotiations at plant level, even while a central agreement was in force, was not suspended. The increase in private consumption was contained by rising indirect taxes resulting in additional wage pressure with a tendency for further rise in consumption. The egalitarian profile of the statutory incomes policy solutions of 1977 and 1979 also resulted in increasing wage pressure and hence the solidary goal of incomes policy contributed in effect to the undermining of the wage restraint target of the same policy.

With the essential strategic coordination not forthcoming, the road to a successful Danish crisis policy was blocked. "Muddling through" was the only alternative.

---

[101] The bourgeois government taking office in 1982 employed this policy style with some success, cf. Damgaard (1989, pp.76-79).

Chapter 4
Unemployment on Demand?

For the sake of reference the average economic performance of the five countries of this study during the first recession period (1974-79) is briefly summarized in table 4.1. by means of four key economic indicators. For comparison
corresponding figures are given for the last full year prior to the first oil price
hike (1972) and for the year marking the transition to the second phase of the
international recession (1979).

Table 4.1.: Economic situation according to four indicators 1972, 1979, and 1974-79

	Austria	Germany	Denmark	Sweden	UK
Average 1974-79:					
Growth (GDP)	3.0	2.5	2.1	1.9	1.4
Inflation (cons. prices)	6.3	4.7	10.8	9.8	15.7
Unemployment	1.8	3.2	6.1	1.9	5.4
B-o-P (pct. of GDP)	-1.9	1.0	-3.3	-1.4	-1.0

	Austria	Germany	Denmark	Sweden	UK
1972:					
Growth (GDP)	6.2	4.2	5.4	2.2	2.2
Inflation (cons. prices)	6.3	5.5	6.6	6.0	7.1
Unemployment	1.2	0.8	1.3	2.7	4.2
B-o-P (pct. of GDP)	-0.8	0.5	-0.3	1.3	0.3

(continued)

	Austria	Germany	Denmark	Sweden	UK
1979:					
Growth (GDP)	4.8	4.1	3.7	4.3	1.6
Inflation (cons. prices)	3.7	4.1	9.6	7.2	13.4
Unemployment	2.1	3.2	6.0	2.0	5.6
B-o-P (pct. of GDP)	-1.6	-0.7	-4.5	-2.2	-0.3

Data: OECD. Economic Outlook (1983; 1990); Danish unemployment: Paldam and
    Rasmussen (1980)

If one concentrates on what must conceivably be the most salient economic
issues from the point of view of the ordinary citizen, unemployment and
inflation, the five countries under study may conveniently be classified according
to their degree of success in fighting off stagflation as in table 4.2.:

Table 4.2.: Crisis performance of the five countries with respect to stagflation 1974-79

		Inflation	
		low	high
Unemployment	low	AUSTRIA	SWEDEN
	high	GERMANY	DENMARK UK

If we turn to the unemployment dimension specifically, the performance of
Austria and Sweden is seen to top the list. In both countries, joblessness was
successfully kept in check throughout the whole period under consideration.[1] In
the three remaining countries, the period 1974-79 saw the return of mass

---

[1] Actually this success was in a sense continued into the 80s, although unemployment did rise
in both countries: Compared to other OECD-countries, Austria and Sweden still managed to
keep unemployment at relatively low levels. This performance is often ascribed to their success
in preventing unemployment to develop during the seventies in the first place.

unemployment.[2] Due to national differences in how unemployment data are collected,[3] more detailed comparisons of the relative extent of joblessness between these three countries are bound to be rather unreliable and shall hence not be attempted. In the following we shall content ourselves with working with two groups of countries only - those which managed to fight off unemployment, and those which did not. For that limited purpose the figures are good enough.

With respect to inflation the ordering of our countries in table 4.2. turns out to be somewhat different. Austria and Germany stand out as low-inflation economies and are in that respect clearly offset from the other three countries.

In the next two chapters I shall try to offer an explanation of the position of the five countries on each of the two dimensions in table 4.2. I shall use the theoretical framework provided by Rational choice theory (or "New Political Economy"). The topic of the present chapter will be unemployment, while inflation is dealt with in chapter 5.

Treating unemployment and inflation separately is not meant to imply that these are totally independent problems. Even a majority of monetarists would probably agree that, at least in the short run, the Phillips-curve need not be completely vertical. On the other hand the empirical relationship between unemployment and inflation is far from being so straightforward that one could claim to have accounted for both phenomena as soon as an explanation of one of them has been provided.

The following analysis will concentrate entirely on what governments did or did not do with respect to unemployment 1974-79, and how to explain inter-country differences with respect to governmental unemployment policy. This is in agreement with conventional Keyensian economic-political thinking where the task of defending or restoring full employment by demand management is assigned to the authorities, primarily the government (Tichy, 1988, pp. 91-93). The role of accommodating or non-accommodating trade union strategies with respect to the employment situation will not be considered in the present context. The contrasting examples of Sweden and Germany have demonstrated that at least in the short run the government can keep unemployment down even when trade unions put in very limited cooperative effort only (Sweden), while the adoption of a cooperative, restrictive wage policy by the trade unions does not necessarily guarantee the restoration of full employment (Germany). With respect to the development in unemployment the government must be treated as the decisive actor.

---

[2] Defined arbitrarily as an average rate above 2 per cent.

[3] Cf. Myers (1975); Hardes (1981, pp. 219-235).

----

1. Political cost versus working class strength as incentive to fight unemployment: Two competing conflict models

In keeping with the "New Political Economy" approach chosen, the central thesis is that *variations in the incidence of unemployment are causally related to variations in the political cost of unemployment. Where the absolute and/or relative political cost of unemployment is high, politicians are induced to keep joblessness down, at least in the short run. Where this incentive is weak or absent, the political cost of unemployment thus being low, politicians can afford to adopt a somewhat more relaxed attitude towards the problem, and unemployment is allowed to rise.[4]*

In the next section the rationale of this thesis - which is actually very simple - will be further elaborated. We will consider a competing "distributive conflict" thesis suggested by Korpi (1990). After this discussion, the empirical evidence from our five countries on the relationship between political cost and the development in unemployment will be presented. In order to further strengthen the empirical results, I finally demonstrate that not only is there a relationship between the political cost and the incidence of unemployment, but there is also a relationship between the political cost of unemployment and the enacting of budgetary policies as well as of active labor market policies. There is a "transmission belt" from political cost faced by governments to the incidence of unemployment.

1.1. Political cost as incentive in anti-unemployment policy

In what follows I assume that politicians and voters are both rational individuals. By this we simply mean that in their respective roles they have individual utility functions which they do their best to optimize.

Voters may be assumed to do so in an essentially Downsian fashion (Downs, 1957). One can imagine that each voter takes up a position in a "policy space", representing his or hers preferred policy-mix. He or she votes for that particular

---

4 A related thesis is proposed by Schmidt (1984). Here the political rewards for fighting unemployment (and punishments for failing to do so) are explicitly included as possible explanatory variables to unemployment alongside a number of others. Schmidt's main conclusion is that since fighting unemployment successfully does not guarantee a political reward (defined as being able to continue in government after election day) and failing to do so does not guarantee punishment (being kicked out of office after the election) - in fact the odds seem to be equal at best - there are no strong political incentives to combat joblessness energetically. Although his study is conceptually as well as empirically too sketchy as to render conclusive results, it is still of value as a point of departure for the present investigation.

party or candidate offering a bundle of policies closest to the voter's own position.[5] In this way, voters try to maximize their utility income.

While in the present context we do not need to concern ourselves with the variables making up the utility function of the voters, we shall have to be somewhat more specific about what defines the utility function of the politicians. I assume (the habitual protestations of politicians to the contrary notwithstanding) that *the probability of re-election* plays a highly prominent part in the utility function of politicians.[6] This, of course, is just a micro-level version of the Schumpeterian definition of politics (Schumpeter, 1947).

Faced with a rational electorate, politicians must take into account the political gains and costs - in terms of increased and diminished probability of re-election - to be expected from policies and policy outcomes.[7] Rational politicians will have every incentive to attempt to redress a state of affairs, if it can be seen to be detrimental to their electoral support, and to enact policies that "pay" on election day. If, on the other hand, a particular state of affairs appears not to have any impact on popular support, then the incentives to do much about it must be supposed to be considerably weaker.[8] In terms of unemployment this implies that if high and/or rising unemployment has political costs in terms of loss of popular support, then rational politicians *ceteris paribus* must be assumed to fight joblessness more energetically than if there is no such cost associated with unemployment.[9]

But even if there are some political costs associated with unemployment, it may still be more rational to leave the situation alone, in case the policies necessary to redress it carry still higher political costs. Assuming, for instance, the usual Phillips-curve trade-off between unemployment and inflation, one should expect the politicians to be less eager to fight joblessness if the political cost of inflation exceeds the political cost of unemployment (provided, of course, inflation cannot be kept down by other means). Nor should one probably expect

---

[5] Empirical research on Danish general elections in the 70s (Nannestad, 1989a) has shown this to be a quite realistic model of voting behavior.

[6] Cf. Campbell et al. (1960, p. 5); Sartori (1973, p. 125).

[7] We thus do not take sides in the debate on whether voters react to policies or to policy outcomes, cf. for instance Fiorina (1981). The reason is that this distinction may be considered mainly an analytical one: what can be seen as policy from one perspective appears as policy outcome when seen from another perspective, cf. Nannestad (1989b, pp. 20-21).

[8] This, of course, does not preclude the possibility that they will have to do something about it for other reasons. A government faced with, e.g., a growing balance of payment deficit may eventually be forced to take counter-measures even though it is well-documented (cf. for example Paldam and Schneider (1980)) that there is no political cost (in terms of diminished chances of re-election) associated with a balance of payment deficit.

[9] This position basically agrees with the point of view expressed by Kalecki (1943, p. 75) according to which "the assumption that a government will maintain full employment in a capitalist economy if it only knows how to do it is fallacious."

rational politicians to be eager to take on the political costs of imposing an unpopular measure like income policies in order to improve employment if they cannot look forward to eventually being able to reap a still greater political profit from bringing down joblessness.

It might be argued, of course, that in the political systems included in this study, most politicians have little opportunity to affect their re-election chances by taking individual standpoints or actions. While the political parties in the five countries are certainly not monolithic entities, voting on bills in parliament usually follows party lines to such a degree that the parties, rather than the individual politicians, should be considered the real actors. The question hence is what the utility function of parties conceived as "unitary actors" (Damgaard and Svensson, 1989) might look like, and how this function relates to the utility functions of the individual politicians.

If - as assumed - all politicians strive individually to maximize their chances of re-election, and if decision making in the parties is democratic, in the sense of being designed in such a way as to make sure that aggregate preferences should reflect individual preferences as closely as possible,[10] then parties as unitary actors should be expected to pursue policies that maximize the chances of re-election for its politicians. Under these assumptions, then, it would not matter if we consider the individual politician or the party as actor.

But political realities are not all that nice and rosy. It might be more realistic to assume that party policies are mainly determined by a leadership group and that the rank and file just follows suit. Party leaders are probably not as much concerned about their re-election prospects as are rank and file politicians, and need not be. After all, party leaders normally have safe seats and can hence face the prospect of an electoral set-back with considerable greater equanimity than backbenchers as far as their personal electoral fate is concerned.

Instead of re-election, influence and power may be assumed to be the central elements in the utility function of party leaders. In order to maximize their utility, they will hence have to maximize (under certain constraints, cf. Nannestad (1989, pp. 195-197)) vote share of their party.

But even if a party, conceived as a unitary actor, pursues a vote maximization policy, this need not collide with the interest of the individual rank and file in the maximization of their re-election chances. Quite to the contrary: under ordinary circumstances, maximizing the party vote will be the best way to maximize the re-election probability of the incumbent politicians. The interests of the leaders and the rank and file do hence converge in this respect. For that reason we may continue to speak of the chance of re-election of the individual politician. We just keep in mind that we might as well have cast the discussion in terms of party vote maximization.

---

10 In the present context we may conveniently disregard the aggregation problem, cf. Arrow (1951).

1.2. A "conflict hypothesis" of unemployment

The "political cost" thesis of unemployment is in some respects rather close to the "conflict hypothesis of unemployment" developed in Korpi (1990). Both theses view the incidence (or lack of incidence) of unemployment as the outcome of a strategic policy choice by government. But there are also important differences some of which have to be made clear.

According to the thesis proposed by Korpi, the incidence of unemployment reflects the outcome of a distributive conflict between the working class and business interests (or capital), mediated through government policies. While the rational interest of the working class is to keep up employment levels, business may well be interested in a certain amount of unemployment in order to keep down wages, curtail inflation, reduce the profit squeeze, and generally discipline the workers by exposing them to the risk of job loss and economic insecurity. The outcome of this conflict, viz. the incidence or non-incidence of unemployment, then logically comes to depend on the relative strength and power of the working class. Where the working class is strong, it can decisively influence government policy making, and unemployment will be kept at bay; where it is less strong, governments may be tempted into using unemployment as a cure to inflation, the profit squeeze, and political unrest (Korpi, 1990, p. 24).

One of the central assumptions behind Korpi's thesis must obviously be that unemployment, by virtue of what it can achieve, is to the advantage of business interests in society. But need that really be so? On closer inspection it turns out to be a rather dubious assumption (although of noble Marxist extraction), for mainly two reasons.

The first reason is that even in case unemployment actually does all those nice things (from the point of view of business interests) it entails costs to capital too. The slow-down of the economy associated with unemployment means reduced demand which may turn out to be fatal to enterprises. In Denmark, at least, a quite reliable relationship between the number of bankruptcies (measured as the number of bankruptcy cases terminated in court) and unemployment can be found for the period 1947-73. Fitting the crude regression model (with the lagged endogenous variable to take into account that one case of bankruptcy may subsequently contribute to others)

$$TERMBNK_t = b_1 TERMBNK_{t-1} + b_2 U_t$$

where

$TERMBNK_t$ = number of bankruptcy cases terminated in court in year (t)

U_t = Unemployment year (t)

the coefficients and statistics given in table 4.3. are obtained.[11] As can be seen, increasing unemployment from about 1 per cent to, e.g., 6 per cent would increase the number of bankruptcies by about 25 per cent compared to the average figure (214 bankruptcies per year) for this period.

Table 4.3.: Coefficient values and statistics for bankruptcy model, Denmark, 1947-73

Variable	Coeff.value	S.E.
TERMBNK$_{t-1}$	0.84	0.09
U$_t$	13.66	6.55
ρ	0.46	0.23
R^2	0.815	
Ljung-Box Q(12)	7.037	

This point is also illustrated in figure 4.1. It shows the development of the number of bankruptcies and of temporary insolvencies together with the development in unemployment figures in Denmark 1970-80.[12] Unsurprisingly [13] - since bankruptcies and forced closures are one of the ways in which redundancies in the labor market are created - unemployment and business closures as well as "near-closures" tend to develop together in this period too. Thus obviously business does not get unemployment for free. If, despite of that, we want to maintain the view that business is interested in creating unemployment, then obviously the gain resulting from, e.g., reduced nominal (and, hopefully, real) wage growth has to be weighted against the losses resulting from reduced aggregate demand. This condition need not be fulfilled at all, or it may be fulfilled only in some sectors of the economy but not in others. In the latter case, which may appear the most plausible one, some business interests might indeed be furthered by unemployment, while others would not. Thus it seems doubtful if business interests (or capital) should really be treated as a homogeneous social force with a unified interest in making the government use unemployment "as a cure to inflation, the profit squeeze, and political unrest", which is the way it is implicitly treated by Korpi.[14]

---

[11] The coefficients are estimated using the Hildreth-Lu method in order to take care of the 1. order auto-correlation in the series.

[12] The figures on bankruptcies and temporary insolvencies are taken from Danmarks Statistik (1982).

[13] Cf. for example Bernanke (1981).

[14] The obvious counter-argument would be that it is not capital as such but the dominating fraction(s) within capital which have their interests served by government. For this argument to stick in the present context, however, empirical evidence would have to be provided to the effect that the dominant fraction(s) of capital do coincide with those segments of business which will

Figure 4.1.: Number of bankruptcies and temporary insolvencies (left scale), with unemployment (right scale, per cent), Denmark, 1970-1980

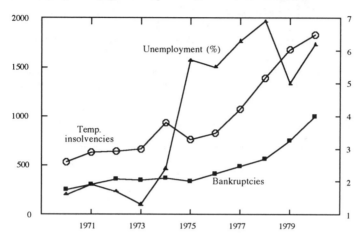

Data: Danmarks Statistik, Statistisk Årbog (var. years)

There is a second reason why unemployment need not suit the interests of capital. Going for unemployment can obviously be a rational strategy only if unemployment does actually alleviate the profit squeeze (by reducing wage growth), discipline the workers, etc. But is that really how unemployment works in the mixed economy of a welfare state? Available historical evidence would seem to raise some doubts about that, at least as far as the countries and the time period under scrutiny here are concerned.

If business, as suggested by Korpi, was in fact interested in making governments use the economic turmoil brought about by the external shocks delivered to Western economies in 1973 as a pretext to create unemployment (or at least let it develop) in order to alleviate the profit squeeze by putting a curb on wage growth and, in general, to discipline the workers, one would have to expect such an interest to have its foundation in previous experiences to the effect that unemployment actually was a reliable means to achieve these ends. With respect to wage growth the "unemployment-strategy" ascribed to business by Korpi seems to lack this foundation, however. As noted by Paldam (1980, p. 216), "(e)ven though many attempts have been made to explain the behavior of the nominal wage rate, it remains one of the ambiguous areas in economics."[15]

---

not be hurt by the loss of aggregate demand due to unemployment.

[15] This is also clearly brought out in the survey of the literature by Santomero and Saeter (1978).

His analysis of the Phillips-curve relationship for 17 OECD-countries in the period 1953-72 highlights this ambiguity, showing (in line with much of the literature) "... that the Phillips curve is a phenomenon which manages, at the same time, to be significant, inadequate and rather shifty."[16] Thus, given the unreliability of the relationship between unemployment and nominal wage growth, and with an eye to the cost aspect alluded to above, there is reason to doubt that pushing for unemployment really was a rational strategy for business by which it could ultimately hope to do something about the profit squeeze.

Figure 4.2.: Development in nominal wage growth in manufacturing 1973-79

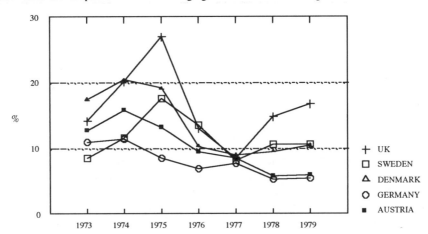

Data: Paldam and Rasmussen (1980)

A second, related question is if unemployment was really central to the development in nominal wage growth once the international recession had become manifest around 1974. We may try to get a hint to the answer by looking at the actual development in nominal wage growth in our five countries during the recession 1974-79 following the first oil price shock. This development is shown in figure 4.2.

As can be seen, the pattern of development with respect to nominal wage growth 1974-79 does not differentiate sharply between full employment and unemployment countries. Everywhere growth rates tended to fall, regardless of the incidence or non-incidence of unemployment. But the strongest similarity, in that respect, is between Germany (an unemployment country) and Austria (a full employment country), while the development in the other full employment

---

16 One of the more puzzling results reported is that for the UK the coefficient to unemployment is positive in two out of three cases (Paldam, 1982, pp. 237-238). The reason is probably that intra- and inter-period tendencies get confounded.

country of this study, Sweden, appears to be closer to the development in the two other unemployment countries, viz. Denmark and the UK, than to the development in Austria. This would seem to raise some doubts as to the relevance of unemployment to the outcome of the distributive conflict over nominal wage growth in that period.

But, still according to Korpi (1990, p. 24), at the eve of the first oil crisis unemployment was viewed not only as a means of bringing down nominal wage growth. It was conceived as a means to "cure political unrest" by which is probably meant working class militancy which had indeed been increasing since the second half of the sixties, cf. Paldam and Pedersen (1982). Here one may ask if there is evidence from post-war experience of a relationship between unemployment and working class militancy. This would be necessary if we were to assume that business interests would seek to exploit the economic situation generated by the first oil price shock to influence the government and get it to allow unemployment to increase.

We shall attempt to shed some light on this question using a simple regression approach. Taking, as an indicator of working class militancy, extent of industrial conflict per year, the following strike model[17] is fitted to three sets of data from 1945 to 1973, using OLS as estimation method:

$$C_t = a + b_1 WM_t + b_2 C_{t-1} + b_3 U_t$$

where

C_t = Extent of industrial conflict in year (t), measured as
   STNA = Number of industrial conflicts (index)
   STDA = Number of working days lost due to
    conflict (index)
   STWA = Number of workers affected by conflict
    (relative to size of population; index)
WM_t = Nominal wage growth
U_t = Unemployment

The results can be seen in table 4.4. The fit varies from a satisfactory level to virtually no fit at all.[18]

---

[17] The model is taken from Paldam and Pedersen (1987), using the same data set. Thanks are due to Martin Paldam for making the data available to me. For a discussion of some problems of validity with connection to strike data the reader is referred to chapter 5.

[18] In general autocorrelation presents no problem, except with the two models (C_t = STDA) and (C_t = STWA) in the case of Sweden and (C_t = STNA) in the case of the UK. Re-estimating these models with the Hildreth-Lu procedure (to take care of the autocorrelation) does not yield substantially different results, so the OLS-estimates are reported here.

Table 4.4.: Coefficient values and statistics from strike model 1945 - 1973 with different
operationalizations of industrial conflict

	Austria	Germany	Denmark	Sweden	UK
C_t = STNA					
CONST	-	-	-1.44	1.70	17.87
(SE)			(7.41)	(3.01)	(7.21)
WM_t	-	-	1.17	0.01	0.97
(SE)			(0.48)	(0.09)	(0.46)
C_{t-1}	-	-	-0.17	0.67	0.56
(SE)			(0.29)	(0.13)	(0.17)
U_t	-	-	0.18	-0.31	-3.38
(SE)			(1.21)	(1.35)	(3.19)
R^2	-	-	0.242	0.733	0.395
Durbin's h	-	-	n.d.[a]	-0.666	2.080
Ljung-Box Q(14)	-	-	14.772	3.634	6.155

	Austria	Germany	Denmark	Sweden	UK
C_t = STDA					
CONST	37.28	1.25	-171.44	-489.45	-94.06
(SE)	(31.74)	(13.60)	(165.71)	(191.33)	(34.37)
WM_t	-1.93	0.93	24.26	-2.67	5.69
(SE)	(2.44)	(1.28)	(11.14)	(11.93)	(3.48)
C_{t-1}	-0.04	-0.07	-0.02	-0.24	0.08
(SE)	(0.26)	(0.22)	(0.28)	(0.16)	(0.17)
U_t	-3.61	2.34	11.22	244.09	79.53
(SE)	(5.57)	(1.61)	(21.41)	(66.68)	(24.35)
R^2	0.040	0.102	0.191	0.431	0.607
Durbin's h	n.d.	n.d.	n.d.	6.092	-0.920
Ljung-Box Q(14)[b]	3.073	6.380	7.396	14.358	5.700

(continued)

	Austria	Germany	Denmark	Sweden	UK
C_t = STWA					
CONST	7.02	1.68	-11.18	-8.08	2.78
(SE)	(11.81)	(2.26)	(11.72)	(2.29)	(8.56)
WM_t	0.02	0.07	2.11	0.17	-0.23
(SE)	(0.90)	(0.22)	(0.77)	(0.14)	(0.90)
C_{t-1}	0.11	-0.12	-0.21	-0.41	-0.13
(SE)	(0.25)	(0.22)	(0.34)	(0.15)	(0.20)
U_t	-0.62	0.15	-0.03	4.38	12.25
(SE)	(2.12)	(0.27)	(2.02)	(0.83)	(6.28)
R^2	0.023	0.029	0.305	0.544	0.159
Durbin's h	n.d.	n.d.	n.d.	4.929	n.d.
Ljung-Box Q(14)[b]	8.968	12.082	10.294	23.725	6.261

[a] not defined
[b] For Austria Q(10); for Germany Q(12)

The figures in table 4.4. indicate that the relationship between unemployment and working class militancy as measured by the extent of industrial conflict in the period 1945 - 1973 is different for different countries. But in no case, no matter how industrial conflict is operationalized, or which of the five countries one looks at, is there a reliable tendency for unemployment to bring down the level of industrial conflict.[19] The only reliable tendencies we have are for growing unemployment in both Sweden and the UK to *increase* the number of working days lost due to industrial conflicts as well as the number of workers affected by such conflicts.[20] From this it appears that prior to the onset of the economic recession unemployment ought to have had a poor record as a cure to working class militancy.

---

[19] This finding looks robust enough, even when taking into account some of the well-known limitations of data series on industrial conflicts.

[20] See Jackson (1987, pp. 137-139) for a survey of recent findings on the relationship between unemployment and strike activity.

Figure 4.3.: Development in two indicators for extent of industrial conflict, 1973-79

(a) Working days lost

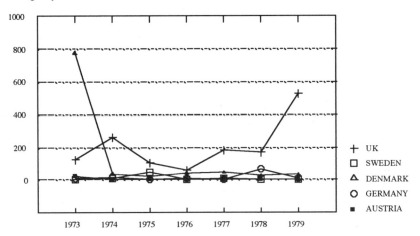

(b) Workers affected

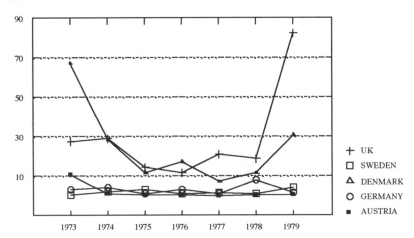

Data: Paldam and Rasmussen (1980)

We may also turn to the actual development with respect to the extent of industrial conflict in our five countries, once the crisis struck, to see if the development in unemployment actually did make for any difference in the extent of industrial conflict. Figure 4.3. shows the development of working days lost due to industrial conflicts and the development of number of workers (relative to population size) affected by conflict from 1973 to 1979.

As the figures indicate, in Austria, Sweden and Germany the level of industrial conflict stayed relatively constant in the period between the first and the second oil price shock (there is a weak tendency of increase in Germany and Sweden towards the end of the period, despite differences with respect to unemployment). In the UK, and, as far as number of workers affected is concerned, in Denmark, the level of industrial conflict remained somewhat higher than in the three other countries. This happened in face of the presence of unemployment in both countries, and there is no obvious relationship between its oscillations and the development in unemployment in Denmark and the UK. Thus, in general, unemployment does seem to be of little relevance to the development in the level of industrial conflict in the period 1974-79, just as it was found to be in relation to the development in nominal wage growth.

To summarize, creating a recession and unemployment (or allowing it to develop) seems on closer inspection to hold mixed blessings to business. It may serve to bring down nominal wage growth, but this reaction is neither automatic nor even particularly reliable. On the other hand it will increase the number of forced closures of enterprises and it will, if anything, tend to increase working class militancy. Thus, from post-war experience, unemployment certainly cuts both ways.

In order to maintain the position that the reappearance of unemployment in the wake of the first oil price hike reflects the outcome of a distributive struggle between labor and capital won by the latter and used by it - with governments in an unspecified mediating role - with the intention of bringing down wage growth (in order to alleviate the profit squeeze) and weakening working class militancy one would have to make an awkward assumption. One would have to assume that business did not possess or did not use the relevant post-war experiences, but rather relied on simplified textbook economics and an OECD policy recommendation (OECD, 1970) as the basis of strategy making. While this possibility cannot be rejected out of hand, it certainly requires some argumentative and empirical support, the provision of which is not the responsibility of those who doubt the thesis.

In fact it seems more likely that government itself (or other authorities with independent control over economic policy instruments, like the German Bundesbank) may occasionally have their own interest in creating unemployment or let it develop, if politically they can afford it. While Korpi treats governments very much as puppets of dominating class interests (another venerable Marxian relict in his model), governments also have their own fish to fry. For instance, creating a recession and unemployment might be a way to "haul the Phillips-curve back in place" by breaking inflationary expectations in both trade unions and business. This is probably what was intended with (and achieved by) the German recession of 1967-68 (Scharpf, 1987, pp. 153-154). Interpreting such government strategy as sheer compliance with the interests of business at the expense of the workers neglects that, in order to work, it has to hurt both.

1.3. Conclusion

In way of conclusion it deserves to be stressed that the criticism put forward above is primarily aimed at the deceptive simplicity of Korpi's dualistic conflict model built upon the (postulated) existence of two homogeneous, opposing social groups (working class and business), rather than at the basic idea that the incidence or non-incidence of unemployment represents the outcome of a conflict of interests and priorities. According to the main thesis underlying the present analysis, however, the basis for this conflict is not primarily that some "want" unemployment in order to strengthen their side in the distributive struggle while others - for identical reasons - do not. Rather it is that full employment in a period of crisis cannot be had for free.[21] Maintaining full employment carries costs, and the conflict is about which other goals must be sacrificed to meet these costs. The conflict is about the priority of competing goals. That is, of course, why there can be a Keynesian coordination problem in economic policy making (Scharpf, 1987) in the first place. It must be stressed that this conflict need not only - or not even primarily - set the working class against business interests. Quite to the contrary, the conflict lines may criss-cross right through the working class itself, setting, e.g., those in secure jobs against those out of job or in danger of losing their job. In the last resort the popular reaction to unemployment expressed in terms of electoral support of the government, i.e. what we have called the political costs of unemployment to government, can be viewed as an indicator of the aggregated or net outcome of this conflict about priorities.

In order to test the thesis relating the political cost and the incidence of unemployment, as a first step we shall hence have to examine the relationship between unemployment and popular support of the government in the five countries and the time period under study. This shall tell us something about the absolute political costs of unemployment in each country and allow us to relate these costs to the extent of joblessness found.

Relative costs are somewhat harder to get a grip on, except for situations where we have a straightforward trade-off, as the one commonly assumed between unemployment and inflation. As one moves beyond that and in the direction of including also what might be called the "political opportunity costs" of fighting unemployment, things quickly get elusive. For that reason, in the present context, we shall consider only the political costs of unemployment relative to the political costs of inflation. While this is certainly a crude simplification of the "relative cost structure" in the real world, it may not be so crude a simplification of how politicians think about these things.

---

21 Cf. Tichy (1988, p. 75).

2. Political cost and unemployment: Empirical findings

Returning to the central thesis of this chapter, we may now specify the empirical relationships that have to hold in order to confirm the "political cost"-explanation of inter-country variation in the extent of unemployment. In order to confirm the thesis we must be able to show that there was a substantial political cost of unemployment (in terms of loss of popular support for the government) to be taken into account in Austria and in Sweden, both in absolute terms and relative to the cost of inflation. On the other hand, as far as Germany, Denmark, and the UK are concerned, we must be able to show that there was either no political cost of unemployment at all, or, that in terms of popular support of the government, the cost of unemployment was lower than the political cost of inflation in these countries.

2.1. Some methodological problems

Since the seminal papers of Goodhart and Bhansali (1970) and of Kramer (1971), the influence of macro-economic variables on the popular support of governments has been intensively studied in many countries, giving rise to an impressive literature on *Vote-* and *Popularity-*functions (VP-functions for short). Today, despite reservations from a small number of die-hards (e.g. Norpoth and Yantek, 1983; Whiteley, 1986a, p. 82), who prefer to view the empirical findings in the literature as evidence of statistical incompetence rather than as evidence of the existence of VP-functions,[22] most scholars would probably subscribe to the conclusion arrived at some time ago in a survey of the literature (Paldam, 1981, p. 194): "The very existence of the VP function should no longer be doubted."

On the other hand it also has to be admitted - and generally is - that the results arrived at in studies of the VP-functions for various countries are in many cases not very stable, neither across time periods, types of data, model and variable specifications, etc. For that reason, evidence from various sources will have to be sifted carefully. With the noticeable exception of Austria, several independent and different studies of VP-functions are available for all countries in the present study. This allows one to cross-check the results quite extensively and in this way - hopefully - to make up for the instability of some of the results.

Strictly speaking, it is the vote function that is of main interest here. To a rational politician, seeking re-election, popularity in the polls - and the variables influencing it - should matter only as far as popularity data have proved them-

---

[22] The basic disagreement is centered around the proper use and interpretation of Box-Jenkins modelling and tests for Granger causality in the study of VP-functions. Kirchgässner (1981; 1983) has convincingly argued that the failure to find significant relationships between macro-economic variables and popular support of the government using tests for Granger causality is primarily attributable to the low statistical power of the tests employed.

----

selves to be reliable predictors of what will happen on election day. Such a politician will not be influenced by polls showing, e.g., that his popularity dwindles with rising unemployment, if from experience he knows this to be an empty threat which in the end will not materialize.

Differences with respect to the influence of unemployment in vote- and in popularity-functions, respectively, can easily be imagined. In fact there is no a priori reason why the influence of unemployment on the expression of government support should be the same when answering an opinion poll question as when actually casting the ballot. The situations from which each type of data emanates are sufficiently dissimilar - as are the possible consequences of a particular answer to a pollster compared to the decision in the vote booth - as to make differences between a vote- and a popularity-function appear entirely reasonable. Essentially, the difference is between "kicking the rascals" (in the polls) and "kicking out the rascals" (in the elections). Because of the lack of any direct and immediate consequences of the act (except for the possibly intended function as a warning shot) it should be easier for many dissatisfied voters to declare their willingness to withdraw support from the party in power in a poll than to actually do so in an election. If one compares Danish polls between elections to the electoral results proper, it appears that actual electoral gains and losses are rarely as big as the difference between the result of the previous election and the parties' standing in the polls between two elections. People obviously do behave somewhat differently in the two situations.

Table 4.5.: Interpretation of various combinations of findings on the political cost of unemployment from vote and popularity functions, respectively

| | | **Popularity function** | |
		cost	no cost
Vote function	cost	Corroboration	Yet to be seen
	no cost	Discard popularity function result	Corroboration

If the strength and, possibly, even the direction of the relationship between unemployment and government popularity in the vote function turns out to be different from what can be found by studying the popularity function, one should suspect the popularity function results of being biased in the direction of a "kick out the rascals"-reaction. Therefore, if we find no relationship between rising unemployment and loss of support of the government in the vote function, but do find such a relationship in the popularity function, the vote function result should nevertheless still be considered valid. On the other hand, if we find the same relationship in both vote and popularity functions, this will obviously strengthen our confidence in the results. Table 4.5. shows the "decision rules" according to which different possible combinations of results from vote and popularity functions will be handled.

In most cases, empirical VP-functions are estimated on the macro-level using time series on government popularity or government vote on one hand and various macro-economic time series (Inflation, unemployment, etc.) on the other. Political scientists (and others) have sometimes expressed uneasiness about this practice, pointing to the dangerous pitfalls of spuriosity.[23] According to this view, macro-level findings on the relationship (or lack of relationship) between, e.g., unemployment and popular support of the government are suspect unless tested on the individual or micro-level as well.

The point of view adopted here is a little different, and it is so mainly for two reasons. The first one has to do with the methodological and practical problems in testing macro-level findings on the relationship between macro-economic variables and popular support of the government by individual-level studies. The second one has to do with the substantive relevance of macro- contra micro-level relationships in the context of the present study. We shall consider both points in turn.

While macro-level VP-functions can be mathematically derived from a set of Downsian micro-level assumptions (cf. Kirchgässner, 1986), testing macro-level findings on the relationship between unemployment and government vote using individual-level data must be considered problematic in several respects. Most importantly, as argued by Kramer (1983, p. 93) "... of the two kinds of analyses, it is the *aggregate* time-series evidence - rather than that based on individual-level survey data - which is most likely to yield valid inferences about the underlying individual-level behavioral effects we are trying to measure." And moreover "(t)he discrepancies between the macro- and the microlevel studies are basically a statistical artifact and do not show any real disagreement about the true values of the underlying behavioral parameters of interest ... (E)ven when the *underlying* behavioral relationship that governs individual voting decisions is the same for every voter in every election, the *observable* aggregate-level and individual-level empirical relationships between measurable economic variables and votes will still differ considerably from each other."

To this two minor, practical points might be added. In the first place, the necessary data for individual-level studies would obviously have to come from opinion polls, and hence the arguments forwarded above concerning the possibility of divergent results from the study of vote and popularity functions, respectively, apply to the possibility of divergent results from macro- and micro-level studies as well. In the case of contradictory macro- and micro-level

---

23 Cf. Miller and Mackie (1973, p. 263): "When two series are correlated either may indeed cause the other, but a third explanation is that they are both dependent on some third variable. Cyclical patterns in both popularity and unemployment can account for the correlation between them and also for the autoregressive nature of the popularity series". Dinkel (1977, p. 143) expresses basically the same view.

findings it would be questionable to consider the macro-level results falsified by the results of micro-level testing. In the second place, besides being of dubious value, micro-level testing may in many cases simply not be feasible, due to the scarcity of relevant data. While today electoral surveys are routinely conducted in many countries, they are often based on an approach to the study of voter behavior very different from a rational choice approach. For that reason they normally contain much information on the voters' social background, personality, attitudes, party identification, etc., but considerably less on the role of "hard incentives".

From the arguments presented it follows that there is not much justification for regarding macro-level results on the relationship between, e.g., unemployment and the popular support of the government as suspect until confirmed by micro-level studies. The unavailability, in some cases, of relevant micro-level evidence should not by itself prevent us from using the macro-level evidence we have. Macro-level findings are valid independently of micro-level corrobation. Micro-level corrobation is nice but not necessary.

More substantive considerations would seem to lead to a similar conclusion. Seen from the perspective of a rational politician, seeking re-election, - which is the basic perspective adopted in this context - what matters is the net or aggregated relationship between the development in unemployment and votes received on election day, and not the particular nature of this relationship. Whatever it may be that causes the (macro-) relationship between unemployment and the vote - or the absence of such a relationship - the politician can happily put it into a black box to be left to political scientists to ponder over.[24] Therefore we shall accept as valid evidence from aggregate-level studies as to the presence or absence of political costs of unemployment to the government in our five countries, even when uncorroborated by individual-level findings.[25]

2.2. The political cost of unemployment: Evidence from studies of vote and popularity functions

To start with what appears to be two rather clear-cut cases from each end of the spectrum of political reaction functions, we have independent, but highly consistent results on the political cost of unemployment from both Denmark and Sweden. For Sweden Madsen (1980) has estimated a vote function for the period 1920-73. He found that the deviation from the "normal vote" of the

---

[24] A similar line of argument can be found in Jacobsen and Kernell (1982).

[25] There is one further point to consider in this matter. In general, the mere reference to the possibility of an empirical relationship being spurious should not be sufficient to dislodge an empirical finding. In such a case, the burden of proof is on the challenger: at the very least (s)he has to suggest a plausible and testable mechanism that might have produced the spurious relationship in the first place.

incumbent party (or parties) was negatively affected by both the level and the change in unemployment, and much more so than by inflation. Thus there used to be a definite political cost to the Swedish government of both unemployment and inflation with the relative cost of unemployment being higher than the relative cost of inflation. While in theory this relationship between unemployment and the vote might, of course, have changed under the impact of the recession after 1974, the results from analyses of popularity data from both pre- and post-1974 surveys suggest a stable relationship, cf. below.

With regard to Swedish popularity functions the central studies are Jonung and Wadensjö (1979) and Hibbs and Madsen (1981). Both are based on opinion poll data from 1967-78, but use quite different modelling strategies. Both studies find popular support for the Swedish government to be significantly negatively affected by rising unemployment, and both show that the government is hurt much more severely by an increase in unemployment than by an increase (of comparable magnitude) in inflation (Jonung and Wadensjö, 1979, pp. 348-351; Hibbs and Madsen, 1981, p. 45). The same result appears in Kirchgässner (1976), who uses opinion poll data from 1967-73. Thus, in this case, the results arrived at by studying the vote and the popularity function, respectively, do agree. This strongly suggests that unemployment in fact did entail political costs to the government in Sweden, both in absolute terms and relative to the political cost of inflation.

For Denmark Madsen (1980), studying the vote function for the period 1920-73, did not find any clear relationship between unemployment and the deviation from the normal vote of the coalition dominant party. The coefficients to the unemployment variable are numerically small and their sign is positive.

The findings and interpretations in Madsen (1980) have been challenged by Paldam and Schneider (1980) who estimated popularity functions for the period 1957 to 1978 from opinion poll data. Their central finding (in the present context) is a sudden change in the direction of the effect of rise in unemployment on government popularity. While there is a significant, negative relationship up to 1973, implying that unemployment had its cost to the government in terms of popular support in the polls, and more so than inflation, the relationship between unemployment and government popularity turns positive hereafter (although it just fails to attain the usual level of statistical significance). The same development was found with regard to the overall trend. Thus it appears that from about 1973-75,[26] unemployment did no longer have adverse effects on the popular support of the Danish government.

The Paldam-Schneider result has been successfully replicated in Nannestad

---

[26] Paldam and Schneider (1980) are not very precise in fixing the time of the shift. The results in Nannestad (1989b) indicate that it took place between the two elections of 1973 and 1975, respectively. That would seem to coincide with the onset of the economic crisis in 1974.

(1990)[27] using ecological vote data from major Danish cities for general elections 1966-77[28] instead of opinion poll data (as the ones used in Paldam and Schneider, 1980). In order to test their result, the following model was fitted:

$$\Delta Gv_{it} = b_1 T + b_2 TD + b_3 \Delta U_{it} + b_4 \Delta U_{it} D + b_5 d$$

where

ΔGv_{it} = Change in vote share of government party (parties) in city (i) at time (t) relative to previous election
T = Trend variable
ΔU_{it} = Change in unemployment in city (i) at time (t)
D = Dummy variable (= 1 for elections 1966-73, else = 0)
d_{73} = Dummy variable for the "landslide"-election of 1973

Here the change in the electoral trend and in the relationship between changes in unemployment and changes in the vote share of the government parties expected to occur in 1975 is modelled using a dummy variable approach.[29] Thus for the elections between 1966 and 1971 the model can also be written:

$$\Delta Gv_{it} = (b_1 + b_2)T + (b_3 + b_4)\Delta U_{it}$$

while for the election of 1973 the model becomes:

$$\Delta Gv_{it} = (b_1 + b_2)T + (b_3 + b_4)\Delta U_{it} + b_5 d_{73}$$

where the dummy variable d_{73} is included because of the very special nature of this election.[30] For the elections from 1975 onwards the model is simply:

$$\Delta Gv_{it} = b_1 T + b_3 \Delta U_{it}$$

In order to be consistent with and to support the Paldam-Schneider results, the signs of the coefficients should then be as shown in table 4.6.

---

[27] Presented at the European Public Choice Society Meeting 1990 in Meersburg, Germany. Thanks are due to the discussant, Gebhard Kirchgässner, for valuable comments and suggestions.

[28] The starting- and endpoints of the period analyzed were determined by breaks in the series.

[29] Cf. Johnston (1963, pp. 221-228).

[30] The 1973-election was a marked "protest"-election where distrust in and discontent with the hitherto dominating parties, which had accumulated in the electorate for some time, erupted. As a result, the "old" parties suffered giant losses in vote shares. For a closer account and analysis see Nannestad (1989).

Table 4.6.: Expected signs of the coefficients

Variable	Expected sign
Trend 75-77	+
Trend 66-73	-
ΔU_{it} 75-77	+
ΔU_{it} 66-73	-
d_{73}	-

Fitting the model by OLS produces the following coefficient values:

Table 4.7.: Coefficient values and statistics

Variable	1966-71		1973		1975-77	
	Coeff.	S.E.	Coeff.	S.E.	Coeff.	S.E.
T	-2.34	0.12	-2.34	0.12	1.56	0.05
ΔU_{it}	-0.09	0.11	-0.09	0.11	0.47	0.04
d_{75}	-	-	-3.37	0.65	-	-
R^2(adj.)	0.941					
D.W.	2.050					

As can be seen, the same shift from a "cost"- to a "non cost"-pattern as found by Paldam and Schneider (1980) can be detected in the ecological vote data as well. Thus again, as one might have guessed (from the fact that Denmark experienced the return of mass unemployment after 1974), there is clear evidence that for the period of interest here unemployment had ceased to have political costs for the Danish government(s).[31]

Some further corroborating evidence can be found in existing survey data covering the general elections of 1975 and 1977, i.e. in individual level data (Nannestad, 1990). In both the 1975- and the 1977-survey[32] the respondents

---

[31] When this result is compared to the results on reactive voting in Danish general elections reported in Nannestad (1989a), it would seem to suggest that as a whole people do react to policies (and policy changes) to a higher degree than to policy outcomes. Recent micro-level research (Nannestad and Paldam, 1990c) indicates that this may be true for some groups in the electorate, but not for all.

[32] The data were originally collected by Gallup Markedsanalyse A/S for a research team consisting of Ole Borre (University of Aarhus), Hans-Jørgen Nielsen, Steen Sauerberg and Torben Worre (University of Copenhagen) and are deposited in the Danish Data Archives (study numbers DDA-0016 and DDA-0166). Ole Borre kindly made his version of the

were asked to indicate which problem they considered the most important for the politicians to do something about, and the employment situation was mentioned by a sufficient number of respondents to permit a more detailed analysis.

If there were a "stability"-reaction at the individual level, i.e. if it were concern about the rise in unemployment that drove voters to the party in government (the Liberals (Agrarians) in 1975 and the Socialdemocrats in 1977), then at the very least we should expect to find a net gain[33] for the party in government among voters who considered the employment situation the most important political problem. Correspondingly, if we find that the party in government has a net loss of voters concerned about the employment situation, that would contradict the notion of an individual-level "stability"-reaction. If the net gain of the government party among those considering the employment situation the most important problem is greater than its net gain among the rest of the voters, this could be interpreted as another indication of an individual-level "stability"-reaction to rising unemployment.

But how should one interpret a situation where the government party has a net gain of voters among those who consider the employment situation the most important problem, but where this net gain is smaller than the net gain among voters who do not consider the employment situation all that important? Two interpretations seem possible here. One may argue that such a finding contradicts the notion of a "stability"-reaction. According to this view, it is because of the rising unemployment that the party in government fails to obtain the same net gain among those most concerned about the employment situation as among those most concerned about other problems. Thus the government party is - in a way - punished for rising unemployment. Alternatively one may argue that such a finding does not invalidate the notion of an individual-level "stability"-reaction to rising unemployment, since it is just indicative of the existence of a still stronger "stability"-reaction to a number of other problems. As there is no way to decide which interpretation is the correct one, we shall have to disregard the situation.

Table 4.8. (first column) shows the net gains of the Liberals in the 1975-survey among respondents considering the employment situation the most important problem and among those who were more concerned about other problems. The figures indicate that in 1975 the Liberals had a net gain[34] among respondents considering the employment situation the most important problem. This suggests an individual-level "stability"-reaction to rising unemployment. On the other

datafiles available to me. Neither he nor the other members of the research team bear any responsibility for the results and interpretations presented in the following.

[33] The net gain is measured on the basis of the recall-questions in the surveys. It is defined as the number of respondents reporting a vote for the party in government in the present election and a vote for any other party (or non-voting) in the previous one, minus the number of respondents reporting a vote for the party presently in government in the previous election and a vote for any other party (or non-voting) in the present election.

[34] Proportion significantly different from zero at 5% level (one-sided test).

hand, the Liberals' net gain among respondents most concerned about problems other than unemployment was clearly greater.[35]

Table 4.8.: Net gains and the concerns of respondents, 1975

	Net gains (%)	
	Liberals (V)	Socialdemocrats (SD)
Employment most important problem	7.27 (33)	4.49 (20)
Other problems most important	11.28 (75)	4.51 (30)

In this situation it is interesting to compare the net gains of the Liberals to the net gains of the Socialdemocrats. Not only were the Socialdemocrats the biggest opposition party; they should also be considered the "natural" party to turn to for respondents who wanted to punish the party in government for the rise in unemployment. From the second column in table 4.8. it can be seen, however, that obviously the party in government (the Liberals) was more successful in recruiting among those most concerned about the employment situation than were the Socialdemocrats.[36] This clearly supports the notion of an individual-level "stability"-reaction.

Table 4.9.: Net gains of party in government and the concerns of respondents, 1977

	Net gains (%) Socialdemocrats (SD)
Employment most important problem	6.59 (49)
Other problems most important	5.41 (21)

In 1977, the picture appears clear. As indicated in table 4.9., the party in government (the Socialdemocrats) had a net gain among respondents considering the employment situation the most important problem,[37] and their net gain in this group of respondents slightly exceeded their net gain among respondents most

---

35 The difference is significant at the 5% level (one-sided test).
36 The difference is significant at the 5% level (one-sided test).
37 Proportion significantly different from zero at 5% level (one-sided test).

concerned about other problems. Thus once more an individual-level "stability"-reaction is suggested.

In comparison with Sweden and Denmark, the empirical evidence relating to the political cost of unemployment in Germany and the UK is rather more complex. For Germany Rattinger (1979; 1980; 1983; cf. Rattinger and Puschner, 1981) has estimated vote functions for the period of interest here, based on cross-sectional ecological data. For the 1976 federal election he finds that in general the Socialdemocrats, who were leading the federal government in a coalition with the Liberals, actually benefitted from unemployment (Rattinger, 1979, p. 60; p. 69),[38] i.e. the same pattern of relationship between unemployment and popular support of the government emerges as was found in Denmark. For the 1980 federal election the results are identical to the 1976-results (Rattinger, 1983, p. 269). Thus these findings appear to support the "no cost" hypothesis, as might have been inferred from the fact that unemployment was allowed to rise in Germany during the period 1974-79.

Furthermore, using survey data Rattinger (1986) has been able to produce supporting evidence for the period 1961-84. With regard to the relationship between individual economic judgements and the SPD-vote he found that "*(c)eteris paribus,* the coefficient which measures the influence of general economic judgements on the SPD-vote (with partisanship held constant) will decrease as unemployment rises. This implies, of course, that a governing SPD will be punished less (or can even benefit from) bad general economic perceptions, while an opposition SPD will benefit more from such judgements if unemployment is relatively high rather than low. In other words, in times of high unemployment negative general economic judgements become more advantageous for this party, no matter whether it governs or not. Electorally, the Socialdemocrats can live with unemployment." (p. 413). With regard to the relative cost of unemployment compared to inflation, the conclusion is also very clear: "Thus, while we found that electorally the SPD could live with unemployment, it has every reason to dread inflation: The higher it runs the more economic dissatisfaction reduces the party's vote when it governs, while in opposition dissatisfaction is not to the SPD's advantage either (rather, votes are attracted to the liberal FDP ...) ... It appears that in the Federal Republic a Socialdemocratic government does not have to be afraid of electoral punishment due to economic dissatisfaction when *unemployment* is high. Rather - just like (and even more so than) a Christian Democratic government - the Socialdemocrats have to attempt to keep *inflation* low when they are in charge of economic policy if they are to avoid this kind of punishment." (pp. 414-415).

If we turn to popularity functions for Germany, the picture becomes rather more blurred. Various studies have produced divergent results which also in a

---

[38] When unemployment is split up into structural and cyclical unemployment and the analysis is conducted at the state-level, the findings have to be modified a little: cyclical unemployment still benefits the Socialdemocrats, while structural unemployment appears to strengthen the locally dominant party.

number of cases appear to contradict the findings reported by Rattinger. Thus Kirchgässner (1977, pp. 524-526) finds that for the period 1971-76 only unemployment has a (negative) effect on the popularity of the Socialdemocrats; the effect of inflation is insignificant. Analyzing the period 1971-82 in a more comprehensive study he finds a different result. In the longer run the rate of inflation seems to affect the respondents' view of the general economic situation (which in turn affects the popularity of the Socialdemocrats) much more strongly than does unemployment (Kirchgässner, 1983, pp. 246-248).[39] A couple of years later, the shoe is on the other foot again (Kirchgässner, 1986). Now the conclusion is that "... even German voters weight unemployment more heavily than inflation" (p. 429). Thus according to the first and the last result, there are political costs of unemployment, both in absolute and in relative terms. According to the second, there are political costs of both unemployment and inflation, but, except for the short run, the political costs of inflation are higher than the political costs of unemployment. Frey and Schneider (1980, pp. 58-65) report results for the period 1970-77 which are similar to the results in Kirchgässner (1977). On the other hand Whiteley (1986a, p. 80), using data from 1950-74, shows both unemployment and inflation to reduce the popularity of the chancellor, with inflation the most important variable.

Thus, if we look solely at the vote function (plus the corroborative micro-level evidence), it seems clear that also in Germany the government might accept unemployment virtually without incurring political costs at election day. If we look at popularity functions as well, the case is less clear. With the chances of re-election in view, however, the vote function would appear to be the most important expression of the effect of unemployment on government popularity and hence to be what rational politicians should be most worried about. As mentioned above, to a rational politician opinion poll results should only matter insofar they can be regarded as reliable indicators of what to expect on election day, which in the case of Germany they obviously could not (to the extent that they indicated that the government would lose electoral support on the account of unemployment). Due to the federal structure of West Germany, which brings with it numerous state elections in between federal elections,[40] German politicians must be assumed to have had lots of chances to learn from experience that whatever the apparent influence of unemployment on government popularity in the polls, it did not materialize in actual elections.[41] Hence we may conclude that,

---

[39] Kirchgässner (1983) suggests that the difference between the short and the long run might be due to the fact that the effects of rising unemployment are felt at once, while it takes some time for the effects of increases in consumer prices to make themselves felt.

[40] v. Beyme (1981, p. 61) claims that due to the frequency of elections in the German federal system the politico-economic cycle is weakened considerably.

[41] The same lesson could be learned from the development in SPD-popularity in 1974-75. "Von 1973 bis Mitte 1974 sank die Popularität der SPD - gemessen durch den Anteil der Befragten, der am nächsten Sonntag sozialdemokratisch wählen würde - ganz dramatisch ab - und zwar auf einen Stand, der von der SPD in den frühen fünfziger Jahren erreicht worden war.

as in Denmark, unemployment did not carry with it political costs to the Social-democratic federal government in Germany.

Also with respect to the UK the evidence is not quite as clear as in the case of Sweden and Denmark.[42] Whiteley (1980, p. 97), using electoral data for 1900-74, finds that there is no political cost associated with unemployment if the conservative vote, as percentage of the total electorate, is used as the dependent variable. On the other hand there seems to be a (very small) cost in two out of three estimations if the dependent variable is the conservative vote as percentage of two party system votes (Conservatives + Labour).[43]

Whiteley's own conclusion (1980, p. 95) is "... that changes in economic variables do not significantly influence voting behavior in Britain from 1900 to 1974. The same conclusion also applies to the post-war period ..." The weakness of that finding in the present context is, of course, that it only includes the first year of the time period under scrutiny here. Extrapolating the result straight-forwardly over the rest of the period may be dangerous due to the profound change in economic conditions that took place in 1974.[44]

Using opinion poll data from 1947-74 to estimate a popularity function, Whiteley (1986a, pp. 78-80) obtains a somewhat different result. Here it turns out that the effect of inflation on government popularity is stronger in magnitude and more rapid in response than the effect of unemployment, but again the analysis does only cover a minor part of the time period of interest here.

One of the most sophisticated analyses of the period's relationship between economic variables, notably inflation and unemployment, and government popularity in the UK is due to Alt (1979, pp. 113-138). His main result (1979, p. 120) is "... that government popularity is determined by two entirely different processes, depending on whether inflation (expected) is in crisis (exceeding its recent trend). When it is in crisis, the effects of inflation expectations ... are marked and significant: independent of cycles, each per cent of expected inflation

---

Ab Mitte 1974, nach dem Kanzlerwechsel (Schmidt anstelle von Brandt), stieg die Populari-tätskurve der SPD dann wieder deutlich an, *und zwar gerade in einer Zeit, in der sich die Wirtschafts- und Beschäftigungskrise auch in der wirtschaftswunderverwöhnten Bundesre-publik ganz drastisch bemerkbar machte.*" (Schmidt 1983b, p. 185).

[42] Alt (1979, p. 114) adopts a somewhat more positive view. According to him, "(d)espite superficially contradictory appearances, the British analyses produce an essentially consistent account".

[43] Due to the inclusion of an incumbency variable with value =1 whenever the Conservatives are in power, and value = -1 whenever they are not, which is used to weight the economic variables, this is equivalent to testing for the political cost of economic developments to the government.

[44] The same applies to an even higher degree to two cross-sectional studies based on constitu-ency data from the general election in 1966. Barnett (1973) found that the vote for the incumbent party (Labour) covaried positively with unemployment. Rasmussen (1973-74), who based his study on 185 constituencies only, found the opposite result, if class was controlled for.

knocks 0.74 of a percentage point off government popularity ... The coefficient of unemployment is not statistically significant in inflation crises, but retains the right sign. In non-crisis periods, government popularity is all cycles and trends: the economic variables have insignificant effects." As can be seen from his figure 6.3. (p. 121), the UK experienced a serious "inflation crisis" from 1973 to 1977. For this period, then, the political cost of unemployment was negligible relative to the political cost of inflation.[45] After that period, government popularity was "all cycles and trends" according to Alt, so also after 1977 there was apparently no political cost attached to unemployment.[46]

While, with respect to the countries considered so far, the main problem in ascertaining the political cost of unemployment to the government has been the relative abundance of (sometimes even partially contradictory) empirical evidence, the problem is the opposite in the case of Austria. Due mostly to the lack or inaccessibility of usable data (Neck, 1988, pp. 50-51), only few attempts at estimating VP-functions for this country and for the period under consideration have been reported (Neck, 1979a; 1979b; 1988; Breuss, 1980). Therefore we shall have to supplement the results with "softer" evidence, mainly from electoral research.

In his 1988-study, Neck estimates both vote- and popularity-functions for Austria. Since there are not enough national-level elections ("Nationalrats-wahlen") to estimate an Austrian vote-function (Austria did regain its sovereignty as late as in 1955), fictitious yearly national election results are constructed from the particular year's state-level election(s), and these data are used in conjunction with "real" electoral data.[47]

On the basis of these data a stable relationship between popular support and macro-economic variables can be found only for the SPÖ in the period 1955-86. Of special interest in the present context is, of course, that there is a clear

---

[45] On a more impressionistic basis, the period's growing popular concern about inflation (at the expense of unemployment) in the UK has also been noticed by others, as for example Clarke (1989, ch. 11, e.g. p. 316; p. 319; p. 320). Whiteley (1986b) also found the level of unemployment and - in particular - inflation to have an influence on the impact of these two variables on government popularity.

[46] In only two out of 18 Gallup polls (3 a year) during the whole period of 1974-79 unemployment was mentioned most frequently as "the most urgent problem facing the Country at the present time". Most of the time it ranked second, cf. Moon (1984, p. 20).

[47] Obviously this construction is open to criticism, but there are other debatable aspects in the analysis. For instance, the models used to estimate the effects of various macro-economic variables on popular support for the Austrian parties contain peculiarities, especially as far as the specification of the lag-structure is concerned. In general these models are built on the assumption that popular support depends on the *level* of the macro-economic variable in the *same* year as the "election". It is also in general difficult to assess to what degree there is misspecification due to autocorrelation in the models, since the D.W.-statistic reported is invalid with models containing lagged endogenous variables (as is the case with the models used by Neck).

negative effect of the rate of unemployment on the support for this party during the whole period. As formulated by Neck (1988, p. 68): "The equation implies that when in government, the SPÖ is hurt by an increase in unemployment and a drop in real economic growth. In opposition it gains in votes when inflation goes up and when real growth goes down."

Estimating popularity-functions on the basis of quarterly data from 1976 to 1986 returns very much the same picture. Once more, a stable relationship between popularity and macro-economic variables can be found only for the SPÖ, and the effect of unemployment on the popularity of this party is negative. "From this one can see that - given the validity of the specification - an increase in unemployment by one percentage point did ceteris paribus cost the SPÖ 7/10 of a percentage point of the valid votes (sic!) ..." (Neck, 1988, p. 58). Increase in real economic growth, on the other hand, increased the popularity of the SPÖ, while there was no systematic impact from inflation. This picture is not decisively changed when the period is split into two in order to take into account the change from a SPÖ-government to a SPÖ-led coalition government in 1983 (and the retirement from prime-ministership of Bruno Kreisky).

Although the analyses of Neck must be used with some reservations, the results seem to fit well into other evidence concerning Austrian politics and political behavior in the relevant period. Throughout the whole period 1974-79 the Socialdemocratic government in Austria managed to maintain a situation of virtually full employment. There seems to be broad consensus among observers that the government was rewarded for this achievement in the general elections of 1975 and 1979, when it won an absolute majority of votes and seats.[48] Obviously the government's full employment policy was an important - maybe even the important - political asset, and in order to stay in office it had any incentive not to waste it, but to keep joblessness at bay.

2.3. Summary and interpretation of the "no cost"-pattern

Summing up the results so far, there seems indeed to be evidence of an empirical relationship between the political cost (in terms of re-election prospects) of unemployment to the government and the extent of joblessness found in the five countries under study in the period 1974-79. In both of the two countries in which the employment situation had a significant impact on the popular support of the government (Austria and Sweden), unemployment was kept at low levels throughout the whole period. In contrast, the three countries in which unemployment obviously did no harm to the governments' stand with the public (Denmark, Germany and the UK), all experienced a significant amount of joblessness.

---

48 Cf. Sully (1976; 1979; 1981); Angermann and Plasser (1979); Schmidt (1983b, pp. 187-188); Schmidt (1984, p. 19); Chalupek (1985).

Table 4.10.: Political cost and unemployment in the five countries

		Political cost	
		yes	no
Unemployment	low	AUSTRIA SWEDEN	-
	high	-	GERMANY DENMARK UK

How should one interpret the fact that the electorate did not punish the government for the return of mass unemployment in Denmark, Germany and the UK? Two rather different alternatives would seem to suggest themselves. According to the first, the lack of a negative voter reaction towards the government in face of unemployment must be interpreted as an expression of weak or non-existing popular demand for and support of anti-unemployment policies: By and large voters did not care sufficiently about unemployment to let it influence significantly on their voting. According to the alternative interpretation, voters who cared about unemployment may have been captives in the sense of Hirshman (1970). With a Socialdemocratic government in power, what party could such voters possibly turn to without risking to make things (i.e. unemployment) even worse?

While the second alternative has a nice familiar ring as well as an intuitive appeal to it, it is, at some points, difficult to square with the facts. In the first place, if one accepts the underlying premise that a Socialdemocratic government is the sole, or at least the best available, guarantee for a full employment policy, then it becomes difficult to explain how there can *ever* be a significant negative effect from unemployment upon the popular support of a Socialdemocratic government. Nevertheless, as witnessed by, e.g., the Swedish and the Austrian case, there can be such a negative effect. Why should it be that Swedish or Austrian voters were less captives than for example their Danish or German counterparts?

Moreover, the Danish and the German cases show that during the period considered here bourgeois governments were not punished for unemployment either. Despite intense efforts from both the Socialdemocratic opposition and the trades unions to blame the upsurge of unemployment on the Agrarian government prior to the Danish general election in January 1975, the government won a smashing victory. At state level in Germany, bourgeois governments were not necessarily hit by unemployment either (Rattinger, 1980).[49] This suggests that the electoral immunity of the government to the development in unemployment

---

49 Nor did the Thatcher government that took over in the UK in 1979 have difficulties in politically surviving soaring unemployment figures, cf. Clarke and Whiteley (1990).

was a much more general trait, not confined - as it should be expected to according to the captivity-explanation - to Socialdemocratic governments alone.

There are other weaknesses in the captivity- or "no alternative"-explanation as well. In assuming that the Socialdemocrats are, in some sense, the "natural" party for voters concerned about unemployment, it seems to build on a rather static view of the relationship between party and voters.[50] The view expressed by the Socialdemocratic Austrian chancellor Kreisky on that matter is probably closer to reality: "Our core constituencies are not people who cast their vote for the Socialdemocrats at any price ... The core constituencies of our party are people who according to their social-economic class position ought to vote for the Socialdemocratic party. But when they get the feeling that the party cares more about everything else than about them, they will stay at home."[51]

Moreover, if we turn to the Danish case specifically, it seems hard to accept that there could be captive voters at all after the fragmentation of the party system occurring in 1973. Voters who felt sufficiently discontent about the development in unemployment under the reign of the Socialdemocrats, but in that respect did not trust the bourgeois opposition either, had at least three left wing parties to turn to.[52] The results reported by Paldam and Schneider (1980) show that prior to 1973 the left wing opposition had indeed gained in popular support from a rise in unemployment, when the Socialdemocratic government had suffered. But despite the rising unemployment, between 1973 and 1979, the vote share of the left wing parties remained remarkably stable (around 11 per cent). During that period they obviously failed to gain from the deterioration in employment.

Everything considered, then, it seems that the absence of an anti-government electoral reaction to the return of mass unemployment in the three Social-democratic countries where such a development took place primarily reflected a - maybe surprisingly - low salience of the employment issue to the electorate, either in absolute terms or relative to other issues of the day. In Denmark, in particular, people grew accustomed to high levels of unemployment with a speed and an ease that shocked observers. Thus a former chairman of the Council of Economic Advisers relates: "In 1974 it was the general opinion of the chairmen that an unemployment figure above 100,000 would be a catastrophe and would be viewed as such by the population. But already in 1976 we had experienced a yearly unemployment level of 125,000 without anything drastic happening for that reason."[53]

---

[50] Besides, the Swedish experience after 1976 shows that a bourgeois government can be as strongly committed to full employment policies as a Socialdemocratic one. Obviously, if the employment issue is salient to the electorate, a rational bourgeois government seeking re-election has not much of a choice here.

[51] Der Spiegel, no. 14, March 4, 1983. Quoted from Visser and Wijnhoven (1990, p. 79).

[52] Besides, of course, the protest party par excellence, the Progress Party.

[53] Rold Andersen (1987, p. 229). Quite appropriately, he chose the heading "The Illusion of Sound Reason".

3. Political cost and unemployment - the policy link

The empirical relationships found above are consistent with the proposed "political cost"-interpretation of inter-country variations in unemployment, but it is not conclusive evidence. There always remains the possibility of the relationship just being spurious: inferences from outcomes to incentives (or motives) are generally not warranted, since actual outcomes need not reflect what was intended in the first place. It could be imagined, e.g., that regardless of the absence of political costs a government did in fact try everything possible to combat unemployment, but failed. Such a case would add to the observed (negative) covariance between political cost and the extent of unemployment, but would nevertheless contradict the "political cost"-interpretation of variations in the extent unemployment.

What is needed in order to make the argument stick is the demonstration of the existence of a policy-link connecting the political cost of unemployment to the government to the extent of joblessness. *It has to be shown that the political costs of unemployment affect government behavior.* Governments act differently if they know that unemployment counts on election day.

This is what we are going to attempt to demonstrate in the following two sections. In the first one, some indirect evidence from an analysis of the Okun-relation in each of the five countries is presented. In the second, we shall examine variations in the extent to which governments in the five countries implemented active labor market policies as part of their fight against unemployment. The reason why active labor market policies have been chosen rather than, e.g., fiscal policies as the policy to be examined in this context is the more discretionary character of the former type of policy. Since automatic budgetary reactions and discretionary government measures are strongly confounded in quantitative figures on fiscal expansion or contraction,[54] and fiscal expansion or contraction does affect unemployment only indirectly, expenditures on active labor market programs that aim directly at reducing the extent of joblessness must be considered superior indicators of the efforts of governments to fight unemployment specifically.

3.1. The relationship between economic growth and unemployment

The relationship we are dealing with here is known as Okun's law (Okun 1970). From a simple macro production function, combined with a labor demand function, one easily obtains the relation (Paldam 1987, p. 306):

$$-\Delta u = gy - z$$

---

[54] This is why it will often be extremely difficult to prove empirically on the basis of fiscal data that governments behave in a vote-maximizing way, cf. Dinkel (1982).

where Δu are the first differences of the unemployment rate u, y is the rate of growth of real GDP, and z is a constant. g then is the employment elasticity with respect to y, i.e. g expresses how much one per cent of growth in real GDP changes the unemployment rate.

The reason why the empirical Okun-relations are of interest here is that this relation may be manipulated politically. While the programmatic politico-economic aim of a Keynesian welfare state will normally be to stabilize real growth in order to keep unemployment down, the next best approach to preventing unemployment would appear to be an attempt by policy means to "isolate" the labor market from the employment effects of the ups and downs of business cycles.

Therefore, if it can be shown empirically that the employment elasticity with respect to real growth is lower in countries where unemployment carries with it political costs to the government than in countries where that is not the case, this would strongly suggest that in countries with political costs of unemployment the Okun-relation has been politically tapered with. This, in turn, would indicate the existence of a policy-link between the political cost of unemployment and the actual extent of joblessness, as required by the "political incentive structure"-interpretation of variations in the extent of unemployment.

Table 4.11. below shows the values of z and of the elasticity, estimated on data from 1960-85. In order to capture possible variations in the employment elasticity due to the crisis 1974-79, the following dummy variable model is estimated[55]

$$\Delta u_t = z + g_1 y_t + g_2 y_{t-1} + g_3 v_t + g_4 v_{t-1}$$

where

$v_t = x_1 y_t$
$x_1 = 0$ for the periods 1960-73 and 1980-85
$\quad = 1$ else

Hence for the periods 1960-73 (and 1980-85) the model becomes

$$\Delta u_t = z + g_1 y_t + g_2 y_{t-1}$$

while for the period 1974-79 we get

$$\Delta u_t = z + (g_1 + g_3) y_t + (g_2 + g_4) y_{t-1}$$

Thus for the periods 1960-73 and 1980-85 the Okun-term (o) can be computed as

---

[55] Cf. Johnston (1963, pp. 221-228).

$o_1 = g_1 + g_2$

while for the period 1974-79 the Okun-term becomes

$o_2 = g_1 + g_2 + g_3 + g_4$

The lagged growth variable y_{t-1} is included here because there is evidence (Paldam, 1987, p. 309) that growth affects unemployment mainly in the same and in the following year. Therefore the total elasticity of unemployment with respect to growth in a given year is the sum of the elasticities with respect to growth in the present and the previous year.

Table 4.11. shows a very clear result: as expected, the Okun-terms for Austria and Sweden turn out to be numerically considerably smaller than for the other three countries.[56] Obviously Austria and Sweden managed better than the other countries to shield their labor markets against the effects of variations in the level of economic activity. This is suggestive of a conscious policy effort to stabilize employment in these two countries.

Table 4.11.: Estimates of constants and elasticities in the Okun-relations

	Austria	Germany	Denmark	Sweden	UK
CONST	0.71	1.34	1.65	0.45	1.57
(SE)	(0.13)	(0.14)	(0.49)	(0.13)	(0.16)
o_1	-0.16	-0.30	-0.43	-0.11	-0.49
(SE)	(0.30)	(0.03)	(0.13)	(0.04)	(0.05)
o_2	-0.21	-0.46	-0.56	-0.27	-0.59
(SE)	(0.05)	(0.06)	(0.25)	(0.07)	(0.11)
R^2	0.600	0.824	0.396	0.439	0.806
D.W.	2.512	1.664	1.511	2.096	2.668
Ljung-Box Q(12)	7.033	12.144	8.132	12.437	15.756

It could be argued, though, that the small values of the Okun-terms in Austria and Sweden are simply caused by the low level of unemployment in these two countries, instead of being an intervening variable in the causal chain running from policy to unemployment as implied by the "shielding"-hypothesis. This is not at all an implausible argument, since diminishing returns with respect to a reduction in unemployment must be expected from accelerating growth as the

---

[56] This result agrees with the results reported in Paldam (1987, p. 312).

level of unemployment approaches its attainable minimum. In such a situation those unable to find employment will probably be mainly a hard core of people with no or the wrong skills, social or physical handicaps, and only a marginal relationship to the labor market.

But it is not quite as clear why diminishing growth should also lead to lower employment elasticities when the economy is running on a low level of unemployment than when unemployment is (already) high. It might be, of course, that in a tight labor market employers will react to lower growth by reducing overtime etc. instead of laying off people. But it might as well be that employers will react by shedding low-productivity workers whom they did only hire in the first place because of the unavailability of others when the economy was booming. Therefore, if we find that the employment reaction to diminishing growth is also weaker in Austria and Sweden than in the other three countries, this would support the "shielding"-hypothesis. Table 4.12. shows the average increase in unemployment in response to a one percentage-point *drop* in real GDP-growth at the lag that produces the strongest correlation between Δu_t and GDP-growth. As can be seen, we again have the weakest reaction in Austria and Sweden. This is suggestive of a conscious policy effort to stabilize employment, to which we shall turn next.[57]

Table 4.12.: Increase in unemployment in response to a one percentage-point drop in real GDP-growth (at the most significant lag)

	Austria	Germany	Denmark	Sweden	UK
$\Delta u_t / \Delta GDP_t$	0.05	0.20	1.54	-0.08	0.08

3.2. Enacting of active labor market policies

Within the framework of (bastard-) Keynesian economic policies the task of keeping (or restoring) employment at high levels is in principle assigned to aggregate demand management by fiscal and monetary instruments. But if demand management threatens to fail or is not feasible, active labor market policies may be called for in order to support or supplement it.

---

[57] Another argument in favor of the "shielding"-hypothesis is that when the Okun-relation is estimated for a period with virtually full employment in all five countries, Austria and Sweden still come out lowest with respect to employment elasticity, cf. Paldam (1987, p. 312). The values estimated for the period 1960-70 are Austria: -0.18, Germany: -0.21, Denmark: -0.21, Sweden: -0.17, United Kingdom: -0.23.

Active labor market policies are specifically aimed at both the supply and the demand side of the labor market. On the supply side they may consist of, e.g., measures like favorable early retirement schemes for elder workers, training and re-training programs for groups of workers, or financial assistances with a view to increasing the geographical mobility of the labor force. On the demand side, they may consist of various schemes for subsidizing the creation of new jobs (or the retaining of existing ones), benefits for taking on members of marginal groups in the work force, etc.

While Swedish economists, labor market organizations and state agencies have pioneered in designing and enacting active labor market policies,[58] all countries considered here did use such policies to some extent to supplement the effects of other economic policy instruments in their fight against the economic crisis 1974-79. They did so, however, in markedly varying degrees. Therefore it is natural to ask if the use of active labor market policies reflects the political cost of unemployment in the various countries. From the central thesis, which has been confirmed so far, one would expect active labor market policies to have been used most vigorously in countries where unemployment carried with it political costs to the government, and somewhat more hesitantly in countries where such was not the case.

Table 4.13.: Expenditure on and "policy deficit" with respect to active labor market policies 1978 (Denmark 1979), in pct. of GDP[59]

	Austria	Germany	Denmark	Sweden	UK
Expenditure on active labor market policy	0.05	0.20	1.54	-0.08	0.08
Additional expenditure needed to achieve full employment	0.06	0.65	1.46	0.12	1.93

At first glance, the first row in table 4.13. may seem to contradict such an expectation. As can be seen, the two countries with considerable political cost of unemployment, Austria and Sweden, make up the opposite extremes with

---

58 Cf. Rehn (1985).

59 For all countries except Denmark, the data are from Scharpf (1987, p. 283). The Danish data have been compiled from various sources, especially Arbejdsdirektoratet (1980) and Budgetrede-gørelsen (1980; 1984). By using data from 1979, the Danish figures have been inflated considerably, since the most important active labour market program of the period 1974-79 (an early and flexible retirement scheme) was not enacted before 1979, cf. Buksti (1984, p. 226).

respect to expenditures on active labor market policies, Sweden spending most and Austria spending least on such measures among our five countries.

Expenditure figures on policy programs are, however, influenced by two factors: they reflect both how much has actually been done, but also how much needed to be done. Thus the low level of expenditures on active labor market policies in Austria certainly reflects that little was done, but possibly also that little needed to be done. In order to take into account inter-country differences in the need for active labor market policies (to supplement traditional Keynesian policy instruments), a "policy deficit" measure has been computed. It expresses the level of additional expenditures on active labor market policies that would have been called for in each country in order to reduce unemployment to a (arbitrarily chosen) level of 2 pct.[60]

As can be seen from table 4.13., the pattern in the second row is exactly as one would have expected if the political cost of unemployment were the main incentive for the enacting of active labor market policies. Taking into account differing needs for active labor market policy, the governments of Austria and Sweden, which both would have had to pay a considerable political price in the case of unemployment, appear to have been using this instrument most vigorously. In the three other countries the use of active labor market policies was limited, not the least so, when compared to what would have been required to retain or restore full employment in these countries.

4. Obstacles on the road to full employment

So far the analysis has exclusively focused on the political reason for inter-country variations in the extent to which unemployment was successfully combatted in the five countries. It has been shown that inter-country variations in the degree to which governments were kept responsible for unemployment by their electorates match variations in the degree to which unemployment was successfully kept down. It has further been shown that inter-country variations with respect to the electoral reaction to unemployment, i.e. with respect to the political cost of unemployment to the government, match inter-country variations in the extent to which specific labor market policies were enacted.

While this demonstration of empirical matches has strengthened the basic thesis, there are conceivably alternative explanations to the inter-country variation in unemployment. Trying to test and to refute them all would for

---

60 For all countries except Denmark, this figure is computed on the basis of data given in Scharpf (1987, p. 283). In order to compute the figure, a number of heroic, simplifying assumptions and rough guestimations have to be made. Hence - despite the two decimals - the figures should be considered rough indicators only. Nevertheless the pattern exhibited by these figures is so clear that it must be considered rather robust.

obvious reasons be an abortive enterprise.[61] Here we shall just take a brief look at two possible alternative explanations: the balance of payment constraint, and the growth of the labor force. The reason for concentrating on these is that in the Danish political debate both have, from time to time, been offered as explanations of and excuses for the poor performance of the Danish economy with respect to the full employment goal.

4.1. Constraints from the balance of payments?

To the analysis presented above it might be objected (by economists and politicians alike) that the governments worked under economic constraints from the balance of payment not equally serious in all five countries. According to such an interpretation inter-country differences with respect to employment performance just reflect differences with respect to the size of the balance of payment problems they faced.

Figure 4.4.: Relationship between BoP-surplus and unemployment, 1960-80

(a) Austria

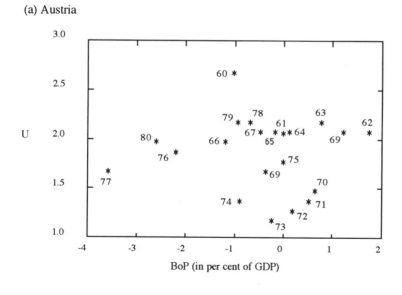

BoP (in per cent of GDP)

(continued)

---

[61] This is nevertheless what is attempted in Therborn (1986).

(b) Germany

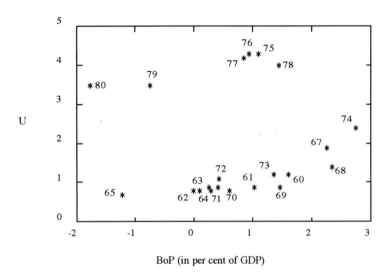

BoP (in per cent of GDP)

(c) Denmark

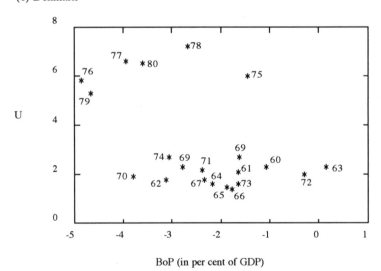

BoP (in per cent of GDP)

(continued)

(d) Sweden

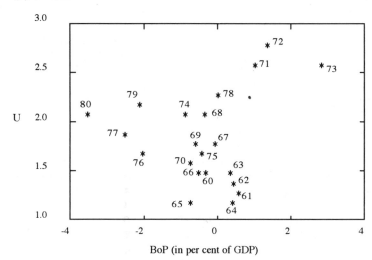

BoP (in per cent of GDP)

(e) UK

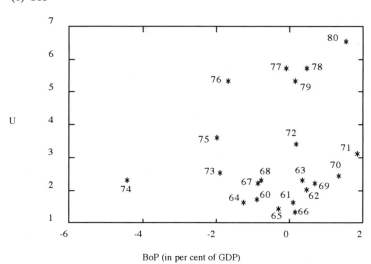

BoP (in per cent of GDP)

Data: OECD, National Accounts (1990)

This type of interpretation suggests that there is a trade-off between balance of payments surplus and unemployment somewhat analogous to the well-known Phillips-curve (Gelting, 1972; 1976). In figure 4.4. the relationship between unemployment (in per cent) and balance of payment surplus (in per cent of GDP) is illustrated by means of "Gelting-curves" for each of the five countries.

The figures show that there has been a parallel development in the trade off between unemployment and the balance of payments in all five countries, full employment and unemployment countries alike. This development is characterized mainly by two traits.

In the first place the price of full employment in terms of a reduced balance of payment surplus (or a greater balance of payment deficit) tended to increase in the 70s: the curves tend to move to the left and upwards. In some countries, e.g. the UK after 1973, this obviously happened in one step, while the development was more gradual in for example Austria, where four phases can be distinguished: 1961-68 (1960 and 1969 are outliers which do not conform to any identifiable pattern), 1970-73, 1974-75, and 1976-80.

In the second place the elasticity of employment with respect to balance of payments changes tends to increase. In general the curves describing the trade off in the 70s tend to be steeper than the curves for the 60s. Thus the employment effects of, e.g., a deterioration in the balance of payment in the 70s tend to be more serious than in the 60s. Conversely, a greater increase in unemployment is called for in the 70s than in the 60s to accomplish a reduction of a certain size in the balance of payment deficit.

The difference between the five countries is, of course, in the balance of payments levels (cf. table 4.1.). Obviously the development in the trade off between balance of payment and employment should be less critical for countries traditionally running a balance of payments surplus, like Germany, than for traditional deficit countries like Denmark. Interestingly, however, the pattern of inter-country variations in balance of payments strength does not match the pattern of inter-country variations in unemployment development. Obviously the relatively poor employment performance of the German economy cannot be straightforwardly explained by balance of payments constraints on full employment policies. On the other hand Austria (and to some extent Sweden) were seemingly willing to "pay" for full employment by running a controlled balance of payment deficit. Thus while Germany did not manage to restore full employment despite a favorable balance of payments,[62] Austria managed to avoid unemployment despite an unfavorable one.

The contrasting examples of Germany and Austria suggest that the degree to which the balance of payment constrains full employment policies depends on

---

[62] The case of Germany clearly refutes an "indisputable" result in Hefting and Nielsen (1983, p. 209): "In the first place it is indisputable that a country faced with a big trade balance deficit and a strong increase in the domestic rate of inflation will be less eager to enact an expansionary policy than a country where inflation is moderate and where there may be a trade balance surplus." (my translation)

what balance of payments saldo is considered acceptable by those in charge - and (within certain bounds) this is a political question as least as much as an economic one.[63]

Moreover, while unemployment may be the easiest remedy to balance of payments problems (if it is politically feasible), it is not the only one. Since the mid-70s the Council of Economic Advisers time and again suggested policies that would have been necessary to solve the Danish unemployment and balance of payment problems simultaneously. By and large their advices went unheeded, and it is tempting to conjecture that this happened primarily because they called for measures that might have been unpopular and hence potentially costly to the government in political terms, which unemployment, by then, had proved itself not to be.

In short then, the trade off between unemployment and the balance of payments is not only economically, but also politically determined. Therefore the balance of payment constraint on closer inspection turns out not to be able to provide an alternative to a political explanation of inter-country variations in unemployment.

4.2. The growth of the labor force

The task of retaining or restoring full employment may obviously be aided or hindered by the development in the size of the labor force. At the same time this development can be politically influenced to a certain extent only.

The demographic basis - conventionally defined as the size of the age group between 15 and 64 - can be manipulated to a minor extent by restrictive government policies towards immigration and foreign workers in order to reduce the size of the labor force. This was actually done in Austria and Germany, but not in the other three countries. Moreover attempts can be made to influence participation rates in particular groups like the young (e.g. by prolongation of comprehensive schooling or by lurking greater fractions into secondary education), the elder (e.g. by early retirement schemes or related labor market policies), or women. But especially with respect to the latter group the development in participation rates is very much a social process not easily controlled or reversed. Hence the question arises if inter-country differences with respect to unemployment can be accounted for on the basis of inter-country differences with respect to the growth of the labor force. The yearly growth (in percentages) is shown in figure 4.5.

As can be seen, the countries can be divided into three groups on the basis of the growth patterns in their labor force. The first group is made up by Germany, where the size of the labor force actually diminished in most of the period

---

63 Here it could be mentioned that Norway did run balance of payments deficits several times the size of the Danish in the middle of the 70s without letting that influence employment levels.

considered here. The average yearly labor force growth was negative (-0.18 per cent). Austria and the UK can be considered a middle group with a rather constant, minor growth in the labor force (on average 0.60 per cent in Austria and 0.62 per cent in the UK). The strongest growth in the labor force is found in Sweden and Denmark (on average 1.47 per cent in Denmark and 1.18 per cent in Sweden). In both countries this development primarily reflects an increase in female participation rates.

Figure 4.5.: Year to year percentage change in total labor force, 1973-79

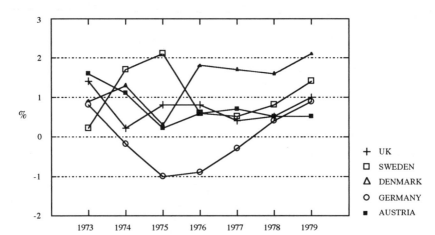

Data: OECD, Historical Statistics (1988); Buksti (1984)

Evidently the inter-country variations in the growth of the labor force do not match the inter-country variations with respect to unemployment: Judged from the development in the size of the labor force Germany did too poorly and Sweden too well with respect to unemployment, and of the two countries with almost identical developments in the size of the labor force, viz. Austria and the UK, one managed to retain a situation of full employment while the other did not. Thus it would seem that inter-country differences with respect to the development in the size of the national labor forces are not sufficient to explain inter-country differences with respect to unemployment.[64]

---

[64] Buksti (1984, p. 219) arrives at the same conclusion as far as Denmark is concerned.

5. Conclusion

This analysis started off from a rather provocative question. While it would probably be driving the point too forcefully to answer it unconditionally in the affirmative, the main result from sifting the empirical evidence is that people certainly did get unemployment where they did not opt against it in the polls.[65]

If this still may seem to be a somewhat startling conclusion, it should be kept in mind that basically it is also a very democratic one.[66] The extent to which anti-unemployment policies were enacted has been shown to be clearly related to popular demand for such policies, as articulated in elections.

This does not necessarily mean that in the three unemployment countries in this study people did not care about unemployment in some ways.[67] As for Denmark, available survey data suggest differently (Nannestad, 1989a). *But as preferences without the backing of money are not effective demand in the economic market, preferences without the backing of votes obviously are not effective demand in the political market either.*

---

[65] Quite recently the lack of political willingness to do something about unemployment in Denmark was pointed to as a reason for the persistence of the problem by the chairman of the Council of Economic Advisers (Jyllands-Posten, October 9, 1990). The analysis in the present chapter indicates that this is not a new situation. The news is that economists see it.

[66] Proponents of a "holistic" conception of democracy (Poulsen, 1986) may have some trouble in accepting unemployment as an outcome of a truly democratic process, since they do not want to separate the procedural and the content aspect in their definition of democracy. More generally the democratic interpretation of the main finding opens up for a lot of theoretical digressions, for example in the field of the theory of representation and the role of the representative (Pitkin, 1967; Eulau et al., 1968) or the history of political thought (Rousseau; Burke). For the sake of brevity we will stay on the main route, however.

[67] Cf. for example the British data reported in Moon (1984, p. 20).

Chapter 5
Wage Structure, Union Pushfulness and Stagflation

In the present chapter we turn to the second dimension in the stagflation complex, i.e. to inflation. Compared to the rather extensive discussion of the inter-country differences with respect to the problem of unemployment and their political causes in chapter 4, however, the inter-country differences with respect to inflation will be given a somewhat briefer treatment.[1]

From table 4.2. in chapter 4 we observe that inflation induces a somewhat different performance ranking of our five countries than does unemployment. With respect to consumer price stability Austria is again a front runner, but it is now joined by Germany; in comparison, the inflation records of Denmark, Sweden and the UK are equally poor. Thus in comparison with employment performance Austria retains its place at the top and Denmark and the UK their place at the bottom of the list, while Sweden and Germany switch positions.

Inflation is a multi-facetted phenomenon and there are various theories of inflation, concentrating on different types and aspects.[2] Several modern economic theories of inflation have stressed the international element in inflation, ascribed to the integration of factor and/or financial markets. There is little doubt that there was a considerable international element in inflation following the first oil price hike. On the other hand, there were also considerable inter-country variations in the level and the time path of inflation. In the present context, given the period under study, it is probably not too controversial,[3] then, to concentrate on inter-country differences in inflation as being mainly the expression of variations in levels of a distributive conflict in society. This was initially set in motion by the loss of national income to the OPEC-countries and by other external price shocks experienced by all oil-importing countries.[4] In that perspec-

---

[1] This, of course, reflects my personal value judgement as to the relative importance of the two issues when seen from the viewpoint of individual welfare. Cf. also Hibbs (1985, pp. 186-188).

[2] For modern economic theories of inflation see Lindbeck (1980) and Frisch (1983). Sociological and institutional approaches can be found in for example Hirsh and Goldthorpe (1978); Lindberg (1985); Maier (1985); Maier and Lindberg (1985).

[3] Actually this interpretation can be found with writers of impeccable socialist leanings, for instance Jubery and Wilkinson (1986, pp. 326-327), as well as with writers of an entirely different persuasion, e.g. SVR (1974, p. 63).

[4] Of course those price shocks hit the different countries in somewhat different ways, depending, i.a., on their dependency on imported oil and on how energy intensive their industries were. Still such factors appear insufficient to explain why inflation could be successfully combatted in Germany and Austria, but not in Denmark, Sweden, and the UK. For the UK, for instance, Dornbusch and Fischer (1980) conclude that rising import prices have been one factor contributing to inflation, but a proportionally weaker one than rising money

tive inflation (above the "unavoidable" level, as it was termed by the German Bundesbank) was the outcome of trade union attempts to avoid income losses for their members and to shift the burden to the employers by claiming wage compensations for the rise in energy prices (and secondary price increases), and of corresponding attempts from the side of the employers to shift (part of) the burden back to wage earners and consumers by raising their prices in response.[5] Where wages were in some way indexed to costs of living, as in Denmark (or in the UK 1973-74),[6] such a process might get started almost automatically.[7]

In a stagflationary situation the unions may at first sight appear to be at a distinct disadvantage in this type of distributive struggle. They will have to take into account the twin goals of defending employment and defending wage levels in the presence of the political unemployment/inflation nexus described above (chapter 2). Governments can use aggregate demand management to fight unemployment *or* to fight inflation, but not both at the same time.[8] When uions press for compensatory wage increases they risk starting an inflationary wage-price spiral. This may jeopardize the possibilities of the government to effectively combat unemployment through demand stimulation by fiscal and monetary policies. In this way inflation may ultimately be hurting the unions' own full employment goal.

If this were the whole story, one should expect to find a uniformly high degree of wage restraint in the trade unions in all five countries, once a stagflationary situation threatened to develop in the wake of the first oil price hike. The fact is, however, that there were considerable differences in that respect between the five countries of this study. The empirical analyses and the estimated wage reaction functions in chapter 2 indicate that trade unions in Germany reacted to unemployment with a much higher degree of wage restraint than did the unions in Denmark and the UK. There was also a strong wage reaction to tightening labor market conditions in Austria. In Sweden, finally, increases in unemploy-

---

wages.

[5] It deserves being stressed that to concentrate on this particular interpretation of inflationary tendencies in the wake of the first oil price hike is not the same as to blame trade unions unilaterally for inflation: where inflation developed there were two parts to the distributive struggle, and once the merry-go-round gets started it is hard to tell who leads and who follows whom.

[6] Cf. Chapter 2, section 5.

[7] This does not mean, however, that the wide-spread use of indexation in collective bargaining agreements in Denmark has to be considered *the* source of inflationary pressures in the Danish economy (although it has quite often been assigned the role of the big culprit). If Danish wage increases over a period are decomposed into their main components, it turns out that close to one half (45 per cent) of the total wage increases are due to wage drift (Pedersen and Søndergaard, 1989, p. 8). About 15 per cent are accounted for by central bargaining, and the rest - about 40 per cent - comes from indexation, cf. also Johansen (1985, pp. 59-66).

[8] This follows from the Tinbergen-rule according to which there have to be as many independent instruments as there are goals in economic policies.

ment led to marked wage restraint only when not accompanied by expansion of labor market programs. The intriguing question hence becomes why such inter-country differences in union behavior did emerge.

There are, of course, numerous conceivable reasons for differences in union reactions and for the lower degree of wage restraint in some of the countries of this study. In the first place, some unions may simply have misjudged the situation and overlooked or underestimated the importance of the unemployment/inflation nexus. Thus Scharpf (1987, p. 167; pp. 171-173) suggests that the German wage explosion in 1974 came about mainly because the unions did not believe, until they had experienced it, in the effectiveness of a monetary contraction to bring about a swift economic down-turn.[9]

Secondly, attempts at, or fears of, exploitation may have played a role. As was mentioned above (chapter 2) Socialdemocratic (or "essentially Socialdemocratic") governments are vulnerable to exploitation by trade unions because, by tradition and ideology, high programmatic value attaches to their full employment goal. Hence trade unions may be tempted to count on the fact that for political reasons a Socialdemocratic government will not refrain from employment stimulating policies, even in the face of strong inflationary pressures that increase the political cost of a full employment strategy to the government. At first sight the situation in Sweden could be interpreted in that way, cf. Scharpf (1987, p. 245) and above.[10] Similarly Andersen (1989) has suggested that trade union policy in Denmark during the last years of the seventies could be interpreted as an attempt to exploit the "demand switch"-policy then enacted, in the (erroneous) belief that it was indeed employment stimulating.

Alternatively unions themselves may also fear to become exploited by the government in the sense that for one reason or another the government may fail to "deliver the goods" so that the trade union membership will not be rewarded by effective full employment policies for exercising wage restraint.[11] This factor may appear to have played a certain role in the UK and Denmark. Trade unions could for obvious reasons not always feel sure of what exactly the various

---

[9] I find this explanation hard to accept, mainly because the Bundesbank had once before demonstrated its ability to turn a boom into a recession at very short notice, when it sent the German economy on a down-turn in 1966. Given the generally very important role played by the experience of the 1966-67 recession in the perception of the post-1973 recession the unions should have known better.

[10] Especially the Haga-agreement and the way it was not honored by the Swedish trade unions in the end seems to lend itself readily to such an interpretation, cf. chapter 2, section 4 above.

[11] This, of course, is one of the main points in the "deferred wage" argument in the neo-corporatist literature when it comes to explaining why neo-corporatist systems of interest intermediation are more successful than others in achieving wage restraint.

parliamentary weak Danish Socialdemocratic minority governments would be able to deliver in return for wage restraint.[12]

In the third place trade unions may simply have disbelieved in the economic wisdom of exercising wage restraint during an economic recession. The point can be made that reducing the purchasing power of wage earners through wage restraint, in a situation characterized by weak aggregate demand, may not be the most self-evident course to follow. This view was intermittently aired by groups of "critical" economists in for example Germany, Denmark, and the UK. While it is clear that wages are an important demand component, the argument tends to overlook that wages are an equally important cost component.

Fourth, unions might also have assigned greater weight to the wage goal than to the employment goal. Sometimes union wage setting behavior has actually been described as an exploitation of the job have-nots by those in (secure) employment.[13] It is obvious that even in periods of high unemployment union members in employment will normally outnumber the unemployed members by a great margin. For that reason alone they have the better chance of having their interests served. Also, unions do normally not represent those who never made it into the labor market or who have been shut out. Thus the point can be made that employment is secondary in actual union policy because it is of secondary importance to the majority of union members. They are employed.

In this respect the relative invisibility of today's unemployment problem may have been a contributing factor. In all five countries considered unemployment benefits were quite generous, so, although it is extremely difficult to draw exact comparisons, it is probably quite safe to say that becoming unemployed in these countries did not (any longer) automatically imply becoming (economically) destitute. Thus the pressure on those in employment to make sacrifices in favor of the jobless may well have been weakened by the existing schemes of income substitution in the case of unemployment.[14]

---

12 On the other hand it has also been argued (within a rational expectation framework) that political uncertainty might actually be conducive to trade union restraint, since unknown government objectives may give a strong trade union an incentive to go for a lower wage rate, cf. Sørensen (1990).

13 This is the well-known insider-outsider model, cf. for example Lindbeck and Snower (1988). Actually this type of accusation has occasionally been raised against trade unions by both leftist and rightist critics.

14 That is the reason why the lachrymose description in Therborn (1986, pp. 14-15) of the plight of the unemployed in a Denmark where "young unemployed were queuing, heads bowed in shame, for morning bread and coffee and for food too stale to sell, which is handed out by the Salvation Army" (the source of which is a Swedish radio reporter) misses the essential point twofold. In the first place it conveys the impression of a Dickens-like situation of readily visible destitution, which is wrong in its own right. In the second place it obscures the fact that it may have been exactly this relative invisibility of the consequences of unemployment that contributed to its persistence. There were some attempts at making unemployment more visible through unemployment marches etc., but they were invariably backed by very few and hence never achieved much of their purpose.

These factors may all, in various mixtures, have contributed to the observed pattern of differences in wage restraint in our five countries. Our main concern, however, is with the strategy choice facing rational union leaders seeking to safeguard their positions. We wantt to determine conditions that might induce rational union leaders to pursue an aggressive wage strategy - even in the face of stagflation. This is an exercise in analytical theory, but with results in hand we turn back to the observable differences between the various countries. Did wage moderation occur *in practice* in those places where wage restraint would be predicted *by theory?*

1. A model of wage structure and trade union behavior

In the following I shall try to shed some light on the question posed above by looking at a crude model of trade union behavior. It describes the strategic choices facing unions when they have to take into account both employment levels and wage levels, and when there is an unemployment/inflation nexus (of the political kind). The model is in many respects quite close to the one found in, e.g., Olson (1982, ch. 7) - as well as to numerous others - although my emphasis and conclusions are somewhat different. Moreover, by way of inspiration the following discussion owes much to the wage structure theory of inflation set out by Paldam (1989) and to the theory of pay forwarded by Wood (1978). No formalized treatment will be undertaken. The model should be considered a framework for common-sense reasoning (offended readers are referred to the Preface of this book for consolation).

1.1. Basic assumptions

Historically trade unions were associations of wage earners with the main purpose of furthering their economic interests vis à vis the employers. Basically these characteristics still apply to Western European trade unions of today.[15] Moreover, in Western countries trade union leaderships are democratically elected.

----

[15] There are, of course, strong inter-country and inter-union variations in the degree to which union membership can be said to be truly voluntary today, depending on, i.a., to what extent trade unions are permitted and able to practice "closed shop"-arrangements. In some blue-collar occupations in the private sector in Denmark, for instance, trade union membership is almost compulsory and the close relationship between trade unions and unemployment insurance funds contributes another strong incentive to join. In Germany, on the other hand, union membership is much more voluntary because "closed shop"-arrangements are illegal and unemployment insurance is taken care of and administered by a federal agency. In the context of the present discussion these differences are of little importance, however.

Thus trade union leaders can be assumed to have a strong re-election motive (as do politicians, and for the same reasons). But unlike politicians trade union leaders may not only be threatened by the vote and the voice, but also by the exit-option (Hirshman, 1970). Discontented members may choose to leave the union and non-members not to join it, ultimately weakening its power base[16] and, consequently, the prestige, influence and power wielded by the trade union leadership. Thus rational trade union leaders will have strong incentives to provide "goods" that attract people into their union, make them stay with it, and make them support the leaders at elections. The two central economic concerns of wage earners must, naturally, be employment and wage, and these are the central goods that union leaderships will have to provide, in some mix, in order to keep membership loyalty intact and to stay in power.

It is reasonable to assume that union members - being rational utility maximisers themselves - will care about their own employment only. But given the highly complex interrelationships between different sectors in a modern economy, employment prospects are strongly interrelated too - if you expand one sector of the economy, you expand them all. Therefore one may assume that in caring about their own employment people are in effect caring about economy-wide full employment.

With respect to wages I assume that what people care about are their relative wages, or their position in the wage structure. This, obviously, is just the time-honored Keynesian argument which, in turn, underlies his central assumption of the downward stickiness of money wages. Since each group of wage earners fears that a cut in their money wage rate would imply a worsening of their relative position in the wage structure vis-a-vis other groups, a reduction in real wages is more easily brought about by an increase in the price of output than by a reduction in money wages.[17] Thus the behavioral assumption with respect to wages is that people know and care about their relative position in the wage structure and that people who feel that their relative wage is too low (has fallen behind) will react by demanding wage increases to themselves (and not wage reductions to all others) in order to restore their position in the wage structure (cf. Paldam, 1989, pp. 64-65).[18]

The situation facing trade union leadership is assumed to be that of the political unemployment/inflation nexus following the first oil price hike. The unions cannot by themselves provide full (or improved) employment. For this they need the government to stimulate aggregate demand. On the other hand there is the

---

[16] There is no doubt that one of the main power resources of a union is the ability to claim that it speaks for all or most members of its constituency.

[17] A formalization can be found in Gylfason and Lindbeck (1984).

[18] As shown by Oswald (1979), basically the same type of union behavior as emerges in the following can be derived without such psychological assumptions ("jealousy effects") by stressing instead the importance of technology and demand, and more particularly the relevance of substitutability between different types of labor (p. 384). But from the broader view of social science there is no compelling reason why psychological assumptions need be inferior.

----

risk that the government will only be politically able and ready to initiate and continue effective expansionary policies if inflation is kept down. This requires a general wage restraint. Thus the strategic choice facing the unions is between the full (or improved) employment goal and the wage goal.

1.2. Strategic choices

It may, initially, be supposed that there are several independent unions, that they enter into collective bargaining at the same time, and that collective bargaining is conducted at the union level throughout. In deciding what goal to go for the leadership in any particular union will then have to take into consideration the possible strategical choices of all the other unions and the effects of these choices on what the union can achieve for itself. There are obviously two possible strategies: the union can choose wage restraint in order to (hopefully) gain in employment, or it can choose an aggressive wage strategy in order to get wage increases.

Now, if union A chooses the aggressive wage strategy and all other unions happen to choose the restrictive wage strategy, union A may get jackpot. It gets a relative wage gain. It may even get improved employment in the bargain. This may happen if the group of wage earners it represents is a minor one so that - thanks to the restraint of the other unions - sufficient wage restraint is still forthcoming economy-wide to allow the government to expand the economy. If the other unions also choose the aggressive wage strategy, union A at least avoids getting ripped off completely. While the employment may deteriorate for all, its members will at least retain their relative position in the wage structure.

If union A chooses wage restraint and all other unions do the same, the pay-off to union A will also be fine. It can then provide its members with improved employment and an unchanged relative position in the wage structure. But if all other unions choose the aggressive wage strategy while union A exercises restraint, it becomes the big looser. There will probably be a general deterioration in employment (no sufficient wage restraint is forthcoming economy-wide to allow the government to lead an accommodating policy), and its members will suffer a relative wage loss in the bargain.

In summary the best choice of union A will be not to exercise wage restraint. Such a strategy may, at best, give jackpot with respect to employment situation and relative wage position, and, at worst, status quo with respect to relative wage position (depending on what other unions do). In contrast, a strategy of wage restraint entails the risk of a big loss to union A. In the worst case nothing is gained with respect to employment in exchange for a relative wage loss. On the other hand, in the best case the strategy gives employment gains with a constant relative wage position. Since the overall worst situation to union A can arise only when it chooses the wage restraint option and the optimal one only when it chooses the opposite, it will be rational for union A to choose the aggressive over the restrictive wage policy strategy.

As the same logic applies to the strategic choice of all other unions, we necessarily end up in the lower right corner of the pay-off matrix. Hence there will be wage pressure, distributive struggle and, as a consequence, inflation despite the known repercussions on employment.

If this result is applied to the real world of stagflationary tendencies developing in the wake of the first oil price hike, it suggests that the inflationary distributive struggle about who was to bear the (main) burden from the loss of national income due to the oil price hike was fought across a battle-line between labor and business, but what happened in this struggle was highly dependent on what was happening on a quite different battlefield, where groups of wage earners tried to shift the burden among themselves and hence confronted each other over relative wage shares.

1.3. Further analysis

So far, the discussion has only demonstrated how unions' concerns about the relative wage shares of their members may have translated into economy-wide inflationary wage pressures. It has not explained the observable differences between the five countries of this study with respect to inflation. To do so, the discussion will proceed in two steps. In the first one the gloom logic of the model will be further elaborated. In the second step the question will be which alterations to the model may help to escape its destructive logic. This will, hopefully, generate some ideas as to where to look for the explanation to inter-country differences with respect to inflation experience.

The reason why aiming at wage gains rather than employment gains is the rational strategy can also be illustrated by taking a closer look at the characteristics of the two goals.

When the government stimulates aggregate demand in order to improve the employment situation it can be seen to provide a collective good in the usual sense of Rational choice theory. When it is provided, it is in principle provided to all, regardless of whether their union contributed, through wage restraint, to its provision in the first place. There can, of course, be structural, sectoral or regional unemployment even in a full employment situation. But the central point is that if you expand one sector of the economy, you expand them all. A group that does not participate (through wage restraint) in bringing about a situation where the government can expand the economy in order to improve the employment situation cannot easily be punished by being prevented from benefitting from improvements in the employment situation.[19] Thus there is no

---

[19] It might be argued, of course, that such a group will "punish itself" by pricing itself out of job. There are two reasons, however, while this effect may not be very central to the strategic choice of the unions. In the first place, there will normally be a lag between wage increases to a group and possible employment effects from this wage increase on the employment situation of this particular group, which will tend to obscure the relationship in the eyes of the rank-and-file. In the second place, the net relationship between wage increase and employment situation in a

----

direct connection between what you "pay" (in terms of wage restraint) and what you gain (in terms of employment). You may gain without paying (free rider), but you may equally well find yourself having paid without gaining (paying non-rider).[20]

Wage rises, on the other hand, come closer to being a private good. In principle at least, what concessions are wrought from the employers by a union are meant to benefit this union's membership only, not members of other unions, and a union will have strong incentives to see to that.[21]

When there is a public as well as a private good in the objective function of decision makers, the rational choice of strategy will be to optimize with respect to the private good. There is no incentive to contribute to the provision of a public good when you can be a free rider as well, and still less so when you may risk ending up as a paying non-rider.

2. Changing the outcome

Despite the model, the empirical analyses in chapter 2 demonstrated that in some countries - namely Austria and Germany - the trade unions seemed to have been highly sensitive to the employment effects of their wage strategies. If this situation is to be accounted for within the present framework of analysis, one must ask how the model and its assumptions might be modified in such a way as to allow for a situation where, under certain conditions, it becomes rational for the unions to take into account the employment consequences of their wage setting strategy. Two approaches will be considered in the following: changing the institutional set-up, and changing the pay-off structure.

---

particular group may well be rather weak. If one looks at the relationship between wage increase and employment in Danish manufacturing 1975-79 (monthly data), it is in fact found to be negative, but only after a 16-months lag, and even at the most significant lag the correlation is as low as $r = -0.11$. Thus considering full employment more of a public rather than of a private good does not seem to be too unrealistic.

[20] From a normative point of view the character of full employment as an essentially public good is a very good reason why determining the employment level should not be left to the market but be assigned to political authorities, as is the case in Keynesianism.

[21] In practice wage rises negotiated by a union may automatically be extended to non-members as well, so to some degree there can be a free rider problem with respect to wage rises too. In Denmark this is an often used argument for the trade unions to practice the "closed shop". On the other hand, such an extension will most often be to the "natural constituency" of the union only, but not to groups which belong to other unions.

2.1. The role of the institutional set-up

Up to now it has been assumed that there are numerous different trade unions participating in the "game". But according to Olson (1982, chap. 7) only "encompassing" organizations can be expected to be able to forego short-term gains to their own members in favor of a long-term growth strategy that will benefit all, and this view is rather widely accepted. In studies both by neo-corporatists[22] and by economists dealing with institutional aspects of labor markets[23] it is often stressed that neo-corporatist countries with few, highly centralized unions have performed above OECD-averages with respect to the economy during the seventies, so possibly the number of trade unions and the degree of centralization is a critical variable.[24]

The strength of the empirical evidence for this hypothesis can be questioned, however. The empirical results use to be quite sensitive to the choice of countries, the measure of economic performance used, and the time period considered.[25] If one looks at the five countries in the present study there is one high-ranking corporatist country among the low-inflation countries (Austria), while the other high-ranking corporatist country belongs to the high-inflation countries (Sweden). The medium-degree corporatist countries (Germany and Denmark) split likewise between the low- and the high-inflation group. There is no low-ranking corporatist country among the low-inflation countries, but an example can easily be found (Switzerland). Thus it seems that, with respect to the countries and the period covered here, corporatism and the degree of trade union centralisation have not been decisive in determining the path of inflation.

This agrees with what can be found if one looks at what happens in the world of the model as one moves from a fragmented to a centralized trade union system. If there are many small unions, the probability of reaping a reward from pursuing an aggressive wage strategy will look great from the point of view of any individual union. The leaders of the union might reason that if all other unions exercise wage restraint, the lack of restraint shown by one or even a small number of minor unions may go more or less unnoticed. If so, there is a good chance of getting away with the jackpot. But since all unions will reason that way, no wage restraint whatsoever will be shown. Thus it appears that with many small unions incentives are strengthened to try for a free ride and hence to choose the aggressive wage strategy.[26]

As the number of unions decreases, so does the individual probability of getting away with the lucky free ride - no wage restraint, but improved employment. If there are only three or four big unions, say, each will realize that, in the

---

[22] Cf. chapter 1, sec. 4.3.

[23] Cf. for example Bruno and Sachs (1985), Bean et al. (1986), Metcalf (1987), Soskice (1988).

[24] The topic of centralized and decentralized wage formation is discussed in Calmfors (1990).

[25] Cf. Calmfors and Driffill (1988, p. 30).

[26] Cf. Calmfors and Driffill (1988, p. 34) for a similar argument.

presence of the political unemployment/inflation nexus, the government will raise employment levels only if all of them choose the restrictive wage strategy, so the free rider incentive for pursuing an aggressive wage strategy does in fact disappear with centralisation. But it is important to notice that the paying non-rider disincentive to pursuing a restrictive wage strategy need not go with it. Even with only two unions in the system and hence no chance of improved employment without wage restraint from both, each of them runs the risk of loosing out on both relative wage position and employment if it chooses a restrictive wage strategy and the other does not.

This leaves the case of one central union. According to Paldam (1989) a central union coordinates wage increases, and hence the possibility of a free ride as well as the danger of paying for a non-ride disappears. The obvious question he does not answer is, however, how a central union can ever manage to do this.

Obviously, if there is consensus about what constitutes a "fair" wage structure, there is no problem. But if such a consensus exists, there would be no problem either if there were many different unions, because consensus about a "fair" wage structure must imply that no group would want to improve its current position in the wage structure beyond what is considered "fair" by all! In the absence of such a consensus it is hard to see how a central union can perform any kind of effective coordination of conflicting wage share claims, not the least because it would continuously be threatened by the exit-option of those who feel "left behind".[27] Thus it appears that *consensus about a "fair" wage structure is much more essential to the possibility of coordinated trade union behavior than is the existence or non-existence of one centralized trade union.*[28] More will have to be said about that topic later.

Another modification in the institutional set-up of the "game" could be to consider it only one instance in a series of identical "games", or part of an on-going interaction process, instead of a one-shot situation. In the neo-corporatism literature this continuing interaction aspect is often stressed as being central to the development of cooperation between various organizations (and between organizations and the state). In a game-theoretical framework Axelrod (1984) has shown how continuous interaction with an indeterminate time horizon may transform even the destructive logic leading to non-cooperative behavior in the "prisoners dilemma" into cooperative behavior.

In the model situation trade unions wanting all unions to exercise wage restraint have only one sanction against unions which do not comply - to give up

---

27 What a central union can do is to coordinate claims to wage increases in time. But, as is shown by the German example, coordination in time is not a necessary condition for wage claim restraint.

28 The same stand-point is taken by Lindbeck (1990, p. 330): "More fundamentally: The degree of centralization of wage formation should perhaps not be regarded as an *exogenous* variable, the consequences of which we are free to study. Maybe countries with centralized wage bargaining are simply countries that have a considerable consensus between employers, employees and the government."

wage restraint themselves in the next round. But this means that if there is a chance of jackpot at all, it must be in the first round, so there is an extra incentive for everybody to try for the free ride in the first round instead of showing wage restraint, as well as an extra fear of getting ripped off altogether. Thus, playing the "game" continuously does not by itself change the way it is played. The experiences from high-inflation Sweden - with its continuous and formalized interaction between organizations within the framework of a neo-corporatist institutional set-up - and low-inflation Germany, where attempts at establishing a similar type of interaction and institutional structure finally broke down in 1977, seem to provide some empirical support to the conclusion that continuous interaction does not by itself guarantee wage restraint, and lack of such interaction needs not automatically lead to a wage-wage race.

It does not change the situation either if it is assumed that the unions do not decide on their strategies simultaneously, but do so in sequence. This is the way wage negotiations are conducted in Germany where one or two unions open the round of collective bargaining and the others follow. Thus the followers know the strategy of the leaders. In theory this should always lead to an aggressive wage strategy, since adopting an aggressive wage strategy is the only way in which the leading unions can protect themselves from the fate of a paying non-rider, and the followers then have to adopt the same strategy in order not to get ripped off. In practice German trade unions have proved themselves able to exercise wage restraint, but obviously despite, rather than because, of their mode of bargaining.

2.2. Changing the pay-off structure

As has been pointed out above, the reason why wage restraint cannot be expected to be forthcoming in the model is that, in the presence of both a public and a private good in the objective function, it will always be rational to optimize with respect to the private good. Therefore the most obvious way to change the pay-off structure must be to change the character of one of the goods involved, i.e. to make employment (more of) a private good or wage rises (more of) a public good.

Changing employment into a private good requires that there be an "employment reward" for groups exercising wage restraint, but not for others, and an "employment punishment" for groups failing to exercise wage restraint, but not for others. This reward and punishment may be meted out, for instance, in terms of changes in the employment situation of the group concerned, or in terms of the group's direct contributions to the social cost of unemployment. Given the inter-relatedness of the various sectors of modern economies, establishing such a link seems an impossible task, however.

In this context it deserves mentioning that the policy of pre-announced money supply targets adopted by the Bundesbank in 1974 did not constitute a "privatization of the risk of unemployment" in the proper sense, although it was promptly denounced as such by German trade unions (Scharpf, 1987, p. 176). It was intended to lead to a rise in unemployment if there was no sufficient wage restraint, but there was - for good reasons - no attempt at hitting only the culprits. If some unions showed wage moderation, while others did not, all would be hit by the Bundesbank reaction, and if such reactions were not forthcoming the aggressive unions would enjoy a free ride, paid for by the more moderate unions.

Neither does a system which links (individual) contributions to unemployment insurance to the level of unemployment within a relevant group of wage earners move unemployment in the direction of becoming a private (non-) good.[29] While it certainly provides an economic incentive to the members of the particular group to try to reduce unemployment expenditures, it need not necessarily lead to wage restraint, or even a realistic assessment of the trade-off between employment and wage increases.

In the first place, what happens to unemployment among the wage earners in one group does not necessarily depend on wage developments in that particular group (alone). For example, wage restraint is not going to help if - for whatever reason - there is a fiscal or monetary contraction. Unemployment will then increase in this group too, and individual contributions to unemployment insurance with it. On the other hand the group may benefit when expansionary fiscal or monetary policies reduce unemployment, whether or not it exercised wage restraint in the first place. Thus the twin possibilities of a free ride as well as of a paid non-ride with respect to employment still exist.

In the second place, instead of trying to reduce individual contributions to unemployment insurance through wage restraint with the vague hope that at last such wage restraint will translate into improved employment levels and lower expenditures on unemployment benefits etc., there is a much more direct, quicker and safer way to accomplish the same goal. It is simply to cut back on unemployment benefits. Since those in jobs will normally outnumber the unemployed by a safe margin, there is a natural constituency for a "welfare backlash" (Korpi, 1980), and if the risk of unemployment is unevenly distributed, meaning that there is a small high-risk group facing a large low- or non-risk group, the welfare backlash is a rational political strategy for the majority.[30] Thus the system, suggested with a view to create economic incentives for those in jobs to exhibit some measure of solidarity with the unemployed, may in the end turn out to produce the opposite result.

The alternative approach to making unemployment into (more of) a private good would be to make wage increases less of a private good. If the wage

---

[29] Such a reform to the predominantly tax-financed Danish unemployment insurance system was recently suggested by the Danish Council of Economic Advisers.

[30] In a mainly tax-financed system the unemployed are to some degree "protected" against a specific welfare backlash by the relative invisibility of the costs of unemployment to the tax payer. On the other hand, unemployment benefit programs - alongside other tax-financed welfare programs - may be hit by a general welfare backlash, cf. Wilensky (1976).

structure were completely rigid, i.e. if the members of all unions automatically got the same proportional wage increase as obtained for the members of any particular union, then there would be no reason for any union to choose the aggressive wage strategy just to avoid getting ripped off. When relative wage shares are no longer a problem, the choice between an aggressive or a restrictive wage policy would solely depend on how (across the board) wage increases are valued relative to employment.

For obvious reasons the idea of a completely rigid wage structure is unrealistic. Nevertheless, existing wage structures may be more or less stable. Following Wood (1978) one may distinguish between two types of pressures on the wage structure, the combined strength of which determines its stability. "Anomic" pressures are pressures due to, e.g., labor shortages and other competitive factors, while "normative" pressures are rooted in the conception of what constitutes a "fair" wage structure, and perceived deviations of the actual from the "fair" wage structure. The following will concentrate on normative pressures.

A compression of wage differentials, accompanied by industrial conflicts, may be indicative of normative pressures on the wage structure. Such conflicts will typically be more local in character than the industry- or economy-wide conflicts that may arise in the context of collective bargaining at centralized levels.

Observable stability of the wage structure, on the other hand, does not necessarily imply the absence of normative pressures. Here it may be useful to distinguish between two different types of wage structure stability which may be termed consensual and competitive stability.

Consensual stability prevails if the existing wage structure is stable because it is by and large accepted as "fair". In that case there will not be many attempts at changing the existing wage structure - typically to compress it - and hence only limited wage share competition between groups of wage earners. As a consequence the wage structure will not generate strong incentives to initiate an inflationary wage race. There will be wage structure stability together with a generally low level of industrial disputes, reflecting the prevalence of consensus.

Competitive stability prevails if the stability of the wage structure reflects a distributional stalemate rather than consensus as to what constitutes a "fair" wage structure. In this situation stability is the momentary outcome because the success of one union in improving the relative wage share of its members triggers off compensating wage claims from other unions which in the end restore (by and large) the previous wage structure ("leap-frogging"). This kind of stability will be accompanied by higher levels of labor market unrest. As mentioned above, there is reason to expect this situation when the trade union system is highly fragmented.

The lower the degree of anomic pressures and the higher the level of consensual stability of the wage structure, the closer wage gains are to becoming a public good where everybody gets (about) the same, and the less compelling the choice of the aggressive wage strategy becomes to any union. Thus one approach to changing the outcome of the "game" and influencing the choice of wage strategy by the unions with a view to reducing inflationary pressures must obviously be to *increase the consensual stability of the wage structure.*

There are mainly two ways of doing this. The first is to use various kinds of symbolic politics, while the other relies on material incentives.

The symbolic politics approach implies the use of positively valued symbols and signals, like the slogan "give a year to Britain" or the frequent invocation of "solidarity", "equality", or "justice".[31] By identifying certain pay-offs with positively valued symbols and others with negative ones, the structure of the pay-offs may effectively be changed in such a way as to contribute to consensual stability in the end. The highly positive value attached to consensus creation in its own right in Austrian politics (cf. chapter 2) may be cited as one (highly success-ful) example of the use of symbolic politics. In a situation where - taken by itself - a consensual outcome would be less profitable (in terms of the pay-off) to a participant than a non-consensual outcome, the symbolic value associated with the mere reaching of consensus pay-offs may suffice to make the consensual outcome the optimal one.

With respect to material incentives the tax system is an example of an instru-ment which may be used to create economic incentives or disincentives to certain kinds of behavior. Extremely high marginal taxes even on moderate incomes may be a way to retain consensual stability even in a situation where the wage structure is being severely compressed. Taxing away 95 or 98 per cent of wage increases to wage earners at medium and higher income levels may be much more effective in making them accept income levelling policies in favor of low incomes groups and a compression of the wage structure than moving appeals to their sense of "justice" and "solidarity". It reduces the value of gains from an aggressive wage strategy to something close to zero for high and medium income groups.[32] Up to the late sixties the situation in Sweden was quite close to this scenario.[33]

In passing it deserves mentioning that it is, of course, equally well possible to destabilize the wage structure and hence to fuel an inflationary wage-wage race

---

[31] In the sense of Edelman (1976, p. 5) these symbols are both referential and condensational. They help to recognize and understand a situation (referential) and they arouse certain emotions in connection with that situation (condensational). In both capacities such symbols are valuable to the rational individual decision maker, because they help to reduce the complexity of the situation and lower information and decision costs. For that reason viewing symbolic politics as simply a way to fool individuals is not adequate, cf. Pirsching (1989).

[32] The effects of this type of policy on labor supply, effectiveness, etc. are a different matter, not to be considered here. Furthermore the policy may become self-defeating if it leads wage earners to set their claims with post-tax income in mind. Actually this is what the union of higher echelon white collar employees in Sweden (SACO) tried to do in the beginning of the seventies.

[33] While Swedish marginal taxes remained excessively high by the standards of most civilized countries, tax reforms during the period 1969-71 implied a certain change, as separate taxation of the incomes of husband and wife was introduced.

by the same means that may be used to stabilize it. This can be done by pressing for, or creating, a situation where the actual wage structure deviates from what is considered "fair" by significant groups of wage earners. Wage levelling policies exceeding the degree of wage structure compression acceptable to strong well-paid groups of wage earners comes to mind. If wage levelling is not widely (enough) accepted the result will become competitive stability or outright instability of the wage structure, and there will hence be a premium on aggressive trade union strategies that will contribute to inflation.

3. A wage structure hypothesis of trade union behavior, and some empirical evidence

Our hypothesis is that *inter-country differences with respect to inflation are strongly related to differences with respect to the degree of normative pressure on the wage structure. In particular, inter-country differences with respect to inflation are strongly related to differences with respect to the extent to which the political-ideological goal of incomes nivellation was pursued.* In a somewhat different terminology the hypothesis states that inter-country differences with respect to inflation are strongly related to differences with respect to the degree of consensus among groups of wage earners in each of the five countries with respect to the distribution of the economic costs of the first oil crisis.

This hypothesis is difficult to test empirically. Obviously it is built on concepts which do not easily lend themselves to quantitative assessment or just plain observation, like "normative pressure", "fair wage structure", or "consensual stability". There are also big problems in comparing the degree of stability of wage structures of different countries. Moreover, the central interest would not be in the mere observable degree of stability of various wage structures over time, but rather in their underlying dynamics. Is an observed stability over time the result of a process of rounds of leap-frogging, or does it reflect that nobody wanted to rock the boat? To answer this question thoroughly would require a strongly disaggregated analysis of wage developments, labor market conflicts, etc., the necessary data for which are simply not available.

Nevertheless, bits and pieces of empirical evidence relevant to judging the validity of the hypothesis can be found. The kind of hypothesis testing they permit is at a highly aggregated level of analysis. Therefore the (substantive) strength of each singular confrontation between hypothesis and evidence is not all that impressive - not many competing hypotheses are eliminated in the process, since findings concerning high level relationships are normally open to a number of different interpretations. But seen in combination the findings nevertheless may support and reinforce each other, if they exhibit a theoretically meaningful pattern. Moreover, not much can be said about the strength of the relationships found and about their explanatory power (in the usual statistical sense). This is a simple consequence of the generally low level of measurement of the variables involved.[34]

The hypothesis formulated above stipulates a (negative) relationship between wage structure stability and inflation, mediated through union pushfulness.[35] This in turn is due to the nature of the bargaining "game" unions are engaging in. In figure 5.1 the central relationships involved are shown in the form of a simple causal model. The signs in parentheses indicate a positive (+) or negative (-) relationship, respectively.

Following the original paper by Hines (1964) there has been much discussion as to the appropriate way of measuring union pushfulness. Strong critique has been levied against his use of the change and the level of union density as a measure.[36] It has been pointed out, i.a., that people may become unionized for many different reasons.[37] No convincing argument is suggested as to why increasing union density by itself should make for increasing union militancy. This may impair the validity of Hines' measure.

On the other hand it seems to be an intuitively plausible assumption that people will tend to join unions in greater numbers when they feel their interests as wage earners threatened - for example by wage structure compression - than when this is not the case, and that such perceived threat will make for higher levels of union militancy as well. Thus there does not have to be any direct causal relationship between increasing union density and increasing union militancy. Both may well have the same root. If this assumption is correct, union pushful-

---

34 As a matter of personal taste, I prefer the honest use of "soft" measurements - e.g. variables allowing only classifications - to the use of coconuts (measurements that appear "hard" from the outside, but are in reality soft inside).

35 This term was coined, to my knowledge, by Hines (1964).

36 See especially Purdy and Zis (1974). It should be noticed that the results of various attempts to test the Hines-model empirically (cf. for example Schnabel, 1989) do not directly apply to the present case. What Hines claims to account for is inflation *per se,* and empirical tests are hence aimed at determining how much of the whole of inflation can be ascribed to union pushfulness. What is dealt with in the present case is, in contrast, inter-country variations in inflation over and above the international element.

37 See Kjellberg (1983, pp. 29-31) for a survey. Recently Pedersen (1989) has forwarded the hypothesis that the level and post-war development of union density in Denmark and a number of other OECD-countries depends on the institutional structure of the unemployment insurance system. In Denmark, Finland, Sweden and Belgium unemployment insurance funds are administered by the trade unions, and in these countries the post-war increase in union density has been high. In the other countries unemployment insurance is taken care of by a state agency and in these countries union density has stayed constant or has even dropped. The rationale behind that finding must be that in countries where the unemployment insurance system is administered by the trade unions, people tend to enter a union when they become insured. But, as pointed out by Darmer (1990), the model of unionization of Danish workers tested in Pedersen (1984), which contains a number of variables relevant to the explanation of why people become insured against unemployment, does fit Danish data for the period 1940-76 poorly ($R^2 = 0.18$).

ness could be measured both by changes in union density and by changes in union militancy, i.e. conflict levels. While both measures are far from perfect, the use of both provides a check on their respective validity.

Figure 5.1.: Causal model of the wage structure - inflation hypothesis

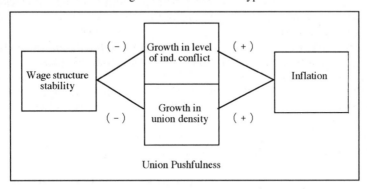

Working backwards in the model in figure 5.1. (from effect to causes) the following empirical propositions for the period 1974-79 can be derived: (i) the level of industrial conflict must be expected to have increased less (or even to have been decreasing) in Austria and Germany (the low inflation countries) than in Denmark, Sweden and the UK. It should have increased in the latter three countries; (ii) the growth in union density is expected to have been lower in Austria and Germany than in the other three countries; (iii) the wage structures in Austria and Germany must show less evidence of compression in the aftermath of the first oil price hike.

In looking for empirical evidence, industrial conflicts may appear the easiest point to start. At least there are data series covering the incidence of industrial conflicts (normally strikes) for all five countries (Paldam and Rasmussen, 1980). For Denmark, Sweden and the UK data on the number of conflicts (STNC), the number of workers affected (STWI), and the number of working days lost due to industrial conflicts (STDL) are available. For Austria and Germany, the total number of conflicts is not reported, but the other two figures are collected.

Using these data directly as an indicator of the level of consensus or conflict in a comparative way would be very problematic, however.[38] In the first place, the data are not collected in the same way in all five countries of this study.[39] In the

---

[38] As a matter of fact, using strike data at all is in some respects highly problematic. As is well known, data do not in general speak for themselves, but strike data may actually lie!

[39] For Denmark, for instance, only conflicts involving at least 100 lost work days are included. "Political strikes" are excluded. For Germany there is a minimum duration of one day, and for the UK at least 10 workers have to be affected, the duration has to be at least one day, and

second place, the number of workers affected and of working days lost does not only reflect the industrial conflict level. It is also influenced by the sheer size of the economy, and this differs widely between the five countries in the present study. In the third place, all five countries, with the UK as sole exception, have rather centralized bargaining systems. This means that the conflict series, especially those on number of workers affected and number of working days lost, also contain instances of those very big conflicts occurring occasionally in connection with periodic collective bargaining in the whole or major parts of the labor market. This type of conflict is less indicative of the extent of relative wage share conflicts than is the extent of minor, local industrial disputes.

One technical way of getting (partially) rid of the last problem is to smooth the series such as to reduce the importance of the big conflicts, and to concentrate on the general trend in the conflict level instead. In the present context this has been done by applying a LOWESS-filter (Cleveland, 1979) to all three series.

To take care of the comparison problem arising from differences in the sheer size of the five economies, the 1974-79 average of each (smoothed) series will be compared to the corresponding 1955-73 average.[40] These relative changes can then be treated as roughly[41] comparable across economies of different sizes, and one would expect to find strong increases in the average incidence of industrial conflicts between 1974 and 1979, relative to 1955-73, in Denmark, Sweden, and the UK (the high-inflation countries), but not in Austria and Germany (the low-inflation countries). The empirical findings are given in table 5.1.

The Austrian strike pattern is exactly as expected: on both measures available. There is a giant drop (to about one-tenth) in the average level of industrial conflicts 1974-79, compared to 1955-73.

Also with respect to Denmark and Sweden a clear picture emerges from table 5.1. In both countries a sizeable increase in the average level of industrial conflict is found. Moreover, the data indicate a certain shift in the pattern of industrial conflicts in both countries. There is a strong rise in the number of conflicts which is not matched by a corresponding increase in the number of working days lost due to the conflicts.

---

political strikes are excluded. Only Austria and Sweden do, in principle, count all conflicts, cf. Paldam and Rasmussen (1980, p. 2).

[40] This period was chosen because by and large it covers the period of uninterrupted prosperity growth in all five countries.

[41] The reservation is due to the fact that - among others - the problem of different inclusion criteria in the collection of conflict data does remain unsolved.

Thus there seems to have been a tendency towards more numerous, but shorter conflicts in these two countries. Intuitively this type of conflict pattern - many conflicts, but of limited extent and duration - seems to correspond well with expectations in the case of (internal) strife about relative wage shares. The (relative) gains to one group of wage earners (typically low paid groups) unleash compensating claims from others in order to restore what the latter consider proper wage differentials.[42]

Table 5.1.: Average incidences of industrial conflicts 1955-73 and 1974-79 (smoothed series)

		STNC*	STWI*	STDL*
AUSTRIA	1955-73	-	24149.09	43078.90
	1974-79	-	2239.98	4529.97
	Δ%	-	9.28	10.52
GERMANY	1955-73	-	100698.52	394290.87
	1974-79	-	129251.26	374041.97
	Δ%	-	128.35	94.86
DENMARK	1955-73	40.40	20581.97	42174.12
	1974-79	202.48	74391.40	160777.41
	Δ%	501.19	361.44	381.22
SWEDEN	1955-73	25.40	3959.52	40607.44
	1974-79	87.57	14446.30	43813.51
	Δ%	344.75	364.85	107.89
UK	1955-73	2491.46	990185.56	5187790.05
	1974-79	2416.49	1055654.49	8944431.83
	Δ%	96.99	106.62	172.41

*See text for explanation
Data: Paldam and Rasmussen (1980); own computations

---

[42] Lewin (1977, pp. 205-206) explicitly rejects the interpretation of the increased frequency of wildcat strikes in Sweden after 1973 which views it as part of a reaction from higher paid groups of wage earners against the effects of the solidaristic wage policy. In his survey he found that wildcat strikes occurred most frequently in trade union sections where wages were low. His results cover only one of the relevant years (1974), however. Moreover, in relation to a series of wildcat strikes 1969-70 Flanagan et al. (1983, p. 329) notice that wage issues were raised by strikers in small firms and in sub-branches where wages were low compared to regional averages, but that most of the strikers were highly paid workers. The same might well be held against Lewin's interpretation of his findings.

Faxén, finally, has pointed out that in 1974 and 1975 more than 70 per cent of all wildcat strikes occurred within four months after the conclusion of the central agreement. This he regards as evidence that a majority of the wildcat strikes were a reaction against the compression of wage differentials (Flanagan et al., 1983, p. 329).

The two cases that, at first view, do not turn out exactly as expected are Germany and the UK. In the German case the evidence appears to be ambiguous. There is an (unexpected) increase in the number of workers affected by industrial conflict 1974-79, and, at the same time, there is a drop in the number of working days lost. These results, for the most part, may reflect the impact of two short, but relatively extensive industrial conflicts in relation to the ordinary rounds of collective bargaining in Germany. The first one occurred among public employees in 1974, and the other one in the Southern German metal industry in 1978. These two conflicts apart, the general level of industrial conflict in Germany 1974-79 was actually lower than in the preceding period 1955-73.

In the UK a very high level of industrial conflict is found for both periods. On two of the three measures (STWI and STDL) there is an increase of the 1974-79 mean over the mean of the previous period, while the average number of industrial conflicts appears to have fallen a bit. The latter is probably explained by a change in the bargaining mode in British coal-mining, which by 1960 was responsible for about 60 per cent of all work stoppages. The changed bargaining mode reduced this proportion to about four per cent by 1970.[43] If this fact is taken into account, then the UK findings do actually show much the same pattern as the findings from Sweden and Denmark, i.e. a tendency towards more numerous, but shorter conflicts in the period 1974-79.

Thus the development in the level of industrial conflicts 1974-79, compared to 1955-73, in the three high-inflation countries (Denmark, Sweden and the UK) turns out to have been remarkably similar in two respects. In the first place, there was an increase in the average level of industrial conflicts in the three countries. In the second place, there was, in all three countries, a certain shift in the pattern of conflicts in the direction of more numerous, but shorter and less extensive conflicts.

In the low-inflation countries (Austria and Germany) the picture is different. In Austria there was a dramatic drop in the level of industrial conflicts 1974-79, compared to the preceding period (where this level was low, too, by most international standards). For Germany the findings are more ambiguous but do allow the (cautious) conclusion that the trend in the level of industrial conflicts in Germany 1974-79 remained approximately constant, compared to the preceding period.

Next we turn to the development in union density. This concept provides a series of measurement problems.[44] As a check on reliability two data sources have been used: Kjellberg (1983) has data on unionization in all five countries, while Scharpf (1987) contains data on unionization in four countries (minus Denmark).

Table 5.2. shows the expected pattern with respect to the development of union density in the five countries of the present study. Independent of data source, growth in union density was considerably lower in the low inflation countries (Austria and Germany) than in the other three. Thus there is the same

----

[43] Tarling and Wilkinson (1977, p. 403, note 4).
[44] See Kjellberg (1983, pp. 33-48) for a discussion.

pattern of development in union density as in the development of union militancy (strike activity).

Finally some evidence concerning the wage structure development in the five countries 1974-79 will be considered. This evidence is drawn together from the country-specific sections in chapter 2 (to which the reader is referred for further documentation).

Sweden and Denmark constitute clear-cut cases of wage structure compression during the period considered.[45] In Sweden, wage differentials within and, to a somewhat lesser degree, between white- and blue-collar groups kept falling during the seventies (Hibbs, 1990, p. 81). By the end of the decade the Swedish wage structure was considerably more compressed than at its beginning.

Table 5.2.: Growth in union density

	Scharpf (1987)	Kjellberg (1983)	
Austria			
1973	59.8	59	
1979	59.3	58	
difference	-0.5	-1	
Germany			
1973	32.7	32	
1979	35.9	33	
difference	3.2	1	
Denmark			
1973	na	62	(69)[a]
1979	na	71[b]	(79)
difference	na	9	(10)
Sweden			
1973	72.2	77	
1979	79.1	85	
difference	6.9	8	
UK			
1973	50.6	48	
1979	57.7	55	
difference	7.1	7	

[a] 1976
[b] 1975

Also in Denmark a considerable compression of the wage structure took place in the seventies. In the private sector the wage differentials between blue- and

---

45 Cf. Faxén (1982, p. 385).

white-collar groups were diminished. While the average yearly income of a male white-collar worker was 128 per cent of the average yearly income of an unskilled male (blue-collar) worker in 1974, this difference had been narrowed down to 118 per cent by 1979.[46] On the other hand, there was almost no change in the wage differentials between unskilled and skilled male workers, despite frequent invocations of solidary principles in wage policies of this period. This indicates that especially skilled male workers were willing, and able, to restore to its previous size the wage differentials vis à vis unskilled male (and female) workers whenever it had been narrowed as a consequence of collective bargaining agreements. There was also a considerable narrowing down of wage differentials in the public sector, mainly as an effect of the change from a percentage to a flat rate CoL-regulation in 1975 and of repeated solidary collective bargaining agreements.

In the UK the wage structure appears to have been stable in the sense that there is no evidence of a general compression of wage differentials - as in Sweden and Denmark - in the period 1974-79.[47] This is remarkable not the least since attempts at a certain levelling of wages were central elements - implemented mainly in the form of flat rate limits on wage increases - in the "Social Contract" between the Labour government and the TUC 1975-77. Hence the surface stability of the wage structure in the UK must be interpreted as the outcome of strong resistance to wage structure compressions by the higher paid income groups (Pond, 1980, p. 97) as well as of the ability of such groups (thanks primarily to the strongly decentralized bargaining system in the British labor market) to evade the consequences of solidary wage policies by local bargaining.

The wage structure stability observed in Austria and Germany[48] in the period considered is of an entirely different kind. In both countries - but most strongly in Austria - it reflects the absence (by and large) of attempts to compress the existing wage structure. Rather to the contrary: if there was any tendency, it seems to have been in the direction of a mild increase of wage differentials.

The variation in wage structure dynamics reflects an important difference in the policy goals and priorities of the labor movements in the five countries. In three of them - Denmark, Sweden and the UK - the policies of the labor movement, i.e. the Socialdemocratic parties and the trade union movement, can be characterized as having been quite strongly distribution-oriented with a view to creating a higher measure of equality in society in general and with respect to

---

[46] Egmose (1985, p. 57). The figures are based on wage data from members of the Danish Employers' Association (DA) only.

[47] Pond (1980, esp. pp. 96-99). The same conclusion is reached in Egmose (1985) on the basis of data on family pre-tax income.

[48] Cf. Faxén (1982, pp. 384-385).

the distribution of income in particular.[49] Attempts at the imposition of solidary wage policies were a natural and central part of this overall orientation. There is little evidence that the onset of the economic recession in the wake of the first oil price hike caused any reconsideration on the part of the labor movements in these three countries.[50]

In comparison, in the period considered here, the policies of the labor movements of Austria and Germany appear to have been much more strongly growth-oriented. While the Socialdemocratic governments in both countries undoubtedly considered "a higher degree of social justice"[51] a policy goal and voiced occasional support of it, it never rose to the same prominence in actual policies as in Denmark, Sweden and the UK.

In this connection the near-total absence of solidary wage policies in both countries deserves special mention. According to v. Beyme (1978, p. 133) German trade unions tended to "praise rather than practice solidary wage policies".[52] Even very moderate attempts at solidary wage formation turned out to be extremely unpopular with both the general public and the union rank and file.[53] With respect to Austria a study of Austrian income distribution and distribution policies (Guger, 1989, pp. 186-187) stresses the difference with explicit reference to the Scandinavian countries that "... *contrary to Austria* (my emphasis) the trade unions of these countries explicitly pursue a more equal income distribution as their goal."

In summary, the empirical relationship between the degree of consensual wage structure stability and inflation performance of the five countries, mediated through union pushfulness, stipulated by the central hypothesis presented above, could be identified empirically. In Denmark, Sweden and the UK the actual development of the wage structure, in the level and type of industrial conflicts

---

[49] In a programmatic way this orientation expressed itself in a number of publications, especially from the early seventies. See for instance for Sweden Nordenstam (1972) and for Denmark Lykketoft (1973).

[50] How all-pervasive the idea of income nivellation was in the thinking of the Danish Socialdemocratic government can for example be seen from the following part of the speech by the Socialdemocratic prime minister Anker Jørgensen in the Folketing on March 7, 1975, when he introduced a bill to stop the outbreak of a large-scale strike by enacting statutory incomes policy measures: "Furthermore we have to accept that there is only limited scope for increases in total incomes in society. This means that there can be no increase for higher incomes groups if the solution is to be socially just. The limited possibilities for increases must as far as possible be reserved for the lower incomes groups only." (Folketingstidende 1974-75, 2. saml., sp. 1068; my translation). There is logic to this sentence only if the goal of income nivellation is accepted as given beforehand.

[51] Jahresbericht der Bundesregierung (1977, p. 7).

[52] My translation.

[53] The derogatory phrase "Klunckers Eintopf" (Kluncker's stew) was coined to characterize (actually very moderate) attempts by the chairman of one of the trade unions of public employees, Kluncker, to get an extra pay raise to low paid members of his organization.

1974-79, and in the growth of union density indicate a lack of consensual wage structure stability in the period under consideration. The predominance of the political goal of equalization in the political strategy of the labor movements in the three countries points in the same direction. But this, as argued, makes a policy of wage restraint non-rational to unions and hence contributes to fuelling inflation: logically enough, in all three countries a rather high level of consumer price inflation persisted during the seventies. In Austria and Germany, on the other hand, the situation has been characterized by a high level of consensual stability of the wage structure, indicated by the observable constancy of wage differentials together with a low level of industrial conflicts (albeit the evidence for Germany is ambiguous on that point), low growth in unionization levels, and the absence of egalitarian aspirations with respect to wages. In such a situation, wage restraint is no longer necessarily a non-rational policy for unions, and wage restraint was in fact forthcoming in both countries. As a consequence inflation was quite quickly brought under control.

One final point deserves to be mentioned. The division line between high- and low-inflation countries in this study coincides with a cleavage between countries with a high and countries with a low level of wage structure consensus. But it does not coincide all the way with a dividing line between countries with a centralized and countries with a decentralized bargaining system in the labor market. Thus it appears (once more) that actual political consensus and conflict was more important to policy choices and political performance than were institutional arrangements.

4. Tying things together: Unemployment, inflation, and strategy coordination

Up till now unemployment and inflation have been treated as if they were independent dimensions of the economic problems to be addressed by crisis policy measures after the first oil price hike. But as has been mentioned already (chapter 4) this separation of unemployment and inflation into two independent problems was chosen merely for analytical convenience. In reality they are closely intertwined, and in the following they will be tied together again.

The concept of political cost, introduced in chapter 4, provides a means for the conceptual integration of the unemployment- and inflation-dimensions of the stagflation problem in the context of the present study. The main way in which trade unions could lower the "price" of employment stimulating policies to the government and hence further the full employment goal was by contributing to the dampening of inflationary pressures through wage restraint. On the other hand they could also raise the price of such policies to the government by adopting an aggressive wage strategy (with inflationary consequences).

Despite this link between trade union wage policy and government demand management (full employment) policy, no actor could by means of its own strategic choice force the other to adopt (or refrain from adopting) a certain type of policy. The relationship is more complex.

In Austria and Germany trade unions quite rapidly adjusted to the economic crisis by (after an initial maladjustment) adopting and staying with restrictive wage policies which strongly contributed to low inflation in both countries. Thus in both Austria and Germany the trade unions adopted cooperative strategies in the interest of governmental full employment policies. In Austria the political cost of unemployment was high enough to make the government use the "room" created for full employment policies by trade union wage restraint to the maximum, and here unemployment was effectively kept down. In Germany, by contrast, the political cost of unemployment was not significant enough to induce the German government to follow similar lines. Here the government, in effect, exploited trade union wage restraint - and the low inflation to which it had contributed - by cashing in the bonus associated with low inflation without combating unemployment sufficiently by demand stimulation.

Table 5.3.: Government - trade union strategic interaction, and policy outcomes

	Unions: Restrictive wage policy	
	strong	weak
Government: Full employment policy — **strong**	*Strong coordination* High employment Low inflation AUSTRIA	*Exploitation* High employment High inflation SWEDEN
Government: Full employment policy — **weak**	*Exploitation* Unemployment Low inflation GERMANY	*Weak coordination* Unemployment High inflation DENMARK UK

In Denmark, Sweden and the UK the trade unions did not, in general, exercise the same degree of wage restraint as can be observed in Austria and Germany. Thus in comparison the wage strategy adopted in these three countries was clearly much less cooperative. Nevertheless the Swedish government was forced by the political cost of unemployment to pursue a demand stimulating full employment strategy. It did so despite the strong inflationary pressures in the Swedish economy which Swedish trade unions did only occasionally try to help to control. In this case the trade unions effectively exploited the government by not showing a higher degree of wage restraint in return for the government's full employment policies. In Denmark and the UK, finally, the political cost of unemployment to the government was not sufficiently high to force it to adopt the amount of demand stimulation necessary to keep down unemployment regardless of union wage strategy and the development in inflation. On the other hand the trade unions were unable to "deliver the goods", i.e. wage restraint, due to the pressures from the wage structure. Thus only weak, if any, coordination of strategies was attained.

In summary the types of strategic interaction between government and trade unions and their different outcomes are as in table 5.3. The degree of strategic coordination is highly important. This should come as no surprise, given the account of what was named the "Keynesian coordination problem" in chapter 2 above. In that respect the findings of the present study agree with, and support, the findings reported in Scharpf (1987). But where Scharpf appears to treat institutions as the main explanatory variable behind inter-country differences with respect to the degree of strategic coordination attained (or even attainable), the present study has stressed the influence of political cleavages, especially those related to distributional problems in society. These cleavages affect the ability of governments and trade unions, as rational actors, to coordinate their particular strategies into a single concerted anti-crisis strategy.

Chapter 6
Conclusion and Some Afterthoughts

1. Summary

The onset of the economic crisis 1973-74 posed a new and different challenge to the economic-political decision makers in Western countries. In order to avoid stagflation, a "Keynesian coordination" of expansive fiscal and monetary policies with a restrictive wage policy became mandatory (Scharpf, 1987). This called for a coordination of economic strategies, primarily between governments and trade unions.

The five countries included in the present study were not uniformly successful in bringing about this vital coordination of strategies. The outcomes of their crisis policies varied accordingly. Austria did best, providing us with the rare, but encouraging, example of a workable solution, made possible through large-scale, coordinated efforts by the main economic actors. In Germany and Sweden coordination partially failed. In Germany the government failed to stimulate the economy sufficiently, even though, after 1974, the German trade unions adapted quickly to the new situation and switched to a moderate wage policy. As a consequence, there was unemployment and, at the same time, relative price stability and a surplus on the balance of payments. In Sweden, on the other hand, the government tried to stimulate the economy (in order to avoid open unemployment) through massive deficit-spending, although the Swedish trade unions did not respond with a policy of sustained wage restraint. As a consequence, Swedish unemployment stayed at low levels, but at the price of high inflation rates and recurring balance of payment problems. In Denmark and the UK, coordination of government and trade union strategies failed even more dramatically. These countries saw neither a sustained policy of demand stimulation nor sustained wage moderation. They came to suffer from high rates of unemployment, high rates of inflation and recurring balance of payment crises at the same time.

The central question has been why the five countries fared so differently in their attempts to achieve the crucial coordination of strategies. Following Katzenstein (1984, p. 31) our aim has been to show "how these strategies and outcomes result from the self-defined interests of actors". In this endeavor the main emphasis has been on the incentives for governments and trade unions to behave cooperatively and to bring about a stable coordination of their strategies.

It has been argued that governments have an incentive to stimulate the economy and enact policies to fight unemployment efficiently when unemployment carries political costs in terms of loss of popular support at the polls. If this is the case, governments may, even in the absence of trade union cooperation, choose to stimulate the economy (in order to combat unemployment) as seen in the case of Sweden. On the other hand, if there is no political cost to unemployment, governments may choose not to stimulate the economy sufficiently, even if the trade unions decide to lead a cooperative wage policy. This was the situation in Germany.

It has further been shown that growth-oriented trade unions have stronger

----

incentives (or weaker disincentives) to behave cooperatively than distribution-oriented trade unions. If unions fight over the wage structure and relative
wage shares, every cooperative union faces the risk of being exploited by free
riders if it opts for a moderate wage policy in order to enable the government to
stimulate the economy (while others do not). If the wage structure is stable, and
existing wage differentials are generally accepted, a wage-wage race becomes less
likely. This is why a moderate wage policy could be initiated and sustained in
Germany and Austria. In Denmark and Sweden, on the other hand, inter-union
quarrels about relative wage shares made wage moderation much more difficult
to achieve. In the UK, inter-union conflict over relative wage shares made a
moderate incomes policy break down when a number of unions decided to try to
recoup part of their losses in relative wage shares, incurred as a consequence of a
solidary incomes policy.

Thus the generally poor results of Danish crisis policy 1974-79 were not
inevitable, the fate of a small, open economy vulnerable to external forces
("beyond our control"). Our analysis shows that policy failure contributed
significantly to the outcome. The government and the trade unions failed to
achieve a "Keynesian coordination" of strategies. In that sense, failure was
chosen, not imposed.

There is no reason for doubting that unemployment was considered a salient
issue both by the Danish governments of the period and by the trade unions and
that they all would have liked to see it disappear. But politically, the government
could live with unemployment (at least for the time being) and afford the attitude
of Mr. Micawber (to wait and hope that something might turn up). The frequent
elections proved, time and again, that it was not "punished" for the unemployment situation. Thus there was no incentive to follow the Swedish example and
keep unemployment levels down, even at the cost of runaway inflation rates and
balance of payment deficits. There was no incentive either to ensure a closer
coordination of strategies by coaxing or pressuring the unions into adopting a
more moderate wage strategy.

The Danish trade unions, on the other hand, also lacked incentives to adopt a
cooperative strategy in order to improve the employment situation. Their
traditional concern about distribution and relative wage shares made moderation
a risky bet for each single union, with only a dubious pay-off in terms of
employment gains and an ever-present danger of losing out with respect to
relative wage shares. No union was keen on seeing others take a free ride on
moderation. Likewise, no union could afford the part of the paying non-rider -
paying the price (in terms of relative wage share losses) without getting the ride
(in terms of an improved employment situation). Evidently, the rational strategy
of the unions had to be to try to protect - or improve - their members' position
in the wage structure and to leave unemployment to the government to worry
about.

2. Some afterthoughts

It is in the nature of inquiry that every answer tends to provoke new questions. This is certainly the case with the present analysis and its results. Provided the answers are accepted as valid,[1] the most obvious questions they raise appear to be (a) why a distributional consensus - or a truce - neither existed nor established itself in Denmark under the impact of the post-1973 crisis, (b) why mass unemployment was so easily and seemingly painlessly accepted in the population, and (c) whether the lack of distributional consensus and the popular acquiescence in mass unemployment are related by a common underlying factor, i.e. should properly be considered just two different expressions of the same thing.

Any answer to these questions must - at present - remain highly tentative and even speculative, although future research may hopefully be able to confirm or reject them. With these reservations in mind I suggest that both the lack of distributional consensus and the high degree of popular acquiescence in mass unemployment should be considered expressions of the weakening of a general sense of solidarity in society. This, in turn, reflects the incipient erosion of the "big compromise"[2] underlying the development of the Danish welfare state after the second world war, and especially after 1958.[3]

There are indeed indications that this consensus was beginning to crack in Denmark in the early seventies, the most spectacular of them undoubtedly being the "landslide election" of 1973 (Nannestad, 1989a, pp. 77-112 and above, chapter 3, sec. 1).[4] The ferments that exploded the Danish party system at that election had, however, been brewing for some time, and the emergence of a new political cleavage line associated with, anti-welfare-state attitudes can be traced back at least to the 1971-election (Nannestad, 1989a, pp. 74-76).

---

[1] Although I think the answers to be valid, it should be stressed that all I can lay claim to is to have found *a* truth, not *the* truth.

[2] The "big compromise" was an implicit understanding. Nobody signed anything at any time. The compromise allowed gradual expansion of the welfare state on condition that private business could continue to operate in a free market unhampered by state interference.

[3] This point of view is not necessarily contradicted by findings from surveys (mostly from the 80s) which show widespread public support for the welfare state and welfare state expenditures, cf. for example Goul Andersen (1982; 1988a; 1988b) or Kristensen (1982). The person taking a free ride on the bus may well be found to be in favor of maintaining or even extending bus services.

[4] A somewhat parallel development was going on in Sweden at about the same time (cf. chapter 2, sec. 4), although there the process was less vehement than in Denmark. Thus the Swedish Socialdemocrats lost power in 1976, but there was never a "landslide election" of the Danish type (or issue content) in Sweden. Also the increase in the level of industrial conflict after 1974 was weaker (on two out of three indices) in Sweden than in Denmark, cf. chapter 5, table 5.2. This seems to agree nicely with the fact that contrary to what happened in Denmark the priority of the full employment goal was retained in Sweden throughout the whole period.

But why should this process of erosion start at the beginning of the 70s? An answer to this question could be that when the "happy 60s" came to a close, it was finally beginning to dawn on a growing number of people that, after all, the welfare state was not a positive-sum game, but rather a zero-sum game (or possibly even a game with a negative pay-off in the long run). Two critical experiences might have contributed to such a re-assessment.

The first experience is the disappointing performance (at least when compared to expectations) of the liberal-bourgeois government 1968-71 (the first non-socialist government in 15 years) in the field of economic policies and, especially, with respect to taxation. While in opposition the three parties in the coalition had criticized - harshly at times - the ever-increasing tax level. "Money is best kept in the pockets of the citizens" had been a catchy conservative slogan. But once in government the parties had presided over the most rapid increase in the level of taxation seen yet. It could no longer be believed that rising taxes were due to the desires or the ineptitude of the Socialdemocrats. Such tax-pressures were endemic to the welfare state.

The second critical experience may have come with the publication in 1971 of a voluminous work on the development of the public sector until 1985 and the associated perspectives (Perspektivplanredegørelsen I),[5] the authors of which were top civil servants from various ministries dealing with economic affairs. With merciless candor they argued that the present growth rates of the welfare state were unsustainable and that the period where conflicts over priorities could be avoided or covered up by just expanding public services and programs had gone. Time had come when developments in the public sector were to be financed, not by an expansion of the budget, but, rather, through reallocation of resources. This had to imply that some interests would be left unserved by the welfare state. The further implication was that some people would pay for the welfare state without getting equivalent returns.

Thus, by the beginning of the 70s it was becoming clear that there was a price tag attached to the welfare state and its services. A bill had to be footed by someone.

Not us, they all said.

---

5 The report received its due share of publicity, much more so than its successor (Perspektivplanredegørelsen II, 1974) which likewise called for better planning within the public sector.

References

Alesina (1988): Alberto Alesina, "Macroeconomics and Politics", *Brookings Macroeconomic Annual 1988*, pp. 14-52.

Alt (1979): James E. Alt, *The Politics of Economic Decline*, Cambridge: Cambridge University Press.

Alt (1985): James E. Alt, "Political Parties, World Demand, and Unemployment: Domestic and International Sources of Economic Activity", *American Political Science Review*, vol. 79, pp. 1016-1040.

Altvater et al. (1979): Elmar Altvater, Jürgen Hoffmann and Willi Semmler, *Vom Wirtschaftswunder zur Wirtschaftskrise*, Berlin: Verlag Olle & Wolter.

Andersen (1987): Torben M. Andersen, "Udviklingslinier i teorien om den økonomiske politik", *Politica*, vol. 19, no. 2, pp. 133-147.

Andersen (1988): Torben M. Andersen, "Makroøkonometriske modeller, prognoser og økonomisk politik", *Økonomi og Politik*, vol. 61, no. 1, pp. 42- 51.

Andersen (1989): Torben M. Andersen, "Stabilization Policies Towards Internal and External Balance - Theory and Some Nordic Experiences", *paper presented to the conference on Unemployment-Inflation Trade-off's in Europe, Stockholm, January 12-14.*

Andersen and Schneider (1986): Torben M. Andersen and Friedrich Schneider, "Coordination of Fiscal and Monetary Policy under Different Institutional Arrangements", *European Journal of Political Economy*, vol. 2, no. 2, pp. 169-191.

Andersen and Åkerholm (1982): Palle Schelde Andersen and Johnny Åkerholm, "Scandinavia", in Andrea Boltho (ed.), *The European Economy. Growth and Crisis*, Oxford: Oxford University Press.

Andersson (1987): Jan Otto Andersson, "The Economic Policy Strategies of the Nordic Countries", in Hans Keman, Heikki Paloheimo and Paul F. Whiteley (eds.), *Coping with the Economic Crisis*, Beverly Hills: Sage.

Angermann and Plasser (1979): Erhard Angermann and Fritz Plasser, "Wahlen und Wähler in Österreich 1972-75", in Andreas Khol and Axel Stirnemann, *Österreichisches Jahrbuch für Politik 1978*, München and Wien: Oldenbourg & Verlag für Geschichte und Politik.

Arbejdsdirektoratet (1980): Arbejdsdirektoratet, *Arbejdsdirektoratets årsberetning 1979*, Copenhagen: Arbejdsdirektoratet.

Arrow (1951): Kenneth J. Arrow, *Social Choice and Individual Values*, New Haven: Yale University Press.

Axelrod (1984): Robert Axelrod, *The Evolution of Cooperation*, New York: Basic Books.

Baring (1982): Arnulf Baring, *Machtwechsel. Die Ära Brandt-Scheel*, Stuttgart: Deutsche Verlags-Anstalt.

Barnett (1973): Malcolm J. Barnett, "Aggregate Models of British Voting Behaviour", *Political Studies 1973*, vol. 2, pp. 121-134.

Barry (1970): Brian M. Barry, *Sociologists, Economists and Democracy*, London: Collier-Macmillan.

Basler (1981): Hans-Peter Basler, "Lohnentwicklung und Lohnpolitik als Bestimmungsgründe konjktureller Verläufe und struktureller Verschiebungen", *Deutsches Institut für Wirtschaftsforschung*, Sonderheft 134, Berlin: Duncker und Humblot.

Bayer (1981): Kurt Bayer, "Funktionelle Einkommensverteilung in Österreich 1954 bis 1979", in Hannes Suppanz and Michael Wagner (eds.), *Einkommensverteilung in Österreich. Ein einführender Überblick*, München: R. Oldenbourg Verlag.

Bean et al. (1986): Charles R. Bean, P. Richard G. Layard and Stephen J. Nickell, "The Rise in Unemployment: A Multi-Country Study", *Economica*, Special Issue on Unemployment, pp. S1-S22.

Bernanke (1981): Ben S. Bernanke, "Bankruptcy, Liquidity, and Recession", *The American Economic Review*, vol. 71, supp. 1, pp. 155-159.

von Beyme (1978): Klaus von Beyme, "Politische und sozio-ökonomische Entwicklungen seit 1974 im Lichte gewerkschaftlicher Interessen", *Gewerkschaftliche Monatshefte*, no. 3, pp. 130-137.

von Beyme (1979): Klaus von Beyme, *Das politische System der Bundesrepublik Deutschland*, München: Piper Verlag.

Beveridge (1944): William H. Beveridge, *Full Employment in a Free Society*, London: HMSO.

Blackaby (1978): Frank T. Blackaby, "General Appraisal", in Frank T. Blackaby (ed.), *British Economic Policy 1960-74*, Cambridge: Cambridge University Press.

Bös, Genser and Holzmann (1979): Dieter Bös, Bernd Genser and Robert Holzmann, "Die finanzpolitische Entwicklung in Österreich 1975-1978", *Finanzarchiv*, Neue Folge, vol. 37, pp. 485-510.

Borre and Katz (1973): Ole Borre and Daniel Katz, "Party Identification and Its Motivational Basis in a Multiparty System: A Study of the Danish General Election of 1971", *Scandinavian Political Studies*, vol. 8, pp. 69-112.

Breuss (1980): Fritz Breuss, "The Political Business Cycle: An Extension of Nordhaus's Model", *Empirica*, vol. 2, 1980, pp. 223-259.

Bruno and Sachs (1985): Michael Bruno and Jeffrey D. Sachs, *Economics of Worldwide Stagflation*, Oxford: Oxford University Press.

Budgetredegørelsen (var. years), Finansministeriet, *Budgetredegørelsen*, Copenhagen: Finansministeriet.

Buksti (1984): Jacob A. Buksti, "Policy-making and Unemployment in Denmark", in Jeremy Richardson and Roger Henning (eds.), *Unemployment. Policy Responses of Western Democracies*, London: Sage.

Buksti et al. (1978): Jacob A. Buksti, Ole P. Kristensen, Karen Siune and Palle Svensson, *ØD-undersøgelsen i Århus kommune*, Aarhus: Arbejdernes Fællesorganisation i Århus.

Burtless (1987), Gary Burtless, "Jobless Pay and High European Unemployment", in Robert Z. Lawrence and Charles L. Schultze (eds.), *Barriers to European Growth. A Transatlantic View*, Washington: The Brookings Institution.

Calmfors (1990): Lars Calmfors (ed.), *Wage Formation and Macroeconomic Policy in the Nordic Countries*, Stockholm: SNS Förlag.

Calmfors and Driffill (1988): Lars Calmfors and John Driffill, "Centralization of Wage Bargaining", *Economic Policy*, vol. 6, pp. 13-61.

Calmfors and Forslund (1990): Lars Calmfors and Anders Forslund, "Wage Formation in Sweden", in Lars Calmfors (ed.), *Wage Formation and Macroeconomic Policy in the Nordic Countries*, Stockholm: SNS Förlag.

Calmfors and Lundberg (1974): Lars Calmfors and Erik Lundberg, *Inflation och arbetslöshet*, Stockholm: SNS.

Cameron (1978): David R. Cameron, "The Expansion of Public Economy: A Comparative Analysis", *American Political Science Review*, vol. 72, pp. 1243-1261.

Cameron (1984): David R. Cameron, "Social Democracy, Corporatism, Labour Quiescence, and the Representation of Economic Interests in Advanced Capitalist Society", in John H. Goldthorpe (ed.), *Order and Conflict in Contemporary Capitalism*, Oxford: Clarendon Press.

Campbell et al. (1960): Angus Campbell, Philip E. Converse, Warren E. Miller and Donald E. Stokes, *The American Voter*, New York: John Wiley & Sons.

Caves and Krause (1980): Richard E. Caves and Lawrence B. Krause, "Introduction and Summary", in Richard E. Caves and Lawrence B. Krause (eds.), *Britain's Economic Performance*, Washington, D.C.: The Brookings Institution.

Chalupek (1985): Günther Chalupek, "The Austrian Parties and the Economic Crisis", *West European Politics*, vol. 8, no. 1, pp. 71-81.

Clarke (1989): Simon Clarke, *Keynesianism, Monetarism and the Crisis of the State*, Aldershot: Edward Elgar.

Clarke and Whiteley (1990): Harold Clarke and Paul F. Whiteley, "Perception of Macroeconomic Performance, Government Support and Conservative Party Strategy in Britain 1983-1987", *European Journal of Political Research*, vol. 18, pp. 97-120.

Cleveland (1979): W.S. Cleveland, "Robust Locally Weighted Regression and Smoothing Scatterplots", *Journal of the American Statistical Association*, vol. 74, pp. 829-836.

Cmnd 3623 (1968): *Royal Commission on Trade Unions and Employers' Associations, 1965-1968*, London: HMSO.

Coen and Hickman (1989): Robert M. Coen and Bert G. Hickman, "Arbeitslosigkeit, Reallohn und Wirtschaftswachstum", in Hanns Abele, Ewald Nowotny, Stefan Schleicher and Georg Winckler (eds.), *Handbuch der österreichischen Wirtschaftspolitik*, 3. ed., Wien: Manz

Cowart (1978): Andrew T. Cowart, "The Economic Policies of European Governments", *British Journal of Political Science*, vol. 8, pp. 285-311 and 425-439.

Czada (1987): Roland Czada, "The Impact of Interest Politics on Flexible Adjustment Politics", in Hans Keman, Heikki Paloheimo and Paul F. Whiteley (eds.), *Coping with the Economic Crisis*, Beverly Hills: Sage.

Damgaard (1977): Erik Damgaard, *Folketinget under forandring,* Copenhagen: Samfundsvidenskabeligt Forlag.

Damgaard (1989): Erik Damgaard, "Crisis Politics in Denmark 1974 - 1987", in Erik Damgaard, Peter Gerlich and J.J. Richardson (eds.), *The Politics of Economic Crisis. Lessons from Western Europe,* Aldershot: Gower.

Damgaard and Svensson (1989): Erik Damgaard and Palle Svensson, "Who Governs? Parties and Politics in Denmark", *European Journal of Political Research,* vol. 17, pp.731-745.

Damgaard et al. (1989): Erik Damgaard, Peter Gerlich and J.J. Richardson, "From the Politics of Abundance to the Politics of Scarcity: Strategic Options", in Erik Damgaard, Peter Gerlich and J.J. Richardson (eds.), *The Politics of Economic Crisis. Lessons from Western Europe,* Aldershot: Gower.

Danmarks Statistik (1982), *Statistisk tiårsoversigt 1982,* Copenhagen: Danmarks Statistik.

Darmer (1990): Michael Darmer, "Arbejdsløshedsforsikringen og dens betydning for organisationsgraden", *Økonomi og Politik,* vol. 63, nr. 4, pp. 52-60.

Dawkins (1980): Peter J. Dawkins, "Incomes Policy", in Peter Maunder (ed.), *The British Economy in the 1970s,* London: Heinemann.

Dencik and Madsen (1978): Peter Dencik and Per Kongshøj Madsen, *Krise og krisepolitik,* Søborg: Forlaget samfundsnyt.

Dennis (1980): Geoffrey E. J. Dennis, "Money Supply and its Control", in Peter Maunder (ed.), *The British Economy in the 1970s,* London: Heinemann.

Dinkel (1977): Reiner Dinkel, *Der Zusammenhang zwischen der ökonomischen und politischen Entwicklung in einer Demokratie,* Berlin: Duncker und Humblot.

Dinkel (1982): Reiner Dinkel, "Ein politisch-ökonomisches Modell der Bundesrepublik?", in *Jahrbuch für Neue Politische Ökonomie,* vol. 1, Tübingen: J. C. B. Mohr.

Dornbusch (1980): Rudiger Dornbusch, *Open Economy Macroeconomics,* New York: Basic Books.

Dornbusch and Fischer (1980): Rudiger Dornbusch and Stanley Fischer, "Sterling and the External Balance", in Richard E. Caves and Lawrence B. Krause (eds.), *Britain's Economic Performance,* Washington, D.C.: The Brookings Institution.

Downs (1957): Anthony Downs, *An Economic Theory of Democracy*, New York: Harper and Row.

Dyson (1982): Kenneth Dyson, "West Germany: The Search for a Rationalist Compromise", in Jeremy J. Richardson (ed.), *Policy Styles in Western Europe*, London: Allen & Unwin.

Easton (1953): David Easton, *The Political System*, New York: Alfred A. Knopf.

Edelman (1976): Murray Edelman, *Politik als Ritual. Die symbolischen Funktionen staatlicher Institutionen und politischen Handelns*, Frankfurt: Campus Verlag.

Edgren, Faxén and Odhner (1970): Gösta Edgren, Karl-Olof Faxén and Clas-Erik Odhner, *Lönebildning och samhällsekonomi*, Stockholm: Rabén & Sjögren; (English edition 1973: *Wage Formation and the Economy*, London: Allen & Unwin).

Egmose (1985): Sven Egmose, "Udviklingen i den personlige indkomstforde-ling", in Sven Egmose, Lisbeth Egsmose, Gunnar Viby Mogensen and Hans Aage (eds.), *Uligheden, politikerne og befolkningen. Sammenligningsundersøgel-sen 2*, Copenhagen: SFI.

Ehrlicher and Rohwer (1979): Werner Ehrlicher and Bernd Rohwer, "Die öffentlichen Finanzen der Bundesrepublik im Jahre 1976", *Finanzarchiv*, Neue Folge, vol. 37, pp. 307-337.

Elvander (1988): Nils Elvander, *Den svenska modellen*, Stockholm: Almänna Förlaget.

Emminger (1986): Otmar Emminger, *D-Mark, Dollar, Währungskrisen*, Stuttgart: Deutsche Verlags Anstalt.

Esping-Andersen (1987): Gøsta Esping-Andersen, "Institutional Accommodation to Full Employment: A Comparison of Policy Regimes", in Hans Keman, Heikki Paloheimo and Paul F. Whiteley (eds.), *Coping with the Economic Crisis*, Beverly Hills: Sage.

Esser (1982): Josef Esser, *Gewerkschaften in der Krise*, Frankfurt: Suhrkamp Verlag.

Eulau et al. (1968): Heinz Eulau, John C. Wahlke, William Buchanan, and LeRoy C. Ferguson, "The Role of the Representative", reprinted in Samuel C. Patterson, *American Legislative Behavior*, Princeton: D. van Norstrand Company.

Faxén (1982): Karl-Olof Faxén, "Incomes Policy and Centralized Wage Formation", in Andrea Boltho (ed.), *The European Economy. Growth and Crisis*, Oxford: Oxford University Press.

Fiorina (1981): Morris P. Fiorina, *Retrospective Voting in American National Elections*, New Haven: Yale University Press.

Flanagan et al. (1983): Robert J. Flanagan, David W. Soskice and Lloyd Ulman, *Unionism, Economic Stabilization, and Incomes Policies: European Experience*, Washington, D.C.: The Brookings Institution.

Fürstenberg (1985): Friedrich Fürstenberg, "Sozialkulturelle Aspekte der Sozialpartnerschaft", in Peter Gerlich, Edgar Grande and Wolfgang C. Müller (eds.), *Sozialpartnerschaft in der Krise. Leistungen und Grenzen des Neokorporatismus in Österreich*, Wien: Hermann Böhlaus Nachfolger.

Furåker (1976): Bengt Furåker, *Stat och arbetsmarknad*, Stockholm: Arkiv.

Franz (1988): Wolfgang Franz, "Viele Indizien, kaum Beweise", *Die Zeit*, no. 48, Nov. 25, 1988, p. 45.

Freeman (1983): John R. Freeman, "Granger Causality and the Times Series Analysis of Political Relationships", *American Journal of Political Science*, vol. 27, pp. 327-358.

Freeman (1988): Richard Freeman, "Labour Markets", *Economic Policy*, vol. 6, pp. 63-80.

Frey (1990): Bruno S. Frey, "Instititons Matter", *European Economic Review*, vol. 34, no. 2-3, pp. 443-449.

Frey and Schneider (1980): Bruno S. Frey and Friedrich Schneider, "Popularity Functions: The Case of the US and West Germany", in Paul Whiteley (ed.), *Models of Political Economy*, Beverly Hills: Sage.

Frey and Schneider (1981): Bruno S. Frey and Friedrich Schneider, "Central Bank Behavior", *Journal of Monetary Economics*, vol. 7, pp. 291-315.

Frisch (1983): Helmut Frisch, *Theories of Inflation*, Cambridge: Cambridge University Press.

Gärtner (1989): Manfred Gärtner, *Arbeitskonflikte in der Bundesrepublik Deutschland*, Berlin: Springer-Verlag.

Gelting (1972): Jørgen H. Gelting, "Betalingsbalancen 1872-1972", *Nationaløkonomisk Tidsskrift*, vol. 110, pp. 379-402.

Gelting (1976): Jørgen H. Gelting, "Skræmmebillede", *Nationaløkonomisk Tidsskrift*, vol. 114, pp. 210-213.

Glastetter et al. (1982): Werner Glastetter, Rüdiger Paulert and Ulrich Spörel, *Die wirtschaftliche Entwicklung in der Bundesrepublik Deutschland 1950-1980*, Frankfurt: Campus Verlag.

Glastetter (1987): Werner Glastetter, *Konjunkturpolitik. Ziele, Instrumente, alternative Strategien*, Köln: Bund Verlag.

Goodhart and Bhansali (1970): C.A.E. Goodhart and R.J. Bhansali, "Political Economy", *Political Studies*, vol. 18, pp. 43-106.

Goul Andersen (1982): Jørgen Goul Andersen, "Den folkelige tilslutning til socialpolitikken - en krise for velfærdsstaten?", in Dag Anckar, Erik Damgaard and Henry Valen (eds.), *Partier, ideologier, väljere*, Åbo: Åbo Akademi.

Goul Andersen (1988a): Jørgen Goul Andersen, "Vælgernes holdning til den offentlige udgiftspolitik", in Karl-Henrik Bentzon (ed.), *Fra vækst til omstilling - moderniseringen af den offentlige sektor*, Copenhagen: Nyt fra samfundsvidenskaberne.

Goul Andersen (1988b): Jørgen Goul Andersen, "The Source of Welfare State Support. Self-Interest or Way of Life", *Rapport #13 fra projektet: Klassestruktur, klassebevidsthed og sociale modsætningsforhold*, Århus: Center for kulturforskning.

Guger (1989): Alois Guger, "Einkommensverteilung und Verteilungspolitik in Österreich", in Hanns Abele, Ewald Nowotny, Stefan Schleicher and Georg Winckler (eds.), *Handbuch der österreichischen Wirtschaftspolitik*, 3. ed., Wien: Manz.

Gunst (1976): Jens Gunst, *Inflation - Stagflation*, Copenhagen: Institute for Political Studies.

Gylfason and Lindbeck (1984): Thorvaldur Gylfason and Assar Lindbeck, "Union Rivalry and Wages: An Oligopolistics Approach", *Economica*, vol. 51, pp. 129-139.

Haas and Svoboda (1978): Erich Haas and Hannes Svoboda, "Ist Österreich ein Steuerstaat?", *Leviathan*, Sonderheft 1/1978, pp. 185-203.

Hansen et al. (1988): E. Damsgård Hansen, Kaj Kjærsgaard and Jørgen Rosted, *Dansk økonomisk politik. Teorier og erfaringer*, Copenhagen: Nyt Nordisk Forlag/Arnold Busck.

Hardes (1981): Heinz-Dieter Hardes, *Arbeitmarktstrukturen und Beschäftigungs-probleme im internationalen Vergleich*, Tübingen: J. C. B. Mohr.

Hedborg and Meidner (1984): Anna Hedborg and Rudolf Meidner, *Folkhems modellen*, Stockholm: Rabén and Sjögren.

Hefting and Nielsen (1983): Tom Hefting and Søren Bo Nielsen, "Makroøkono-miske effekter af olieprischok", *Økonomi og Politik*, vol. 57, no. 3, pp. 203-214.

Hibbs (1977a): Douglas A. Hibbs, Jr., "Political Parties and Macroeconomic Politics", *American Political Science Review*, vol. 71, pp. 1467-1487.

Hibbs (1977b): Douglas A. Hibbs, Jr., "On Analyzing the Effects of Policy Intervention: Box-Jenkins and Box-Tiao versus Structural Equation Models", in David R. Heise (ed.), *Sociological Methodology*, San Francisco: Jossey-Bass.

Hibbs (1979a): Douglas A. Hibbs, Jr., "The Mass Public and Macroeconomic Performance: The Dynamics of Public Opinion Toward Unemployment and Inflation", *American Journal of Political Science*, vol. 23, no. 4, pp. 705-731.

Hibbs (1979b): Douglas A. Hibbs, Jr., "Communication", *American Political Science Review*, vol. 71, pp. 185-190.

Hibbs (1985): Douglas A. Hibbs, Jr., "Inflation, Political Support, and Macroeco-nomic Policy", in Leon N. Lindberg and Charles S. Maier (eds.), *The Politics of Inflation and Economic Stagnation*, Washington D.C.: The Brookings Institu-tion.

Hibbs (1990): Douglas A. Hibbs, Jr., *Wage Compression Under Solidarity Bargaining in Sweden*, Stockholm: FIEF.

Hibbs and Locking (1991): Douglas A. Hibbs, Jr. and Håkan Locking, *Wage Compression, Wage Drift, and Wage Inflation in Sweden*, Stockholm: FIEF.

Hibbs and Madsen (1981): Douglas A. Hibbs, Jr. and Henrik J. Madsen, "The Impact of Economic Performance on Electoral Support in Sweden, 1967-78", *Scandinavian Political Studies*, vol. 4 (New series), no. 1, pp. 33-50.

Hines (1964): A. G. Hines, "Trade Unions and Wage Inflation in the United Kingdom, 1893-1961", *Review of Economic Studies*, vol. 31, pp. 221-252.

Hirsh and Goldthorpe (1978): Fred Hirsh and John H. Goldthorpe (eds.), *The Political Economy of Inflation*, Cambridge (Mass.): Harvard University Press.

Hirshman (1970): Albert O. Hirshman, *Exit, Voice, and Loyalty*, Cambridge (Mass.): Harvard University Press.

Ibsen and Jørgensen (1979): Flemming Ibsen and Henning Jørgensen, *Fagbevægelse og stat*, vol. 2, Copenhagen: Gyldendal.

Ifo (1974; 1975): Ifo-Institut für Wirtschaftsforschung, *Wirtschaftskonjunktur. Monatsberichte des Ifo-Instituts für Wirtschaftsforschung*, Berlin: Duncker und Humblot.

Jackson (1987): Michael P. Jackson, *Strikes*, New York: St. Martin's Press.

Jacobson and Kernell (1982): G. Jacobson and S. Kernell, *The Structure of Choice: a Theory of Congressional Elections*, New Haven: Yale University Press.

Jahresbericht der Bundesregierung (1977): *Jahresbericht der Bundesregierung 1976*, Bonn: Presse- und Informationsamt der Bundesregierung.

Johansen (1985): Steen Johansen, *Lønudvikling*, Copenhagen: Fremad.

Johnston (1963): J. Johnston, *Econometric Methods*, New York: McGraw-Hill.

Jonung (1989): Lars Jonung, *Inflation och ekonomisk politik i Sverige*, Lund: Universitetsförlaget Dialogos.

Jonung and Wadensjö (1979): Lars Jonung and Eskil Wadensjö, "The Effect of Unemployment, Inflation and Real Income Growth on Government Popularity in Sweden", *Scandinavian Journal of Economics*, 81, pp. 343-353.

Jørgensen (1989a): Anker Jørgensen, *Bølgegang*, Copenhagen: Fremad.

Jørgensen (1989b): Anker Jørgensen, *I smult vande*, Copenhagen: Fremad.

Kaarsted (1988): Tage Kaarsted, *Regeringen, vi aldrig fik*, Odense: Odense University Press.

Kalecki (1943): Michael Kalecki, *The Last Phase in the Transformation of Capitalism*, New York and London: Monthly Review Press (reprinted 1972).

Katzenstein (1984): Peter J. Katzenstein, *Corporatism and Change. Austria, Switzerland and the Politics of Industry*, Ithaca: Cornell University Press.

Katzenstein (1985): Peter J. Katzenstein, *Small States in World Markets*, Ithaca: Cornell University Press.

Kirchgässner (1976): Gebhard Kirchgässner, *Rationales Wählerverhalten und optimales Regierungsverhalten*, Konstanz: Unpublished dissertation.

Kirchgässner (1977): Gebhard Kirchgässner, "Wirtschaftslage und Wählerverhalten. Eine empirische Studie für die Bundesrepublik Deutschland von 1971 bis 1976", *Politische Vierteljahresschrift*, vol. 18, pp. 510-536.

Kirchgässner (1981): Gebhard Kirchgässner, *Einige neuere statistische Verfahren zur Erfassung kausaler Beziehungen zwischen Zeitreihen*, Göttingen: Vandenhoeck und Ruprecht.

Kirchgässner (1983): Gebhard Kirchgässner, "Wirtschaftliche Entwicklung, Wirtschaftslage und Popularität der Parteien", in Max Kaase and Hans-Dieter Klingemann (eds.), *Wahlen und politisches System*, Opladen: Westdeutscher Verlag.

Kirchgässner (1986): Gebhard Kirchgässner, "Economic Conditions and the Popularity of West German Parties: A Survey", *European Journal of Political Research*, vol. 14, pp. 421-436.

Kjellberg (1983): Anders Kjellberg, *Facklig organisering i tolv länder*, Lund: Arkiv förlag.

Kloten et al. (1985): Norbert Kloten, Karl-Heinz Ketterer and Rainer Vollmer, "West Germany's Stabilization Performance", in Leon N. Lindberg and Charles S. Maier (eds.), *The Politics of Inflation and Economic Stagnation. Theoretical Approaches and International Case Studies*, Washington, D.C.: Brookings.

Kock (1975): Heinz Kock, *Stabilitätspolitik im föderalistischen System der Bundesrepublik Deutschland. Analyse und Reformvorschläge*, Köln: Bund Verlag.

Korpi (1980): Walter Korpi, "Social Policy and Distributional Conflict in Capitalist Democracies. A Preliminary Comparative Framework", *West European Politics*, vol. 3, no. 3, pp. 296-316.

Korpi (1990): Walter Korpi, "Unemployment and Distributive Conflict in a Longterm Perspective - a Comparative Study of 18 OECD Countries", *Paper presented to the 9th Nordic Political Science Congress, Reykjavik August 16-18, 1990*.

Kramer (1971): Gerald H. Kramer, "Short-Term Fluctuations in US Voting Behavior 1896-1964", *American Political Science Review*, vol. 65, pp. 131-143.

Kramer (1983): Gerald H. Kramer, "The Ecological Fallacy Revisited: Aggregate- versus Individual-level Findings on Economics and Elections, and Sociotropic Voting", *American Political Science Review*, vol. 77, pp. 92-111.

Kristensen (1982): Ole P. Kristensen, "Voter Attitudes and Public Spending: Is There a Relationship?", *European Journal of Political Research*, vol. 10, pp. 35-52.

Leaman (1988): Jeremy Leaman, *The Political Economy of West Germany, 1945 - 1985*, New York: St. Martin's Press.

Lehner (1987): Franz Lehner, "Interest Intermediation, Institutional Structures, and Public Policy", in Hans Keman, Heikki Paloheimo and Paul F. Whiteley (eds.), *Coping with the Economic Crisis*, Beverly Hills: Sage.

Lehner (1982): Gerhard Lehner, "'Deficit-spending' in Österreich", *Wirtschaftspolitische Blätter*, vol. 29, pp. 24-35.

Lessmann (1987): Sabine Lessmann, *Budgetary Politics and Elections: An Investigation of Public Expenditures in West Germany*, Berlin: Walter de Gryter.

Levacic and Rebmann (1989): Rosalind Levacic and Alexander Rebmann, *Macroeconomics* (2. edition), London: Macmillan.

Lewin (1977): Leif Lewin, *Hur styrs facket?*, Stockholm: Rabén och Sjögren.

Lewin (1984): Leif Lewin, *Ideologi och strategi. Svensk politik under 100 år*, Stockholm: P. A. Norstedt & Söners förlag.

Lind (1985): Jens Lind, *Arbejdsløshed og velfærdsstat*, Aalborg: Aalborg University Press.

Lindbeck (1979): Assar Lindbeck, *Inflation. Global, International and National Aspects*, Louvain: Presses Universitaires de Louvain.

Lindbeck (1990): Assar Lindbeck, "Comment", in Lars Calmfors (ed.), *Wage Formation and Macroeconomic Policy in the Nordic Countries*, Stockholm: SNS Förlag.

Lindbeck and Snower (1988): Assar Lindbeck and Dennis J. Snower, *The Insider-Outsider Theory of Employment and Unemployment*, Cambridge (Mass.): MIT Press.

Lindberg (1985): Leon N. Lindberg, "Models of the Inflation-Disinflation Process", in Leon N. Lindberg and Charles S. Maier (eds.), *The Politics of Inflation and Economic Stagnation*, Washington D.C.: The Brookings Institution.

Lundberg (1983): Erik Lundberg, *Ekonomiska kriser förr och nu,* Stockholm: SNS.

Lykketoft (1973): Mogens Lykketoft (ed.), *Kravet om lighed,* Copenhagen: Fremad.

Madsen (1980): Henrik J. Madsen, "Electoral Outcomes and Macro-Economic Policies: The Scandinavian Cases", in Paul Whiteley (ed.), *Models of Political Economy,* Beverly Hills: Sage.

Madsen (1981): Henrik J. Madsen, "Partisanship and Macroeconomic Outcomes: A Reconsideration", in Douglas A. Hibbs, Jr. and Heino Fassbender (eds.), *Contemporary Political Economy,* Amsterdam: North-Holland Publishing Company.

Maier (1985): Charles S. Maier, "Inflation and Stagnation as Politics and History", in Leon N. Lindberg and Charles S. Maier (eds.), *The Politics of Inflation and Economic Stagnation,* Washington D.C.: The Brookings Institution.

Maier and Lindberg (1985): Charles S. Maier and Leon N. Lindberg, "Alternatives for Future Crises", in Leon N. Lindberg and Charles S. Maier (eds.), *The Politics of Inflation and Economic Stagnation,* Washington D.C.: The Brookings Institution.

Mandel (1978): Ernest Mandel, *The Second Slump,* London: NLB.

Martin (1985): Andrew Martin, "Wages, Profits, and Investment in Sweden", in Leon N. Lindberg and Charles S. Maier (eds.), *The Politics of Inflation and Economic Stagnation,* Washington D.C.: The Brookings Institution.

Mazier (1982): Jacques Mazier, "Growth and Crisis - a Marxist Interpretation", in Andrea Boltho (ed.), *The European Economy. Growth and Crisis,* Oxford: Oxford University Press.

McCleary and Hay (1980): Richard McCleary and Richard A. Hay, Jr., *Applied Time Series Analysis,* London: Sage.

McCracken et al. (1977): Paul McCracken, Guido Carli, Herbert Giersch, Attila Karaosmanoglu, Ryutaro Komya, Assar Lindbeck, Robert Marjolin, Robin Matthews, *Towards Full Employment and Price Stability. A Report to the OECD by a Group of Independent Experts,* Paris: OECD.

Meidner (1974): Rudolf Meidner, *Samordning och solidarisk lönepolitik,* Stockholm: Prisma.

Meidner (1984): Rudolf Meidner, "Sweden: Approaching the Limits of Active Labor Market Policy", in Knut Gerlach, Wilhelm Peters and Werner Sengenberger (eds.), *Public Policies to Combat Unemployment in a Period of Economic Stagnation*, Frankfurt: Campus Verlag.

Metcalf (1987): David Metcalf, "Labor Market Flexibility and Jobs: A Survey of Evidence from OECD Countries with Special Reference to Europe", in Richard Layard and Lars Calmfors (eds.), *The Fight Against Unemployment*, Cambridge (Mass.): MIT Press.

Miller and Mackie (1973): W. L. Miller and M. Mackie, "The Electoral Cycle and the Asymmetry of Government and Opposition Popularity: An Alternative Model of the Relationship between Economic Conditions and Political Popularity", *Political Studies*, vol. 21, pp. 263-279.

Moon (1984): Jeremy Moon, "The Responses of British Governments to Unemployment", in Jeremy Richardson and Roger Henning (eds.), *Unemployment. Policy Responses of Western Democracies*, London: Sage.

Mosley (1976): Paul Mosley, "Towards a Satisficing Theory of Economic Policy", *Economic Journal*, vol. 86, pp. 59-72.

Mueller (1989): Dennis C. Mueller, *Public Choice II*, Cambridge: Cambridge Uinversity Press.

Myers (1975): Robert J. Myers, "International Comparison of Unemployment", *The Banker*, 1975, pp. 1257-1262.

Nannestad (1973): Peter Nannestad, "Den tyske Forbundsrepublik", in Asger Lund-Sørensen (ed.), *Den centrale statsadministration i Danmark og enkelte fremmede lande*, Aarhus: Institute of Political Science.

Nannestad (1989a): Peter Nannestad, *Reactive Voting in Danish General Elections 1971-79. A Revisionist Interpretation*, Aarhus: Aarhus University Press.

Nannestad (1989b): Peter Nannestad, "The Blessing of Ignorance? On the Problem of (Non)Information in Models of Rational Voting Behavior", *Paper presented at the annual meeting of the European Public Choice Society 1989*, Aarhus: Institute of Political Science.

Nannestad (1990): Peter Nannestad, "Rally around the Rascals? Unemployment and the Vote in Danish General Elections 1966-77", *Paper presented at the annual meeting of the European Public Choice Society 1990*, Aarhus: Institute of Political Science.

Nannestad and Paldam (1990a): Peter Nannestad and Martin Paldam, "The Economic Dimension of Political Distrust", *Working Paper #1 from the Project "Economic Foundations of Mass Politics: Information, Expectations and Political Reactions"*, Aarhus: Institute of Political Science and Institute of Economics.

Nannestad and Paldam (1990b): Peter Nannestad and Martin Paldam, "Inflation in Denmark, May 1990. What Do People Know and Expect?", *Working Paper #6 from the Project "Economic Foundations of Mass Politics: Information, Expectations and Political Reactions"*, Aarhus: Institute of Political Science and Institute of Economics.

Nannestad and Paldam (1990c): Peter Nannestad and Martin Paldam, "Personal vs. Sociotropic Grievances and Anti-Government Stance: The Danish Case", *Working Paper #3 from the Project "Economic Foundations of Mass Politics: Information, Expectations and Political Reactions"*, Aarhus: Institute of Political Science and Institute of Economics.

Neck (1979a): Reinhard Neck, "Gibt es einen politischen Konjunkturzyklus in Österreich?", in C.C. von Weizsäcker (ed.), *Staat und Wirtschaft*, Berlin: Duncker und Humblot.

Neck (1979b): Reinhard Neck, "Wirtschaftliche Bestimmungsgrößen des Wählerverhaltens", *Wirtschaftspolitische Blätter*, vol. 26, no. 3, pp. 39-47.

Neck (1988): Reinhard Neck, "Wahl- und Popularitätsfunktionen für Österreich", *Quartalsheft der Girozentrale*, vol. 23, 1988, pp. 43-73.

Neck (1989): Reinhard Neck, "Politisch-ökonomische Bestimmungsgrößen der österreichischen Finanzpolitik", in *Jahrbuch für Neue Politische Ökonomie*, vol. 8, Tübingen: J.C.B. Mohr.

Nielsen (1984): Søren Bo Nielsen, "Olieprischock og beskæftigelse", in Udvalget vedr. arbejdsløshedsforskning (ed.): *Arbejdsløshedsforskning IV. Strukturproblemer og økonomisk politik*, Aalborg: Aalborg Universitetsforlag.

Nordenstam (1972): Gunnar R. Nordenstam (ed.), *Värde, välfärd och jämlikhet*, Lund: Studentlitteratur.

Nordhaus (1975): William D. Nordhaus, "The Political Business Cycle", *Review of Economic Studies*, vol. 42, pp. 169-190.

Norpoth and Yantek (1983): Helmut Norpoth and Tom Yantek, "Von Adenauer bis Schmidt: Wirtschaftslage und Kanzlerpopularität", in Max Kaase and Hans-Dieter Klingemann (eds.), *Wahlen und politisches System*, Opladen: Westdeutscher Verlag.

Nowotny (1989): Ewald Nowotny, "Institutionen", in Hanns Abele, Ewald Nowotny, Stefan Schleicher and Georg Winckler (eds.), *Handbuch der öster-reichischen Wirtschaftspolitik*, 3. ed., Wien: Manz.

NU (1984): "Arbejdsløshedens omkostninger i Norden", *NU 1984:9*, Stockholm: Gotab.

Nyboe Andersen (1989): Poul Nyboe Andersen, *Det umuliges kunst. Erindringer fra dansk politik 1968-77*, Odense: Odense University Press.

OECD (1970): OECD, *Inflation: The Present Problem. Report by the Secretary General*, Paris: OECD.

OECD, Economic Outlook (1983): OECD, *Economic Outlook*, vol. 33, Paris: OECD.

OECD, Economic Outlook (1990): OECD, *Economic Outlook*, vol. 47, Paris: OECD.

OECD, Historical Statistics (1988): OECD, *Economic Outlook. Historical Statistics 1960-1988*, Paris: OECD.

OECD, National Accounts (1984): OECD, *National Accounts: Detailed Tables*, vol. 2, 1970-72, Paris: OECD.

OECD, National Accounts (1990): OECD, *National Accounts: Main Aggregates*, vol. 1, 1960-88, Paris: OECD.

Offe (1984): Claus Offe, "'Crises of Crisis Management': Elements of a Political Crisis Theory", in Claus Offe, *Contradictions of the Welfare State*, London: Hutchinson.

Okun (1970): A. M. Okun, *The Political Economy of Prosperity*, Washington: Brookings Institution.

Olson (1965): Mancur Olson, *The Logic of Collective Action*, Cambridge (Mass.): Harvard University Press.

Olson (1982): Mancur Olson, *The Rise and Decline of Nations*, New Haven: Yale University Press.

Olsson (1986): Sven Olsson, "Sweden", in Peter Flora (ed.), *Growth to Limits. The Western European Welfare States Since the World War II*, vol. 1, Berlin: De Gryther.

Oswald (1979): Andrew J. Oswald, "Wage Determination in an Economy with Many Trade Unions", *Oxford Economic Papers*, New Series, pp. 369-385.

Paldam (1979a): Martin Paldam, "Danmark og den internationale konjunktur 1948-75", in *Vækst og kriser i dansk økonomi i det 20. århundrede*, vol. II, Aarhus: Skrifter fra Aarhus Universitets Økonomiske Institut.

Paldam (1979b): Martin Paldam, "Is There an Electional Cycle? A Comparative Study of National Accounts", *The Scandinavian Journal of Economics*, vol. 81, no. 2, pp. 323-342.

Paldam (1980): Martin Paldam, "The International Element in the Phillips Curve", *The Scandinavian Journal of Economics*, vol. 82, no. 2, pp. 216 - 239.

Paldam (1981): Martin Paldam, "A Preliminary Survey of the Theories and Findings on Vote and Popularity Functions", *European Journal of Political Research*, vol. 9, no. 2, pp.181-199.

Paldam (1987): Martin Paldam, "How Much Does One Percent of Growth Change the Unemployment Rate?", *European Economic Review*, vol. 31, pp. 306-313.

Paldam (1989): Martin Paldam, "A Wage Structure Theory of Inflation, Industrial Conflicts an Trade Unions", *Scandinavian Journal of Economics*, vol. 91, no. 1, pp. 63-81.

Paldam (1990): Martin Paldam, "The Development of the Rich Welfare State of Denmark, an Essay in Interpretation", *Memo 1990-5*, Aarhus: Institute of Economics. Also in: Magnus Blomström and Patricio Meller (eds.), *Diverging Paths. A Century of Scandinavian and Latin American Economic Development*, Baltimore: John Hopkins University Press.

Paldam and Pedersen (1982): Martin Paldam and Peder J. Pedersen, "The Macro-Economic Strike Model: A Study of Seventeen Countries 1948 - 1975", *Industrial and Labor Relations Review*, vol. 35, pp. 504-521.

Paldam and Pedersen (1987): Martin Paldam and Peder J. Pedersen, *Wages and Industrial Conflicts: The OECD-Countries, 1920-84* (Unpublished).

Paldam and Rasmussen (1980): Martin Paldam and F. L. Rasmussen, "Data for Industrial Conflicts in 17 OECD Countries 1948-77", *Memo 80-5*, Aarhus: Institute of Economics.

Paldam and Schneider (1980): Martin Paldam and Friedrich Schneider, "The Macro-Economic Aspects of Government and Opposition Popularity in Denmark 1957-78", *Nationaløkonomisk Tidsskrift 1980*, pp. 149-170.

Paldam and Zeuthen (1988): Martin Paldam and Hans E. Zeuthen, "The Expansion of the Public Sector in Denmark - A Post Festum?", in J.A. Lybek and Magnus Henrekson (eds.), *Explaining the Growth of Government*, Amsterdam: North-Holland.

Paloheimo (1984): Heikki Paloheimo, "Distributive Struggle, Corporatist Power Structures, and Economic Policy in the 1970s in Developed Capitalist Countries", in Heikki Paloheimo (ed.), *Politics in the Era of Corporatism and Planning*, Tampere: The Finnish Political Science Association.

Panitch (1976): Leo Panitch, *Social Democracy and Industrial Militancy*, Cambridge: Cambridge University Press.

Payne (1979): James L. Payne, "Inflation, Unemployment, and Left-Wing Political Parties: A Reanalysis", *American Political Science Review*, vol. 73, pp. 181-185.

Pedersen (1977): Mogens N. Pedersen, "Om den rette brug af historiske materialer i statskundskaben: Nogle didaktiske overvejelser", in Erik Damgaard, Carsten Jarlov and Curt Sørensen (eds.), *Festskrift til Erik Rasmussen*, Aarhus: Forlaget Politica.

Pedersen (1988): Mogens N. Pedersen, "The Defeat of all Parties: The Danish Folketing Election, 1973", in Kay Lawson and Peter H. Merkl (eds.), *When Parties Fail*, Princeton: Princeton University Press.

Pedersen (1984): Peder J. Pedersen, "Aspekter af fagbevægelsens vækst i Danmark 1911-1976", in Peder J. Pedersen *Arbejdsmarkedet - langtidstendenser og internationale perspektiver*, Aarhus: Aarhus Business School.

Pedersen (1989): Peder J. Pedersen, "Langsigtede internationale tendenser i den faglige organisering og den politiske venstrefløj", *Økonomi og Politik*, vol. 62, no. 2, pp. 91-100.

Pedersen and Søndergaard (1989): Peder J. Pedersen and Jørgen Søndergaard, "Det inflationære danske arbejdsmarked", *Nationaløkonomisk Tidsskrift*, vol. 127, no. 1, pp. 1- 20.

Pedersen and Westergård-Nielsen (1984): Peder J. Pedersen and Niels Westergård-Nielsen, "Arbejdsløshed og understøttelse - nogle foreløbige resultater", in Udvalget vedr. arbejdsløshedsforskning (ed.): *Arbejdsløshedsforskning IV. Strukturproblemer og økonomisk politik*, Aalborg: Aalborg Universitetsforlag.

Pirsching (1989): Manfred Pirsching, *Rational Politicians and Symbolic Politics*, unpublished manus.

Pitkin (1967): Hanna F. Pitkin, *The Concept of Representation*, Berkeley: UCLA Press.

Pommerehne (1990): Werner W. Pommerehne, "The Empirical Relevance of Comparative Institutional Analysis", *European Economic Review*, vol. 34, no. 2-3, pp. 458-469.

Pond (1980): Chris Pond, "Low Pay", in Nick Bosanquet and Peter Townsend (eds.), *Labour and Equality. A Fabian Study of Labour in Power, 1974-79*, London: Heinemann.

Poulsen (1986): Jørgen J. Poulsen, *The Holistic Conception of Democracy*, Michigan: UMI (Ph. D.-dissertation).

Przeworski and Teune (1970): Adam Przeworski and Henry Teune, *The Logic of Comparative Social Inquiry*, New York: John Wiley and Sons.

Purdy and Zis (1974): David L. Purdy and George Zis, "Trade Unions and Wage Inflation in the UK: A Reappraisal", in David Laidler and David Purdy (eds.), *Inflation and Labour Markets*, Manchester: Manchester University Press.

Putnam and Bayne (1987): Robert D. Putnam and Nicholas Bayne, *Hanging Together. Cooperation and Conflict in the Seven-Power Summits*, 2. rev. edition, London: Sage.

Rasmussen (1973-74): Jorgen Rasmussen, "The Impact of Constituency Structural Characteristics Upon Political Preferences in Britain", *Comparative Politics 1973-74*, vol. 1, pp. 123-145.

Rattinger (1979): Hans Rattinger, "Auswirkungen der Arbeitsmarktlage auf das Ergebnis der Bundestagswahl 1976", *Politische Vierteljahresschrift 1979*, vol. 20, pp. 51-70.

Rattinger (1980): Hans Rattinger, *Wirtschaftliche Konjunktur und politische Wahlen in der Bundesrepublik Deutschland*, Berlin: Duncker und Humblot.

Rattinger and Puschner (1981): Hans Rattinger and Walter Puschner, "Ökonomie und Politik in der Bundesrepublik", *Politische Vierteljahresschrift*, vol. 22, pp. 264-279.

Rattinger (1983): Hans Rattinger, "Arbeitslosigkeit, Apathie und Protestpotential: Zu den Auswirkungen der Arbeitsmarktlage auf das Wahlverhalten bei der Bundestagswahl 1980", in Max Kaase and Hans-Dieter Klingemann (eds.), *Wahlen und politisches System*, Opladen: Westdeutscher Verlag.

Rattinger (1986): Hans Rattinger, "Collective and Individual Economic Judgements and Voting in West Germany 1961-1984", *European Journal of Political Research*, vol. 14, pp. 393-419.

Regini (1984): Marino Regini, "The Conditions of Political Exchange: How Concertation Emerged and Collapsed in Italy and Great Britain", in John H. Goldthorpe (ed.), *Order and Conflict in Contemporary Capitalism*, Oxford: Clarendon Press.

Rehn (1985): Gösta Rehn, "Swedish Active Labor Market Policy: Retrospect and Prospect", *Industrial Relations*, vol. 24, pp. 62-89.

Ringen (1987): Stein Ringen, *The Possibility of Politics*, Oxford: Clarendon Press.

Rold Andersen (1987): Bent Rold Andersen, "Perioden 1976-78: Illusionen om den sunde fornuft", in Det økonomiske Råd, Formandskabet, *Dansk økonomi. Råd og realiteter 1967-87*, Copenhagen: DøR.

Rothschild (1989): Kurt W. Rothschild, "Ziele, Ereignisse und Reaktionen: Reflexionen über die österreichische Wirtschaftspolitik", in Hanns Abele, Ewald Nowotny, Stefan Schleicher and Georg Winckler (eds.), *Handbuch der österreichischen Wirtschaftspolitik*, 3. ed., Wien: Manz.

Rubery and Wilkinson (1986): Jill Rubery and Frank Wilkinson, "Inflation and Income Distribution", in Peter Nolan and Suzanne Paine (eds.), *Rethinking Socialist Economics*, Cambridge: Polity Press.

Sandmo (1990): Agnar Sandmo, "Noen refleksjoner om public choice-skolens syn på økonomi og politikk", *Norsk Økonomisk Tidsskrift*, vol. 104, pp. 89-112.

Santomero and Saeter (1978): Anthony M. Santomero and John J. Saeter, "The Inflation-Unemployment Trade-off: A Critique of the Literature", *Journal of Economic Literature*, vol. 16, no. 2, pp. 499 - 544.

Sartori (1973): Giovanni Sartori, *Democratic Theory*, Westport (Conn.): Greenwood Press.

Sawyer (1976): Malcolm Sawyer, "Income Distribution in OECD Countries", *OECD Economic Outlook, Occasional Studies*, Paris: OECD.

Scharpf (1985): Fritz W. Scharpf, "Die Politikverflechtungs-Falle: Europäische Integration und deutscher Föderalismus im Vergleich", *Politische Vierteljahresschrift*, vol. 26, nr. 4, pp. 232-356.

Scharpf (1987): Fritz W. Scharpf, *Sozialdemokratische Krisenpolitik in Europa*, Frankfurt: Campus Verlag.

Scharpf (1988a): Fritz W. Scharpf, "Inflation und Arbeitslosigkeit in Westeuropa. Eine spieltheoretische Interpretation", *Politische Vierteljahresschrift*, vol. 29, no. 1, pp. 6-41.

Scharpf (1988b): Fritz W. Scharpf, "Weltweite, europäische oder nationale Optionen der Vollbeschäftigungspolitik?", *Gewerkschaftliche Monatshefte*, vol. 39, no. 1, pp. 14-25.

Scherf (1986): Harald Scherf, *Enttäuschte Hoffnungen - vergebene Chancen*, Göttingen: Vandenhoeck und Ruprecht.

Schmid et al. (1987): Günther Schmid, Bernd Reissert and Gert Bruche, *Arbeitslosenversicherung und aktive Arbeitsmarktpolitik*, Berlin: Edition Sigma Bohn.

Schmidt (1979): Manfred G. Schmidt, *Determinanten der staatlichen Politik in industriell-kapitalistischen Demokratien. Ein Überblick über den Stand der vergleichenden Policy-Forschung*, Konstanz: Konstanz University Press.

Schmidt (1982): Manfred G. Schmidt, "Does Corporatism Matter? Economic Crisis, Politics, and Rates of Unemployment in Capitalist Democracies in the 1970s", in Gerhard Lehmbruch and Philippe E. Schmitter (ed.), *Patterns of Corporatist Policy Making*, London: Sage.

Schmidt (1983a): Manfred G. Schmidt, "The Welfare State and the Economy in Periods of Economic Crisis: A Comparative Study of Twenty-Two OECD Nations", *European Journal of Political Research*, vol. 11, pp. 1-26.

Schmidt (1983b): Manfred G. Schmidt, "Politische Konjunkturzyklen und Wahlen. Ein internationaler Vergleich", in Max Kaase and Hans-Dieter Klingemann (eds.), *Wahlen und politisches System*, Opladen: Westdeutscher Verlag.

Schmidt (1984): Manfred G. Schmidt, "The Politics of Unemployment: Rates of Unemployment and Labour Market Policy", *West European Politics*, vol. 7, no. 3, pp. 5-24.

Schmitter (1981): Philippe E. Schmitter, "Interest Intermediation and Regime Governability in Contemporary Western Europe and North America", in Suzanne Berger (ed.), *Organizing Interests in Western Europe: Pluralism, Corporatism, and the Transformation of Politics*, Cambridge: Harvard University Press.

Schnabel (1989): Claus Schnabel, *Zur ökonomischen Analyse der Gewerkschaften in der Bundesrepublik Deutschland*, Frankfurt: Peter Lang.

Schumann et al. (1971): Michael Schumann, Frank Gerlach, Albert Gschlössl, and Petra Milhoffer, *Am Beispiel der Septemberstreiks - Anfang der Rekonstruktionsperiode der Arbeiterklasse?*, Frankfurt: Europäische Verlagsanstalt.

Schumpeter (1947): Joseph A. Schumpeter, *Capitalism, Socialism, and Democracy*, 2nd edition, New York: Harper and Brothers.

Sjøqvist (1965): Viggo Sjøkvist, *Peter Vedel*, Copenhagen: Gyldendal.

Smith (1980): Eric Owen Smith, "Collective Bargaining", in Peter Maunder (ed.), *The British Economy in the 1970s*, London: Heinemann.

Soskice (1988): David W. Soskice, "Industrial Relations and Unemployment: The Case for Flexible Corporatism", in J.A. Kregel, E. Matzner and Alessandro Roncaglia (eds.); *Barriers to Full Employment*, New York: St. Martin's Press.

SOU (1984): "Arbetsmarknadspolitik under omproving", *Statens Offentliga Utredningar 1984:31*, Stockholm: Arbetsmarknadsdepartementet.

Spahn (1976): Heinz-Peter Spahn, "Keynes in der heutigen Wirtschaftspolitik", in Gottfried Bombach, Hans-Jürgen Ramser, Manfred Timmermann, Walter Wittmann (eds.), *Der Keynesianismus I*, Berlin 1976: Springer-Verlag.

Spahn (1988): Heinz-Peter Spahn, *Bundesbamk und Wirtschaftskrise*, Regensburg: Transfer Verlag.

Statistisches Handbuch für die Republik Österreich 1980, Wien: Österreichische Staatsdruckerei.

Steiner (1972): Kurt Steiner, *Politics in Austria*, Boston: Little, Brown and Company.

Sully (1976): Melanie A. Sully, "The Austrian Parliamentary Election of 1975", *Parliamentary Affairs*, vol. 29, pp. 293-309.

Sully (1979): Melanie A. Sully, "The Austrian Parliamentary Election of 1979: A Socialist Victory", *Parliamentary Affairs*, vol. 32, pp. 437-447.

Sully (1981): Melanie A. Sully, *Political Parties and Elections in Austria*, New York: St. Martin's Press.

Suppanz and Wagner (1981): Hannes Suppanz and Michael Wagner (eds.), *Einkommensverteilung in Österreich. Ein einführender Überblick*, München: R. Oldenbourg Verlag.

Surrey (1982): Michael Surrey, "United Kingdom", in Andrea Boltho (ed.), *The European Economy. Growth and Crisis,* Oxford: Oxford University Press.

SVR (1974): Sachverständigenrat zur Begutachtung der gesamtwirtschaftlichen Entwicklung, *Vollbeschäftigung für morgen,* Stuttgart and Mainz: Verlag Kohlhammer.

Sørensen (1990): Jan Rose Sørensen, "Political Uncertainty and Macroeconomic Performance", *Memo 1990-26,* Aarhus: Institute of Economics.

Tarling and Wilkinson (1977): Roger Tarling and Frank Wilkinson, "The Social Contract: Postwar Incomes Policies and their Inflationary Impact", *Cambridge Journal of Economics,* vol. 1, no. 4, pp. 395-414.

Teschner and Vesper (1983): Manfred Teschner and Dieter Vesper, "Die Budgetpolitik Österreichs im internationalen Vergleich", *Deutsches Institut für Wirtschaftsforschung: Beiträge zur Strukturforschung,* Heft 75, Berlin: Duncker und Humblot.

Therborn (1986): Göran Therborn, *Why Some Peoples are more Unemployed than Others. The Strange Paradox of Growth and Unemployment,* London: Verso.

Therborn (1987): Göran Therborn, "Does Corporatism Really Matter? The Economic Crisis and Issues of Political Theory", *Journal of Public Policy,* vol. 7, no. 3, pp. 259-284.

Thygesen (1979): Niels Thygesen, "Udviklingstendenser i tilrettelæggelsen og virkningerne af dansk pengepolitik", in *Vækst og kriser i dansk økonomi i det 20. århundrede,* vol. II, Aarhus: Skrifter fra Aarhus Universitets Økonomiske Institut.

Tichy (1984): Gunther Tichy, "Strategy and Implementation of Employment Policy in Austria. Successful Experiments with Unconventional Assignment of Instruments to Goals", *Kyklos,* vol. 37, pp. 363-368.

Tichy (1988): Gunther Tichy, *Konjunkturpolitik,* Berlin: Springer-Verlag.

Topp (1987): Niels-Henrik Topp, *Udviklingen i de finanspolitiske ideer i Danmark 1930-45,* Copenhagen: Jurist- og Økonomforbundets Forlag.

Tufte (1978): Edward R. Tufte, *Political Control of the Economy,* Princeton: Princeton University Press.

Vejrup Hansen (1982): Per Vejrup Hansen, "Lønforskelle, lønpolitik og beskæftigelse i 1970'erne", *Arbejdsløshedsundersøgelserne 4,* Copenhagen: SFI.

Visser and Wijnhoven (1990): Wessel Visser and Rien Wijnhoven, "Politics Do Matter, but Does Unemployment? Party Strategies, Ideological Discourse and Enduring Mass Unemployment", *European Journal of Political Research,* vol. 18, pp. 71-96.

Webber (1983): Douglas Webber, "Combatting or Acquiescing in Unemployment? Crisis Management in Sweden and West Germany", *West European Politics*, vol. 6, no. 1, pp. 21-43.

Westaway (1980): Thomas Westaway, "Stabilisation Policy and Fiscal Reform", in Peter Maunder (ed.), *The British Economy in the 1970s,* London: Heinemann.

Whiteley (1980): Paul F. Whiteley, "Politico-Econometric Estimation in Britain: An Alternative Interpretation", in Paul Whiteley (ed.), *Models of Political Economy*, Beverly Hills: Sage.

Whiteley (1986a): Paul F. Whiteley, *Political Control of the Macro-Economy*, Beverly Hills: Sage.

Whiteley (1986b): Paul F. Whiteley, "Macroeconomic Performance and Government Popularity in Britain: the Short Run Dynamics", *European Journal of Political Research,* vol. 14, pp. 45-61.

Whiteley (1987): Paul F. Whiteley, "The Monetarist Experiments in the United States and the United Kingdom: Policy Responses to Stagflation", in Hans Keman, Heikki Paloheimo and Paul F. Whiteley (eds.), *Coping with the Economic Crisis*, London: Sage.

Wilensky (1976): Harold Wilensky, *The New Corporatism. Centralization and the Welfare State*, Beverly Hills: Sage.

Wilensky (1981): Harold Wilensky, "Democratic Corporatism, Consensus, and Social Policy: Reflections on Changing Values and the 'Crisis' of the Welfare State", in OECD (ed.), *The Welfare State in Crisis: An Account of the Conference on Social Policies in the 1980s*, Paris: OECD.

Wilson (1979): Harold Wilson, *Final Term*, London: Weidenfeld and Nicolson.

Winckler (1985): Georg Winckler, "Sozialpartnerschaft und ökonomische Effizienz", in Peter Gerlich, Edgar Grande and Wolfgang C. Müller (eds.), *Sozialpartnerschaft in der Krise. Leistungen und Grenzen des Neokorporatismus in Österreich*, Wien: Hermann Böhlaus Nachfolger.

Winckler (1989): Georg Winckler, "Geld und Währung", in Hanns Abele, Ewald Nowotny, Stefan Schleicher and Georg Winckler (eds.), *Handbuch der österreichischen Wirtschaftspolitik*, 3. ed., Wien: Manz.

Wood (1978): Adrian Wood, *A Theory of Pay*, Cambridge: Cambridge University Press.

Åsard (1985): Erik Åsard, *Kampen om löntagarfonderna. Fondutredningen från samtal till sammanbrott*, Stockholm: P. A. Norstedt & Söners förlag.